A DANCE CALLED AMERICA

In the evening the company danced as usual. We performed, with much activity, a dance which, I suppose, the emigration from Skye has occasioned. They call it *America*. Each of the couples, after the common involutions and evolutions, successively whirls round in a circle, till all are in motion; and the dance seems intended to show how emigration catches, till a whole neighbourhood is set afloat.

James Boswell, *Journal of a Tour to the Hebrides*, 2 October 1773

A DANCE CALLED AMERICA

The Scottish Highlands
the United States and Canada

JAMES HUNTER

MAINSTREAM
PUBLISHING

EDINBURGH AND LONDON

For Iain and Anna

First published in Great Britain in 1994 by
MAINSTREAM PUBLISHING COMPANY (EDINBURGH) LTD
7 Albany Street
Edinburgh EH1 3UG

ISBN 1 85158 639 3

A catalogue record for this book is available from the British Library

The publisher gratefully acknowledges the financial assistance of
The Scottish Arts Council in the production of this volume

Typeset in Linotype Sabon by Servis Filmsetting Ltd, Manchester

Printed in Great Britain by Butler & Tanner Ltd, Frome

CONTENTS

Acknowledgments

THIS BOOK'S TITLE, though it derives from a comment made long ago by James Boswell, acquired the form I have used as a result of a Runrig song. I am grateful to this most successful Highland band for allowing me to apply their song title to my book. I am also grateful to Runrig for permission to borrow one of my chapter headings from another of the band's songs, 'Rocket to the Moon'.

The other obligations I have incurred in the course of working on this book in Scotland, the United States and Canada are so numerous as almost to defy listing. I am particularly grateful to John Angus MacKay, Margaret MacKelvie and their colleagues at Comataidh Telebhisein Gaidhlig in Stornoway. But for their having commissioned me to report to them on the nature of Highland links with North America, this book would not have been written. I trust that my findings will help bring to television audiences some appreciation of the Scottish Highland role in the development of the United States and Canada.

John Foster and John Prebble were prominent among the friends who encouraged me to press ahead with this project. Norman Gillies, John Norman MacLeod and their colleagues at Sabhal Mor Ostaig, Skye's Gaelic-medium business college, gave me the run of a very fine library. Rob McDonald Parker and Margaret MacDonald at the Clan Donald Centre, also in Skye, did likewise. Roger Miket of Skye and Lochalsh District Council's museum service were similarly helpful. The staffs of the National Library of Scotland in Edinburgh, Aberdeen University Library and the Public Library in Inverness helped track down a wide range of North American publications. Sir Donald Cameron of Lochiel kindly supplied me with copies of correspondence in his family archives. Norman Macdonald, a long-standing Skye friend and a man who has lived and worked on both sides of the Atlantic, provided me with material I should not otherwise have discovered. Alasdair MacEachen from Benbecula did the same.

I am grateful to Cailean Maclean, William Hunter, Wallace Ellison, Peter Langer, William Munoz, the Scottish Highland Photo Library, the National Trust for Scotland, the US National Parks Service, the New York State Department of Economic Development, the Canadian Tourist Office, Parks Canada, Gouvernement du Quebec and Alberta Tourism for kindly supplying me with the photographs which illustrate this book.

To the US National Parks Service staffs at Moore's Creek Bridge in North Carolina and at Saratoga in upstate New York, my thanks for their courtesy in dealing with my frequently protracted questions. Equal gratitude is due to the staffs of Parks Canada at Fortress Louisbourg in Cape Breton Island, at Grosse Ile in the St Lawrence, at the Plains Interpretation Center in Quebec City, at the North West Company warehouse in Lachine, Montreal, and at Lower Fort Garry in Manitoba. The staffs of a wide range of other more locally managed historic sites were every bit as co-operative. This was especially the case at Fort King George in Darien, Georgia; at the Miners Museum in Glace Bay, Cape Breton Island; at Johnson Hall in Johnstown, New York; at the Nor'Westers and Loyalist Museum in Glengarry County, Ontario; at Old Fort William in Thunder Bay, Northern Ontario; and at Spokane House in Washington State.

My interest in the connection between the Scottish Highlands and North America dates back to a summer course which I taught some ten years ago at the University College of Cape Breton under the auspices of Ora McManus and Sheldon MacInnes. I have been kept in touch with more recent Cape Breton Island developments by Frances MacEachen of *Am Braighe*, a periodical which is essential reading for anyone wanting to be informed about the Highland diaspora.

I am enormously indebted, of course, to the many historians and other writers whose works are cited in my bibliography. I am especially grateful to Marianne McLean whose book, *The People of Glengarry*, is a model of its kind. Both Marianne and her husband, Philip Goldring, received me very warmly in their Ottawa home. As well as making a series of most helpful comments on a typescript version of this book's earlier chapters, Marianne took time to show me round Glengarry County on the sort of dreadfully hot day when she could very easily have found something more enjoyable to do. Other Glengarry County residents who helped freely with this project include Harriet MacKinnon, David G. Anderson and Ken and Ann McKenna.

The hospitality which I received in Glengarry County was replicated everywhere I went in North America. In Thunder Bay, Northern Ontario, I was generously entertained by Jean Morrison and her colleagues in the Thunder Bay Historical Society. I am grateful to Kathryn Beach of the Museum of the Cape Fear in Fayetteville, North Carolina, and to Barry Hillman of the Manitoba Museum of Man and Nature in Winnipeg for having so enthusiastically responded to my requests for assistance. I am thankful to John Currie who farms near Moosomin in Saskatchewan for the way in which he took a wandering Highlander in from the cold. And I am grateful to Maureen Lyons and her colleagues in the Vancouver Gaelic Choir for having allowed me to disrupt a choir practice with much genealogical questioning.

My trip to Vancouver also provided me with the chance to meet for the first time some of my own North American relatives. My third cousin, Anne Harper, and Anne's mother, Ina Harper, drove me to the Fraser Canyon, plied me with food and made me appreciate the extent to which kinship links between the Scottish Highlands and North America are capable of surviving the stresses placed on them by distance.

I shall always remember the warmth of the welcome accorded to me by Charlie MacDonald, Tom and Beverly Branson, Eileen Decker and other members of their family on the Flathead Reservation in Montana. With me on that occasion was my good friend, Jim McLeod. Jim and his wife, Judy, have generously assisted with this project ever since it began to take shape. Their home in Coeur d'Alene, North Idaho, will forever be associated in my mind with the happiest of memories.

Bill Campbell, Peter MacKenzie and others at Mainstream have once more encouraged me to keep writing. Evelyn, my wife, has been strongly supportive as always. And my teenage children have put up with their father absenting himself from their lives for rather longer than he should have done. To both of them, with love, this book is dedicated.

Names Personal and Otherwise

THE SPELLING OF both Scottish and North American place names has varied greatly in the course of the last 250 years. I have mostly used the forms which appear on modern maps. I have imposed a similar uniformity on surnames which, in any book dealing with Scottish Highlanders, cause particular difficulties. In the case of a name like MacKay – which might also appear, even at different phases in the career of the same person, as Mackay, McKay or even M'Kay – I have preferred the MacKay form except in instances when it would be totally perverse to do so. Thus John A. Macdonald, the Canadian statesman, to take an obvious example, has been allowed to retain his lowercase 'd' on the grounds of long-standing usage, familiarity and fame. I have tried to be similarly tolerant of the foibles of the still living individuals mentioned in ensuing pages. Most of the dead, however, have had their surnames standardised along the lines just indicated. From their shades, descendants and biographers, I request both mercy and forbearance.

CHAPTER ONE

King George and Broadswords!

ONCE IT WAS a road of sorts. Now it is a neatly maintained US National Parks Service footpath which takes you towards the spot where a narrow bridge carried the original, more rough-and-ready, thoroughfare across Moore's Creek. Tall trees protect this path from the full force of a North Carolina summer's sun. But it is desperately hot here all the same. Nothing stirs except mosquitoes. The air is as motionless as the creek's dark waters which, in this tidewater landscape, are already on a level with the distant sea.

On so sweltering an August afternoon, more than two centuries after the event, it is difficult to imagine men dying here in the altogether colder, misty half-light of a February dawn; difficult to recreate in your mind the fear and the confusion that always go along with battle; difficult to think of Moore's Creek Bridge and its surroundings as they were at the time of the fighting which caused this otherwise unimportant tract of swamp and forest to be designated one of modern America's foremost historic sites.

But some small indication of what went on here eight weeks into 1776 can still be picked out on the ground. That long and slightly curving mound near the crest of the low ridge which overlooks Moore's Creek was then a freshly constructed embankment, smelling strongly of raw earth. The ridge's defenders sprawl full-length behind this all too scanty piece of cover. Their muskets are cradled to their cheeks, each musket barrel pointing towards the bridge not very many paces down below.

The visibility is poor. But it is not poor enough to shelter those other troops who are known to be just north of Moore's Creek and who are seen suddenly to be getting to this side of it. One of those attackers, shouting something in a language none of the waiting men can understand, is far before the rest. Clutching in one hand an upraised sword, he comes running full tilt up the gentle incline from the creek. 'He was a brave soldier,' one of his opponents will soon be writing of this man, 'and would have done honour to a good cause.' But these are sentiments of the sort that flourish only in the aftermath of combat. Just now there is no room for generosity. Fingers tighten on a score of triggers. The swordsman, it seems probable, is dead before he falls.[1]

Many of the other individuals shortly to be killed beside Moore's Creek cannot nowadays be named with any certainty. But the man whose courage so impressed even his enemies is among the few who can be satisfactorily identified. He was called Donald MacLeod and he was in charge that February morning of several hundred troops whose names, like their commander's own, were redolent of Scotland. MacLean, MacNeil, MacDougall, runs a list of some of those soon to be taken prisoner here. Campbell, Stewart, MacEachen, this long list continues, Cameron, MacPhail, MacLennan and MacRae.[2]

These men were not full-time soldiers. Mostly, in fact, they were farmers. But they were also Gaelic-speaking Scottish Highlanders. And so they had been turned out to fight in the familiar Scottish Highland manner. This meant that they had been pressed or persuaded, by Donald MacLeod and by others of their officers, to leave behind their homes, their wives, their families and to march away to war.

Such had been the pattern in their homeland for a dozen or more generations. Such, so far at least, remained the pattern here in their new country. For all this country's distance from the glens and islands where the largest number of them had been born, it was as if the men who mustered here beside Moore's Creek felt still that matters of this kind ought to be ordered in accordance with tradition. Something clearly of the customs of their people had survived the ocean crossing; that something which had brought them – in some instances, it seems certain, against their better judgment – to this spot where they found themselves expected to unleash one of those pell-mell Highland charges which had put to flight so many overwhelmingly superior formations in the past.

And there was now, for just a moment, a glimpse of what had been experienced at Prestonpans, at Killiecrankie, at all the other Old World battlefields where Highlanders had been victorious. Among the long-leaf pines, it would later be reported, the polished blades of broadswords glinted in the first, faint light of morning. There was the sound of bagpipes. Not since Scotland's final Jacobite rebellion, thirty years before, had an army quite like this prepared for battle. No such army ever would exist again.

Command this day should have belonged to Donald MacDonald,

a professional military man who had most recently been in action at a place called Bunker Hill in Massachussetts. But the elderly MacDonald – who, had the times been better ordered, might have already retired to his family home in the southern corner of the Isle of Skye – had been exhausted by forced marches through unsettled, trackless country. The previous evening, with his health clearly giving out, MacDonald had summoned his senior subordinates and told them that, for the time being, they would take their orders from the one remaining regular soldier at the ailing Skyeman's disposal, this Donald MacLeod whose unenviable task it was to storm Moore's Creek Bridge.

Also in attendance at that anxious conference, where there had been taken the decision to secure this vital crossing, was the man now serving as MacLeod's second-in-command. His name was Allan MacDonald. As was equally true both of Donald MacDonald and Donald MacLeod – to the former of whom he was, in fact, closely related – Allan belonged to one of those families who stood just below the region's chieftains in the Scottish Highland scheme of things. All three men, like several others readying themselves for combat in the woods adjacent to Moore's Creek, were of the class to which Scotland's clans had customarily looked for leadership. In their own Gaelic language the members of this class were *daoine uaisle*, a phrase denoting elevated rank and status. In English, just then beginning to be heard more often in the Highlands, they were usually called tacksmen – a tack being one of the names given to the piece of land which a man such as Allan MacDonald generally expected to occupy in return for such services, military or otherwise, as his chief might from time to time exact. There being no small prestige to be gained in Scotland from territorial designations of this sort, the name of his tack or tenancy was habitually linked to the tacksman's own. So Allan, though he had recently put the breadth of the Atlantic between himself and Skye, still called himself MacDonald of Kingsburgh. By thus advertising his connection with the locality of that name, Allan proclaimed himself a man of standing in his hierarchically organised community.

Now, just as so many others of his background and position had previously done in Scotland, this archetypal Highland gentleman was about to lead the men of his community into battle. Little glory would accrue to Allan from what was about to follow. But it was of some small subsequent consolation to him, perhaps, that it was as MacDonald of Kingsburgh that he would be formally identified, even when the captive of those aggressively egalitarian Americans whose steadily mounting challenge to British rule this far-travelled Skyeman was so disastrously determined to resist.

Allan MacDonald's Scottish home, in its sheltering grove of wind-bent trees just to the east of the fiord-like inlet of Loch Snizort, looks out on a typical Skye patchwork of sea and moor and hill; all blues and greens on a fine summer's morning; a less enticing blend of washed-out greys and browns on one of those winter days when slanting sheets of rain are marched across the landscape by an Atlantic storm of the sort so common here at the north-western end of Europe.

This was one of the places sought out by Dr Samuel Johnson, then England's foremost man of letters, when he journeyed to Skye in the company of his Scots friend and future biographer, James Boswell. Theirs was an extraordinary adventure, undertaken in the steadily deteriorating weather of an island autumn at a time when Johnson was well into his sixties and at a period when this part of Scotland, now given over very largely to tourism, possessed no roads and not much in the way of inns. But on reaching Kingsburgh at the end of a day when, as Boswell remembered, 'it rained very hard' and 'Dr Johnson appeared to be somewhat out of spirits', the two travellers were promptly taken in for the night by Allan MacDonald, 'completely the figure of a gallant Highlander', in Boswell's recollection. 'He had his tartan plaid thrown about him, a large blue bonnet with a knot of black ribband like a cockade, a brown short coat of a kind of duffil, a tartan waistcoat with gold buttons and gold buttonholes, a bluish philibeg and tartan hose. He had jet black hair tied behind him and was a large, stately man with a steady, sensible countenance.'[3]

This, then, was the Highland tacksman in his native setting: lavishly dressed, perhaps a trifle self-important, certainly hospitable. But Allan's literary visitors, as is made clear by their separately published accounts of their island jauntings, were much more interested in Kingsburgh's wife than in her husband. She was, Boswell noted of this lady in the journal he kept by him while in Skye, 'a little woman, of a genteel appearance, and uncommonly mild and well bred'. Johnson concurred. His hostess's name, he added a little portentously, would 'be mentioned in history and, if courage and fidelity be virtues, mentioned with honour'.[4]

The name in question was that of Flora MacDonald. And its fame – which was clearly sufficient to have persuaded even Samuel Johnson to set aside his curmudgeonly tendency to treat with insistent scepticism each and every Scottish claim to merit or distinction – derived from events in the summer of 1746. Then it was that Flora had famously come to the assistance of the fugitive Jacobite prince, Charles Edward Stuart, whose arrival in Scotland, some twelve months before, had precipitated the Highland uprising which ended so calamitously at the Battle of Culloden. Flora's own closest kin in Skye had not participated in the rebellion, preferring to take the side, officially at least, of the Hanoverian monarchy which the Jacobites were attempting to overthrow. This, however, had not prevented her helping the beaten Charles make his way from Uist across the Minch to Skye and on to Raasay in the course of the prince's protracted, but ultimately successful, escape to France.

It was to be claimed in the aftermath of the Moore's Creek Bridge engagement that Flora – mounted, or so the story went, on a white horse – had pronounced a Gaelic blessing on Donald MacDonald's soldiers prior to their setting off to confront those of their fellow colonists who had chosen openly to defy the American rule of King George III and his ministers. This particular tale, to be sure, was very possibly the product of further runaway romanticism of the sort which had so enormously overblown the now middle-aged Mrs MacDonald's earlier role in the affair of Charles Edward Stuart. But there was certainly no doubting her husband's prominent part in the proceedings which, at this same Moore's Creek Bridge, were to result in a decisive setback for the cause which both Allan and Flora had so eagerly adopted almost from the moment of their setting foot in North America.

Johnson and Boswell had discovered the Kingsburgh family to be contemplating emigration. That was in September 1773. The MacDonalds duly left the following summer, taking what was getting to be a well-worn route from Skye to the Cape Fear River country of North Carolina. Pausing briefly in Cross Creek, the little town at the centre of an increasingly extensive set of Highland settlements in the valley of the Cape Fear River, Allan and Flora had pushed westwards to a locality then known as Mount Pleasant, afterwards renamed Cameron's Hill. Here, through the winter of 1774–75, they made a temporary home on a plantation owned by relatives, also of the name MacDonald, who had emigrated from Cuidreach – maybe four miles north of Kingsburgh – some three years before.[5]

The terrain in the vicinity of Cameron's Hill is just a little bit more undulating than the countryside around Moore's Creek. It looks to be considerably more fertile also. That is why substantial numbers of Scottish Highland emigrants – MacLeods, MacQueens, MacKinnons, Campbells, Camerons, MacNeils and MacDiarmids among others – had been gravitating here for twenty years or more before the Kingsburgh MacDonalds became Mount Pleasant's newest residents.[6]

Not far away, at Barbecue Creek, is the church maintained by North Carolina's oldest Presbyterian congregation. This congregation's modern redbrick building, surrounded by trim lawns and topped off by a slender spire, is very different from the place of worship first constructed on this site in 1765. That church was made from nothing more elaborate than logs. But the people now in charge here remain sufficiently connected with the original church's founders to have paid those founders an appropriate public tribute. *Ceud Mile Failte*, their roadside noticeboard proclaims in the Gaelic spoken by this Barbecue Church's earliest preachers. One hundred thousand welcomes.

In a corner of the immediately adjacent graveyard are the tombstones marking the last resting place of men and women whose lives began in eighteenth-century Scotland. 'Jennie McLean, who died May 6,

1823, aged 84', reads the barely legible inscription on one plain slab of hand-carved rock. On this particular grave there has not long before been placed a bunch of flowers. Although North America's preoccupation with the present and the future is one of the things that make a country like the United States attractive to the visitor from a more history-ridden continent like Europe, it seems somehow heartening to come across this evidence of a community retaining still some linkage with its origins.

Cameron's Hill came to be so called, of course, because Highland families of that name – families from the Cameron homeland of Lochaber – first undertook the task of carving out of old growth forest all the fields you see around you here today. Six, seven, eight or more generations on from that beginning, some at least of these same families – as can be demonstrated simply by conducting a quick check of the names on farm mailboxes – are still living on the North Carolina homesteads to which their folks were given title some twenty, thirty, forty years before the USA existed.

Allan and Flora MacDonald, as is evident from the descriptions of their Skye lifestyle provided by Johnson and Boswell, were no humble pioneers, having sufficient cash at their disposal to avoid the desperately hard work which other, much more typical, Highland emigrants had to undertake immediately on reaching North America. The MacDonalds felled no trees and built no log cabins. Instead, in the spring of 1775, they bought an already existing plantation and its accompanying house. Here Allan and Flora installed their children, their eight servants and such furniture, books and other possessions as they had been able to ship with them from their previous home beside Loch Snizort.

The Kingsburgh family, it is clear, intended to occupy as prominent a position in North Carolina as they had occupied in Skye. Wider events, however, were to get in the way of this ambition, the MacDonalds having arrived in the Cape Fear River country at just the moment when the gradually developing crisis in relations between Britain's increasingly assertive American colonies, on the one side, and one of Britain's more than usually incompetent governments, on the other, came finally to a head. This was arguably a good time for newly settled immigrants to lie low politically. But the Kingsburgh MacDonalds – who had got themselves into considerable financial difficulty when in Skye and who were to make no better a job of managing their lives in North Carolina – promptly chose to involve themselves personally and directly in the ensuing conflict.

Quarrels about colonial taxation – turning eventually on the very basic issue of whether or not the imperial parliament was constitutionally entitled to raise revenues in Britain's overseas possessions – had begun in the 1760s and, by the early 1770s, when Allan and Flora were just starting to consider emigration, American resistance to London's ever more insistent claims was being co-ordinated and directed by a steadily spreading network of Committees of Correspondence. These, for all their innocuous title, were to be the means of organising revolution – first in Massachussetts, where separatist feeling was strongest, and afterwards in almost all the several other British colonies then strung out along North America's Atlantic coast.

Following a number of Bostonians deciding in December 1773 to dump a consignment of tea in their city's harbour rather than pay the duty which London ministers had levied on it, the imperial authorities began to impose a series of increasingly coercive measures on their American subjects – only to find the Committees of Correspondence convening a Continental Congress to give voice to their more and more far-reaching demands. These demands, couched in terms which implied that Britain should immediately abandon its claims to fiscal overlordship of the colonies, were wholly unacceptable – as the more radical spirits among the Americans clearly hoped would be the case – to the British government. Thus there commenced a seemingly unstoppable drift to war, with actual fighting breaking out at Lexington, near Boston, on 19 April 1775.

Within a very few weeks of the news from Lexington having reached North Carolina, Allan MacDonald, though then resident in the colony for not much more than six months, was offering his active support to the loyalist side in the developing military contest. MacDonald's close collaborator in this enterprise was one more member of Skye's Gaelic-speaking gentry, Alexander MacLeod, son-in-law to the Kingsburgh MacDonalds and, like them, a recent addition to the Scottish Highland community in the Cape Fear River country. MacDonald and MacLeod, the authorities in London were informed by their North Carolina representative, Governor Josiah Martin, were 'men of great worth and good character'. They had 'most extensive influence over the Highlanders here', Martin wrote. With these two estimable gentlemen's freely available assistance, the governor went on optimistically, he could readily raise three thousand 'effective men' to counter the growing rebel activity in the colony.[7]

The prospect of recruiting such a force was naturally of interest to senior officers at the British army's American headquarters in Boston. It was at their instigation that two Highlanders then serving with the British forces in that quarter, Donald MacDonald and Donald MacLeod, were despatched to North Carolina in the autumn of 1775. MacDonald was promoted, for the occasion, from colonel to brigadier-general and given the task of rallying the Cape Fear Highlanders to his colours. MacLeod was to have the rank of colonel and serve as the general's second-in-command.

The two men's further instructions were that the Highland militia detachment which Britain's commanders in America hoped thus to have placed at their disposal should, in the early weeks of 1776, march eastwards to the sea where General MacDonald would make contact, or so it was intended, with regular troops to be conveyed to North Carolina by the Royal Navy. This combined force was then to set about the business of securing both North Carolina and its neighbouring colonies for the Crown.

It was as a first step towards the attainment of these ambitious objectives that General MacDonald, in January 1776, issued from Cross Creek, North Carolina, a 'manifesto' which invited 'every well-wisher to that form of government under which they so happily lived . . . to repair to His Majesty's royal standard, erected at Cross Creek, where they will meet with every possible civility and be . . . engaged in the best and most glorious of all causes, supporting the rights and constitution of their country'.[8]

The general, of course, had the enthusiastic backing both of his cousin, Allan MacDonald of Kingsburgh, and Kingsburgh's own kinsman-by-marriage, Alexander MacLeod. But for all their efforts and for all Governor Martin's continued assurances that the 'Scotch Highlanders' were 'generally and almost without exception staunch to government', it proved no easy matter to get men to enlist. When General MacDonald eventually marched out of Cross Creek in the direction of the Atlantic coast on 18 February 1776, therefore, he had only some 1,500 troops – and poorly armed troops at that – under his command.[9]

Those much more numerous North Carolinians who felt themselves to have less in common with the British monarchy than with the Continental Congress had meanwhile been making their own preparations for battle. The colony had eagerly organised an early contribution to the Continental Army which Congress had established under the leadership of General George Washington. And by 15 February, one of the Continental Army's locally raised units, the First North Carolina Regiment, commanded by Colonel James Moore, had taken up position some seven miles outside Cross Creek – on the route which MacDonald was expected to follow eastwards. Reinforcements were joining Moore daily. Soon it was clear that the Highland loyalist detachment, of which so much had been expected by the like of Governor Martin, was going to have to engage in a good deal of stiff fighting if it was ever to win through to the sea.

On 19 February, partly with a view to spying out the nature of Moore's troop dispositions and partly perhaps with a view to delaying a battle which he may have already suspected that he might not win, MacDonald, whose first day's march had ended – a little ingloriously – a mere four miles from his Cross Creek base, sent a letter-carrying emissary to his Continental Army counterpart. The general's message was couched in his now customary style. 'I must suppose you unacquainted,'

Moore was informed by MacDonald, 'with the . . . proclamation commanding all His Majesty's loyal subjects to repair to the king's loyal standard . . . else I should have imagined you would ere this have joined the king's army.' MacDonald, however, seriously misjudged his man. James Moore, whose family had been settled in North America since the seventeenth century, had already been described by a more discerning loyalist than the general as a soldier whose 'unblemished character', 'amiable manners' and 'virtuous life' made him one of the colony's most popular and most trusted leaders. Such a commander was clearly most unlikely to be intimidated by bombast of the type which Donald MacDonald had made his speciality. And so it proved. He had consulted his officers, ran Moore's despatch of 20 February to MacDonald, and he had been pleased to discover that they were of one mind with himself. 'We consider ourselves engaged in a cause the most glorious and honourable in the world, the defence of the liberties of mankind, in the support of which we are determined to hazard everything dear and valuable.'[10]

To this the First North Carolina Regiment's colonel added a comment which could not have done other than make some impact on MacDonald's recently recruited troops – if they were ever made aware of it. No small proportion of the Cape Fear Highlanders, as James Moore knew very well, had received considerable financial aid from the North Carolina legislature on their arrival in the colony. Now, the American officer pointed out, these same Highlanders were 'about to make . . . ungrateful return for their favourable reception in this country'. And if reflection on this circumstance was not sufficient to persuade General MacDonald's soldiers that they ought, in fact, to be on the side of Congress and the Continental Army, then, Moore suggested, MacDonald might perhaps be good enough to inform his troops that they were 'engaged in a cause . . . which must end in their utter destruction'.[11]

That destruction was necessarily to be delayed, however. For on the morning of 21 February, Moore awoke to be informed, to his considerable surprise, that the Highland army had suddenly withdrawn. Under cover of darkness, it transpired, the loyalist force had been got over to the further bank of the Cape Fear River. All available boats, it also became evident, had been destroyed to delay any attempt at pursuit. Donald MacDonald, it was clear, was intent on giving the Americans the slip and continuing his push for the Atlantic through forest country where he hoped to avoid any out-and-out confrontation before effecting his planned junction with the stronger force promised by British headquarters.

This latest plan James Moore and other Continental Army commanders now set out to frustrate with deadly effect; deploying their forces in such a way as effectively to encircle the loyalist army, leaving the Highlanders with little alternative but sooner or later to walk into a trap of the sort which their American opponents set for them at Moore's Creek.

At first light on 27 February, the morning after the worn-out General MacDonald's decision to surrender his command to Donald MacLeod, the loyalist advance guard found themselves among the pine trees just beside that sluggish watercourse. The creek had to be crossed if the Highlanders were ever to reach the coast. But Continental Army units, it was immediately obvious, were already in the vicinity. The bridge, which was the one sure way to get across a channel much too deep and treacherous ever to be forded, had been partially demolished. Its roadway had gone entirely. All that remained were the three squared timber beams which had been used by the bridge's builders to provide their structure with a frame to which decking planks had then been nailed. Less imaginative men than the Americans responsible for this piece of sabotage would no doubt have removed even the bridge's supporting timbers. Instead these timbers had been left as an enticement to the unwary. But by way of adding to any attack force's difficulties they had also been carefully smeared with home-made soap and tallow. This was a simple stratagem. But it was to prove quite shattering in its impact.

An exchange of shouted challenges and counter-challenges had already made clear to Colonel Donald MacLeod and his men that some sort of American detachment was in possession of the far bank of the creek. But MacLeod had no means of knowing at this stage just how well-defended a position he was up against. As his enemies intended, therefore, the fact that a crossing of Moore's Creek could still be attempted had the effect of persuading this loyalist commander of less than one day's standing to mount an immediate attack. But what was left of the bridge had been so treated by the Americans, of course, as to make it impossible for the Highlanders to make one of those massed, screaming charges which were their favourite tactic. Being unable to advance at speed and in large numbers, MacLeod's troops were equally prevented from engaging in the close-quarter, hand-to-hand fighting in which Scotland's clans had long excelled.

A more cautious – and maybe a better – soldier, foreseeing at least some of this, would surely have paused to consider his next move. But that was not Donald MacLeod's way. Running on to the remnants of Moore's Creek Bridge, MacLeod set out across one of its slippery wooden beams, digging his sword point into the beam's surface to retain his balance, yelling at his men to hurry. From the woods behind the colonel came the shouted rallying cry agreed among the loyalists prior to their going into battle: 'King George and Broadswords!'[12]

From the rising ground on the far side of the creek there was at first no answering sound of any kind. Then, just as the Highlanders began in more substantial numbers to attempt the crossing of Moore's Creek, a volley of small arms fire rang out – followed, a few seconds later, by the deeper and still more alarming din of the several artillery pieces which the Americans had just had time to get dug in behind their earth embankment.

Donald MacLeod, one of the few Highlanders to get clear across Moore's Creek that morning, was also the first to die, nine musket balls and twenty-four pellets of swan-shot afterwards being taken from his mangled body. Several dozen of MacLeod's soldiers, struggling to maintain some sort of foothold on the greasy bridge supports which had been so efficiently transformed into a deathtrap, were quickly killed in the ensuing chaos. Then, a mere two or three minutes after the first shots had been heard and seeing that they were quite literally lining up to be slaughtered, the dead men's surviving comrades took precipitately to their heels, throwing away both their swords and their muskets – the victorious Americans, whose casualties numbered only two, swarming in their turn now across the half-demolished bridge to set off in hot pursuit of the retreating Highlanders.

A few of the loyalist troops escaped entirely. Among this group was Torquil MacLeod who, having served previously with one of Britain's regular regiments, was employed by Donald MacDonald to train and drill his little army in the weeks before the general started on his eastward march out of Cross Creek. MacLeod somehow managed, or so it was afterwards reported, 'to secret himself from the enemy in the back parts of North Carolina', going on eventually to join the British forces once again.[13]

More typical, however, was the experience of John MacRae, no more than twelve months in North Carolina when the Revolutionary War began and so unsure of English as to require an interpreter to make his eventual claim to the British government in respect of the losses – including ownership rights to an extensive tract of land – which he had incurred as result of taking up that government's cause. MacRae, according to the man employed to translate and set down his subsequent appeal for some financial compensation, had 'lost his right arm by a gunshot after which he suffered captivity'.[14]

Several hundred of MacRae's fellow Highlanders were also taken prisoner by the Continental Army in the hours immediately following the Moore's Creek débâcle. The private soldiers among them were mostly released and allowed to return to their Cape Fear River farms on swearing an oath that they would not again take up arms in opposition to the Continental Congress. Those of higher rank, however, were to receive less lenient treatment, the Americans suspecting, quite correctly, that the former tacksmen who loomed so large in the defeated loyalist contingent's command structure were the principal source of such counter-revolutionary feeling as existed in the Cape Fear River country. Thus it came about that Allan MacDonald of Kingsburgh, who had been theoretically in command of this last Highland army in the minutes following Donald MacLeod's death, was conveyed from Moore's Creek to an overcrowded prison at Halifax, near North Carolina's border with Virginia.

It was at Halifax in April 1776 – as this tidy little town takes care to inform all its modern visitors – that the North Carolina Provincial Congress, its members much encouraged by what had occurred at Moore's Creek Bridge, became the first representative body in all of North America to vote in favour of ending constitutional links between the colonies and Britain. What Allan MacDonald thought of this development is not recorded. Nor is there any way of knowing what the Kingsburgh tacksman made of subsequent events in Philadelphia – to where he had been transferred, along with other loyalist prisoners, at about the time the Continental Congress was meeting in that Pennsylvanian city to consider its next move.

Not only had all men been created equal, Congress proclaimed on 4 July 1776. They had also been endowed by their creator with certain inalienable rights, among them life, liberty and the pursuit of happiness. It was in order to secure these same rights, the Continental Congress went on to agree, that governments had been instituted among men, deriving their just powers from the consent of the governed. And it was because King George III and his ministers had so signally failed to honour their side of that bargain, so Congress now concluded, that Americans were both legally and morally entitled to opt for independence.

Admirably democratic though they might be, these were sentiments which more socially elevated Highlanders like the MacDonalds of Kingsburgh were not at all inclined to take to heart – their background and upbringing being such as to make them much more favourably disposed to aristocracy and monarchy than to the revolutionary concept of a sovereign people. Allan and Flora aspired now only to return as soon as possible to Scotland. And back to Skye they were eventually to go. This was, however, most untypical of emigrants to North America from the MacDonald family's homeland. Innumerable other Scottish Highlanders would warm to this continent in ways which the Kingsburgh tacksman and his wife never did quite understand.

CHAPTER TWO

What, Then, is the American, This New Man?

THE ENORMOUS SIZE of the United States has long been one of this country's most obvious characteristics. And there are plenty of American localities where the traveller is constantly aware of the apparent limitlessness of the surrounding landscape. But the tidewater region, just behind the Atlantic seaboard between Virginia and Florida, is not one of them. After several hours on Interstate 95, heading through South Carolina and on into Georgia, seeing nothing all the while but the solid-seeming walls of forest which loom over the highway, the prospect of a brief diversion is so tempting as to give Darien, a community of less than two thousand people, an allure it might not otherwise have.

Darien, you quickly gather from the brochures on offer at the municipality's Welcome Center, is one of those numerous tidewater towns which did rather better economically in the nineteenth century than they have ever managed to do in the twentieth. A timber and cotton trade of international significance was once handled here. Now Darien's waterfront, on the north branch of the Altamaha river delta, comes to life only when the local fishing fleet puts into port.[1]

The Welcome Center stands on what is known in these parts as a bluff. Although not much more than twenty feet above the chocolate-coloured Altamaha, which threatens hereabouts to lose itself among a mass of swampy and reed-covered islands, the bluff in question is a vantage-point of real significance. That is why, when Darien began to acquire its first European settlers, this little piece of rising ground was promptly fitted out with cannons, bastions, half-bastions, stockades,

23

blockhouses and all the other paraphernalia thought appropriate to an early eighteenth-century fortification.

Nor was there anything exaggerated about the fears which lay behind these military preparations. The men who manned this Darien outpost, together with the wives and families they brought here, were positioned on the southern edge of Britain's colonial territories in North America. Beyond this point, some 250 years ago, political dominance belonged either to the Creeks, a native people, or to Spain, a country which, since the time of Christopher Columbus, had maintained an active presence in the general vicinity of Florida and the Gulf of Mexico. Both the Creeks and the Spaniards, more especially the latter who had their own imperial claims on Georgia, were rightly thought to threaten Britain's hold upon this then very sparsely populated region. Thus the need for strongpoints of the sort constructed on that slope above the Altamaha. And thus James Edward Oglethorpe's evident sense of being among soldiers when he came here to Darien in February 1736.

Oglethorpe, as Georgia's governor, was responsible to the privately managed trust on which King George II had bestowed effective owner-ship of the colony in 1732. And it was to the trust's directors, back in London, that the governor now reported on Darien's resident troops who, Oglethorpe wrote, presented 'a most manly appearance with their plaids, broadswords, targes and firearms'. He had been offered 'a very good bed', complete with holland sheets and curtains, for the duration of his stay, the governor continued. But in deference to his hosts, whose uncompromisingly spartan lifestyle he had clearly made up his mind to adopt as completely as possible, Oglethorpe, himself an army officer by profession, had opted instead to sleep in the open. Although 'the night was very cold', his superiors were informed, he had been content to stretch out on the ground 'under a great tree'. There he had lain, right through the hours of darkness, keeping close to the 'guard fire' and, for additional warmth, wrapping around himself the 'Highland habit' with which his Darien troops had presented him.[2]

The technique of conscripting tribal levies at one end of an empire and deploying those same levies on some other imperial frontier several thousand miles away is one at least as old as Rome. But it was James Edward Oglethorpe, on his being sent from England to Georgia as governor, who can be said to have first grasped the possibilities which Scottish Highlanders thus offered to those attempting to enforce British rule in North America.

The Highlands, as far as governments in London were concerned, constituted a much bigger military problem than anything likely to be faced by Oglethorpe. Many Highlanders still hankered stubbornly after the exiled Stuart monarchs who had been deprived of both the Scottish and English crowns in 1689. Hence the tendency for Britain's principal European enemies, France and Spain, to look on the Scottish Highlands as a perennially promising invasion route. Hence, too, the close association between a number of Highland clans and the long series of Jacobite risings brought finally to an end by the defeat of the Stuart prince whom Flora MacDonald helped protect in the months following his flight from Culloden.

Where others – quite understandably – saw only the danger posed to Britain by Highland disaffection, Georgia's governor discerned an opportunity. Although he was eventually to get back to England in time to take an active part in operations against Prince Charles Edward Stuart's mostly Highland army in 1745, Oglethorpe was himself to be accused at various points in his career of clinging secretly in adulthood to the Jacobite doctrines which he was known to have embraced openly in his youth. Irrespective of the truth or otherwise of such allegations, the governor's lifelong interest in everything to do with the Scottish Highlands – an interest demonstrated by the fact that a Gaelic grammar was among the many purchases he made at the 1785 sale in London of Samuel Johnson's library – was clearly real enough. It was certainly sufficient to make Oglethorpe well aware of the undoubted military prowess of Scottish Highlanders. It is by no means surprising, therefore, that Georgia's governor should have decided that his struggling colony might effectively be safeguarded from possible Creek and Spanish incursions by a force of Scottish clansmen.[3]

The first such clansmen left for Georgia in October 1735 from Inverness, the principal town in the Highlands and a place where Oglethorpe was afterwards to be made an honorary burgess. This particular party – whose names are listed in a pamphlet produced in 1986 by the great-great-great-great-granddaughter of two of these Highland pioneers in order to mark the 250th anniversary of her people's arrival in North America – numbered 177 individuals. Perhaps 100 of these were soldiers or potential soldiers, most of them young men of about twenty years of age. It was this group that Georgia's governor was to visit in their newly fortified settlement on the Altamaha River in the early part of 1736.[4]

These people are commemorated nowadays by the Highlander Memorial near Darien's civic buildings, just across the street from the carefully preserved remnants of what is traditionally reputed to have been the tree mentioned by Governor Oglethorpe when reporting on his first trip here. Large oaks, their branches draped in ragged streamers of the Spanish Moss which is one of the most distinctive features of the American South, are still to be seen in various parts of Darien. But this one must have been a more than normally grand specimen. It had a girth of more than fifteen feet when measured in 1895, according to the metal plaque beside its stump. And the spread of its branches was then such as to have made it possible for this huge tree to have provided no less than five thousand men with shelter of the sort which James Edward

Oglethorpe and his Highland troops were seeking that chilly February night in 1736.

The governor, for all that he might well have wished his vulnerable colony could muster such resources, never had more than a fraction of this number of soldiers at his disposal. But Oglethorpe was able to go at least some way towards overcoming his paucity of military muscle by ensuring that several hundred more Highlanders – women and children as well as fighting men – were established here on the north bank of the Altamaha between 1737 and 1741. As was true of their predecessors, the bulk of these new arrivals – MacIntoshes, MacPhersons, Grants, Frasers and the like – belonged originally to the hill country in the immediate vicinity of Inverness. Others – and MacKays predominated in this category – came from the north-western corner of Sutherland, a place as cold, treeless and windswept as Georgia is typically humid, well-wooded and hot.[5]

It usually took the best part of three months to make the sea voyage here in the 1730s. Now, in summer anyway, you can reach Darien from Inverness by air in the space between the same day's sunrise and sunset. Nor is Georgia, of course, the untamed territory it was in 1736. For all its having gone back a bit commercially since its exporting heyday, modern Darien boasts all the standard amenities of smalltown America. And as happens always in this hemisphere, its banks, food marts, insurance agencies, drugstores, high school, gas stations and hamburger restaurants have spread across so large a slice of real estate as to make Darien – actually no more than a village – seem like a relatively substantial urban centre.

'Industrious, laborious and brave', James Edward Oglethorpe called Darien's Highlanders, his strongly proprietorial feeling for this wholly Gaelic-speaking community which he had done so much to establish being such as to cause him – in the course of his despatches to Georgia's London-based trustees – to compare its progress very favourably with that of the English and Lowland Scots settlers who had installed themselves in the rather less rigorous setting of Savannah. 'Darien has been one of the settlements where the people have been most industrious as those of Savannah have been most idle,' the governor reported on one occasion. 'The trustees have had several servants there who, under the direction of Mr Moore McIntosh, have not only earned their bread but have provided the trust with such quantities of sawed stuff as has saved them a great deal of money.'[6]

Such were the beginnings of Darien's long connection with the lumber business, the town eventually relying very largely on its sawmilling of the millions of pine and cypress logs which were to be rafted down the Altamaha from forests deeper in the Georgia interior. Such, too, was the commencement of the American career of 'Mr Moore

McIntosh' whose Gaelic designation, *Iain Mor*, meaning simply Big John, was to cause endless difficulty to practically every colonial official required to set down in English the name of this man who was to play no small part in the development of colonial Georgia.

MacIntosh, though a much better soldier and a more successful settler than Allan MacDonald of Kingsburgh, belonged, like that later immigrant, to one of those gentry families who were to forge so many links between the Scottish Highlands and North America in the course of the next hundred years. A younger brother of William MacIntosh of Borlum, who was easily the most daring commander produced by the Jacobites in the course of their 1715 rising in Scotland, and a grandson of that other MacIntosh of Borlum who had fought beside the Marquis of Montrose in the cause of the Stuart kings some seventy years earlier, Iain Mor had spent his boyhood on the MacIntosh family estate near Kingussie in Badenoch – his upbringing, one may safely guess, laying considerable stress on the martial qualities which he was afterwards to demonstrate in the course of his several campaigns on the Georgia frontier.[7]

The military formation which John MacIntosh led to war on Governor Oglethorpe's behalf, following the more general outbreak of hostilities between Britain and Spain in the later 1730s, became known in time as the Georgia Highland Rangers. And though there were to be several other ranger corps – the term denotes a sort of mounted militia – on active service in the American colonies both then and later, none was ever to be quite as distinctive as this one. Provided by Oglethorpe with horses, saddles and weapons, MacIntosh and his soldiers favoured a uniform, if that is the right word in the circumstances, which was the product of a unique blend of Scottish and American influences. Troopers wore both the buckskin breeches of the frontier and the tartan plaid – made from cloth stocked especially for this purpose in Savannah – of the Highlands. While their favoured weapon was probably a musket with its barrel sawn off to make for easier handling on horseback, these Georgia rangers, whose language remained the Gaelic of the glens and straths where they had been born, also carried broadswords, dirks and targes, or shields, of the type which James Edward Oglethorpe observed during his 1736 excursion to Darien and of the type which he was to see again, no doubt, when in action against the Jacobites in 1745.[8]

The conditions in which colonial Georgia's Highland troops both lived and fought, one recent American historian has commented, were not dissimilar to those encountered by his own generation in Vietnam. This was then true wilderness: unmapped, uncharted and, by Europeans at any rate, by no means thoroughly explored; a place where sunlight brought out clouds of flies and where darkness, or the forest shade, belonged to swarms of mosquitoes. Nor were Georgia's hurriedly constructed forts any more comfortable than the surrounding woods. Men and horses were crowded together inside ramparts made from roughly sharpened tree-trunks. Such shelter as existed was provided by crudely built huts which were stiflingly hot when the sun shone and relentlessly damp when it rained. Always there were rats. Always there was the stench and filth resulting from the cramped and confined circumstances of the typical frontier garrison's existence.[9]

Sometimes also there was combat to be endured; the sort of combat that took place after long treks through country where men took care to leave blaze marks on the trees for fear of their otherwise becoming hopelessly lost; the sort of combat that could result, as happened at Fort Musa on the contested borders between the British and Spanish spheres of influence, in many Highlanders being killed or taken prisoner.[10]

That was in the summer of 1740, during the frequently confused preliminaries to those international hostilities which the American colonists called King George's War and which the British were to call the War of the Austrian Succession. The Battle of Fort Musa, which took place in what is now the northern part of Florida, marked the commencement of what was soon to be an extensive Highland involvement in this particular contest. Among the many Highlanders drawn into the steadily widening conflict were those men who died while serving with the British army's first Highland regiment, the Black Watch, on continental European battlefields like Fontenoy. Among the war's other Highland casualties were the Gaelic-speaking soldiers who were to be killed while fighting against this same British army following France's decision, on its becoming embroiled in the wider struggle, to take a certain Stuart prince by sea to Scotland.

If it had ever been possible for the people of the Scottish Highlands to isolate themselves from international developments, such isolation, as their various entanglements in the War of the Austrian Succession showed so clearly, was certainly possible no longer. The social, political and other transformations now beginning to take place across the world were to undermine and destroy the traditional, still recognisably tribal, society of the Highlands every bit as much as they were to destroy those other tribal societies which John MacIntosh and his comrades encountered among Georgia's various native peoples. And in the radically altered situation produced by those global convulsions, of course, huge numbers of Highlanders were to leave the Highlands – to leave, in particular, for North America.

Moving to distant lands was no new concept in the eighteenth-century Highlands. Both the region's people and this people's Celtic culture were the product of a previous exercise in colonisation which had involved considerable movement to Scotland from Ireland in the period following the collapse of the Roman Empire. Among these early migrants were Gaelic-speaking monks who were to travel on through the Minches to

Orkney, Shetland, Faroe, Iceland and, or so some traditions suggested, to other territories still farther to the west. Gaelic tales about a land beyond the sunset possibly required no basis other than the American tree-trunks which were washed ashore from time to time on the Atlantic beaches of islands like Tiree, Barra, Uist or Lewis. But when America was actually reached by voyagers from Viking settlements in Greenland, it was, so Icelandic sagas insist anyway, to be explored in part by people belonging to those other Norse realms which had been established during the ninth and tenth centuries in the Hebrides.[11]

Nor had there been any lack of subsequent ventures from the Scottish Highlands to overseas countries. The soldiers who were to become one of the region's principal human exports to North America were the successors of those other Highland military men who waged war in Ireland in the fifteenth and sixteenth centuries. They were the successors also of the later generations of Highland troops who fought in seventeenth- and eighteenth-century Germany, Poland and France. Although there were few stronger influences on Highlanders than their attachment to their homeland, there was nothing in this same people's history, therefore, to indicate that, should circumstances suggest such a course, they were congenitally unwilling to travel to faraway places. Rather the reverse.

While North America was certainly the destination favoured by most of the many eighteenth-century Highlanders who decided to make a fresh start elsewhere, there was one essential precondition to such emigration. This precondition was the union between England and Scotland in 1707. Prior to that date, despite the fact that both countries had shared the same monarch since 1603, Scots were legally barred from entry to England's transatlantic colonies. There were Scots in English North America to be sure. But their position was always inherently precarious. And it was by way of trying to gain formal entry to the New World that Scotland's seventeenth-century governments made a series of attempts to provide the country with its own possessions in the western hemisphere. The failure of the last of these attempts – involving Scotland's transient occupation of the Panamanian locality of Darien which was subsequently to have its name applied, in commemoration of what had gone before, to the first distinctively Highland settlement in North America – helped convince much influential Scottish opinion that accommodation with England was essential if the more northerly country was ever to obtain a meaningful share of colonial opportunities. This explains Scotland's reluctant agreement to the Treaty of Union. It explains also the significance of the treaty's fourth article: 'That all the subjects of the United Kingdom of Great Britain shall from and after the union have full freedom and intercourse of trade and navigation to and from any port or place within the said United Kingdom and the dominions and plantations thereunto belonging.'

Thus there was created a common market which embraced Scotland, England and those imperial territories which had previously belonged exclusively to the latter. And thus, from a purely Scottish perspective, there was opened a door on a whole range of novel possibilities. Now merchants from Lowland towns like Glasgow and Greenock began to acquire the important positions which they were to occupy in colonial America. Now Scottish Highlanders, too, began to put in an appearance – not least in Georgia where Darien, becoming more civilian and less military in its purpose as the Florida frontier gradually stabilised, was to retain its Highland character right through the eighteenth century.

In the autumn of 1739, at about the time that John MacIntosh and his ranger troops were beginning to become caught up in intensified fighting with Spain, there arrived in the recently established port of Wilmington, North Carolina, a ship carrying some 350 emigrants from Argyll. These people had formerly lived in the Kintyre peninsula and the adjacent islands of Islay and Gigha – the part of the Scottish Highlands, as it happens, which had initially attracted those other Gaelic-speaking colonists who had left Ireland more than a thousand years before. Now Argyll's population was on the move again. And while these latest emigrants were apparently content to remain for some months in the little town of Wilmington, then barely six years old, it was evident from the outset that what they really wished to obtain here in America was what their ancestors from Ireland had also been prepared to cross the sea to find: land which they could occupy and farm; land of the sort soon granted to them in the valley of the Cape Fear River.[12]

Quite why this immigrant group, whose leader was a man called Neil MacNeil, should have come to North Carolina in preference to other North American destinations is not known for certain. But the connection now starting to be made between the Cape Fear River country and Argyll, just like the link already forged between Darien and more northerly parts of the Scottish Highlands, possibly had its origins in the interests and attitudes of the relevant colonial governor. In the North Carolina case this man was Gabriel Johnston who had taken up office in the later part of 1734.

One of the several similarities between Governor Johnston and his Georgia counterpart, James Edward Oglethorpe, is to be found in the fact that Johnston, like Oglethorpe, was accused occasionally of harbouring Jacobite sympathies – on such grounds, for example, as his having taken no visible pleasure in what his colonial critics called the 'glorious victory of Culloden'. Such allegations, which were sometimes combined with the suggestion that his politics accounted for his having made room in North Carolina for so many Scottish Highlanders, may or may not have been securely founded, the charge of Jacobitism tending to serve much the same politically malevolent purpose in mid-eighteenth-century America as the charge of Marxism was to serve some two hundred years later. What is clear, however, is that Johnston was anxious to have the Cape Fear River district opened up to settlement. And it is possible that the governor, being a Scot himself, knew something of contemporary developments in Kintyre. There the ruling landlord, the Duke of Argyll, a man whose politics were as fervently Hanoverian as those of certain other Highland noblemen were passionately Jacobite, was showing a keen interest in innovative types of farming. Instead of being left automatically in the occupation of tacksmen whose families had long looked upon their tenancies as something approximating to an irrevocable right, Kintyre farms were now being let by the duke to comparative strangers offering higher rents. The consequent dissatisfactions – paralleled exactly in the Isle of Islay which lies westwards of Kintyre and which was also beginning to have its traditional tenures overturned by its proprietor – made this south-western corner of the Scottish Highlands an obvious source of settlers of the type Gabriel Johnston wanted to establish in the Cape Fear River territory.[13]

Nor did Kintyre and Islay people have to look very far for a potent suggestion as to how they might best escape the clutches of landlords seeking to levy increased rents. In Ulster, the part of Ireland which is nearest to Argyll and a place with which Argyll's population had maintained close contact through the centuries, rising rents had already caused extensive emigration on the part of those Presbyterian Scots farmers who had been settled there in the seventeenth century by English and Scots politicians looking to discover some permanent means of suppressing rebellion among the native, and Catholic, Irish. These Ulster emigrants, for whom Ireland was merely a staging-post on a journey which began in Scotland and ended on the far side of the Atlantic, have long been known to Americans – on whose history they exercised a profound and lasting influence – by the unlovely appellation of Scotch-Irish. The Scotch-Irish were mostly of Lowland origin, their forebears having come originally from localities like Ayrshire and Galloway. But Highlanders, too, participated in this Ulster exodus – one eighteenth-century visitor to Islay, Iona and Mull remarking, for instance, on the extent to which these Argyll islands were being denuded of people by the growing tendency of their young men and women to travel first to Ulster in search of casual employment and then to 'join the emigrants which now go annually in great shoals from the north of Ireland to America'. Irish stopovers of this sort were soon to be unnecessary, however – whole families and communities from Argyll, with their ever more discontented tacksmen to the fore, simply emulating the Ulster example and organising their own departure for America.[14]

Ulster talk to the effect that there was 'good land' to be got in the American colonies 'for little or no rent' was bound sooner or later to reach the ears of those of the Duke of Argyll's tacksmen whose own rents, just like those of Ulster farmers, were being pushed ever upwards. 'Several persons in Kintyre,' one of the duke's estate managers accordingly noted in 1729, 'in imitation of their neighbours in Ireland show a great inclination to go to New England to settle there.' The same man, Archibald Campbell, was soon reporting emigration actually getting under way. 'The adventurous disposition of going to America which has for some years prevailed in Ireland,' Campbell wrote in 1737, 'has at length come over the water and seized our people in Argyleshire to that degree that some of our landed men are about to sell their concerns and are determined to try their fortunes in that country.' Prominent among the 'landed men' in question, it is hardly necessary to add, was Neil MacNeil who was to bring those 350 emigrants from Argyll to North Carolina no more than two years later.[15]

The hundreds of Highlanders who were to come here in the 1740s and the 1750s, like the many thousands who were to follow in the 1760s and 1770s, first landed either at Wilmington or Brunswick on the Cape Fear River's lower reaches. Brunswick, though the prior settlement, was the less prepossessing of the two. 'Very poor,' one Scottish visitor called it in 1775, 'a few scattered houses on the edge of the woods without street or regularity.' But Wilmington, some sixteen miles further upstream, was wealthier, more attractive. And the countryside beyond, to that 1775 visitor whose name was Janet Schaw, seemed more appealing still. 'Nothing,' she wrote a little gushingly, 'can be finer than the banks of this river; a thousand beauties both of the flowery and the sylvan tribe hang over it and are reflected from it with additional lustre.' [16]

Most seagoing ships of the time could get as far as Wilmington. There immigrant families transferred to one of those longboats, lighters or large canoes which were the principal mode of travel on the Cape Fear River's upper reaches. Journeys which had commenced on Scotland's western seaboard, many weeks or even months before, consequently culminated in the several days spent slowly making headway in the direction of the steadily expanding North Carolina communities which were becoming the Highland people's main means of entry to America.

Whatever drew these folk to the Cape Fear River territory, it was certainly not the region's similarity to Scotland. North Carolina is far warmer than any part of Britain. Its physical appearance, too, must have struck eighteenth-century Highlanders as strange. People used to mountains, moorland, rocky coasts and the wide vistas generated by such places, now found themselves in a flat, low-lying countryside where such slightly higher ground as could be seen by emigrants coming up the Cape Fear River was covered in undisturbed pine forest and where the landscape's many swampier depressions were a mass of quite impenetrable brushwood. To make a farm here, these emigrants must have realised, would be no simple matter.

But there was one huge advantage which eighteenth-century North Carolina had over Scotland as far as any intending agriculturalist was concerned. Here land could be got for no more than the few shillings it cost to have a holding formally surveyed and registered with the colonial authorities. Men whose hold on their native country consisted increasingly of nothing more substantial than an insecure, high-rented tenancy of the kind being offered to Kintyre's population by the Duke of Argyll now transformed themselves, by the act of emigration, into the outright possessors of several hundred acres. It was little wonder, given such advantages, that these new arrivals should have immediately set to work with an energy and enthusiasm which Highlanders back home were often said by their many critics to lack entirely.

Farming methods, to be sure, were as primitive on the American frontier as they were in much of northern Scotland. Janet Schaw, who belonged to one of those Scottish Lowland districts then adopting the innovative techniques which were eventually to produce an agricultural revolution, was surprised, on taking the emigrant route up the Cape Fear River in 1775, to find that 'every instrument of husbandry' seemed 'unknown' to colonists. 'The only instrument used is a hoe with which they till and plant the corn,' Schaw commented. It did not follow that North Carolina farming was unproductive, however. The simple technologies observed by Janet Schaw were very well adapted, in fact, to the task of establishing an agricultural economy in what was naturally a forest country.[17]

A settler began by felling only a tiny proportion of the thousands of trees on his concession – cutting down, in the first instance, only enough to provide him with the timber needed for a house. Other trees were ringed, or barked, to kill them where they stood. The Indian corn, wheat, oats, beans and sweet potatoes which were the staple crops of the Cape Fear region were subsequently planted among the original woodland's all-too-evident remains. Extensive, open fields of the European sort, then, were initially non-existent. And a hoe or *cas-chrom*, the latter being the manually operated plough which Highlanders had earlier developed in response to their own unyielding terrain, proved the ideal means of coping with the sort of ground with which this same people now had to deal here in North Carolina.

That ground, as can be seen today by anyone driving through North Carolina's Bladen, Cumberland, Harnett, Scotland and Anson Counties – the localities settled mainly by Highlanders – is of a light and sandy texture, making it far easier to work by hand than the heavier soils to which immigrants from places like Argyll had previously been accustomed.

This was anyway stock-rearing country where grain and the like were grown mainly for domestic consumption and where a farmer looked more to animals than crops for a money income. The cultivated plots which gradually spread along the banks of the Cape Fear River and its various tributaries served merely as a frontage to huge tracts of mostly uncleared territory. This wilderness was treated as a shared resource by settlers long accustomed to the notion of keeping their beasts on common grazings of the type which have survived into modern times in northern Scotland's crofting, or smallholding, areas. It was on these North Carolina equivalents of a crofting township's hill and moorland pastures that the first generation of Cape Fear farmers developed cattle herds which, in some individual instances, ran to as many as 2,000 head.[18]

Nor was this newly established population's success in the livestock business the only indication of its growing prosperity. As well as trading in cattle, salted beef and hides, the Scottish Highland communities in the Cape Fear country were soon exporting several other commodities. And as timber, turpentine, beeswax, barrel staves, cotton and tobacco began to be shipped down the Cape Fear River, so the region that was the source of these materials began to develop its own commercial centre.

This was the little settlement known originally as Campbelltown or Cross Creek and today called Fayetteville in honour of the French aristocrat who was George Washington's close ally and collaborator during America's Revolutionary War. Here in the 1760s and 1770s came wagonload after wagonload of goods which were afterwards sent downriver to Wilmington on the first stage of a journey due to terminate eventually in London, Bristol or Glasgow. Here were the gristmills which converted the district's grain into flour and meal. Here were the stores where farmers and their wives came to buy those axes, saws, gunpowder, pots, pans, needles, thread and other manufactured goods which they could not provide for themselves. Here was Neil MacArthur's sawmilling plant. Here were the business premises of merchants like William Campbell and Robert Gillies. Here those many people falling victim to the 'fluxes, fevers and agues' of an eighteenth-century North Carolina summer could buy, with what results one can but guess, the various medicaments on offer at the shop belonging to Murdock MacLeod, surgeon and apothecary.

Nothing now remains of the original Cross Creek. Not a lot remains of nineteenth-century Fayetteville either. The metal plaque attached to a granite boulder at one end of Hay Street announces to such passers-by as might be interested that this rock's function is to 'commemorate the settlement of the Upper Cape Fear by the Highland Scotch'. But Hay Street, though once the premier place to be in Fayetteville, now has the sadly run-down air of so many of those American city centres which have fallen victim to this continent's tendency to turn all its urban areas inside out. Modern Fayetteville's shopping malls, like most of its many motels, are located near the freeway interchanges some five miles out of town.

But here and there across this sprawling city, larger by far than any town in the Scottish Highlands, it is possible to capture something of the character of the much earlier settlement. Step into the Museum of the Cape Fear which includes among its exhibits a battered Gaelic bible brought here by one emigrant and the waterproofed carrying-pouch used by another pioneer to protect his personal papers from the penetrating damp which was an invariable feature of an eighteenth-century Atlantic passage. Next take a stroll along MacGilvary Street in the direction of Highlander Avenue. Look at the way this district's older buildings are equipped with wide stoops and verandas, carefully shaded by high, leafy, spreading trees. Such arrangements were essential, in times previous to our own air-conditioned era, to give some protection from the unremitting heat of this region's long, long summers.

What is missing from those streets, of course, are the jostling crowds, the wagons, horses, smells, dirt, dust and racket of Cross Creek as it would have been when this was still a frontier outpost. To that Cross Creek there came, in search of some additional earnings, those poorer settlers who combined their farming, just as their crofting counterparts did back in Scotland, with some other occupation. Among them were men like John Campbell, surveyor; Angus MacDougall, weaver; Allan Cameron, millwright; John Clark, tailor; Patrick MacEachen, black-smith; men with Scottish Highland surnames of the sort which still occupy column after column in the Fayetteville telephone directory. To Cross Creek, too, came people of higher social standing: professionals like Revd James Campbell, the Cape Fear River district's first Presbyterian clergyman; well-dressed and comfortable-looking indi-viduals of the still more affluent planter class to which the like of Allan MacDonald of Kingsburgh belonged.

Men of this type had not soiled their hands with manual labour on their farms or tacks in Scotland. Nor did they personally work the land which they obtained on coming to America, entrusting that task to their immigrant Scottish Highland servants or to black slaves who, this being eighteenth-century North Carolina, could very readily be bought.

Georgia's first Highland settlers had stood out against the adoption of slavery which, as late as 1775, Darien residents were condemning as 'an unnatural practice . . . founded in injustice and cruelty'. But their Cape Fear counterparts showed no such inhibitions. A census of 1790 found several hundred Afro-Americans in the neighbourhood of Fayetteville, most of them belonging to men with Scottish Highland names. Farquhard Campbell, John MacLean, Archibald MacKay, Archibald MacNeil and Alexander MacAlister had 180 slaves between them. And many of those slaves, it was noted as a curiosity by travellers to the Cape Fear River region, were distinguished from other North American blacks by the fact that they spoke Gaelic – this being, of course, the everyday language both of their white owners and of practically everyone else in the vicinity.[19]

* * *

The earlier Scottish Highland emigrant trickle to North Carolina had, by the 1770s, become a flood. The outflow, moreover, now had its origins not only in Argyll but in several more northerly localities also. Allan and Flora MacDonald, for example, were but two of hundreds, maybe thousands, of people to leave Skye in the years immediately prior to the American Revolution. And since a nation's economic as well as its military strength was thought then to depend primarily upon its having as large a population as possible, much printer's ink began to be expended in Scotland on the contentious issue of why so many Highlanders were abandoning their own country.

Longstanding anti-Highland feeling provided the editor of the *Edinburgh Advertiser* with all the explanation that was needed. An imagined dialogue which appeared in the paper's pages in September 1773 begins with a Highland emigrant being asked why he is leaving the place where his ancestors have lived for a thousand years. 'Because I want food,' the man replies. But are there not fish to be had in his neighbourhood? 'Amazing plenty,' the departing Highlander agrees. Why, then, does he not launch a boat and catch them? 'Because I am lazy,' the Highlander is made to admit, the *Advertiser* then adding, by way of conclusion, 'It is well known that you are lazy and 'tis honest in you to acknowledge it.'[20]

Not even the most prejudiced observer, however, could plausibly sustain for very long the fiction that Highlanders were leaving for America solely in the hope of discovering a more congenial setting for the layabout lifestyle to which their Lowland critics believed them so addicted. Such an idea simply could not be reconciled with the effort and risk involved in getting across the Atlantic. Hence the enthusiasm with which opponents of emigration were to leap on the alternative, if scarcely more credible, thesis that emigrants were not so much idle as deluded. Most departing Highlanders, it now began to be suggested, were the inherently gullible and dimwitted victims of those various individuals who, for their own allegedly self-interested purposes, were filling Highland heads with all sorts of exaggerated expectations of life in North America.

Then and later, of course, naïve and credulous emigrants undoubtedly existed. They might not quite have expected American streets to be paved with gold and American meadows to flow with milk and honey. But they certainly failed entirely to realise, as one colonist noted caustically in the 1770s, 'that a man may possess twenty miles square in this glorious country and yet not be able to set a dinner'.[21]

Nor is there any question as to the existence, even in the eighteenth century, of the dubious practice to which a later generation of Americans were to give the name of boosterism – the business of inflating wildly, usually with speculative intent, the economic and other attractions of some newly opened-up locality. At least one of the publications which were intended to make the Cape Fear River district better known to Scottish Highlanders was, in fact, a prime example of the booster's art. North Carolina, this particular pamphlet stated, was 'the most temperate part of the earth on the north side of the equator'. Its winter skies were 'commonly clear and serene'. Spring brought 'gay and glowing colours . . . promising rich fruits in their appointed seasons'. Summer might 'indeed be called hot . . . but, by not exposing the body to the warm sunbeams at noon, a man may always keep himself cool and comfortable in the hottest day'. As for autumn, 'there cannot be a . . . finer climate than here, the weather being . . . dry for the space of forty or fifty days'.[22]

Such stuff, printed in Scotland in 1773 under the title of *Informations Concerning the Province of North Carolina*, was as clearly calculated as any modern travel agent's advertisements to appeal to a readership accustomed to ceaseless cold and wet. As was readily conceded even by this pamphlet's author, however, much more than the beckoning prospect of better weather was always going to be required to dislodge from their Scottish glens and islands a people who, as the *Informations* put it, 'have always been remarkable for their strong attachment to the place of their nativity'. Not even the 'most flattering accounts' of North America, the eighteenth-century pamphleteer continued, would have turned Highlanders into 'adventurers to other climes and regions far remote' had not something also happened 'to make their home intolerable and disagreeable to them'.

That something, concluded Scotus Americanus, as the author of the *Informations* styled himself, was to be found in the greatly altered outlook and conduct of Highland Scotland's 'landholders and proprietors'. It was to be found, more especially, in this class's growing tendency 'to squeeze and oppress' their tenants. And it was to be found more especially still, or so Scotus Americanus contended, in the landowning fraternity's 'tyrannic' determination to impose a larger and larger rent burden on their estates.

Scotus Americanus had himself travelled to the Cape Fear country where he had found, he reported, 'the banks of the rivers from Wilmington to far above Cross Creek . . . agreeably adorned with fine seats, villas and pleasant farmhouses'. And since the whole tenor of his pamphlet is such as to suggest that he was one of the victims of the new estate management policies about which he complained so bitterly, the compiler of the *Informations* was naturally delighted that Highlanders, whom he considered to be fleeing from their landlords in much the same spirit as the Israelites once fled from Pharaoh, should have found 'refuge . . . on some more hospitable shore where freedom reigns and where, unmolested by Egyptian taskmasters, they may reap the produce of their own labour and industry'.

In marked contrast to Scotus Americanus, the young and rising politician, Henry Dundas, soon to be the most powerful man in Scotland, would greatly have preferred those same Highland emigrants to desist from wanderings which threatened, in his opinion, to empty a large part of the country. But Dundas was at one with the pro-emigration pamphleteer on the underlying reasons for the Highland exodus. The 'cherishment and protection' which Scottish Highlanders had once received from their chiefs had become hopelessly outmoded, Dundas wrote in 1775. The relationship between landlord and tenant was now strictly commercial. And the 'precipitate and injudicious rise in rents' which was one result of this transformation had proved, on investigation, to be the 'immediate cause' of so many people leaving the Highlands for the colonies.[23]

Few actual emigrants were themselves asked officially about their motives and fewer still had the capacity to set these motives down on paper. But the families from Glen Orchy and Kintyre who gave 'high rents and oppression' as the causes of their having decided to take ship from Greenock to North Carolina in the summer of 1774 were not untypical of the minority who left some record of their thinking. That same thinking is very generally reflected in the published comments of those contemporary observers who had both a first-hand knowledge of the Scottish Highlands and some sympathy with the aspirations of the region's Gaelic-speaking population.[24]

Northern Scotland, it was beginning to be almost universally agreed, was in the grip of social and cultural upheavals so far-reaching in their implications as to amount practically to a revolution. 'There was perhaps never any change of national manners so quick, so great and so general,' remarked Samuel Johnson, 'as that which has operated in the Highlands by the last conquest and the subsequent laws . . . The clans retain little now of their original character, their ferocity of temper is softened, their military ardour is extinguished, their dignity of independence is depressed, their contempt of government subdued, and their reverence for their chiefs abated.'[25]

Following their narrow escape in 1745, when Prince Charles Edward Stuart had marched his Highland army to a point well within striking distance of London, Britain's ruling orders, as Johnson observed, had gone on to occupy and pacify the previously unruly localities where the rebel prince's soldiers had mostly been recruited. But government ministers did not stop there. They also set out to make the north of Scotland much more completely than ever before an integral part of the British state created by the Scottish-English union. The largely tribal traditions and institutions which had characterised the Highlands and Islands for the better part of a millennium were wholly rooted out and set aside. A clan chief was now to be regarded simply as a proprietor of land and he was to be encouraged to conduct his affairs in exactly the same way as similar landed proprietors did elsewhere. The many ancient ties of kinship, as Samuel Johnson noted sadly, were thus inevitably severed. 'Their chiefs . . . have already lost much of their influence; and as they gradually degenerate from patriarchal rulers to rapacious land-lords, they will divest themselves of the little that remains.'[26]

In such developments, Johnson was convinced, there were to be found the causes of the 'epidemical fury of emigration' which he encoun-tered so frequently in the course of his travels in the Highlands – that passion to be off to America which, as was remarked by the doctor's friend and companion, James Boswell, had begun to be reflected in every aspect of the popular life of a locality like Skye. 'In the evening the company danced as usual,' Boswell noted during his stay with one island family. 'We performed, with much activity, a dance which, I suppose, the emigration from Skye has occasioned. They call it *America*. Each of the couples, after the common involutions and evolutions, successively whirls round in a circle, till all are in motion; and the dance seems intended to show how emigration catches, till a whole neighbourhood is set afloat.'[27]

The north of Scotland, as the Hebridean poet Iain MacCodrum so bitterly reflected in the 1760s, was becoming a place much like any other. Its landed magnates felt no obligation towards those tenantries who had loyally defended their predecessors. An estate's value was now reckoned in terms of its income-generating capacity rather than, as had previously been the case, in terms of the number of fighting men it could support. 'The warrior chiefs are gone, who had a yearning for the truth, who had regard for their faithful followers.' So runs a prose translation of one of MacCodrum's most striking Gaelic verses. 'Look around you and see the nobility without feeling for poor folk, without kindness to friends; they are of the opinion that you do not belong to the soil and, though they have left you destitute, they cannot see it as a loss.'[28]

Among the first victims of this transformation were the tacksmen who had occupied such a prominent position in traditional hierarchies which were more and more withering away. Once tacksmen had been charged only a nominal money rent for their lands – on condition that they provided from among their generally numerous dependents the manpower needed by their clan in time of war. Now members of this gentry class, these *daoine uaisle*, found themselves regarded primarily as a ready source of cash by chiefs who, in their own new role of landlords, were necessarily committed – as was so plainly recognised by men as varied as Henry Dundas, Samuel Johnson and Iain MacCodrum – to maximising their revenues. With land beginning to be let competitively, tacksmen found themselves paying higher and higher rents. These rents they could attempt to pass on, with no great success very often, to those other and lowlier clansmen to whom they had traditionally sublet the greater proportion of their tacks. Alternatively, and increasingly frequently, having become disgusted with the behaviour of their former chiefs and having had the possibility of emigration drawn to their attention by Scotus Americanus and his fellow propagandists, tacksmen might simply 'throw up their tacks, convert the remainder of their subject into cash' and resolve 'to try their fortunes in another country'.[29]

Nor did tacksmen leave for America entirely by themselves. In the clan society which was now being steadily dissolved, the *daoine uaisle*, as Samuel Johnson put it, 'held a middle station by which the highest and lowest orders were connected'. That is not to imply that they were necessarily popular. Far from it. But it is to hint at this social grouping's traditional leadership role. Tacksmen had earlier exercised this role most obviously when their clans had mobilised for war. Now they were to deploy their leadership skills for a quite different, but equally important, purpose in the face of the economic and other changes which had begun to erode the foundations of clanship itself.[30]

The typical tacksman, as was commented by various eighteenth-century travellers in the Scottish Highlands, was a man 'of education and of considerable endowments'. His home, as Johnson and Boswell certainly discovered, was usually well supplied with books, fine furniture and other evidence of his generally superior standing. His knowledge of the wider world was anything but limited. Such individuals, many of them already dabbling in trade and commerce of one kind or another, were ideally placed to finance their own emigration by chartering substantial ships and explicitly encouraging their less affluent neighbours, many of whom were as anxious as the tacksmen themselves to escape the clutches of Highland landlords, to take this once-and-for-all opportunity to be off to America. Some tacksmen undoubtedly earned substantial profits on transactions of this type – by the simple expedient of recovering from their fellow emigrants rather more than these people's fair share of total chartering and provisioning costs. Others seem to have promoted wholesale emigration not so much with a view to cashing in on it as in the hope of dealing a mortal blow to those chieftains who were now so busily adopting the grand landlord manner. 'Emigrations are likely to demolish the Highland lairds and very deservedly,' wrote a Moidart tacksman, John MacDonald of Glenaladale, in the course of organising the passage of more than two hundred people from the Highlands to North America in 1772.[31]

The one thing the eighteenth-century tacksman did not have to do was to persuade the mass of Highlanders to leave for North America against their will. 'This idea of going to that country is at present a sort of madness among the common people,' one estate manager reported from Sutherland in the early 1770s. The departing tacksman, in such circumstances, had merely to provide a ship in order to see it quickly filled.[32] That is what Argyll tacksmen like the North Carolina immigrant Neil MacNeil began to do in the 1730s. That is what tacksmen from much of the rest of the region took to doing in the course of the twenty or thirty years following the Battle of Culloden. And that is why so many of the former *daoine uaisle*, Allan MacDonald of Kingsburgh prominent among them, were eventually to be found in the Cape Fear territory. There, as they were informed by the ever-helpful Scotus Americanus, probably a tacksman himself and certainly a resident of the Argyll island of Islay which was one of the places first affected by this type of emigration, a plantation 'consisting of 640 acres . . . with a good mansion house and all the necessary offices upon it, may be purchased for £160'. It was just such a property which Allan and Flora MacDonald acquired in North Carolina in 1775.[33]

The plantation-owning Scottish Highlanders of the Cape Fear River country were no match, financially at least, for the Scottish aristocrats whose estates they had recently left. But they were substantial men of property all the same. Allan MacDonald, for example, was reckoned to have brought with him assets valued at over £1,000 – no mean fortune at that time. Others of MacDonald's stamp may well have been similarly cushioned. But it was not people of this sort whom a longer-established colonist had in mind when he commented of those Highlanders whom he had encountered in the New World that 'it was not poverty or necessity which compelled but ambition which enticed them to foresake their native soil'. The people to whom this American was almost certainly referring were the many more modestly placed individuals and families whom the tacksmen, so to speak, brought to places like North Carolina in their wake.[34]

These were people of the type encountered by a visiting English clergyman in Perthshire in the 1770s: people unwilling to put up any longer with what was happening in the Highlands; families with just enough spare cash to pay for their passage in one of the ships which emigrating tacksmen were now regularly chartering; farm tenants who were looking forward to taking on holdings of their own; 'men who were able to carry their health, their strength, and little property, to a better market'. There was to be no lack of such Scottish Highlanders in British North America in the years immediately preceding the Revolutionary War. One of them, in fact, was to help provide its eighteenth-century originator with an answer to that still occasionally nagging question, 'What, then, is the American, this new man?'[35]

The solution to the conundrum thus posed by the French-born Hector St John de Crevecoeur, whose *Letters from an American Farmer* appeared in 1782, began, as far as Crevecoeur himself was concerned, with a recital of colonial accomplishments. The American, he wrote, was the person responsible for the fact that this 'mighty continent' now contained 'fair cities, substantial villages, extensive fields . . . decent houses, good roads, orchards, meadows and bridges where a hundred years ago all was wild, woody and uncultivated'. America's politics, it seemed to Crevecoeur, were as new-minted as its homes and settlements.

Here was a 'modern society . . . not composed, as in Europe, of great lords who possess everything and of a herd of people who have nothing'. Here were no vast and unbridgeable distinctions of class and position. Each and every American was well-clothed, well-housed, dignified, self-assured and, above all, free. 'We have no princes for whom we toil, starve and bleed; we are the most perfect society in the world.'

No emigrant need fear failure or rejection in the colonies, insisted Crevecoeur, who had himself arrived in New York in 1759. 'There is room for everybody in America. Has he any particular talent or industry? He exerts it in order to procure a livelihood and it succeeds. Is he a merchant? The avenues of trade are infinite . . . Does he love a country life? Pleasant farms present themselves . . . Is he a labourer, sober and industrious? He need not go many miles . . . before he will be hired, well fed at the table of his employer and paid four or five times more than he can get in Europe.'

The validity of these claims Crevecoeur now demonstrated, to his own satisfaction at any rate, by 'relating . . . the history of an honest Scotch Hebridean who came here in 1774'. This man, whose name is Andrew, belonged originally to Barra, an island where, he tells Crevecoeur, conditions are 'bad enough', the weather cold, the land thin. 'We have no such trees as I see here,' he says, 'no wheat, no kine, no apples.'

But Andrew is no poverty-stricken refugee of the sort that Barra will produce in plenty in the nineteenth century. A legacy from an uncle and money saved from a job he took for a time in Glasgow have together enabled him to pay the full cost of his family's emigration, while leaving the sum of 'eleven and a half guineas' to be expended on establishing himself, his wife and children in America. To this task Andrew the Hebridean, as Crevecoeur calls the Barraman, promptly applies his considerable energies. He finds employment, learns to use an axe and masters the handling of a plough before going on to acquire the occupancy of 'a hundred acres of good arable land' in first-rate farming country where, with the help of his new neighbours, Andrew has soon constructed one of those log-built homes which were standard fixtures right across the colonies.

Crevecoeur leaves 'honest Andrew' at the end of the Scotsman's fourth year in America; 'become a freeholder possessed of a vote'; appointed 'overseer of the road'; accustomed to serve regularly on local juries; the possessor of six cows, two breeding mares and various other livestock, to say nothing of wheat, pork, beef, wool, flax and miscellaneous agricultural implements. There could be no more eloquent testimony, Crevecoeur concludes, to 'the happy effects which constantly flow in this country from sobriety and industry when united with good land and freedom'.

In the achievements of this Scottish Highland emigrant of 1774, then, we have the first literary embodiment of what would subsequently be called the American Dream – the enduring conviction that, once liberated by American residency from the restraints and oppressions of Europe, there was nothing to stop any halfway competent individual gaining the material and other rewards which were denied to the majority of mankind by less progressive, less enlightened social systems than America's democracy.

Nor is this vision of America to be idly mocked. The franchise which Andrew obtained here so readily, after all, would not be gained by those of his relatives who remained in Barra for more than a hundred years. His comparative security and prosperity would not be theirs for several decades after that. And while not every eighteenth-century Scottish Highland emigrant would do as well as Andrew, there were others who did even better.

In this latter category, for example, was Neil MacArthur who came to Cross Creek in 1764 with no more starting capital than Andrew the Hebridean but who held property worth some £4,600 just ten years later. North Carolina was 'the best poor man's country I have heard in this age', another rapidly prospering Cape Fear Highlander, Alexander MacAllister, informed one of his relatives in Scotland. 'You would do well to advise all poor people whom you wish well to take courage and come to this country.' The alternative was simply to remain in the Highlands and Islands where 'the landlord will sure be master' and where 'the face of the poor is kept to the grinding stone'.[36]

'We are all freeholders here,' one of the earliest of North America's English settlers had remarked in 1621. 'The rent day doth not trouble us.' Even more strongly than it had done to people from seventeenth-century England, this notion of a country without landlords appealed to eighteenth-century Highlanders – who, by the early 1770s, were accounting for almost a fifth of all emigration to British North America. The Gaelic song which advocated *dol a dh'iarraidh an fhortain an North Carolina*, going to North Carolina to seek a fortune, is one indication of America's growing attractiveness to the former commons of the clans. Equally illuminating is the tenor of the many letters sent back to Scotland by men like Alexander MacAllister. 'Copies of letters from persons who had emigrated several years before to America to their friends at home, containing the most flattering accounts of the province of North Carolina, were circulated among them,' one Highland clergyman wrote in the course of an attempt to account for the number of departures from his own parish. 'The implicit faith given to these accounts made them resolve to desert their native country, and to encounter the dangers of crossing the Atlantic, to settle in the wilds of America.'[37]

It was in response to a letter of this kind that a man by the name of John MacRae, *Iain MacMhurchaidh*, emigrated from Kintail to North Carolina in 1774. And though he found his departure no simple thing to contemplate, the Gaelic song which he composed on leaving his birth-place makes its own small contribution to the concept of America as a place of liberation.

'Let us go and may God's blessing be with us,' MacRae's composition begins. 'Let us go and charter a vessel. Better that than to remain under landlords who will not tolerate tenantry, who would prefer gold to a brave man . . . We shall all go together . . . to where we shall find game of every kind, the most beautiful game to be seen. We shall get deer, buck and doe, and the right to take as many as we wish. We shall get woodcock and woodhen, teals, duck and wild geese. We shall get salmon and . . . white fish if it pleases us better. Imagine how prosperous they are over yonder; even every herdsman has his horse.'[38]

More than two hundred years after the publication of Hector St John de Crevecoeur's *Letters from an American Farmer*, Jonathan Raban, novelist and travel writer, was to make his own crossing of the Atlantic in search of what it is that continues to attract so many people to North America; people of the sort who, in their thousands, make the hazardous crossing of the US-Mexican border under cover of darkness; people of the type who fly into Los Angeles, San Francisco or Seattle from countries like Vietnam, the Philippines, Korea. 'Guy in Korea make three–four hundred dollar a month,' one such immigrant tells Raban. 'No house his own, no business his own. *This* is country of opportunity. No comparison. Chance of self-employment: maybe one thousand per cent better! Look. '73. I am in Washington DC with 400 dollars. Now? My business is worth one million dollars – more than one million. Heh? Isn't that the American Dream? And I am only a small! Yes, I am a *small*.' To that man of our own time, in exactly the same way as it did in the case of Iain MacMhurchaidh two centuries ago, America offered both a degree of freedom and a degree of material prosperity which were simply not to be got in his own country. This continent, of course, has not always made good that particular promise. But it has done so often enough to make the promise always plausible.[39]

So why, then, to pose a question which goes some way to rival Crevecoeur's in the complexity of its answer, did Scottish Highlanders, many of whom owed America a great deal, take the loyalist, or Tory, side when their fellow colonists made their break in 1775 and 1776 for independence? How did it come about that John MacRae, within a year of getting here, was fighting for King George III?

Not every Highlander in America, it should be made clear, was unquestioningly supportive of those men – the Kintail poet among them – who followed General Donald MacDonald to Moore's Creek. Georgians of Highland extraction in and around Darien were solid for the revolution and one of them, thought by no less a personage than George Washington himself to be 'an officer of great worth and merit', actually held the rank of general in the Continental Army. This was John

Mor MacIntosh's son, Lachlan, who, when still a teenager, had served at his ranger father's side at the Battle of Fort Musa and who had afterwards attempted – vainly as it turned out – to smuggle himself to Scotland in order to take part in Charles Edward Stuart's rising.[40]

Nor was this republican descendant of the Jacobite lairds of Borlum without his counterparts in the Cape Fear River country. The district's original Presbyterian cleric, John Campbell, decamped to a more patriotic neighbourhood – a Scotch-Irish one as chance would have it – rather than have anything to do with the activities of the men responsible for raising the army which was to go down to defeat at Moore's Creek Bridge. Other eminent Cape Fear Highlanders – including one Cross Creek merchant who was later to sit in the North Carolina senate – managed somehow to keep a foot in both camps. No small number of less elevated citizens responded to General Donald MacDonald's appeals for troops by decamping to the back country. Others who agreed initially to join MacDonald afterwards deserted. For all the general's boasting and bravado, therefore, the army which he put together at Cross Creek in the early weeks of 1776 was neither as large nor as effective as he and his superiors had hoped it would be. That was why MacDonald was so anxious to postpone an actual confrontation with his Continental Army opponents. That was why this force of 'tattered Scotch Highlanders', as the general's troops were dubbed by one American patriot, was in the end so easily defeated. The conduct of the men led into battle at Moore's Creek Bridge by the unfortunate Donald MacLeod was not the conduct of soldiers whose heart was in the cause to which they were formally pledged.[41]

Most of North Carolina's Scottish Highland settlers, had they been left to their own devices, would probably have preferred simply to keep out of the war. Like other minorities – Pennsylvania's Germans, for example – who were separated from the English-speaking colonial majority by cultural and linguistic barriers, they were not fully acquainted with patriot objectives and possibly suspected that they might be marginalised still further in an independent America. Some Cape Fear Highlanders, of course, were Jacobite veterans and it seemed odd to many Americans, then and later, that they should now be prepared to fight for the same royal family as had previously defeated them. But to be a Jacobite was, by definition, to be conservative politically – to favour enhancing, not detracting from, the power of kings. Wanting to replace George II or George III with Charles Edward Stuart was not at all the same as wanting to do away with monarchs altogether.

The conduct of those Highlanders who, having been overwhelmed militarily by the Hanoverian ascendancy in Scotland, became defenders of Hanoverian power in America was, in this respect, not dissimilar to the behaviour of that other North American minority, the French-Canadians or Québécois. They, too, had been conquered not long previously by the British army. But they were even more unanimously disinclined than Highlanders to rally to American republicanism.

Both Quebec and the Cape Fear River country were places where significant numbers of people, not least because so many of them were separated from the American mainstream by their knowing little English, still tended to cling strongly to their European heritage. While this did not mean that either French-Canadians or Scottish Highlanders necessarily revered King George III, it did mean that both groups were inclined to follow the lead given by those men in their communities to whom there was traditionally owed at least some semblance of obedience. In French-speaking Quebec this leadership was supplied by the Catholic hierarchy whose position, much to the outrage of the Protestant majority in other North American colonies, had been guaranteed by the British – and who consequently adhered staunchly to the loyalist camp throughout the Revolutionary War.[42]

A comparable stance was taken in North Carolina's Gaelic-speaking localities by those former tacksmen who, from the outset, were the dominant figures in the effort to rouse the Cape Fear River country for a British king. Had those tacksmen lived in America as long as their Georgia counterpart, Lachlan MacIntosh, their political outlook may have been different. But men like Allan MacDonald of Kingsburgh were newly come to America and had not yet shed their Scottish attitudes. Those attitudes might once have been Jacobite – as they had been, for instance, in the case of the MacIntosh family in Darien. But now the tacksman class, like the rest of the Scottish gentry, was increasingly identified with the Hanoverian ascendancy. Some tacksmen were carving out careers in the expanded commerce made possible by the union with England. Others were eagerly taking commissions in the British army. The Skye-born Donald MacDonald held just such a commission. MacDonald's Kingsburgh cousin, with whom the general worked so closely at Cross Creek, was soon to hold one also. Individuals of this sort, for all that some of them had once been Jacobite in sympathy, now had a vested interest in the maintenance of the British Empire. And they still possessed enough of the tacksman's customary influence over other Highlanders to make their loyalist campaign possible.

The problem with the Cape Fear Scottish Highlanders, observed one Pennsylvanian revolutionary, was that their 'attachment to *names* keeps them servile'. Although his point could have been put more sympathetically, that Pennsylvanian had made no mean stab at understanding what motivated a clan society. He had certainly understood what it was that persuaded North Carolinians of Highland origin to turn out, as their ancestors had turned out for centuries past, when a tacksman of their clan announced the time had come to go to war.[43]

But if there lingered in North Carolina a sense of clanship strong enough to have persuaded some Cape Fear settlers to rally to General

Donald MacDonald's standard in 1776, that feeling was not for very much longer to get in the way of this expatriate Highland population's growing identification with its new homeland. Allan MacDonald and several other tacksmen, once freed from the prisons to which they had been consigned in the immediate aftermath of the fighting at Moore's Creek Bridge, were either to return to Scotland or to move to those parts of North America, such as Nova Scotia and New Brunswick, which were to remain British. But most survivors of the Moore's Creek episode, those common soldiers who were the Cape Fear equivalents of Crevecoeur's Andrew the Hebridean, simply went home to the American farms they had made their own.

Movement from Scotland to North Carolina was banned by the government in London at the start of the Revolutionary War. And postwar emigration would mostly take other directions. But the area around Cross Creek or Fayetteville, as it now became, would long retain its Highland character – one recent historian of North Carolina going so far as to assert that the Cape Fear Valley is 'still known' as 'the land of the Macs'. Visitors in the 1790s, the 1820s, even the 1860s, were to hear Gaelic sung and spoken in the Cape Fear River country. And something of this locality's Scottish Highland tradition and culture was also to be taken across the the Appalachian Mountains by those North Carolina folk who were among the pioneer settlers of new frontier territories like Tennessee and Mississippi.[44]

A modern descendant of the Buie family, who left Jura for the Cape Fear territory in the 1730s, has painstakingly traced his people's migration from North Carolina to Alabama, Kentucky, Arkansas and Texas. And the Buies certainly did not move on alone. From Mississippi, for example, it was reported in the 1840s that the southern part of the state, in particular, still contained many of 'the old Scotch families that originally settled this country'. In Greene County there were 'yet living . . . some of the original immigrants who speak nothing but the Gaelic'.[45]

'Here individuals of all nations,' Crevecoeur wrote of North America, 'are melted into a new race of men.' That was as true of the Cape Fear Highlanders as of the Italians, Poles, Ukrainians and others who were afterwards to follow them across the Atlantic. When the United States went to war with Britain in 1812, North Carolina men of Highland extraction 'enlisted readily' in the American forces – the loyalist dissent shown by those of their fathers and grandfathers who had fought at Moore's Creek Bridge now long forgotten. What remained of their Highland identity was no doubt important to these soldiers, just as it is important to those of their descendants who flock each year to the Grandfather Mountain Games and other celebrations of the Scottish Highland contribution to North Carolina. But these 1812 recruits clearly were, and felt themselves to be, Americans first and foremost – their political attitudes neatly symbolised by one of their contemporaries who,

born in the Scottish Highlands in 1769 and having been taken to North
Carolina not long afterwards by his parents, migrated in due course to
Tennessee, a state which was eventually to send him to the United States
Congress. George Campbell was how this man was christened. George
Washington Campbell was how he preferred to be known.[46]

The westward movement of which this Cape Fear Highlander was
part would gather pace as the nineteenth century advanced. Eventually
it would result in the United States, as the former colonies now called
themselves, extending all the way to the Pacific. The Cape Fear River
families who participated in this new migration no doubt met up, from
time to time, with other folk who – although they might have travelled
by very different routes – also belonged originally to the faraway places
from which the Cape Fear people's own ancestors had come. Those later
emigrants would develop their own ways of getting to this continent. But
it was largely due to what had filtered back across the ocean from North
Carolina's eighteenth-century settlements that the idea of America was
now so firmly planted in the Scottish Highland mind.

CHAPTER THREE

A Hardy and Intrepid Race of Men

SOME SEVEN OR EIGHT miles from Culloden, where Prince Charles Edward Stuart and his largely Highland following fought their last battle in April 1746, a flat, exposed peninsula juts northwards into the grey waters of the Moray Firth. Here, on a site selected solely for strategic reasons, certainly not picked with any eye to shelter, stands the most imposing monument in the United Kingdom to the king the Jacobites were trying to overthrow. Fort George, still a British army base, is regarded by most soldiers as a bleak and cheerless place. So it is. No set of determinedly utilitarian barracks exposed always to the wind could be anything else. But to walk below Fort George's high stone walls, its bastions and its batteries, is immediately to be impressed. Those black-painted artillery pieces pointing out to sea may be entirely obsolescent. They seem none the less menacing for that.

This is exactly the effect Fort George's builders clearly wanted to create. Constructed on the orders of politicians who were determined, in the immediate aftermath of Culloden, to eradicate such Jacobite feeling as persisted in this part of Scotland, and named after the monarch whose younger son, the Duke of Cumberland, had commanded the Hanoverian troops responsible for Charles Edward Stuart's defeat, Fort George was meant to demonstrate to Highlanders just how much power eighteenth-century Britain's ruling orders now had at their disposal. Not even the towering steel platforms produced for the United Kingdom's offshore oil-fields at nearby Ardersier have detracted from Fort George's air of looming over its surroundings. Nearly two-and-a-half centuries after work on it began, this particular piece of military architecture looks as formidable as ever.

One early English visitor here, in October 1751, was Colonel James Wolfe of His Majesty's 20th Foot. When completed, Wolfe commented in a letter to his father, himself a former army officer, Fort George would be 'the most considerable fortress and the best situated in Great Britain' – though that, the colonel added, aiming a typically scathing sideswipe at the ministers responsible for his country's national defences, was not 'saying much'.[1]

A tall, red-haired, unhealthy man who seems seldom to have been at ease with either his surroundings or his colleagues, James Wolfe had first seen action in 1743 at the Battle of Dettingen, one of the series of engagements fought by Britain in the Low Countries during the war in which John Mor MacIntosh in distant Georgia had also become embroiled. Wolfe was then only sixteen. But already he was anxious to make a name for himself. It was with some disgust, therefore, that he found his continental soldiering curtailed, some two years afterwards, when his regiment was one of several recalled urgently to Britain to be given the essential, but less than glorious, task of countering Prince Charles Edward Stuart's thrust into the English Midlands.

The young James Wolfe's detachment was one of those sent north when the Jacobites began eventually to retreat, Wolfe being involved in fighting with the Highlanders at Falkirk in January 1746 and at Culloden three months later. There then followed, to this most ambitious officer's obvious horror, several years in Scotland: years of garrison duty in small country towns; years spent supervising the construction of those mountain roads which were one more element in the British government's plans for the long-term pacification of the Highlands.

Scotland was then no very popular place with Englishmen. 'The sink of the earth,' one southern politician called the country. And that description would most certainly have struck a chord with Wolfe. 'When I am in Scotland,' he wrote to a friend, 'I look upon myself as an exile.' The 'villainous nature' of the place and the 'brutality' of its people were sources of constant complaint. And while there was plenty of opportunity for the study of military theory, there seemed no certainty that the bookish but promotion-hungry Wolfe – now that war in Europe had once more ended – would ever get a chance to put his growing knowledge of strategy and tactics to the test.[2]

There were occasional diversions, admittedly. At Inverness, during those dreary months when the 20th Foot was providing some of the fifteen infantry companies then employed on Fort George's construction, the colonel attended a ball where he 'had the honour', as he put it, 'to dance with a daughter of a chieftain who was killed at Culloden'. The girl's dead father was MacDonald of Keppoch who had been at the forefront of a desperate Jacobite charge which had ended with the Highland

dead piled up in front of Cumberland's infantry. Maybe there is a certain
frisson to be got from guiding round a ballroom the offspring of a man
with whom one has done battle. Or perhaps Miss MacDonald was
simply not the sort of company a lonely officer expected to come across
so far from home. On recalling this social encounter, at all events,
Colonel Wolfe was less derogatory than usual about Highlanders. 'They
are as perfectly wild as the hills that breed them,' he wrote. But he did
not, this time, appear to think his adjective an insult.[3]

Scottish Highland vigour, it was beginning to occur to James Wolfe,
might yet be made to serve a British purpose in places other than an
Inverness dance-floor. 'I should imagine that two or three independent
Highland companies might be of use,' the colonel commented to another
military man in 1751. 'They are hardy, intrepid, accustomed to rough
country and no great mischief if they fall.'[4]

It was significant, perhaps, that this particular remark should
appear in a letter sent by James Wolfe to a colleague then in Nova Scotia.
Highlanders, after all, had already been deployed on the American frontier by Governor Oglethorpe of Georgia. And in 1746 a New Englander
by the name of William Pepperrell – a man then freshly returned from a
successful expedition against a French fortress on Cape Breton Island
where, as it happened, Wolfe himself was eventually to make his name –
had suggested to one of King George's ministers, the Duke of Newcastle,
that Jacobite prisoners might be sent as soldiers to the North American
colonies. Newcastle, at this point, was more interested in hanging
Jacobites than in enlisting them. But the idea that the Scottish Highlands,
for all the region's longstanding rebelliousness, might one day supply the
British Empire with a reservoir of troops was nevertheless beginning to
catch on with people in authority.[5]

Antedating even Oglethorpe's Gaelic-speaking ranger corps was the
Black Watch. Recruited mainly in Perthshire, the Watch's original role
was that of a paramilitary police force whose task it was to keep in check
the various freebooters and bandits who had long enjoyed a virtually free
run of those glens and passes which, in the years following the Anglo-
Scottish union of 1707, became the principal arteries of a flourishing
trade in cattle. In 1739, however, the United Kingdom being as ever short
of soldiers, the Black Watch – both its officers and men kitted out still in
the dark check of the government-issue tartan to which it owed its name
– had been transformed into a regiment of the line and sent abroad. A
mutiny had followed among men who had not understood, or who had
not been informed, that they were eligible for service overseas. And some
among the mutineers, ironically enough, were despatched to join the
Georgia Highland Rangers. But the bulk of the Black Watch had finally
gone, whether willingly or not, to Flanders. There the 43rd, as the regiment was now officially known, performed very well. So heroically did
its men fight in the course of their encounters with the French, in fact,

that they found themselves at the centre of the first public celebrations of Highland bravery in a British cause – a popular print telling the story of how a Black Watch private, James Campbell, had distinguished himself at the Battle of Fontenoy by singlehandedly killing nine Frenchmen prior to having his own arm removed by an enemy cannonball.[6]

Before 1745 had ended, of course, other Highlanders, serving now in a Stuart and French-supported army, were again making their part of Scotland, as far as most of the United Kingdom's inhabitants were concerned, seem more synonymous with treason than with patriotism. No more was heard in the south of James Campbell's bravery. The Black Watch, the loyalty of its place of origin being once more considered suspect, was stationed for several years in Ireland where, so English politicians no doubt thought, one set of ceaselessly troublesome Celts might usefully be kept in order by another. For all that Colonel James Wolfe might have been toying with the notion of incorporating the male relatives of his Inverness dancing partners into new regiments of foot, there was not the least sign that his superiors might shortly be about to embark on just such a course of action.

What led to a sudden change of attitude in this regard was a developing strategic crisis in North America where Britain and France, having collided more than once before in the course of their respective pushes westward, were beginning to be engaged in what would turn out to be a final struggle for continental supremacy.

The British presence in the New World was by far the larger one – extending all the way from Nova Scotia to Florida and including a colonial population starting to be counted now in millions. But the French, though not so numerous in America as the British, had developed a much longer reach. From New France, as they called their well-established settlements on the St Lawrence, French traders and missionaries had voyaged into the Great Lakes and then gone on to travel down the Ohio and the Mississippi to the Gulf of Mexico. So enormous were the distances involved, and so tiny were the numbers participating in these feats of exploration, that France, in fact, exercised little real control over the huge territories its nationals had opened up to European influence. But matters did not look like that from the perspective of Britain's seaboard possessions where the more commercially ambitious colonists were already firmly convinced that it was their people's manifest destiny to expand all the way across the continent. This expansion, it was now suspected, France was aiming to prevent.

The particular bout of fighting between France and Britain which the latter's American colonists called King George's War – and which encapsulated, of course, Scotland's last Jacobite rebellion – ended with the Peace of Aix-la-Chapelle in 1748. But in North America, even more so than in Europe, the cessation of hostilities proved brief. Renewed jostling for position in the Ohio country resulted, in the summer of 1754, in a 22-year-old Virginia militia officer, one George Washington by name, becoming involved in exchanges of fire with the French – to whom Washington was eventually forced to surrender at that most inauspiciously named frontier encampment, Fort Necessity.[7]

Something of the flavour of the more widespread fighting which followed – fighting during which the French came to rely increasingly on auxiliary troops recruited from among the native peoples then inhabiting the regions to the south of Lake Ontario and Lake Erie – is embodied in the conflict's still enduring American designation, the French and Indian War. The Ohio territory was like no European theatre of operations. As was remarked some seventy years afterwards by the novelist James Fenimore Cooper, who knew the area well and whose pioneer hero, Hawkeye, was modelled on those frontier scouts – most notably Daniel Boone – who served the British side, 'It was a feature peculiar to the colonial wars of North America that the toils and dangers of the wilderness were to be encountered before the adverse hosts could meet.'[8]

The French, though theoretically outnumbered, had the better of things to begin with – British generals like the hopelessly incompetent Edward Braddock simply blundering about in virgin forest until, on finally encountering the better-acclimatised French, they met defeat and, in poor Braddock's case, death also. Then, with the fighting spreading from America to the West Indies, to Europe and to India, on its becoming, in effect, a world war, Britain suddenly found itself possessed of that most rare of individuals, a politician capable of carrying everyone and everything before him. 'I know that I can save this country and that no one else can,' William Pitt is reputed to have said. The new prime minister's chosen means of national salvation were such as to involve Scottish Highlanders inextricably in North America.[9]

Previous holders of Pitt's office had invariably regarded events in America as little more than a distraction from much more important happenings in Europe. But Pitt reversed this ordering of priorities. The expulsion of French power, not just from the Ohio country but from the entire North American continent, became for the prime minister a personal crusade, almost an obsession. Pitt consequently took risks. He propelled through the army's rigid and cautious hierarchies a younger and more innovative set of generals, one of whom would turn out to be James Wolfe. He looked around, too, for new sources of military manpower.[10] 'I sought for merit wherever it was to be found,' Pitt was to inform parliament. 'It is my boast that I was one of the first ministers who looked for it and found it in the mountains of the north. I called it forth and drew into your service a hardy and intrepid race of men . . . Those men . . . were brought to combat on your side; they served with fidelity, as they fought with valour, and conquered for you in every part of the world.'[11]

This was said with hindsight. The prime minister's mobilisation of Highlanders on the side of the state which, as he himself admitted, they 'had gone nigh to have overturned' not so many years before, was less an act of carefully considered policy, and more a desperate expedient. The British, in truth, armed the Highland clans in much the same reluctant spirit as the French armed North American native peoples, doing so because they thought themselves to have no alternative. 'The only business I shall have with these companies,' Lord Barrington, the government's secretary of war, remarked of the several other Highland regiments which now took their place alongside the Black Watch, 'is to see that they be well accoutred and sent out of Scotland as soon as possible.' The Highlander of the 1750s was no more to be relied upon, in other words, than his predecessor of the 1740s – especially when that Highlander, whom the government had so forcefully disarmed in the period following Culloden, had once more got a musket in his hand.[12]

Barrington's anxieties, from the war minister's point of view, were amply justified. Just three or four years before Pitt began looking to the 'mountains of the north' in search of troops, after all, the British government had ordered the execution – by means of the hanging and quartering devised in medieval times – of a prominent member of the Highland gentry class to whom the same government was now appealing for military assistance. This was Archibald Cameron who, in the summer of 1745, had helped his elder brother, who was also his chief, to mobilise Clan Cameron in the cause of Charles Edward Stuart. Cameron's execution had been delayed until 1753 for the simple reason that he had previously evaded capture. But it was not surprising – this same execution and the rebellion which had preceded it being such comparatively recent events – that a cabinet minister charged in 1756 with the task of getting Highlanders to enlist in the royal service should have wanted to get these same Highlanders out of harm's way as soon as possible. Might they not otherwise be tempted to launch yet another of their periodic uprisings?[13]

What neither Barrington nor Pitt could have anticipated, however, was the extent to which the more eminent men of the Scottish Highlands – the dead Archibald Cameron's surviving counterparts – had now concluded that their future, if they were to have one, lay in putting any lingering Jacobite sympathies firmly behind them and getting on to better terms with the Hanoverian establishment. This the French and Indian War was to enable them to do.

In 1756, less than ten years after he had been found guilty of high treason and confined to Edinburgh Castle as a result of his having helped bring reinforcements to the beleaguered Charles Edward Stuart at Culloden, Simon Fraser was given the rank of colonel in the British army and instructed to raise a Highland regiment for service in America. This, from Fraser's standpoint, was the vindication of all he had done from the moment of his imprisonment. The Hanoverian authorities might have had Simon's father, the 79-year-old Lord Lovat, chief of Clan Fraser, dragged from his hiding-place beside Loch Morar prior to ordering his beheading on Tower Hill. The same authorities might have declared forfeit both the Lovat lands and titles. But Simon sought for no revenge. Instead the son attempted ceaselessly to ingratiate himself with his father's killers. He endeavoured always to prove himself worthy of their trust. He looked forward constantly to nothing other than the moment which had now arrived, this moment of political and social rehabilitation.

Within months of his father's execution, Fraser was instrumental in engineering the Hanoverian ministry's victory in an Inverness-shire election, helping thereby to defeat a man who was his own close relative. Such small gestures having secured his early release, Simon, now in his twenties, studied law at Glasgow University. From there, the better to please those government ministers whom he wished so desperately to cultivate, Fraser went on to join the prosecution team at the trial, in 1752, of a man who clearly stood for the old Highland order on which the young Simon was so anxious to turn his back.[14]

This was James Stewart of Acharn, half-brother to Charles Stewart of Ardshiel, the man who had led his Appin clansmen into battle at Culloden and who had afterwards fled, like the Jacobite prince himself, to France. James Stewart, who had remained in contact with his exiled kinsman, had been accused, on slim and unconvincing evidence, of being implicated in the assassination of one of the officials appointed to manage those lands which the British government had removed from the possession of prominent Jacobites. The estates which Simon Fraser would otherwise have inherited had themselves been confiscated in just such a manner. But Fraser displayed not a shred of sympathy for the man charged with involvement in the killing of this government agent who, when he was shot, was on his way to supervise evictions in the township of Auchindarroch, immediately adjacent to James Stewart's farm.[15]

James Stewart's mistake was to have continued clinging to traditional Highland loyalties; loyalties which had made him a Jacobite; loyalties which led him to risk both his position and, as things turned out, his life in a vain attempt to protect those of his neighbours who had fallen foul of a government-appointed functionary. But such loyalties, in the Highlands of the 1750s, were beginning to look badly out of date. James Stewart was found guilty and hanged. Simon Fraser, in contrast, went on to be put in charge of his own infantry regiment.

This regiment – the 78th, or Fraser's, Highlanders – was to consist of 88 commissioned officers, 65 non-commissioned officers, 30 pipers and drummers and 14 companies with 105 men in each, making a total strength in excess of 1,500. Several hundred of its soldiers were recruited personally by the 78th's newly designated commander from the many little communities scattered across the former Fraser lands around the Inverness end of the Great Glen. The remainder were found by other

Highland gentlemen who, in the same manner as Simon Fraser, saw in the British government's manpower crisis an opportunity to prove both their loyalty and their use. There was no scarcity of such individuals. Indeed it was indicative of the far-reaching nature of the changes which the Highlands had experienced in the decade following Culloden that the 78th included, among its captains and lieutenants, many leading members of those clans which had long been staunchly Jacobite.[16]

Donald MacDonald, whose father, MacDonald of Keppoch, had died at Culloden and whose sister had so impressed James Wolfe in Inverness, was an officer in Fraser's Highlanders. So were senior representatives of the Glengarry MacDonells, the Camerons, the Appin Stewarts, the Clanranald MacDonalds and the family of Cluny MacPherson. The latter, having hidden himself away in the hills and woods of Badenoch for several years after the collapse of Prince Charles Edward Stuart's rising, had made his way eventually to France, that habitual Jacobite refuge. Now France was again at war with Britain. But far from involving themselves in yet another round of Jacobite conspiracy and rebellion, Cluny's clansmen, like the clansmen of so many other previously Jacobite chieftains, were being organised by Simon Fraser to do battle on behalf of Britain against the French king's armies in America.

Although several of them were closely connected with those other Highlanders who had found it politic to remain in Paris ever since 1746, war with their former French allies was not without its own perverse attractions to the many Jacobite veterans in the ranks of the 78th. Thus Malcolm MacPherson, one of Cluny's people, feeling still that the Jacobite cause had been fatally undermined by France's failure to honour its pledges of support to those Highlanders who had risen on behalf of Charles Edward Stuart, saw in the American campaign an opportunity to get something of his own back. On returning home at the end of his field service with Fraser's Highlanders, and on being presented to William Pitt in recognition of his bravery under fire, this grizzled warrior – who was said to have been 'seventy years of age' at the time – remarked that he had enlisted with the 78th, in part at least, with a view to 'being revenged on the French for their treacherous promises in 1745'.[17]

To the author who took the trouble to set down Malcolm MacPherson's comments, the old soldier's valour seemed one more piece of evidence to the effect that Fraser's Highlanders constituted 'a superior body of men'. This author was the Perthshire laird, David Stewart of Garth, whose own rather later service with another Highland regiment was to last for a full quarter of a century. Stewart, by his own self-deprecatory account, was simply 'a plain practical soldier'. In fact, he was a highly perceptive, warm-hearted man who – in reaction to the land management policies responsible for the depopulation of so many of the glens and straths which had provided the British army with some its most effective troops – devoted his retirement to a literary crusade intended to end in general acceptance of the Highland people's claim to a secure and permanent stake in the country which had called them to its colours.[18]

David Stewart's writings, predictably enough, did not persuade Scotland's landlords that the families of former infantrymen were automatically to be preferred to the sheep which displaced those same families from their homes. But the two volumes which Stewart turned out in this brave cause were nevertheless to be of lasting value. They remain the most sensitive account of what it meant in eighteenth-century circumstances to be a Highland soldier.

Because he had been 'nursed in poverty', Stewart observed, such a soldier had 'acquired a hardihood which enabled him to sustain severe privations'. Physically attuned to the military life, the Highlander, in Stewart's opinion, was mentally and culturally fitted for it also. 'He was taught to consider courage as the most honourable virtue, cowardice the most disgraceful failing.' Other infantry regiments of the time, Stewart went on, consisted mostly of men who had no prior connection with one another; men swept into the army, very often, from city slums and other breeding grounds of crime and lawlessness; men who, as Stewart put it, had 'scarcely any other stimulus to the performance of duty . . . than the fear of chastisement'. A Highland infantryman, in contrast, was 'surrounded by the compatriots of his youth and the rivals of his early achievements; he feels the impulse of emulation, strengthened by the consciousness that every proof which he displays, either of bravery or cowardice, will find its way to his native home . . . Hence he requires not artificial excitements. He acts from motives within himself.'[19]

There was an element of wishful thinking in all this, of course. The Black Watch was not the only eighteenth-century Highland regiment to mutiny. And not every Highland soldier went voluntarily, cheerily and courageously to war. 'The zeal with which the followers of any chieftain then came forward to enlist,' as one of David Stewart's more cynical contemporaries commented of those men who served with regiments like Fraser's Highlanders, 'was prompted not only by affection and the enthusiasm of clanship, but likewise by obvious views of private interest. The tenant who, on such an occasion should have refused to comply with the wishes of his landlord, was sensible that he could expect no further favour and would be turned out of his farm. The more considerable the possession he held, the more was it his interest, as well as his duty, to exert himself. The most respectable of the tenantry would, therefore, be among the first to bring forward their sons; and the landlord might, upon an authority almost despotic, select from among the youth upon his estate all who appeared most suitable for recruits.'[20]

Although his family properties were in government hands rather than his own at the time of Simon Fraser's raising of the 78th, it would be naïve to presume that a degree of coercion did not, therefore, play a part in the regiment's recruitment – it being as much in the government's interest as Fraser's own to get men to come forward. But there was an unusual sense of solidarity, an especially high degree of comradeship, among Gaelic-speaking soldiers all the same. The regular floggings and beatings which were to result in English troops being nicknamed 'bloodybacks' by American colonists were hardly known in Highland regiments. And there is a ring of authenticity to David Stewart's story of how, as a newly enlisted ensign in one such regiment, he was provided with a servant – 'a steady old soldier' – whose task it was to introduce him to the regimental way of doing things. This man's approach to knocking the young Stewart into shape involved an overturning of all accepted military form, with the private soldier taking it upon himself to correct and chide the officer. 'These admonitions,' Stewart wrote of his tutor, 'he always gave me in Gaelic, calling me by my Christian name, with an allusion to the colour of my hair, which was fair, or *ban*, never prefixing *Mr* or *Ensign*, except when he spoke in English.'[21]

The early Highland regiment, then, possessed something of the nature of the clan armies of earlier times. Its officers and men belonged, as David Stewart stressed, to the same locality. They knew one another. They felt themselves connected in some subtle and complex sense by those traditional ties which made it possible for an elderly soldier to give the man who was his military superior the friendly, almost intimate, name of *Daibhidh Ban*. For the laird of Garth to have been addressed in an English-speaking unit as anything other than Ensign Stewart would have been a flogging offence. But relationships between Highland troops and their officers rested on something more profound than military discipline. Regiments of the sort which David Stewart knew, for all that men like Simon Fraser might wish to utilise them as a means to personal advancement in the wider world into which Highlanders were now being drawn, retained at least a little of the very different character of the more traditional social order whose passing Stewart observed with such regret.

Among Colonel Simon Fraser's more active subordinates in the 78th Highlanders, during those hectic weeks when the regiment was just beginning to be formed, was Captain Charles Baillie whose task it was to gather in men from the low-lying farmlands between the Cromarty and Dornoch Firths. Baillie's recruits included the captain's own cousin, James Thompson, whose home was in the little market town of Tain and who was taken on as a sergeant at a shilling a day – one of this non-commissioned officer's attractions, from the point of view of a largely Gaelic-speaking regiment operating in the context of an essentially English-speaking army, being his linguistic capabilities. 'I spoke English and wrote a tolerably fair hand,' James Thompson was to recall in the course of a subsequent memoir of his military service.[22]

From Tain the new sergeant took the road, by way of Dingwall, to the Highland capital of Inverness, then a town of some six thousand people. 'We staid some days at Inverness,' he remembered, 'walking the streets to show ourselves, for we were very proud of our looks.'[23]

This pride derived, in no small part, from the fact that the traditional Highland dress, banned after Culloden by a government wishing to eliminate everything that distinguished the more northerly parts of Scotland from the rest of Britain, was now restored to those Highlanders who were being readied for the American war. 'We were allowed the garb of our fathers,' Sergeant Thompson wrote.[24] This consisted primarily of a plaid made from twelve yards of heavy-duty tartan cloth which was slung over one shoulder and fastened at the waist by means of a black leather belt. To this standard outfit, which included also a linen shirt and a pair of buckled shoes, the more fastidious Highland infantrymen, according to James Thompson, added – 'at their own expense' – a purse or sporran of the traditional type. If acquired prior to the regiment leaving Scotland, these sporrans were most commonly made from otterskin or badgerskin. But if obtained in America they were more likely to have been manufactured from beaver pelts.[25]

And it was to America that Fraser's Highlanders were now despatched. From Inverness, in April 1757, the regiment tramped down the Great Glen – by way of Fort Augustus and Fort William which, like Fort George, were heavily symbolic of the British military's successful subjugation of the clans – on the first stage of a journey which, in the conditions of the time, could not take less than several months. Through Glasgow they marched and on to Port Patrick. From that Wigtownshire village the 78th were shipped across the North Channel to Donaghadee in Ireland. Then there followed still more gruelling miles on roads that took them south to Dublin and finally, at the end of June, to Cork.

Next came the misery of an Atlantic passage made on troopships on which eight men out of every hundred died in the course of the average ocean crossing; troopships which served rations that were usually both old and rotten; troopships on which each soldier had to make what shift he could in cramped and miserable conditions. 'A tall man could not stand upright between decks, nor sit up straight in his berth,' it was afterwards observed of the typical military transport of that era. Half a dozen soldiers were habitually allocated to a single bunk designed for four. There they slept 'spoon fashion', the head of the one beside the feet of the other. 'When they tired on one side, the man on the right would call, *About Face*, and the whole file would turn over at once; then, when they were tired again, the man on the left would give the same order, and they would turn back to the first side.'[26]

Nearly eight weeks out of Cork, and the better part of five months after taking leave of Inverness, the men of Fraser's Highlanders stepped ashore in Halifax, Nova Scotia, Britain's principal forward base for operations against the French forces still commanding the approaches to the St Lawrence River, Quebec and Montreal. From Halifax the British had originally planned that summer to mount a major expedition against France's key installation in the vicinity, Fortress Louisbourg on the Atlantic coast of the place the French called Isle Royale and the British knew as Cape Breton Island. But that particular stratagem, like so many others attempted in this phase of the war, did not succeed. And in October, with cold weather coming on, the 78th were sent south to New York and, from there, to winter quarters in and around Schenectady, a few miles beyond Albany and near the junction of the Mohawk River with the rather larger Hudson.

Now constituting, along with Albany, an urban complex of some 165,000 people, Schenectady was described by one British visitor in 1760 as a 'little dirty village'. For all its unprepossessing appearance, however, Schenectady occupied a position of considerable strategic importance. The direct route between France's St Lawrence strongholds and Britain's principal colonial territories in America lay along the north –south line of the Richelieu River, Lake Champlain, Lake George and the Hudson Valley. It was in order to counter French probes along this natural communications artery that so many British troops were concentrated, at one time or another, in the particular piece of territory where Fraser's Highlanders now found themselves.[27]

The countryside in this vicinity, though much more thickly settled today than in the eighteenth century, is peculiarly reminiscent of Scotland. Its mountains, which rise to much the same height as Highland hills, are more thickly wooded than their Scottish counterparts. But the region's numerous lakes and rivers – which nowadays make this a leading vacation destination for families weekending out of Boston and New York – give it something of the look of Deeside, Perthshire or Strathspey.

Nothing they had known in Scotland, however, could have prepared the men of the 78th for their first North American winter. The same British traveller who thought so little of Schenectady was to report that, as early as the first days of December, the Mohawk River was 'full of ice'. By January the temperature had fallen so low that 'strong punch in twenty minutes is covered with a scum of ice and ink on a table is frozen before the fire'. This was weather of the sort in which troops were frequently 'rendered incapable of service' as a result of 'having lost toes and fingers and some feet' to frostbite. Soldiering around Schenectady, it seems, could be miserable enough even during those periods when the French, for all that many of them had been in North America a good deal longer than Fraser's Highlanders, were driven by the cold to suspend military operations.[28]

Despite the severity of its winters, spring comes quickly in this part of the world. As the four-foot-deep snows of February gave way to the broiling heat of June and July, the forest country to the north of Schenectady resumed its longstanding role as 'the bloody arena in which most of the battles for the mastery of the continent were contested'. Those words are Fenimore Cooper's. And they are as good a summary as any of what long ago occurred around these lakes where so many American families now keep summer cabins, sailboats, cruisers, canoes and all the other things thought necessary for a twentieth-century vacation on this continent. Here, in much wilder times, fort after fort was built, fought over, taken and destroyed. Here, as well as in the Ohio country, much further to the west, soldiers from one or other of the three Highland regiments now deployed in North America were to be engaged in much fierce fighting.[29]

Those different battles, though occurring seemingly at random on a long and utterly disjointed front, were the product of a well-considered strategy conceived by William Pitt and now unfolding on his orders. From the Ohio territory and from the Hudson, the prime minister envisaged, British forces would advance in the direction of Quebec – being joined there, or so Pitt planned, by yet another British expedition pushing up the St Lawrence River from the sea. To take Quebec, the centre of French influence in North America, would be to win the continental war. The necessary prelude was to capture Fortress Louisbourg. It was to this campaign that the 78th were directed in the spring of 1758, marching overland from Albany to Boston, taking ship again for Halifax.

The expeditionary force which the 78th now joined, and which consisted of no less than 41 warships and 116 troop transports, arrived off Gabarus Bay on Cape Breton Island's eastern coast at the beginning of June – to confront, when a Cape Breton fog had finally dispersed, a much larger, more spectacular, version of Fort George. Nor was Louisbourg merely a military strongpoint of the sort which had been built at the same time on the Moray Firth. This Cape Breton fortress was a flourishing commercial centre also; one of the three busiest seaports in North America; a merchant colony in its own right. There were fishermen, administrators, business people, wives, children, priests, nuns, lawyers, surgeons, prostitutes and innkeepers in Louisbourg as well as several thousand soldiers. Black slaves had been brought here from Guadaloupe and Martinique in the West Indies. Seamen from half a dozen European countries could be found along the settlement's bustling wharves. Micmac Indians, the original inhabitants of Isle Royale, some serving now with the Louisbourg garrison, were to be met with strolling through streets which, if one were to take account only of the design of their surrounding buildings, would have fitted readily into any town in France.[30]

Something of the bustling, cosmopolitan atmosphere of this little city can be sampled in today's painstakingly recreated Louisbourg, now among the leading visitor attractions in all of maritime Canada and one of several such pieces of testimony in North America to the possibility, given the necessary resources and sufficient expertise, of making the eighteenth-century world seem suddenly less abstract, less remote.

Here is the Louisbourg magazine, complete with powder barrels, bales of wadding, piles of shot; here the Duhaget home, the Carrerot home, the Dugas home and the De la Villière property; here the King's Battery, an artillery forge, the Frederic Gate, a limekiln, the Destouches residence, the garrison stables, the Hotel de la Marine and an artillery storehouse. Fishermen are drying their catch on wooden racks a little to the west of the fortress walls. Soldiers muster to the beat of drums and to the shouted orders of their sergeants. Women talk at corners. Children play in the street. You catch a chord or two of music from an open window. There is a sudden clattering of dishes in a nearby coffeehouse. A bonneted lady wishes you – in French – good morning.

It is not, of course, exactly as it would have been; not so smelly, noisy, smoky, rowdy, blasphemous and downright unhealthy as the original. But when you look across the grey and windscuffed waters of its harbour, and see Louisbourg's spires and high walls silhouetted against lowering cloudbanks of the kind that greeted Fraser's Highlanders here in 1758, it is easy to understand how Louisbourg's defenders – and some of its prospective capturers also – might have come to think this fortress unassailable.

Much money had been spent by France in order to produce just this effect. So great, in fact, were Louisbourg's demands on the French treasury that Louis XV, the king whose name the fortress bore, is said to have remarked, in his mounting exasperation at its costs, that he expected one morning to open his bedchamber window at Versailles and see his American outpost's soaring towers peeping over the western horizon. But like many similar strongholds, like Singapore in a much later war, for instance, Louisbourg – for all the huge sums lavished on it – was less impregnable than its designers thought. In 1745, at about the time the French were slipping Charles Edward Stuart into Scotland, the place was taken, after only a brief siege, by a far from lavishly equipped force of New England militiamen commanded by that same William Pepperrell who had given it as his opinion that Highland troops might one day serve some useful function in America. Now just such troops, in the shape of the 78th, had been brought here in the hope of their assisting in a repetition of Pepperrell's feat of thirteen years before. And in overall command of the larger formation to which the 78th had been attached for the forthcoming landings was a still-youthful brigadier who had also wondered, some time previously, about the possibility of incorporating Highland soldiers into the British army. James Wolfe was shortly to fight his way ashore here on Cape Breton Island alongside men he had confronted both at Falkirk and Culloden.[31]

Wolfe and his fellow commanders aimed to take Louisbourg in the rear, so to speak, by landing their several thousand troops some four or five miles to the south-west of the French fortress and then going on to establish a strong cordon right across the stubby, eastward-projecting peninsula on which Louisbourg sits in much the same way as Fort George occupies its own very similar promontory in Scotland. With the British army thus in control of its overland access, and with the Royal Navy choking off the possibility of relief arriving from the sea, the Louisbourg garrison, according to the military planners anyway, would be quickly forced into capitulation.

This was straightforward enough in theory. To get a glimpse of how desperately hard it was to accomplish in practice, it is necessary only to drive down the comparatively unfrequented dirt road which skirts around the fringes of the main tourist area at Louisbourg and then heads in the direction of Gabarus Bay's north shore. This coast, when you reach it, turns out to be both rocky and exposed. Atlantic waves are breaking loudly all along its cliffs. From far away, just audible above the noisy sea and the occasional shrieks of gulls, there comes the sound of a foghorn. A less propitious-seeming landing-site would be extremely hard to find.

It is not surprising, therefore, that a heavy surf held up the British for a week. But at last, on the morning of 8 June and under a heavy covering fire from its supporting men-o'-war, Britain's invasion force was launched against Cape Breton Island.

The men of Fraser's Highlanders were taking part in no surprise attack. The French had been given plenty of time to marshal their artillery and generally dig in their infantry above the Coromandière Cove – nowadays Kennington Cove – beaches which were the 78th's preliminary objective. There consequently followed all the horrors which invariably attend a seaborne assault on carefully prepared positions.

'We were so closely packed together,' Sergeant James Thompson recalled of the time he spent in the clumsy lighter taking both himself and his comrades slowly landwards, 'there was only room . . . to stand up.' The one partial exception to this highly dangerous congestion, the sergeant added drily, was to be found 'in the back of the boat' where he and several others of some modest seniority – pulling, no doubt, all the rank they possessed – had 'contrived to sit down in the stern sheets'. This arrangement, Thompson continued, 'left no room for rowing' – his party's overcrowded craft depending for such slight forward momentum as it managed to develop on the naval longboat which had it under tow. It was inevitable, under such dreadfully disadvantaged circumstances and with the invasion force at the mercy of those French guns mounted on the clifftops high above, that casualties began immediately to mount.[32]

It was more by good luck than by careful design that the 78th eventually found their way to one of the Gabarus Bay shoreline's few reasonable landing areas. This is a little sandy beach, now used for bathing in fine weather, just westwards of the spot where a stream known as Kennington Brook flows swiftly to the sea. The ocean breakers are a

lot less dangerous here than they are in the vicinity of this relatively sheltered beach's partially enclosing headlands. And so sheer are the cliffs to
the west that the French gunners on these heights found it impossible to
direct any worthwhile fire on the men immediately below them.[33]

Having reached so favoured a locality, the Highlanders made the
best of their unlooked-for opportunity. They grounded their boats. They
quickly seized a bridgehead big enough to let others follow them ashore.
They somehow managed to clear the French from the nearby vantage-
point where you can nowadays lie full-length in the grass by the cliff's
edge while trying to form in your mind some impression of how
Coromandière Cove would have looked from here when filled, as it was
certainly filled that morning back in 1758, with splintered boats, abandoned gear and the gruesomely shattered bodies of the many British
soldiers who never made it to the shore.

For James Thompson, clambering with his men across those slopes
above the beach which are today set out with wooden picnic tables, it
had been a very close-run thing. 'One twenty-four pound shot did a great
deal of mischief,' this man from Tain remembered. 'It passed under my
haunches and killed Sergeant MacKenzie, who was sitting as close to my
left side as he could squeeze, and it carried away the basket of his
broadsword which, along with the shot, passed through Lieutenant
Cuthbert, who was on MacKenzie's left, tore his body into slivers and
cut off both legs of one of the two fellows that held the tiller of the boat,
who lost an astonishing quantity of blood and died with the tiller grasped
tight in his hand . . . Although this shot did not touch me, the thighs and
calves of my legs were affected and became as black as my hat and, for
some weeks, I suffered a great deal of pain.'[34]

At this juncture, making a bad situation still worse, Thompson's
party were abandoned by the sailors whose job it was to convoy their
otherwise helpless lighter towards its destination. French sharpshooters
now took over where the French artillery had left off, pouring musket-
balls into the wallowing craft and killing still more of the Highlanders.

But on at least one of those snipers – one of the French army's native
auxiliaries, as it happened – James Thompson's company were to be
avenged following their drifting vessel's eventual rescue by another naval
detachment. 'There was a rascal of a savage on top of a high rock that
kept firing at the boats as they came within his reach,' runs the sergeant's
account of this episode, 'and he kill'd Volunteer Fraser of our regiment
. . . There was next to Fraser in the boat a silly fellow of a Highlander,
but who was a good marksman for all that, and, notwithstanding that
there was a positive order not to fire a shot during the landing, he
couldn't resist this temptation of having a slap at the savage. So the silly
fellow levels his fuzee at him and, in spite of the unsteadiness of the boat,
for it was blowing hard at the time, faith he brought him tumbling down
like a sack into the water . . . This shot was the best I have ever seen.'[35]

That he and his fellow soldiers of the 78th were to be considered in some sense more civilised, more cultured, than that dead sniper seemed unquestionable, no doubt, to James Thompson. To the French, however, it appeared to be the English rather than themselves who had entered into an alliance with barbarity. *Sauvages d'Ecosse*, they called the Scottish Highlanders. And in those French colonies, in the West Indies as well as North America, where regiments like the 78th were now being deployed, there began to gather around the Highlanders the sort of tales which were also told about France's own Indian detachments. 'They believed,' it was reported of French attitudes to Highlanders, 'that they would neither take nor give quarter and that . . . they were so nimble nobody could escape them; that no man had a chance against their broadswords; and that, with a ferocity natural to savages, they made no prisoners and spared neither man, woman nor child.' The soldiers of the 78th, some Frenchmen added in the particular case of Louisbourg, were also cannibals.[36]

Similar fears had once been generated in England and the south of Scotland by those Gaelic-speaking troops who had served with Charles Edward Stuart. But Highland clansmen were now being utilised in such a way as to advance the strategic interests and ambitions of the Hanoverian-ruled United Kingdom which they had formerly threatened. And this fundamental change in their military role was naturally producing an equally large shift in the way that Highlanders were regarded by the wider British public. The clansman was acquiring now a new – but, as matters turned out, enduring – reputation as a heroic fighter in the cause of Britain's rapidly expanding empire.

The Highlander's exoticism, from this perspective, was a positive attraction. When the 78th first got to North America, staff officers in Halifax suggested that the regiment might appropriately exchange its plaids for standard-issue British uniforms. This proposal had been fended off with difficulty. But following actions of the Louisbourg variety, no more was heard of kitting Highlanders in the red coats and white trousers then worn by other British troops. Instead their tartan, which Pitt's cabinet was still pledged formally to eradicate from Scotland, was transformed into one of the most potent of all imperial symbols – while their military prowess, previously a source of constant ministerial anxiety, became now a matter of considerable British pride.[37]

From Coromandière Cove there came reports of how the soldiers of the 78th had employed their plaids to staunch the holes left by French cannonballs in the boats which carried them ashore; reports of how they had waded waist-high through a surging surf and through a withering fire, each man clutching a Brown Bess musket in one hand and a broadsword in the other; reports of how they had swept effortlessly through the French lines above the beaches; reports of how they had pursued the breaking and retreating enemy to the very gates of the soon to be surrendered Louisbourg.[38]

Even James Wolfe was belatedly warming to this people whom he had so cordially detested when obliged to live among them back in Scotland – finding time, according to one persistent story, to press guinea pieces into the hands of the two men of the 78th who were the first British troops actually to set foot on the Coromandière Cove beaches. It would not have done, of course, for an officer like Wolfe to have had nobody to complain about. It consequently comes as no surprise to find colonial Americans featuring in the brigadier's correspondence as 'the dirtiest, the most contemptible, cowardly dogs you can conceive'. For the 78th, however, this most irascible of men had only praise. 'The Highlanders are very useful, serviceable soldiers and commanded by the most manly corps of officers I ever saw,' Wolfe wrote while in Cape Breton Island.[39]

With Louisbourg in British hands, Quebec itself lay open to assault. When the coastal ice began to break in the spring of 1759, therefore, a further expeditionary force, including both Fraser's Highlanders and the newly promoted General James Wolfe, was flung against New France. Soon Cape Breton Island had been left far behind by one of the largest British fleets ever to be assembled. Soon that fleet's 49 warships, together with its still more numerous and deeply laden transports, were probing westwards into the gradually narrowing estuary of the St Lawrence River which, since the sixteenth century, had provided the French with their principal route to the North American interior; to the Great Lakes; to the Ohio country; to that vast network of inland waterways which, stretching ever onwards to the prairies and beyond, had proved to be the means of gathering in a staggeringly rich crop of furs.[40]

The sons, grandsons and other descendants of soldiers of the 78th were eventually to control a large proportion of the fur trade out of the St Lawrence. And even in 1759 something of the possibilities inherent in their surroundings was maybe starting to be grasped by Colonel Simon Fraser's men. Neither this great river nor the territories to which it gave such valuable access had been so much as glimpsed, before the British army brought them here, by any significant number of Scottish Highlanders. But the soldiers of the 78th had now been nearly two years in North America. They had seen something of New York, New England and Nova Scotia as well as the approaches to New France. The thought of settling permanently on this continent must by now have been beginning to occur to some of them.

That thought would not have been dispelled from any Highland soldier's mind by the landscapes coming steadily more into focus as Britain's new invasion fleet reached the eastern end of the Ile d'Orleans where the banks of the St Lawrence draw that bit nearer to each other. Even here, just thirty miles below Quebec City, the river is more than ten miles wide. But the view from mid-channel is spectacular. On the southern skyline are the Monts Notre-Dame. To the north are the higher peaks of the Laurentides, looking not at all unlike the mainland hills of northern Scotland as seen, for instance, from the Minch. Ahead, meanwhile, the river is still broad enough to make its own wide junction with the western sky.

This is the country which the French called Canada. Jacques Cartier, a Breton skipper in the pay of King François I, had begun its exploration as long ago as 1535 when searching, like most Europeans who came to this part of the world at that time, for a new route to Asia. This aim Canada's French settlers were eventually to commemorate in the ironic title they gave to those swift and broken waters – situated just beyond a spot the local Iroquois called Hochelaga and the French, in due course, christened Montreal – which kept Cartier and his successors taking their oceangoing vessels any further west. Lachine, or China, these rapids were now designated. And they proved a formidable obstacle. Not until the early decades of the seventeenth century – having meanwhile mastered the essential technology in the shape of the birchbark canoe – were the French in a position to resume their push up the St Lawrence and its tributaries in the direction of the faraway Pacific.

As for the St Lawrence's own tidal reaches, when Fraser's Highlanders first got here in the early summer of 1759 the lower river valley had already taken on something of its modern, domesticated character, with the many little farms of the *habitants*, as French-Canadian settler families were known, stretching mile after mile along low riverbanks from which the forest, over several generations, had gradually been felled and driven back.

Because communication mostly still took place by water, the typical *habitant* concession was in the shape of a highly elongated rectangle, thus ensuring that every cultivator acquired both a reasonable amount of land and his own river frontage. Such farms, measuring maybe 300 or 400 yards across but as much as a mile or two in length, are still to be seen by anyone travelling through – or flying over – the more eastern parts of the St Lawrence Valley. And they are extraordinarily reminiscent of the very similar pattern of landholding which was to be imposed on much of the Scottish Highlands when the region's nowadays characteristic crofting system began to be developed by its landlords towards the end of the eighteenth century. Driving towards Quebec from Rivière du Loup, through the many linear settlements produced by each 300-yard-wide farm being entitled to its own house, you begin to wonder if the crofting concept could conceivably have been brought back to Scotland by one of those several landowning families who were represented among Simon Fraser's officers. Here, at any rate, farmhouses are strung out along the highway – which has long since replaced the river as the district's principal thoroughfare – in exactly the same manner as you find long lines of croft homes by the roadside in places like Skye, Sutherland, Lewis, Uist and Wester Ross.

But these *habitant* farms, though small by North American standards, are significantly larger and more fertile than their crofting equivalents. Indeed it was because of their potential contribution to keeping New France's armies properly supplied with food that James Wolfe – having laid siege now to Quebec City – ordered his troops to devastate as much of the surrounding countryside as they could conveniently reach. 'We marched 52 miles,' the general was accordingly informed by one of his subordinates, 'and in that distance burned 998 good buildings, two sloops, two schooners, ten shallops and several bateaux and small craft.' Thus it came about that Scottish Highlanders now found themselves applying to the Québecois exactly the same brutal and intimidatory measures which, in Culloden's aftermath, had been applied to their own homeland.[41]

Anse au Foulon – called Wolfe's Cove until the politically and linguistically assertive Québecois population of recent decades caused that name to be excised from their province's maps – is some three miles upriver from Quebec's original walled town. Between Anse au Foulon and the virtually sheer slopes of the towering escarpment on which the French had built their fortified settlement, there is a narrow strip of flatter land. Today it is occupied by a road, some railway sidings, a yacht club and a variety of industrial concerns. In 1759, however, there was no habitation here – and no very worthwhile military presence either.

Wolfe's landing at Anse au Foulon under cover of darkness in the early hours of a moonless 13 September was the British commander's latest – and, some thought, unnecessarily foolhardy – move in a campaign which had already lasted for nearly three months and which had been characterised, until this moment, by no very great success. An initial thrust on Quebec from the east in the early part of July had been beaten back after stiff fighting, some of it involving the Highlanders of the 78th, along the line of the Rivière Montmorency. Neither the intermittent skirmishing of subsequent weeks nor the fact that the British had been able to begin bombarding Quebec from the opposite bank of the St Lawrence had noticeably dented French morale nor brought the garrison's commander, the Marquis de Montcalm, any nearer to defeat. Such an outcome, it was clear, was likely to be produced only by the full-scale engagement which Wolfe was now attempting to force upon his opponent.[42]

According to some at least of the many accounts of the confused and confusing events surrounding the British advance guard getting ashore at Anse au Foulon, the one French sentry in a position to give the alarm was duped by a Highland officer who, perhaps as a result of earlier Jacobite affiliations, was fluent in the sentry's native language.

Irrespective of the truth or otherwise of such assertions, the cliff path –
now a zigzagging road so steep as to make walking up it a stiff climb –
was both taken and scaled. When dawn broke that September morning,
therefore, the Marquis de Montcalm found himself confronting several
thousand British troops drawn up in line of battle not much more than
a mile from Quebec City's western gate.

This place, as millions of schoolchildren right across the world
would learn in the British Empire's heyday, was called *les Plaines
d'Abraham*, the Plains of Abraham, its designation deriving from a
seventeenth-century Québecois, Abraham Martin, who, though born in
France in 1589, was known as *l'Écossais*, the Scot. As to Martin's links
with Scotland, there can now be only speculation. What is clear about
the piece of land to which he gave his name, however, is that it is less a
plain, more a gently undulating plateau, its surface marked out by a
series of shallow hollows and low ridges where, in winter, the residents
of the nowadays enormously expanded Quebec City can try out their skis
and where, in summer, families sunbathe and picnic within easy walking
distance of the downtown shopping area.

Here, on the British left and in the drizzling rain that had come on
with daylight, stood Fraser's Highlanders, their Brown Bess muskets
loaded, on General Wolfe's instructions, 'with an additional ball' – the
better to wreak havoc among the advancing French who, as the general
had intended, now had no alternative but to launch an immediate attack
on an enemy who had so clearly seized the tactical advantage.

Some thirty or forty paces in front of the 78th, the regiment's non-
commissioned officers placed markers on the ground to indicate the
point at which a French charge was most likely to be broken by concerted
musket fire. In mid-morning the French duly came, Fraser's Highlanders,
like the rest of the British line, holding fire until, at a given signal, there
rang out the carefully prepared and short-range musket volley which
observers later claimed to be the most effective such discharge ever
accomplished. So perfectly was it timed, people said afterwards of the
British volley, that it sounded like a single cannon shot, *comme un coup
de canon*, as one French survivor put it. And if this was an exaggerated
claim, there was certainly no doubting the consequences of that initial
and highly disciplined discharge. It broke the French attack, provided the
time the British needed to reload and allowed a second, more ragged,
volley of musket-balls to wreak further havoc among Montcalm's troops.

Montcalm himself was now dying and James Wolfe, too, had been
mortally wounded. But the day's overall outcome was clear. The French
were in retreat – pursued, almost needless to say, by the men of the 78th
who, in the customary Highland manner, had flung their muskets aside,
drawn their swords and raced down on Montcalm's increasingly
demoralised soldiers. He would 'never forget Fraser's Highlanders flying
wildly after them', one of these soldiers, Joseph Trahan, would

subsequently remark, 'with streaming plaids, bonnets and large swords, like so many infuriated demons'. It was a comment reminiscent of those made by the English troops who had been on the receiving end of similar assaults at Prestonpans and Falkirk only fourteen years before. Now these same English troops, in one or two instances at any rate, were reaping the benefit of the 'great slaughter' reported to have resulted from this latest Highland charge.

'Different nations have different excellencies and defects in war,' David Stewart of Garth observed. 'The power of the Highlander lies in close combat. Close charge was his ancient mode of attack . . . and if he can grasp his foe, as man with man, his courage is secure.' So it was at Quebec in September 1759. And it was symbolic of the extent to which these Highland qualities had begun to be positively regarded back in Britain that the monument raised to James Wolfe's memory in Westminster Abbey, the country's foremost imperial shrine, should have incorporated the distinctive, plaided figure of a soldier of the 78th.[43]

Serving as the Marquis de Montcalm's aide-de-camp on the day which brought about the fall of Quebec was the self-styled Chevalier James de Johnstone, an exiled Scottish Jacobite who had gone into battle at Culloden alongside some of those MacDonalds whose fighting skills now made their contribution to this decisive French defeat. Also serving on the French side was Jean-Baptiste Roche de Ramezay whose unhappy role it was to surrender Quebec formally to Britain. Roche de Ramezay's father had emigrated from Burgundy to Canada in 1685. His remoter ancestors, whose name was Ramsay, had left Scotland for France a century before.[44]

Like James de Johnstone, Roche de Ramezay had survived the battle for Quebec. What had not survived that battle, however, was the world to which, in their different ways, these two French officers belonged – a world in which it was plausible to maintain that a properly patriotic Scot ought to identify with France and not with England. Scotland's future – as underlined by the inclusion of that sculpted Highlander in the Westminster memorial to James Wolfe, conqueror of Canada – was now almost universally considered, and was certainly so considered by everyone who mattered in the Scottish Highlands, to be inextricably bound up with the progress both of the United Kingdom and the still wider empire to which Scotland's union with England had provided such profitable access. In the autumn of 1759 those English church and cathedral bells which had once pealed in gratitude for Culloden were rung out in celebration of a North American battle won, in part at least, by the force of Highland arms.

There was no better testimony to the rewards to be got from this Scottish collaboration in the developing imperial design than the career of Simon Fraser, state prisoner turned regimental commander. While still on active service in Canada – where, by no means lacking courage, he was wounded twice – Fraser was elected MP for Inverness-shire. Sent in 1761 from North America to Portugal, Britain's ally in the more general war of which the Quebec campaign was but one episode, he rose eventually to the rank of major-general. That was achievement enough. But a still more spectacular coup was to follow. Ten years in advance of its decision to restore to other formerly Jacobite families those estates which had been declared forfeit in the aftermath of Charles Edward Stuart's rising, parliament conceded that Simon Fraser's military service merited 'some particular act of grace' and returned to him the extensive lands of which his executed father had been so summarily deprived.[45]

In Quebec itself, meanwhile, Simon Fraser's soldiers, who had suffered more casualties than any other regiment involved in the battle for the city, were making what shift they could in a town which has now become a scrubbed and polished tourist mecca but which was then a desperately bedraggled place where provisions were extremely scarce and where practically every building had suffered badly during the earlier artillery bombardment. 'I contriv'd somehow to procure six blankets,' Sergeant James Thompson from Tain – a survivor if ever there was one – remembered of the months he spent in a half-demolished house, 'so that notwithstanding that I was almost frozen during the day . . . I passed the nights pretty comfortably, though 'twas funny enough to see every morning the whole surface of the blankets covered with ice from the heat of my breath and body.'[46]

As the exceptionally severe winter of 1759–60 dragged on, it became increasingly evident to General James Murray who now found himself in command – following Wolfe's death – of all the British forces then in Canada, that there was no guarantee of his fending off any counter-attack that might be mounted by the French forces still holding out upriver in Montreal. In September 1759, Murray had a total of 5,653 troops at his disposal. Six months later, however, nearly 700 of these men had died – while frostbite, scurvy and other diseases had left more than 2,000 of the remainder quite unfit for duty.[47]

In April there was further fierce fighting with the French. And again the 78th suffered heavy losses. But for all its garrison's many difficulties, Quebec remained in British hands. And when the ice broke that spring on the St Lawrence, allowing Royal Navy convoys to resupply James Murray with both men and munitions, it was clear that what remained of New France could not long survive. Montreal, the last bastion of French power in the region, was now under pressure from the west and south as well as from the east. In September, one year after Quebec's capture, Montreal's defending forces also capitulated, leaving Britain in control, as William Pitt had intended from the first, of huge new territories.

In less than twenty years, of course, much of Pitt's legacy was to be squandered by politicians lacking totally his breadth of vision. For the moment, however, the imperial government's priority was to promote the permanent British occupation of those North American localities which its troops had so recently taken from the French. And where better to find the necessary settlers than from among the ranks of these same soldiers? Thus it was that the men of Fraser's Highlanders, who received finally in Montreal the back pay owed to them for the entire period of their overseas service, now found themselves encouraged to remain here in North America.

CHAPTER FOUR

To Found in the New Land
a New Glengarry

OFFERED LAND ON the highly favourable terms embodied in a royal proclamation of 1763, some former soldiers of the Highland regiments which had seen so much action in the course of the French and Indian War chose to settle near Montreal or Quebec where they afterwards married into the *habitant* community and where, more than two centuries later, it is still possible to find French-speaking families with Scottish Highland names. A number headed east to Nova Scotia and Prince Edward Island. Others chose to return to one of the other North American localities with which so many Highland soldiers had become familiar some years earlier, moving south from Canada, where their units were generally disbanded, to the highly attractive hill country where the Mohawk and the Hudson Rivers meet.[1]

Originally inhabited by the Iroquois, this part of North America was reached by Europeans in 1609 when one of that era's more indefatigable explorers, Henry Hudson, looking vainly for a way to the Pacific, made his way here by means of the great watercourse which was afterwards named in his honour. Settled to begin with by the Dutch, taken subsequently by the British, coveted for the first half of the eighteenth century by the French, and joining, in the end, the United States, the region was remembered by James Fenimore Cooper, who was born and raised on its south-eastern fringes, as consisting in 1793 of 'beautiful and thriving villages . . . and neat and comfortable farms'. These were the end product of a pioneering effort to which families from the Scottish Highlands, for a period at least, made no small contribution.[2]

73

The first Highland settlers to reach colonial New York consisted of eighty or so families brought here in the 1730s by Lachlan Campbell who had previously held land in Islay, the Argyll island which was also home to the pro-emigration pamphleteer, Scotus Americanus. The Highland connection with the colony consequently antedated the French and Indian War by more than twenty years. But it was the novel set of circumstances created in America by the destruction of New France, together with the impact in Scotland of the Highland discontents articulated so effectively by Scotus Americanus, which resulted in New York becoming, in the 1760s and 1770s, the leading destination, after North Carolina, of the many Highlanders now wishing to take themselves beyond the reach of landlords whose conduct was increasingly regarded as intolerable.[3]

A key figure in this process was that most colourful of colonial characters, Sir William Johnson, who had himself arrived in New York in 1738 and who, in his several overlapping roles of fur trader, land speculator, superintendent of Indian affairs and militia commander, had made himself the effective ruler of much of the lower Mohawk Valley. Johnson's position, though already strong, had been made still stronger by the British army's removal of the threat posed previously to his domains by French soldiers and traders pushing south from the St Lawrence. It is appropriate, therefore, that the most successful of New York's territorial magnates should have marked the end of the French and Indian War by ordering, in 1763, the construction of Johnson Hall on the Mohawk Valley's northern slopes. The house still survives. And even the briefest look around Sir William's creation – its architecture of a type that would be more at home in rural England than in modern upstate New York – is sufficient to give something of an insight into the social aspirations of this quite extraordinary man.[4]

It may not be quite literally the case that Johnson, as has occasionally been suggested, bedded at least a thousand Iroquois women. But he clearly liked to live in something approximating to the roistering style of a medieval baron all the same; surrounding himself at Johnson Hall with hosts of supplicants and dependents; looking to have himself recognised as lord, as well as master, of the Mohawk territory. In principle, any sort of settler would have met Sir William's urgent need to develop the 700,000 acres of wild country which he had at his disposal by the 1760s. In practice, one suspects, Scottish Highlanders especially suited the Mohawk Valley baronet precisely because he hoped to take the place of a clan chieftain in this particular immigrant group's affections. It may well have been with some such purpose in mind, therefore, that Sir William Johnson began to offer land on his estates to a number of the Highland military men he had first encountered in the course of the French and Indian War.

Among the more prominent members of this group was Hugh

Fraser who had held the rank of lieutenant in the 78th Highlanders and who was one of about three hundred officers and men of the regiment to settle permanently in North America. Fraser, having first returned to Scotland to get married, brought both his new wife and her younger brother to the Mohawk Valley in 1763. Along with those other Highland veterans of the recent fighting who were to make their homes in the same general area, Hugh Fraser and his family were consequently to help establish what was soon to become one of the more sizeable Scottish Highland communities in North America.[5]

This community was boosted substantially in the early part of 1774 by the arrival of some 425 settlers who had sailed the previous September from the West Highland town of Fort William. The leaders of this emigrant party, which was very similar in its social composition to those other groups of Highlanders then establishing themselves in the Cape Fear River country, may or may not have obtained some previous knowledge of the Hudson and Mohawk Valleys during the French and Indian War. What is certain is that they felt themselves to be leaving Scotland for reasons more or less identical to those which were commonly mentioned by their counterparts in North Carolina. The 'hardships and oppressions of different kinds imposed . . . by the landholders' had 'obliged them to abandon their native country', the Fort William party maintained in a letter published on their arrival in New York City in October 1773.[6]

For all their unwillingness to pay the high rents now demanded of them in Scotland, these latest additions to the Highland population in America were by no means lacking in resources. Some were described by the *New York Journal* as 'genteel people of considerable property'. Others were said by the *New York Gazette* to have 'ready money to purchase each man his freehold'.[7]

These, then, were immigrants whose ambitions were firmly in line with those which Hector St John de Crevecoeur was to attribute to his Andrew the Hebridean; people who were determined to better themselves here in the New World; farming families looking to get hold of their own land. Indeed it is by no means impossible that there stepped ashore from the *Pearl*, the ship which conveyed this particular set of emigrants from Scotland to New York, the very man whom Crevecoeur was to make a symbol of so many American aspirations. It was in 1774, after all, that Andrew the Hebridean was reported by Crevecoeur to have settled in his neighbourhood. And it was in the spring of that year that the men, women and children who had landed from the *Pearl* the previous October made their way from New York City to the Mohawk country by way of the Hudson Valley where Crevecoeur was then resident.

Neither the author of *Letters from an American Farmer* nor the Scottish Highlanders whose progress he reported in his book were destined to remain long in the place where they now found themselves, however. For all that he had served as a young officer with the French forces defeated by the British at Quebec, and for all his evidently deep and genuine affection for the American colonies, Crevecoeur chose to align himself with the loyalist side in the political crisis which was now developing into open war. And in New York, as in North Carolina, most Scottish Highland immigrants did likewise.

As always, of course, there were exceptions. Prominent among these was Alexander MacDougall who was born in Islay in 1732 and whose parents had shortly afterwards joined the emigrant party led here by Lachlan Campbell. MacDougall's father had eventually gravitated towards New York City where he found employment as a milkman. But Alexander, a recklessly adventurous young man, became in turn a privateering seaman, a businessman, a banker and one of the earliest advocates of American independence. Jailed by the colonial authorities in 1770 on charges of sedition, MacDougall was eventually to represent New York in the Continental Congress and to hold the rank of major-general in the Continental Army.[8]

But Alexander MacDougall, like that other Continental Army commander of Highland extraction, Lachlan MacIntosh, had left Scotland when still a child. The principal organisers of the *Pearl* emigration – the three brothers, John MacDonell of Leek, Allan MacDonell of Collachie, Alexander MacDonell of Aberchalder, with their cousin, John MacDonell of Scotus – were of a very different stamp from this New York City radical. As was also true of the loyalist leadership in the Cape Fear River region, the MacDonells were tacksmen. That did not mean that they were without their rebellious tendencies, belonging as they did to a clan which was traditionally Jacobite and which had suffered heavy losses at Culloden. In New York as in North Carolina, however, to have been a Jacobite did not by any means disbar a man from being a loyalist. The cause of King George III, in fact, was to have few more committed adherents in all of North America than those West Highland tacksmen who reached the Mohawk Valley at just the moment when colonial difficulties were clearly tending towards a violent resolution.[9]

Their religion, it should be said, was an additional factor in the thinking of the *Pearl* emigrants. The MacDonells were Roman Catholics. That had been one reason for their Jacobitism – the exiled Stuart monarchy being of the same persuasion. But it was not a circumstance likely to make them the natural allies of colonial revolutionaries who were motivated partly by a conviction that the Quebec Act of 1774, which legally sanctioned the continuation of the Catholic Church in the former New France, was but one element in a wider conspiracy to subvert Protestantism in all of British North America.

It was certainly the case, as noted by one of colonial New York's Presbyterian ministers, that the Scottish Highlands had become by the mid-1770s a place where the population was 'generally discontented' and where 'the spirit of emigration' was consequently becoming steadily more prevalent. But wishing to be out of Scotland, and believing America to offer much more attractive prospects than the Highlands, was not at all the same thing, from the perspective of the tacksman class, as desiring to sever all connections with the United Kingdom. Many tacksmen, several MacDonells among them, had been eager to embrace the opportunities provided by service in the British army during the French and Indian War. Those tacksmen who were still in Scotland in 1775 were, in very many instances, joining the new Highland regiments now being drilled at Fort George prior to their being sent to confront American revolutionaries. And others from among the *daoine uaisle* were no doubt just as ready as the rest of the Scottish gentry to append their signatures to the numerous 'loyal addresses' which Scotland's local authorities were ostentatiously submitting to parliament as a token of their unstinting support for British policy in the colonies.[10]

A Highland soldier whose unit was forced to surrender to the Continental Army during the Revolutionary War was afterwards to give some account of the hostility which he and his comrades endured at the hands of the American public while being marched under escort through one colonial locality. 'On our journey,' this Highlander recalled, 'no slaves were ever served as we were; through every village, town and hamlet that we passed, the women and children, and indeed some men among them, came out and loaded us with the most rascally epithets . . . But what vexed me most was their continual slandering of our country on which they threw the most infamous invectives.' The country thus singled out for abuse, that soldier went on to make clear, was not so much Britain as Scotland.[11]

The conduct of the Highland settler community in the Cape Fear River country, and particularly that community's support for Allan MacDonald of Kingsburgh and those other individuals responsible for the events which culminated in the Battle of Moore's Creek Bridge, had helped engender this very general American detestation of Scots. But the Highland population in and around the Mohawk Valley was to become, if anything, more strongly identifed with unremitting enmity to the cause of American independence. The Cape Fear Highlanders, after their Moore's Creek experience, had prudently kept their heads down for the duration of the war. But their Mohawk Valley counterparts – those Gaelic-speaking residents of frontier settlements which have since developed into placid little towns with names like Broadalbin, Scotchbrush and Edinburg – became highly effective guerilla fighters who, over several years, managed to keep much of the New York countryside beyond Albany in a state of constant turmoil, terror and disorder.

Initially responsible for rallying the Mohawk country's Highland settlers to the cause of maintaining British rule in North America was

Alexander MacDonald who had been one of the few men of his name to serve on the Hanoverian side in the course of the last Jacobite rebellion and who had afterwards gone on to become an officer in Montgomery's Highlanders, one of the regiments which helped finally to expel the French from both the Mohawk and the Hudson Valleys in the later 1750s. For all that he had afterwards settled in the vicinity of New York City where he had married into an American family of decidedly patriot views, MacDonald remained stubbornly loyalist in his opinions, concluding by 1774 that 'nothing can cure the madness that prevails all over America but the sternest of measures'. Convinced that war was coming and that his fellow Highlanders would have a substantial part to play in it, MacDonald accordingly travelled first to the Mohawk Valley and then, in the spring of 1775, to Boston. There, having sought out General Thomas Gage, Britain's supreme commander in America, he was able to assure the general that Highland fighting men in plenty might readily be recruited in the Mohawk territory.[12]

Also present in Britain's Boston headquarters at this critical juncture was Colonel Allan MacLean, another veteran of the heavy fighting which had gone on around the Mohawk Valley during the French and Indian War. MacLean belonged originally to Mull and his military career – in contrast to that of Alexander MacDonald – had begun with his joining the Jacobite army in 1745. Having survived Culloden, MacLean subsequently fled to Holland where he served for some years with the Dutch army prior to taking advantage of the amnesty eventually offered by the British government to those former Jacobite officers now willing to deploy their swords, so to speak, in the Hanoverian interest. Hence this former Jacobite's subsequent involvement in Britain's battles with New France. And hence his strong conviction that he, and not the lower-ranking Alexander MacDonald, should now take charge of operations in the Mohawk country.[13]

Two distinct military formations were quickly to result from these manoeuvres, the Royal Highland Emigrant Regiment, commanded by Allan MacLean, and the King's Royal Regiment of New York, commanded by Sir John Johnson whose father, the rumbustious Sir William, had died in 1774. The Johnsons, in spite of their tendency to run things in the Mohawk Valley very much in their own way, had always been solidly pro-British, not least because of their well-founded suspicion that their own patriarchal role in the upper part of colonial New York was unlikely to survive American independence. Sir John accordingly became Allan MacLean's close ally in the recruitment drive which the latter launched in the Mohawk Valley in the summer of 1775. Among the men who consequently emerged as holders of commissions in either the Highland Emigrant Regiment or the King's Royal Regiment were those most recent arrivals in the Mohawk territory, Allan MacDonell of Collachie, John MacDonell of Scotus and Alexander MacDonell of

Aberchalder, together with several of their sons, nephews and other relatives.[14]

Whatever else they may have been, the MacDonells were no novices in the business of war. In his account of the Battle of Culloden, Chevalier James de Johnstone, afterwards on the Marquis de Montcalm's staff at Quebec, recalled how an earlier MacDonell of Scotus, *Domhall nan Glean*, Donald of the Glen, was killed by his side as the two of them took part in a final and futile Jacobite charge that April morning in 1746. And it was indicative of this particular clan's reluctance to come to terms with Culloden's wider consequences that another MacDonell veteran of this last Jacobite campaign, Archibald MacDonell of Barrisdale, instead of fleeing to France with the Chevalier de Johnstone and so many others in 1746, had remained at large for several years in his native Knoydart. There, for all that he had been found guilty of treason and was in constant danger of being captured and hanged, Archibald MacDonell contrived to maintain a considerable degree of control over an estate which was theoretically in possession of the British government. 'They have the insolence,' a government agent reported of the Knoydart people in 1753, 'ever since the year 1746 to pay their rents to the attainted Barasdale who since that time absolutely rules them and ranges up and down that country . . . with a band of armed men dressed, as well as himself, in the Highland habit.'[15]

The MacDonell country, though its heartland was the comparatively sheltered Glen Garry, some forty or fifty miles to the south-west of Inverness, also included an altogether wilder tract of mountain country extending all the way from the southern end of Loch Ness to the Atlantic coast. This was as inaccessible and impenetrable a place as existed in Scotland – 'a perfect den of thieves and robbers', according to a military intelligence report of 1750. Its inhabitants, who tended to be as intractable as their surroundings, had long been bred in a tradition of cattle rustling and general freebootery. That was why MacDonell of Barrisdale – whose younger brother, incidentally, was one of the several officers of Fraser's Highlanders to die in the course of the battle for Quebec – had been able to avoid his Hanoverian pursuers for so long. And that was why this new generation of MacDonells who had now aligned themselves with the Hanoverian, or Tory, cause in America were to take so readily to the type of war in which they rapidly became engaged in those territories stretching northwards from the Mohawk River to the Adirondack Mountains. Not only is this ideal guerilla country, but it has something of the look and feel of those Scottish Highland landscapes where the Glen Garry people first learned how to fight.[16]

This latest MacDonell campaign, just like those which went before in Scotland, was a war of long marches through rough terrain; a war of sudden attacks on isolated homesteads; a war in which the loyalist

Highlanders operated in close alliance with those native peoples, most especially the Iroquois, who had also been persuaded to take the British side in a conflict from which most Indians had tried initially to remain aloof. 'They were sent out on scouting parties and employed in picking up intelligence and in harassing the back settlements of the enemy,' one of his contemporaries reported of the unit commanded by that most effective loyalist raider, Captain John MacDonell, son of Alexander MacDonell of Aberchalder. Described as 'rather below the middle size, of a fair complexion and . . . uncommonly strong and active', John MacDonell, still a teenager when the Revolutionary War began, was also said to be the loyalist officer 'best liked' by the British army's Iroquois auxiliaries. That makes this young man, born in 1758 at Aberchalder House beside Loch Oich, the most likely subject of a despatch sent to the Continental Congress in Philadelphia by one of the American patriots on the receiving end of an especially destructive loyalist attack. The raiders in question, this man reported from the Mohawk Valley, consisted of 'about twenty Indians and one MacDonald, a Tory'.[17]

This may sound faintly glamorous. In fact, the fighting around the eastern end of the Mohawk Valley was of the bloody, brutal, unforgiving variety always generated by guerilla warfare. 'No other sector or district of country in the United States,' one nineteenth-century American was to observe, 'suffered in any comparable degree as much from the War of the Revolution as did the Mohawk. For month after month, for seven long years, were its towns and villages, its humbler settlements and isolated habitations fallen upon by an untiring and relentless enemy until, at the close of the contest, the appearance of the whole district was that of widespread, heartsickening and universal desolation . . . It was the computation, two years before the close of the war, that one-third of the population had gone over to the enemy; that one-third had been driven from the country or slain in battle and by private assassinations; and yet among the inhabitants of the remaining third, in June 1783 it was stated at a public meeting held at Fort Plain, that there were 300 widows and 2,000 orphan children.'[18]

The burnings and killings organised by the Mohawk country's Highland loyalists, though they tied down a number of Continental Army detachments which might more profitably have been deployed elsewhere, had no very major impact on the wider outcome of this latest struggle for America. But it was practically impossible, of course, for people like John MacDonell or their comrades and their sympathisers to remain in the former colony of New York when that colony eventually became part of the United States. On Britain finally admitting defeat and accepting the reality of American independence, therefore, most of the Scottish Highlanders still living in the Mohawk Valley were left with little alternative but to undertake the long and difficult journey to what remained of British North America. There they were promised, by the colonial officials in charge of providing for the many thousands of American loyalists then making their way north, a fresh start. That was exactly what was wanted by those MacDonells and others who, since leaving Scotland on the *Pearl* in 1773, had been almost constantly on the move. They now hoped, one of these people is reputed to have written in 1785, finally to settle down and 'to found in the new land a new Glengarry'.[19]

Driving towards Toronto from Montreal by way of Lachine, the St Lawrence always on your left, you cross, after an hour or so, the border separating the Canadian provinces of Quebec and Ontario. The countryside adjacent to the river here is flat and clearly fertile. Its wide fields grow corn and other crops. Its skyline is everywhere dominated by the concrete and steel grain silos which nowadays tower above most one-and-a-half-storey farmhouses of the type long characteristic of these parts. Linking one farm with another in this quarter is a road network in the shape of a grid. One set of highways and dirt roads run inland at right angles to the St Lawrence. Another set, as ruler-straight as the first, precisely parallel the great river's course from south-west to north-east.

Venture into this chequerboard-like collection of quiet and mostly minor thoroughfares – as different as they could possibly be from the ceaselessly turning, twisting, sharply rising, steeply falling roads of either the Mohawk Valley or the Scottish Highlands – and you find yourself directed towards a whole series of familiar-sounding destinations. There is a Glen Nevis hereabouts and a Lochiel; a Laggan, Fassifern and Glenroy; an Eigg Road, a Skye Road and a Dunvegan. For maybe twenty miles along the St Lawrence, and for a slightly greater distance back from it, place names of that sort are common. Equally plentiful, it quickly becomes evident, are family names which also have their origins in Scotland.

The co-ed soccer team fielded by one of this district's high schools, you gather from the weekly newspaper on sale for 65 cents at McCrimmon, includes John MacSweyn, Stephen Cameron, Dave MacDonald, Glen Campbell, Bridget Cameron, Jewel Morrison, Anne Ferguson, Lisa MacDonald, Todd MacDonald and Isabel Campbell. Elsewhere in the paper's columns there is word of Gaelic choir and pipe-band practices. John MacAskill, auctioneer, will be presiding at a forthcoming sale of antiques and collectibles belonging to Karen and Harold MacLeod. Anna-Mae MacMillan is celebrating her ninetieth birthday. Karen MacCallum has just got married. And Brody Alexander MacDonald's christening took place at St Raphael's Church last Sunday.[20]

This being the eastern end of Ontario, there are also plenty of Québecois names to be seen in *The Glengarry News*. But the Scottish Highland influence on this part of North America is, to say the least, considerable. It has been so ever since the 1780s when there finally settled here in Glengarry County most of those emigrants who had originally left the Scottish Glen Garry for New York in 1773.

It was no simple matter, in the chaotic conditions of that time, to get from the Mohawk country to Upper Canada – as the modern province of Ontario was then called. And it is perfectly understandable that the former loyalist guerilla commanders who led column after column of refugees through the Adirondack Mountains should have been extremely proud of their having made it possible for so many Highlanders to make a second North American beginning in Glengarry County. When, towards the end of his life, someone sought to compliment one of those loyalist heroes by comparing his Adirondack trek with the exodus of the Israelites from Egypt, the old man, or so the story goes, was highly indignant. 'Moses be damned,' this veteran exclaimed. 'He lost half his charges in the Red Sea. I brought all my folk through without losing a man, woman or child.'[21]

Since the beginnings of such emigration in the 1730s, it had been characteristic of people leaving the Scottish Highlands for North America that they tended, as was commented in 1805 by the Earl of Selkirk, author of a highly perceptive book on the subject, to be of an 'uncommonly gregarious disposition'. Highland emigrants, Selkirk pointed out, chose almost always to travel with, and to settle alongside, others of their own original community. The Highland population's 'peculiar language and manners', the earl explained, resulted in their being reluctant to mingle in North America with the continent's other immigrant groups. Once established, or so Selkirk's investigations had convinced him, this tendency towards a degree of Highland isolationism became rapidly self-reinforcing. 'The communication arising from repeated emigrations, and the continual correspondence between these settlers and their relations in Scotland, have given the people of every part of the Highlands a pretty intimate acquaintance with the circumstances of some particular colony,' the earl wrote. And because Highlanders, according to Selkirk, 'always show great distrust of any information which does not come from their own immediate connexions', it was usually the case that where an initial band of pioneers had led, many more of their relatives and neighbours were likely to follow.[22]

Selkirk, as later events were to show, was not without his own axe to grind in these matters. But his conclusions as to the preferred destinations of Highland emigrants were clearly founded on the facts. There had been an especially close link, as the earl commented, between Argyll and Skye on the one hand, and the Cape Fear country on the other. A similar connection was soon to be established between Glengarry County, which Selkirk visited in 1804, and a number of Highland localities. These included places – as can be seen by reading just a few of the nineteenth-century gravestones in Glengarry County's neatly kept churchyards – as far apart as Skye and Glen Lyon. But the bulk of the earliest European settlers in this part of Ontario were to come from the district bounded on the south by the narrow waters of Loch Shiel, on the east by the Great Glen and on the north by the high mountains of Kintail.

This was an area where landed proprietors, in accordance with the requirements of the new economic order which had been established in the Highlands in the aftermath of Culloden, were endeavouring by the 1780s to increase the commercial potential of their estates by turning more and more of those estates over to the sheep-farmers who were then beginning to move into the Highlands from other parts of Scotland. It was little wonder, in such circumstances, that long-established tenants who were deprived of their land to make way for these incomers, together with those of their neighbours who feared that they might soon suffer a similar fate, now decided to try their luck in this 'new Glengarry' of which they were beginning to hear from the loyalist refugees who were already resident there.[23]

In 1785, partly as a result of wholesale evictions ordered by men who were now more inclined to behave as landlords than clan chieftains, some three hundred people left the Scottish Glen Garry and the adjacent Glen Moriston for what one contemporary called 'the banks of the St Lawrence'. Several hundred more were to follow in 1786 – most of them drawn, in this instance, from the more westerly districts of Knoydart and Morar. By way of bearing out the general validity of Lord Selkirk's observations on the mechanisms governing such emigrations, it is worth noting that relatives of the MacDonell tacksmen who had forged the initial connection between this part of the Highlands and North America in 1773 were also prominent among the leaders of a number of later groups – one such party including, for example, Father Alexander MacDonell, a younger son of MacDonell of Scotus.[24]

Something of the regret, bordering on sorrow, which such Highland emigrants felt on leaving their homeland is evident in the Gaelic songs composed by a member of that particular contingent, Anna Gillis. But something of the typical emigrant party's hopes and aspirations is evident in these songs also. Her people might be taking leave, as Anna put it, 'of Morar, Arisaig and mountainous Moidart, Eigg, and fair, surf-swept Canna, beautiful, lovely Uist'. But it was good to be bound for *Canada Ard*, Upper Canada, that country of 'joy and delight', where wheat required 'only three months to bring it to full season', where, thanks to the prevalence of maples, 'sugar may be got from a tree' and where neither the singer nor her friends from Scotland would ever again want for anything.[25]

They were putting behind them the 'land of the lairds', Anna Gillis continued, and were bound now for 'the land of contentment'. *Maighstir Alasdair og, mac Fear Scotais*, young Father Alexander, son of Scotus, was bringing them out of Scotland, 'so that we would be free as were those who followed Moses out of Egypt'. In Canada they would get farms of their own; there 'landlords will no more oppress us'.

In their less lyrical moments, of course, its prospective settlers fully understood that Glengarry County – still largely covered by dense stands of old growth forest in the 1780s – was not the sort of place where a good living was to be earned without effort. 'I know . . . from personal communication with them,' the Earl of Selkirk remarked of such emigrants, 'that they are aware of the laborious process that is necessary for bringing the forest lands into a productive state. But this is not sufficient to deter men of vigorous minds when they are incited by . . . powerful motives.' Not the least of such motives, in Selkirk's opinion, was the Highlander's deep-seated desire to acquire a piece of land which neither he nor his successors would ever be obliged to relinquish in the manner that so many people were just then being forced to give up their ancestral landholdings in Scotland.[26]

The numerous agricultural tenants being displaced by changes of the sort which were occurring in Glen Garry, Glen Moriston, Knoydart, Arisaig and Morar could easily have moved south, as Selkirk readily acknowledged, to those Lowland towns where labour was much in demand as a result of the beginnings of industrialisation. And there were those, it should be underlined, who did indeed leave the Highlands for places like Glasgow and Paisley rather than make the ocean crossing to North America. But there was no doubt in Selkirk's mind as to those nearer destinations being, in comparison with North America, very much a second choice – a choice which, or so the earl insisted, 'can have no attraction except in a case of necessity'.

Their poverty might compel some Highlanders to take jobs in Scotland's growing number of urban 'manufactories', Selkirk went on. But those possessing the resources needed to finance an ocean crossing were much more likely to emigrate to North America. Such emigration certainly required 'a great momentary effort', Selkirk conceded. But it also held out to Scotland's Gaelic-speaking population 'a speedy prospect of a situation and mode of life similar to that in which they have been educated'. Being 'accustomed to possess land' and 'to derive from it all the comforts they can enjoy', Highlanders, in Selkirk's opinion, 'naturally consider it as indispensable and can form no idea of happiness without such a possession'. Industrial employment, while fairly easy to obtain, was consequently lacking altogether in appeal. 'The situation of a mere day-labourer,' as Selkirk put it, 'is one which must appear degrading to a person who has been the possessor of a portion of land, however small, and has been accustomed to consider himself as in the rank of farmer.' Hence the allure of North America where the lowliest of Highlanders, assuming only that he could afford to get there, had some 'prospect', in Selkirk's words, 'of holding land by a permanent tenure instead of a temporary, precarious and dependent possession'.

It is in this sense that the movement from the Scottish Highlands to North Carolina, to the Mohawk Valley, to Glengarry County, to Nova Scotia, to Prince Edward Island and to all the other North American localities which received so many Highland settlers in the several decades following Culloden can be understood as a gesture of defiance, maybe even of rebellion. Those Highlanders who remained at home were increasingly liable both to eviction and to the various other forms of exploitation which were inseparable from the new types of estate management now being introduced by their landlords. Those Highlanders who removed themselves to North America, in contrast, were successful in rejecting and avoiding such a fate. 'Their emigration,' as has been remarked by Glengarry County's leading modern historian, Marianne McLean, 'registered a radical protest against the impact of economic transformation in the Highlands.'[27]

There are few more scenically spectacular journeys to be made in Britain than the one which takes you from the Great Glen through Glen Garry to the edge of the Atlantic. You start beside Loch Oich near Aberchalder, once the tack, or farm, occupied by one of the organisers of the 1773 emigration from this part of the Highlands to New York. You make your way along the densely wooded north shore of Loch Garry. You traverse the altogether more exposed slopes high above Loch Quoich. Eventually, at the point where a gradually deteriorating road gives out completely, you begin to get the seaweed-laden scent of Loch Hourn's strongly tidal waters. You now have six or seven miles to walk along the coastal path to Barrisdale – home at one time to that especially elusive Jacobite veteran who managed for several years in the 1740s and 1750s to keep always one step ahead of the Hanoverian troops whose job it was to hunt him down and see him hanged. You have been travelling, all these several hours, among the high hills and along the river valleys that were home for centuries to those hundreds and hundreds of families who considered themselves a part of the clan whose lands these were – this Clan MacDonell which, for more than two hundred years now, has loomed larger in the history of North America than in the history of Scotland.

In our now arguably overpopulated world, there is is something very peculiar about Glen Garry – just as there is something equally strange about Glen Moriston and Glen Shiel to the north, Glen Dessary and Glen Pean to the south or Knoydart, Morar, Arisaig and the islands of Eigg, Muck, Rum and Canna to the west. These places contain far fewer people in the twentieth century than they did in the eighteenth. Possibly this is a good thing. Certainly there are those who can be found to say, or write, of what occurred here in the 1770s and 1780s that it added up to something in the nature of improvement; that it was, in any case, unavoidable; that it makes no sense now to regret what happened in the past. But it is hard, on making that long trip from Loch Oich to

Loch Hourn and seeing almost nothing in the way of human habitation, not to wonder if it really represented any advance on what had gone before to have 'tenants . . . dismissed from their habitations', as one victim of this transformation put it, 'and numbers of small farms . . . united in one for the purpose of making a sheepwalk which was given to a stranger'.[28]

All such upheavals have their beneficiaries, however. The most immediate of these, as far as this part of the Scottish Highlands was concerned, was a sheep-farmer by the name of Thomas Gillespie, in his way as much a pioneer, it must be said, as any North American frontiersman. One of the first south country sheep producers to venture into territories which less than twenty years before his arrival were still regarded as so lawless and disorderly as to require regular patrolling by the military, Gillespie profited exceedingly from his bold decision to take on those lands from which the MacDonells were then being steadily expelled. Things had not always gone exactly as he might have wanted, the sheep-farmer made clear to James Hogg, the Scottish novelist and poet with whom Gillespie spent a few days in the course of a visit Hogg made to the Highlands in the summer of 1803. But he had made good all the same. 'Mr Gillespie,' Hogg recorded, 'with a perseverance almost peculiar to himself, continued to surmount every difficulty and at the expiration of every lease commonly added something to the extent of his possessions. He is now the greatest farmer in all that country and possesses a tract of land extending from the banks of Loch Garry to the shores of the Western Ocean.'[29]

Today, should you venture beyond Barrisdale into the Knoydart peninsula, now one of the most isolated localities in all of Europe, you will find in its 200 square miles no more than two or three dozen human beings. So completely have this district's original communities been obliterated, there is among the modern Knoydart's population not a single person who can claim descent from any of the hundreds of families who lived here in the period before Thomas Gillespie drove his sheep into these parts. As any visitor from Scotland to Ontario's Glengarry County is promptly made aware, however, you can find here, an ocean's breadth removed from Knoydart and its neighbouring localities, any amount of folk who, to some small but ineradicable extent, still think of themselves as belonging – in the way this most emotive word is used by Highlanders – to those faraway glens and shorelines which no more than a few of them have ever seen.

It is easy, of course, for that same visitor from Scotland to adopt a slightly – or maybe not so slightly – condescending attitude to the ways in which so many Glengarry people's continuing affection for the Highlands is made visible in the twentieth-century's last decade. It is a simple matter, for example, to make fun of the enormous pomp and ceremony surrounding events like the Glengarry Highland Games. It is no difficult thing to get a cheap laugh back home at the expense of this or that Glengarry resident's confusion as to the pronunciation of this or that phrase in either Gaelic or Broad Scots.

But to adopt such an attitude is simply to demonstrate one's own failure to comprehend the distinction between symbol and substance. What is being celebrated at the Glengarry Highland Games and similar festivals is the profound sense of community generated over the last two hundred years in the homesteads and the villages established with such difficulty in this little bit of North America. The dancers, the pipebands, the hammer-throwers, the fiddlers and the singers have the vital role of making clear that the Glengarry Games are a Highland occasion. But what matters much more than the formal proceedings is the opportunity which such an event provides each year for many thousands of men and women, many of them living now in other parts of Canada or in the United States, to renew their acquaintance with the place which, for several generations, their people have called home.

The Glengarry sense of identity, as far as the county's Scots-descended families are concerned, is certainly Highland in origin. But that same sense of identity – and it is a very powerful one – is rooted also in experiences which owe little or nothing to Scotland; in the act of emigration; in the loyalist exodus from the Mohawk Valley; in the years, the lifetimes really, spent turning forest into farmland; in all the myriad happenings which have made Glengarry County what it is today. No, they do not do things here quite in the style thought proper back in Scotland. Why should they? Glengarry folk go partying on their games day not because they want to play at being Scots but because they want to celebrate the fact of their being North American Scottish Highlanders. That is – and it should be recognised as such – an absolutely key distinction.

'Go not to Glengarry if you be not a Highlandman,' prospective emigrants were warned by the author of an 1829 publication. And with some reason. Of the 8,500 or so people living in Upper Canada's easternmost county at that time, around three-quarters were of Scottish Highland extraction and many were still largely Gaelic-speaking. Much the same was true of the 17,500 Glengarry residents of twenty years later – when, as is revealed by census data, one such resident in every six was named either MacDonell or MacDonald.[30]

Among the latter large category, or so it would afterwards be claimed in Glengarry County, was a certain Duncan MacDonald who, when a young man in Scotland, had enlisted as a piper in one of the British army's several Highland regiments. This regiment was posted to India and such was the customary toll then taken there by disease that, when a report of Duncan's death reached Scotland, it did not occur to any of his relatives to question it. In fact, Duncan did not die. But he did lose contact with his family who, in the course of his long absence, had left the Highlands for Glengarry County.

On Duncan finally returning to Scotland and discovering what had occurred, according to the standard story of his wanderings, he decided to follow his people to North America: taking ship for the St Lawrence; tramping the last fifteen miles from the riverfront to the spot, near McPhee's Bridge, where his family had settled; announcing his arrival by playing, on the bagpipes which he had brought from Scotland, that most haunting of emigrant airs, *Lochaber No More*.

The first, faint notes of Duncan's playing reached the MacDonald homestead just as its occupants, so this particular tale continues, had sat down to their evening meal. 'Near and nearer came the music and soon they saw a kilted figure, travel-stained and weary, approaching the house. They scarcely knew him after twenty-one years of service, tall, broad in shoulder, bewhiskered. Yet they did recognise him and threw themselves upon him in an abandonment of happiness and thankfulness.'[31]

It may not have been quite like that. But what is significant about the tradition of how Duncan MacDonald came to Canada is not its authenticity or otherwise. What is of interest is the extent to which the story's account of Duncan's reunion with his family conveys a strong impression – which you get from lots of other sources also – of Glengarry County, rather than the Scottish Highlands, having become home to the community of which the piper was a part.

Here on the St Lawrence there had been recreated something of the Scottish Highland social order which was then being destroyed so comprehensively in places like Knoydart. Now it was rather more with Glengarry County, rather less with the increasingly deserted glens of the West Highlands, that folk like Duncan MacDonald and his kin identified. The pride taken by such people in their piece of Ontario was identical to that taken in Moidart, Arisaig or Glen Moriston by earlier generations of their families. The new Glengarry's attributes were celebrated by the county's Gaelic-speaking population, through story-telling and through music, in exactly the same way as their predecessors, on the other side of the Atlantic, once celebrated those districts which so many Highlanders had now abandoned in favour of North America.

What is most striking about the way in which Glengarry County was regarded by its Scottish Highland settlers is the extent to which it appeared to these immigrants to be a marked improvement on the country they had put behind them. Here in North America, remarked Iain Liath MacDonald, there was none of the 'harassment' which, by implication, he had suffered in Scotland. Here there were some three thousand farms of about two hundred acres each – from none of which a family could ever be evicted. Here a Highlander, who could readily be jailed for doing such a thing in Scotland, might 'kill a deer . . . without fear or control from any superior power'. Here that same Highlander, just like Crevecoeur's Andrew the Hebridean in a slightly earlier period, quickly found himself the possessor of a vote – Glengarry County being entitled to return two representatives to the Upper Canada assembly in the first assembly election of 1792. 'The candidates couldn't speak english very well,' it was reported of that election by one Glengarry man whose own grip of the language did not run to a full understanding of its spelling, 'and their efforts at speachifying were comical.'[32]

Maybe. But Glengarry County nevertheless sent to the first representative body to be convened in this part of North America two most serious-minded men. One was John MacDonell, the former soldier whose wartime exploits had terrorised the Mohawk Valley. The other was John's brother Hugh, another veteran of the Revolutionary War. And though both these Aberchalder MacDonells were certainly Gaelic-speaking, it is hardly possible to reconcile their alleged deficiencies in English with the fact that John, now a lawyer by profession, was shortly to be chosen by his fellow assemblymen as the Upper Canadian parliament's first speaker.[33]

There was arguably nothing very democratic about John MacDonell. To the Highland tacksman's longstanding consciousness of his own status he seems to have added the fierce pride which the self-made North American has always taken in his or her achievements. At least a little of this is evident in the still impressive ruins – the place was accidentally burned in 1813 – of the home which MacDonell had built for him on the banks of the St Lawrence not far from Summerstown. Glengarry House, the former soldier turned politician called this pile, reputedly the largest private residence in the Ontario of its day and, according to one slightly later account, 'renowned for its hospitality'.[34]

It is easy to imagine John MacDonell riding out from here to solicit electoral support in much the same way as his immediate ancestors had dragooned the lowlier sort of clansman into war. But what is really important about that 1792 election is neither its conduct nor its outcome. What matters is the extent to which the taking place of such a democratic contest was symbolic of what it was that caused so many Highland emigrants to North America to highlight – whether in their letters, their Gaelic poetry or their public statements – their strong sense of having, by the act of coming to this continent, made themselves free. The year which was marked in Glengarry County by Highland settlers electing two of their number to a representative legislature was marked in Scotland, after all, by the deployment of the Black Watch against those other, still unenfranchised, Highlanders then protesting against the expansion of sheep-farming in Easter Ross and Sutherland. 'The present race of Highland tenants,' it was remarked complacently by one of the landlords whose policies had provoked that particular crisis, 'will yet find themselves much happier, and more comfortable, in the capacity of servants to substantial tenants than in their present situation.' Such sentiments, had they known about them, would certainly have found no backing among the freeholding Highland farmers of Glengarry County. It was precisely to avoid becoming other men's dependents that they had been so anxious to come here to Upper Canada.[35]

'Here men fare well enough, with fine prosperous homes, something they would not see in their lifetime had they remained on the other side.' So runs Hugh MacCorkindale's *Oran le seann Ileach*, Song of an old Islayman, the title given by this nineteenth-century emigrant to the verses he composed in praise of Ontario. 'The settlers have stone houses, brick houses, frame and log houses,' MacCorkindale's song continues, 'and most of those have an orchard, well branched, up to their eaves.' It had been hard work clearing his Canadian farm of its trees, MacCorkindale remembered, 'but it was heartening to see their tops bending, then causing a tremor all around, falling in the direction I thought best'. It had been good to take in the land in this way and to see it bearing a 'heavy crop of wheat'. But what was more important still to this elderly Islayman was his feeling of having made himself the master of his own destiny in a manner that would have been quite impossible if he had remained in Scotland: 'This is a free land for people who suffered extortion in the country they left . . . They are free from the summons of agents and from the landlord's arrogance; from every factor and baillie who used to harass them and bring the roof down over their heads.'[36]

From South Lancaster, the landing place used by Highlanders coming here by way of Quebec and Montreal, you look across the wide and lakelike waters of the St Lawrence to the hazy shapes of the distant Adirondacks. Behind, its farmland shimmering in the summer heat, Glengarry County rises gradually in a series of gently undulating ridges. Some of those more northerly and slightly higher sections of the county are every bit as worthy of acquiring as the lower land a little to the south. Other parts are stonier, less productive. The families who took on these less desirable localities in the years around 1800 consequently had to remove many thousands of glacial boulders, as well as the more usual tree-stumps, before their fields could be cultivated with the help of horse-drawn ploughs. Here and there across the modern Glengarry you are shown the resulting piles of rock – each of these piles constituting its own highly eloquent memorial to the immense demands made of Glengarry County's Scottish Highland pioneers.

The 'first operation' undertaken by each new settler, one of the county's nineteenth-century residents recalled, was to construct a log cabin on his 200-acre lot. As it had been in those other North American colonies which had now become the United States, this was a collaborative exercise: 'Each, with his axe on his shoulder, turned out to help the other.' And the result – something of which can still be glimpsed, for instance, in the surviving log-built church at St Elmo near Glengarry's western boundary – was a reasonably snug home.[37]

'Round logs, roughly notched together at the corner and piled one above another to the height of seven or eight feet, constituted the walls,' goes on that nineteenth-century Glengarrian's account of the typical Canadian cabin. 'Openings for a door and one small window . . . were cut out. The spaces between the logs were chinked with small splinters and carefully plastered, outside and inside, with clay for mortar. Smooth straight poles were laid lengthwise of the building on the walls to serve as supports for the roof. This was composed of strips of elm bark, four feet in length by two or three feet in width, in layers, overlapping with each other . . . An ample hearth, made of flat stones, was then laid out, and a fireback of field stone or small boulders, rudely built, was carried as high as the walls. Above this the chimney was framed of round poles, notched together and plastered with mud. The floor was of the same materials as the walls, only that the logs were split in two and flattened so as to make a tolerably even surface.'

Log cabins were eventually to give way to those one-and-a-half-storey, timber-framed or occasionally brick-constructed houses which are scattered today right through the Glengarry countryside. But that took time; just as it took time also – at least one human lifetime and maybe a bit longer – to clear the land of forest.

There are woodlands still in Glengarry County. But those are composed of second-growth, third-growth, fourth-growth descendants of the district's original trees. And they are a very pale reflection of the sort of forest found here in earlier times. 'When some dozen or more of the crossroads . . . which lead off to the east and west have been passed,' runs one description of Glengarry as it would have appeared to a northbound traveller in the middle decades of last century, 'the road seems to strike into a different world. The forest loses its conquered appearance and dominates everything. There is forest everywhere. It lines up close and thick along the road, and here and there quite overshadows it. It crowds in upon the little farms and shuts them off from one another and from the world outside, and peers in through the little windows of the log houses, looking so small and so lonely.'[38]

As these comments amply indicate, tree cover of this type was thought by almost all of North America's European settlers to be hostile, menacing, something to be eradicated as soon as possible. New England's woods, William Bradford had reported at the beginning of the seventeenth century, gave that locality the frightening character of a 'hideous and desolate wilderness full of wild beasts and wild men'. Later venturers into the interior were equally unimpressed, indeed appalled, by what they found there: commonly applying adjectives like 'howling', 'dismal', 'dreary', 'terrible' and 'unhallowed' to their surroundings; looking forward always to the 'populous cities, smiling villages, beautiful farms and plantations' which would one day take the place of 'solitude and savageness'.[39]

For all that Highland emigrants were familiar in their Scottish homeland with landscapes which were themselves unusually untamed by European standards, they tended to regard those natural woodlands which they encountered on their arrival in North America with the same sort of loathing as was demonstrated by their English-speaking counterparts. That much is evident from many of the Gaelic songs composed here. It is evident, too, from the many tales told of Glengarry people's hazardous encounters with the wolves and bears which the wildwood contained. North America, both to Scottish Highlanders and to the wider settler population of which they were but one component, seemed requiring, therefore, of being as far as possible domesticated, beaten into shape. This process necessarily began with the destruction of those forests which had reigned uninterruptedly in places like Glengarry County since the ending of the Ice Age.

Such of the resulting timber as was not required for the construction of homes, barns and bridges was, to begin with, simply burned or left to rot. Soon, however, it began to be borne in upon the Glengarry people that their forests were every bit as valuable an asset as the farmland which they had been endeavouring to create by removing the county's tree cover. North American timber, it was apparent by the 1790s, could now be sold at a profit on the other side of the Atlantic Ocean.

Britain's own original forests having been largely worked out by the eighteenth century, the country had become increasingly dependent for its timber requirements on Scandinavian and Baltic sources of supply. This caused no difficulty in peacetime. But since the United Kingdom was pre-eminently a naval power, and since its men-o'-war were built entirely of wood, an enemy had only to interfere effectively with Britain's timber imports to bring the country to a very parlous state. This was exactly what happened in the course of the long series of wars involving the United Kingdom, on the one side, and first revolutionary and then Napoleonic France, on the other. One result was the development of a transatlantic timber trade – a trade which British governments took care to protect from renewed Baltic competition even after the eventual restoration of peace in Europe.[40]

British North American timber was shipped to the United Kingdom mostly from the ports of Saint John and Quebec, the former drawing on the forests of New Brunswick, the latter on the still more extensive resources of the St Lawrence basin. And in all the vast hinterland of the St Lawrence, which drained some 400,000 square miles of British territory, there was no better prospect, as far as Canada's emergent timber barons were concerned, than the valley of the Ottawa River which, its lower reaches being just a few miles to the north, was within easy reach of Glengarry County's Scottish Highland settlements.

Of the 850,000 tons of cargo shipped annually from British North America to Britain in the early 1840s, some 600,000 tons consisted of timber. Of those 600,000 tons, no small proportion originated in the vicinity of the Ottawa River. And much of this Ottawa River cut of white pine, oak, hickory, maple, butternut and cedar was both felled and conveyed to Quebec by men from Glengarry County; men who now 'lumbered a lot and farmed a little'; men whose fathers and grandfathers had sometimes never seen an axe before their arrival on this continent; men who had made themselves some of the most skilled lumberjacks and river drivers in all of North America.[41]

Theirs was a desperately tough existence, 'a demi-savage life', one nineteenth-century visitor to Canada called it. Its centre was the shanty, a term which derived from *chantier*, the French-Canadian word denoting what, in North American English, might be called a lumberyard. And nothing was more indicative of the transient nature of this frontier industry than the typical shanty's jerry-built appearance.[42]

Makeshift bunkhouses, stores, and a blacksmith's shop were hastily and roughly thrown together on the edge of some timber contractor's latest woodland concession. Here the same contractor's workforce was accommodated through the winter, each bunkhouse or caboose – as such rudimentary living quarters were called in the Ottawa Valley – containing its several tiers of bunks and its 'cook's corner' where there were heated the porridge, potatoes, salt pork, beans, molasses and black tea on which shantymen subsisted.

His diet left the shantyman constantly liable to boils or even scurvy. The almost unimaginably heavy nature of his daily work – which involved both cutting and moving huge weights of timber entirely by hand – was such as to exhaust the strongest individual. And there was little that was homelike in those cabooses where a felling squad might have to bunk down, night after night, for several long months at a time. Because few such cabins were equipped with chimneys – the smoke from the cook's fire being left to find its way through a hole in the roof – and because they were generally crammed with wet clothes, unwashed bodies, hastily discarded boots and the general clutter of the shantyman's existence, by far the most memorable quality of any caboose was invariably its quite appalling smell.

But it was to the shanty rather than to their farms that many Glengarry families were to look for the bulk of their livelihood during the greater part of the nineteenth century. 'There isn't an old family in the county that hasn't had men in the bush someplace,' the compilers of one modern history of Glengarry were informed. And though Glengarry shantymen began by venturing no further than the Ottawa Valley, they were eventually to follow the lumber business to Northern Ontario, Michigan, Wisconsin, British Columbia and several other parts of North America.[43]

They were exploited, of course, exploited ruthlessly on occasion. But they took a tremendous pride in their achievements all the same: in their ability to bring down the biggest of big trees; in working through the snows and sub-zero temperatures of winter; in taking time off only on Sundays and – for they were Scottish Highlanders, after all – on New Year's Day. They levered, sledged and hauled their timber to the nearest riverbank and, with the spring break-up of the river ice, they floated that same timber many miles downstream. They risked their lives to clear the logjams which invariably developed at each river rapid. They went on finally to guide their rafts of prime Canadian lumber towards tidal waters and the waiting cargo ships.

Such were the 'raftsmen from Glengarry' encountered by a newly arrived Scots emigrant on the St Lawrence in 1827. 'They were sons of the men who had come from the Highlands and Islands of Scotland,' it was said of them in a late Victorian novel featuring their exploits. 'Driven from homes in the land of their fathers, they had set themselves with indomitable faith and courage to hew from the solid forest homes for themselves and their children that none might take away from them. These pioneers were bound together by ties of blood, but also by bonds stronger than those of blood. Their loneliness, their triumphs, their sorrows, born of their common lifelong conflict with the forest and its fierce beasts, knit them in bonds close and enduring. The sons born to them, and reared in the heart of the pine forests, grew up to witness that heroic struggle and to take part in it. And mighty men they were. Their life bred in them hardiness of frame, alertness of sense, readiness of resource, endurance, superb self-reliance, a courage that grew with peril, and withal a certain wildness which at times deepened into ferocity.'[44]

Ralph Connor, author of *The Man from Glengarry*, the source of these remarks, was born in 1860 in the county to which this and others of his novels were to give a modest international renown in the period just before the First World War. Although he left his birthplace while still a boy, several of Connor's fictional creations were clearly rooted in actual shantymen whom the novelist had known. This was certainly true of MacDonald More, hero of *The Man from Glengarry* and very much the sort of bare-knuckle bruiser around whose exploits the shanty balladeers, in verses altogether earthier than Connor's best-selling prose, constructed songs which are still sung in various parts of North America.

MacDonald More, his slightly anglicised Gaelic nickname denoting his large stature, was one of many lumberjacks of Highland origin who, according to Ralph Connor, 'carried the marks of their blood in their fierce passions, their courage, their loyalty'. There is an element of romance in this, of course. Romance was Connor's business. But when his creator comments of MacDonald More that 'fighting was like wine to him', when this Canadian novelist goes on to reproduce the Gaelic choruses sung by Ottawa Valley lumberjacks, or when he tells how Scots-

Canadian shantymen rallied to the shouted battlecry, *Glengarry*, then it is difficult not to feel, as Ralph Connor clearly felt, that something of the ethos of the eighteenth-century Scottish clan still lingered here in nineteenth-century Ontario.[45]

CHAPTER FIVE

Such of Them as Did Not Die While Going Across the Ocean

NORTH AMERICAN TIMBER was not the only material required to fuel Britain's breakneck economic expansion in the years around 1800. Wool was also in demand and the Scottish Highlands – where landlords were turning more and more territory over to men like the Glen Garry sheep-farmer Thomas Gillespie – was to have a key role in its provision. 'In this as in every other instance of political economy,' remarked James Loch, business adviser to Lord and Lady Stafford whose Sutherland properties were among the most extensive in the United Kingdom, 'the interests of the individual and the prosperity of the state went hand in hand. And the demand for the raw material of wool by the English manufacturers enabled the Highland proprietor to let his lands for quadruple the amount they ever before produced to him.'[1]

The men who paid these hugely inflated rents originated mostly, as Glen Garry's Gillespie had done, in more southerly parts of Scotland. They came north with a view to exploiting Highland pastures every bit as uncompromisingly and as aggressively as others of their time and class were exploiting comparable resources in Britain's overseas possessions. Northern Scotland, to that extent, was now being treated rather like a colony. It was maybe fitting, therefore, that the incoming sheep-farmers who were beginning to exercise such a critical influence on Highland affairs should have regarded the Highlanders they displaced in much the same way as many of their counterparts in North America regarded that continent's native peoples.

To Patrick Sellar, who established an especially extensive sheep-rearing empire on those same Sutherland estates with which James Loch had such a close connection, 'the aborigines', as the newly arrived Sellar habitually called Highlanders, were characterised mainly by their 'sloth, poverty and filth'. They were a 'parcel of beggars' whose 'obstinate adherence' to Gaelic – a 'barbarous jargon' Sellar called it – had deprived them of both 'knowledge and cultivation' and left them in that 'state of society' which one might expect to encounter among 'savages'.[2]

Not everyone concerned with the promotion of large-scale sheep production in the the north of Scotland was as casually callous as Patrick Sellar, who seems at times to have taken an almost sadistic delight in personally supervising the enforced removal of the hundreds of families whose homes and landholdings happened to be in the way of one or other of his own extensive farms. Irrespective of the personal outlook or motives of their originators, however, changes of the sort now affecting the Highlands could not produce anything other than enormous social dislocation. Sellar's mass-evictions or clearances, as all such population transfers came to be called, were more notorious than most. But there was little that was unique about them. The Sutherland clearances, for all that they have often been singled out for particular censure, were simply one example of a much more general process which emptied glen after glen, strath after strath, of people whose ancestors had lived in these places for very many centuries.

'All was silence and desolation,' runs a contemporary account of the eradication of one Highland community. 'Blackened and roofless huts still enveloped in smoke, articles of furniture cast away as of no value to the household, and a few domestic fowls, scraping for food among hills of ashes, were the only objects that told us of man. A few days had sufficed to change a countryside, teeming with the cheeriest sounds of rural life, into a desert.'[3]

Homes were commonly destroyed in this way to forestall any attempt to reoccupy them. But the landlords who were ultimately responsible for all such proceedings, while they certainly intended to depopulate those parts of their domains which were most suited to sheep-farming, did not wish the families whom they had thus set adrift to move away completely. This would have been to deprive those same landlords of the workforce which they needed to have readily to hand if they were to cash in on the one commodity to rival wool as a means of obtaining a worthwhile revenue from the typical Highland estate.

This commodity was kelp. It was a form of industrial alkali made from seaweed. And it soared suddenly in price in the years around 1800 for reasons identical to those which were then making Ottawa Valley timber such a valuable asset.

The alkaline materials required for the manufacture of soap, glass and the like had previously been imported into the United Kingdom from continental Europe, mainly from Spain. But the French had deprived their British enemies of Spanish alkali by means which were very similar to those adopted to sever the trade in Baltic timber – with the result that Scottish kelp, which had been selling for not much more than two or three pounds a ton in the 1780s, became worth £10 a ton in the 1790s and £20 a ton just after the turn of the century.[4]

Since kelp was made from seaweed and since seaweed belonged legally in Scotland to the owners of the coastlines on which it grew, Highland landlords now found themselves in possession of a whole new source of wealth. But because the business of making kelp necessarily involved large numbers of people in harvesting and incinerating the raw material from which this wealth derived, landed proprietors were obliged to cast around for a way of securing the necessary labour.

Persuading people to engage voluntarily in this peculiarly Highland industry was never going to be easy. Making kelp, nineteenth-century observers agreed unanimously, was both an unattractive and an arduous occupation. 'If one figures to himself a man, and one or more of his children, engaged from morning to night in cutting, drying, and otherwise preparing the seaweeds, at a distance of many miles from his home, or in a remote island; often for hours together wet to his knees and elbows; living upon oatmeal and water with occasionally fish, limpets and crabs; sleeping on the damp floor of a wretched hut; and with no other fuel than twigs or heath; he will perceive that this manufacture is none of the most agreeable.'[5]

In comparison with the typical kelping labourer's existence, one visitor to the Highlands commented in 1807, 'the state of our negroes is paradise'. While that may have been an exaggerated view, it was certainly the case that the landlords who controlled the kelp trade found it necessary to engage in far-reaching restructuring of their estates in an attempt to leave as many people as possible with no real alternative but to participate in making kelp. Central to all such restructuring was the development of the novel type of tenure which was known as crofting and which, in the early decades of the nineteenth century, became the standard means of organising the occupancy of those parts of the Highlands not given over totally to raising sheep.[6]

Below the level of the tacksman class, whose farms were held on an individual basis, Highland tenancies tended traditionally to be of an intricate and usually communal type. Many different families might have some sort of stake in the same piece of land. And the relationship between these families and the chief to whom they ultimately owed allegiance frequently had much more to do with their being ready to turn out on his behalf in times of inter-clan hostility than it had to do with the payment of money rents. Now all of these older complexities – together with their associated implication that the connection between clansman and chief, tenant and landlord, was more than a merely commercial one – were brushed brutally aside.

Where an entire community might previously have shared the tenancy of a tract of arable land beside a bay or around a sea loch, that land was typically divided into separate smallholdings or crofts. Each croft was placed in the occupancy of a single family and, to that extent, the crofter who headed such a family approximated to the status of a farmer. There was one key distinction between farmers and crofters, however. The latter were not full-time agriculturalists – their landlords, for purposes which can be readily deduced from the key role of the kelp industry in all such tenurial changes, having taken care to ensure that no croft was large enough to enable its crofter tenant to earn an adequate livelihood from the cattle-rearing and associated activities in which Highlanders had traditionally engaged.

The standard crofting township consequently tended to contain many more people than the communally tenanted farm it generally replaced. Some of these people were drawn from among families who had lived on the original farm. Others were refugees from inland communities of the sort being cleared by men like Patrick Sellar. And because those crofting townships which were created by subdividing older settlements could not accommodate all such refugees, additional townships were brought into existence by the simple expedient of establishing further smallholdings on what had previously been moorland or rough grazing.

What was common to every crofter, no matter his origin, no matter his location, was the pressing need to find some means of supplementing the meagre income-generating potential of his croft. The only such means available, in all too many instances, was to become a kelp producer. That involved turning out ton after ton of alkali. It meant being paid one, two or three pounds per ton by a landowner who might very well be selling each such ton for four or five times as much. It meant also returning to this same landlord, in the form of rent, a substantial proportion of such little cash as came in the crofter's direction. It is not surprising, therefore, that Lord Macdonald of Sleat, owner of most of Skye and all of North Uist, should have been informed by his tenants in 1801 that, rather than transform themselves into kelp-producing crofters, they would 'much rather try their chance in other countries'. Nor was it surprising that the many other Scottish Highlanders then being treated similarly to those Skye and Uist people should once again have been thinking about being off to North America.[7]

The war between Britain and France which commenced in 1793, and which had made it difficult for civilians to get transatlantic passages, was ended – temporarily at least – by the Peace of Amiens in March 1802. The impact of this development on the north of Scotland was both immediate and dramatic. 'The emigrations from the Highlands, which had been of little account during the continuance of the hostilities,' one commentator noted at the time, 'recommenced upon the return of the peace, with a spirit more determined and more widely diffused than on any former occasion.'[8]

Repeated clearances, on the one hand, and the dragooning of so many men and women into the understandably detested kelp business, on the other, were snapping those cultural and other ties which connected Scottish Highlanders with the places they had always regarded as home. Emigration, to be sure, remained a hugely disruptive experience and, for that reason, was not undertaken lightly. As a result of the constant flow of information from those who had gone before, however, the notion of leaving for North America was now much less intimidating to Scottish Highlanders than it had been originally. 'We begin to look upon America as but one of our islands . . . and on the sea that intervenes as but a little brook that divides us,' remarked a Uist clergyman in 1801.[9]

As the idea of emigration began again to take hold, it was men of the tacksman class – their social position threatened now not just by rent increases but by the actual loss of their lands to south country sheepfarmers – who once more assumed the organising role which had been theirs since Scottish Highlanders had first left in large numbers for North Carolina and New York. 'Whenever the circumstances of any part of the country induced people to think of emigration,' the Earl of Selkirk wrote of these tacksmen's contribution to the managing of such departures, 'the usual procedure has generally been that the leading individuals have circulated a subscription paper to which all those who agreed to join in chartering a ship for the purpose signed their names; and whenever they had thereby ascertained their number, they called together all those who had declared their intention to emigrate. If previous information had been obtained of the price at which shipping could be procured, it was usual for some person of the most respectable situation and property among the associates to make proposals to transact the business for them at a certain rate for each passenger; if his offer was accepted, one half of the price agreed upon was deposited by each in his hands. With the money so collected, he proceeded to some of the great commercial ports where he made the best bargain he could with a shipowner, contracting for such provisions and accommodations as was customary, and giving security that the rest of the passage money should be paid previous to embarkation.'[10]

So it was in the case of the 450 or so people who left the Lochaber district for Glengarry County in 1802. The principal planners in this instance were Archibald MacMillan of Murlaggan and Allan MacMillan of Glen Pean. These men were cousins. They were also tacksmen on the estate belonging to Cameron of Lochiel whose family their families had served loyally for some three centuries – not least in the course of the last Jacobite rebellion which might never have got off the ground but for men

100

like the MacMillans having rallied to their Cameron chief when he agreed in 1745 to put his clan at Charles Edward Stuart's disposal.

More than half a century on from these events a Cameron was still in charge at Achnacarry, the narrow neck of thickly wooded land between Loch Arkaig and Loch Lochy where this particular laird's people had for generations maintained their principal stronghold. That stronghold had been destroyed by the Duke of Cumberland's troops in the summer following Culloden. Now this latest Cameron – in outlook less a chieftain than a landlord – had begun to build a grand house where his Jacobite grandfather's more utilitarian dwelling had once stood. 'The whole scene is romantic beyond conception,' that early Highland tourist, James Hogg, remarked of Achnacarry in June 1803. He had 'spent the middle of the day viewing the new castle of Lochiel, the building of which was . . . going briskly on,' Hogg continued. 'The castle is on an extensive scale and promises to be a stately structure.'[11]

The people who had traditionally occupied Clan Cameron land were meanwhile viewing these developments less favourably than Hogg. 'The grand castle at Achnacarry is going on with great speed,' one local tacksman wrote. It was likely to cost its builder some £9,000, the same man reported. And there was little question as to how the necessary money would be raised. 'Lochiel's lands are in the papers to be let at Whitsuntide first . . . and I am afraid the tenantry have no chance . . . The highest bidder of rent . . . will be preferred.'[12]

So it proved. And the MacMillan tacks towards the head of Loch Arkaig – just a few miles to the south of Glen Garry where sheep-farming had been firmly established for some twenty years already – were among the first casualties. Clearances had begun around Loch Arkaig in 1801. And with more evictions evidently in the offing, Archibald and Allan MacMillan decided to make new lives in Upper Canada both for themselves and for as many of their neighbours as wished to join them.

Archibald MacMillan had worked for some time in London and consequently knew his way around the world of business. He was nevertheless to incur 'considerable trouble and expense', as he reflected ruefully, in getting such a large number of people safely to the St Lawrence. MacMillan travelled to Leith, Glasgow and Port Glasgow to make enquiries of various shipping firms. He held meetings with prospective emigrants in different parts of the West Highlands. He carefully calculated costs and began collecting fares. He chartered three ships, the *Jane*, the *Helen* and the *Friends*, at a total cost of £1,861 and went on to make various stipulations as to how they were to be modified to ensure as safe as possible a passage – endeavouring to minimise the risk of shipboard illness, for example, by insisting that ventilation be installed 'for the benefit of conveying air to the hold'.[13]

All such preparations finally concluded, MacMillan, with his dozens of accompanying family groups, sailed from Fort William on 2

July 1802. Just over nine weeks later, on 5 September, the *Jane* and the *Helen* reached Quebec, the *Friends* taking a further ten days to complete the crossing. In October, with a North American fall already turning into winter, the bulk of this latest emigrant detachment were safely settled in Glengarry County. And the news which soon reached them of continuing developments on Cameron of Lochiel's estate must have convinced these new arrivals that, in taking themselves to Upper Canada, they had made the right decision. 'Everything is turned upside down since you left Lochaber,' Archibald MacMillan was informed in a letter he received from the son of one of his fellow tacksmen, Cameron of Invermallie. 'Families who have not been disturbed for four or five hundred years are turned out of house and home and their possessions given to the highest bidders. So much for the Highland attachment between chief and clans.'[14]

The 'unfortunate poor people' who were thus being evicted, Cameron of Invermallie continued, 'you will see emigrating to America . . . or at least as many of them as have the means in their power'. And for all that Highland landlords were certainly not motivated by concern for their tenants, emigration – which Invermallie had himself decided on – was clearly preferable to remaining on an estate geared only now to raising cash for its proprietor. 'My own opinion,' Invermallie commented of Cameron of Lochiel and his fellow landowners, 'is that the great gentlemen alluded to are doing a great deal of good, without the intention of doing so, by driving . . . people to desperation and forcing them to quit their country.'

These were Archibald MacMillan's own beliefs exactly. It had been no easy thing to leave his home beside Loch Arkaig, he reflected. 'We cannot help looking at our native spot with sympathy and feelings which cannot be described. Yet I have no hesitation in saying that, considering the arrangements that daily take place and the total extinction of the ties betwixt chief and clan, we are surely better off to be out of the reach of such unnatural tyranny.'[15]

Where there had once been a sense of kinship between Scottish Highlanders and their chiefs, there was now, and not only on the part of Archibald MacMillan, the antipathy which had invariably been engendered by the conduct of Cameron of Lochiel and all those other individuals who, as Samuel Johnson had predicted thirty years before, were responding to their new situation by ceasing to be 'patriarchal rulers' and becoming instead 'rapacious landlords'. The Earl of Selkirk neatly summarised the outcome. 'The progress of the rise of rents and the frequent removal of the antient possessors of the land have nearly annihilated in the people all that enthusiastic attachment to their chiefs, which was formerly prevalent, and have substituted feelings of irritation and disgust proportionately violent.'[16]

Not just Archibald MacMillan's party but as many as several thousand other people were preparing to leave the Highlands in the spring of 1802, the government was informed by Thomas Telford who had been instructed to report to the relevant authorities on the economic and social conditions then prevailing in the Highlands. He was personally in no doubt, Telford continued, that the most 'powerful cause' of the rapidly accelerating outflow was to be found in the practice of 'converting large districts of the country into extensive sheep walks'. Because the cattle which departing emigrants traditionally sold to raise their passage money were just then fetching a 'very high price', Telford added, there was little to prevent a continuing exodus.[17]

'If the government or the legislature do not speedily interpose,' one Highland landlord warned, 'the Highlands will be depopulated.' This would deprive the United Kingdom of what had become, since William Pitt had first turned to the region in search of additional troops, one of the country's main sources of military manpower. Even more to the point, as far as the owners of Highland estates were concerned, was the threat which emigration posed to their enormous earnings from kelp. 'If emigration from Uist took place to a great extent,' the chief of Clanranald was informed by his business managers at this time, 'it would prove most hurtful to the interest of Clanranald as thereby the kelp would remain unmanufactured from which Clanranald at present draws his principal revenue.'[18]

Since Clanranald's income from kelp was almost twice as large as his total land rental, these anxieties were clearly justified. They go some way to accounting for the key role of Clanranald's factor or estate manager, Robert Brown, in the campaign which now developed to have emigration halted.

This campaign was co-ordinated by the Highland Society of Edinburgh. The society was composed largely of the north of Scotland's landed proprietors and their legal agents. Its leading political ally was Charles Hope, the government's chief law officer in Scotland and a man who, as an Edinburgh lawyer himself, was the close friend and colleague of those now acting on behalf of the kelping interest.

The Highland Society's chosen means of preventing the departure to America of discontented crofters and kelp producers was to advocate the imposition of stringent regulations on the owners and masters of emigrant ships. It followed that the emigrants themselves had to be cast in the role of victims: as victims, first, of those emigration agents who were said to be 'leading the poor people on to ruin, disturbing their enjoyments, rendering them ripe for a revolt, deluding them by false hopes and, of course, inspiring them with discontents of the most dangerous kind'; as victims, second, of those skippers who were alleged to be packing their ships with many more emigrants than could be safely carried; as victims, third, of propagandist accounts of conditions in that faraway North American continent which every person of sense knew, in

the opinion at least of Highland landlords and their friends, to be an altogether less agreeable place than early nineteenth-century Scotland.[19]

The Highland Society's lobbying paid off. On 18 May 1803, at the
start of a summer which some said would see 20,000 people leave the
Scottish Highlands, the House of Commons passed the legislation for
which Robert Brown and his colleagues had so energetically been pressing. The legislation in question took the shape of an Act 'for regulating
the vessels carrying passengers from the United Kingdom to His
Majesty's plantations and settlements abroad'. By insisting that many
fewer people than previously could be carried on the typical emigrant
ship, this 1803 measure, which parliament found scarcely any time to
debate, had the effect of sharply increasing the cost of a passage from
Scotland to the St Lawrence. Emigration from the Highlands had been
effectively curtailed.[20]

Charles Hope and its other promoters insisted in public that
nothing other than 'common principles of humanity' had inspired the
Passenger Vessels Act. In private, however, Hope was more forthcoming.
Remarking in a letter of 1804 that his had been the 'chief hand in preparing and carrying through parliament' this particular piece of legislation, Hope readily acknowledged that, although the Act had been
'professedly calculated merely to regulate the equipment and victualing
of ships carrying passengers to America', it had also been 'intended . . .
to prevent the effects of that pernicious spirit of discontent against their
own country, and rage for emigrating to America, which had been raised
among the people'.[21]

In the localities most affected by the Passenger Vessels Act, the measure's originators were regarded as dissemblers from the outset. One
Highland priest, Father Alexander MacDonell, who had given it as his
opinion in 1794 that 'our Highland lairds are more . . . than any other
set of men upon the face of the earth actuated by self-interest', saw in the
legislation of 1803 yet one more confirmation of this most uncharitable
verdict. The landowning fraternity's 'specious pretext of humanity and
tender benevolence', according to Father MacDonell, who was certainly
not alone in his suspicions, had concealed altogether baser motives.[22]

Something of the nature of such motives can be deduced from the
fact that landlords now felt free to proceed with plans which the threat
of wholesale emigration had threatened to disrupt. All along the coastal
fringes of the mainland Highlands, and throughout the Hebrides, the
crofting system was peremptorily imposed on thousands of families who
had no alternative but to accept both this innovation and the enforced
kelp-making which was its practically universal adjunct. 'These poor
people, unable to get to America, are glad to get any sort of plot and hut,'
it was noted by one observer in 1813. Prominent among this emergent
crofting population, of course, were those people expelled from their
homes as a result of clearances of the sort which Archibald MacMillan

of Murlaggan was anticipating when he took so many folk to Canada in 1802.[23]

These clearances had duly taken place. 'The proprietor encourages extensive grazing which is greatly against the poor tenants who would incline to go to America,' MacMillan was informed by one of his Lochaber correspondents in the summer of 1803. 'But the government has fallen on a plan to stop their career, as they will not be able to pay freight.'[24]

Loch Arkaig, according to one nineteenth-century traveller in these parts, 'though considered by many to equal, if not excel, the most picturesque of our Scottish lakes, is seldom visited and almost unknown'. That remark remains as true as ever. The shores of this long, lovely stretch of water, running practically due west from Achnacarry, are as lonely and deserted as they have been since 1804. Then it was, as Archibald MacMillan learned from a letter reaching him in Canada, that Cameron of Lochiel completed the depopulation of this part of his estate: 'Great are the changes that have taken place along both sides of Loch Arkaig. Every single small tenant is to be dispossessed.'[25]

The stone and turf cabins occupied by those unfortunate 'small tenants' have left little in the way of imprint on the modern landscape. But Archibald MacMillan's own home at Murlaggan, being of the more substantial type which tacksmen of his sort constructed, still survives. The house has been much altered in two centuries, of course, being rented nowadays to holidaymakers. But standing just beside it on a sunny summer's morning when the only sound to be heard is the steady rush of the fast-flowing stream from which the tacksman's household would have drawn their water, it is easy to see why MacMillan felt, in North America, a continuing affection for this place.

To the right is Monadh Gorm and the several other high tops – snow lingering in their corries even in June – which enclose Glen Pean and Glen Dessary. Leftwards are those other hills which separate Murlaggan from Loch Lochy and the Great Glen. Opposite, just across the narrow waters of Loch Arkaig itself, are remnant fragments of the birchwoods and pinewoods which once flourished hereabouts but which have struggled for two centuries now to survive in the face of that most ecologically disastrous animal, the sheep.

Between what remains of his house and the loch's shore are Archibald MacMillan's fields. Here the tacksman would have grown his crops and kept his cattle when his herds were brought in at the back end of the year from the hill pastures stretching northwards from Murlaggan to the watershed which separated the various MacMillan tenancies from those of their MacDonell neighbours in Glen Garry. Murlaggan's fields, of course, have long been uncultivated. Wild irises are flowering in their damper corners. Everywhere are the rushes and other intrusive vegetation which, throughout the Scottish Highlands, quickly swallows up abandoned crofts and farms.

This is the sort of utterly depressing scene which inspired the nineteenth-century Gaelic poet, John MacLachlan, to compose his own lament to what it was that had been destroyed by clearance and eviction. It was impossible to be other than deeply moved, MacLachlan wrote, on 'seeing the mountain a wilderness with no tillage on its face'. In one glen after another, the poet continued, there were to be glimpsed innumerable signs of habitation in places now bereft of people. 'As I look down over the pass, the view I have is very chill. There is many a poor hut levelled, a green site on every side . . . Where the fire and children were, the rushes grow the highest.'[26]

How could either his people's ancient speech or their equally age-old traditions survive the eradication of so many of the communities which had treasured them, another nineteenth-century poet wondered: 'It is not surprising that the sweet mother tongue should die. The deer in the wilderness do not speak and the white sheep have no language.'[27]

Nor was depopulation to be confined to places like Murlaggan and Glen Pean. Soon those coastal communities which landlords had been initially so anxious to protect from the effects of emigration were themselves being cleared even more ruthlessly than inland areas had previously been. Peace had returned to Europe in 1815. This had allowed the import trade in continental alkali to be resumed at much the same time as scientific advances had made it possible for most industrial consumers of kelp to switch to chemically produced alternatives. There followed an almost total collapse in the price of the very commodity on which the proprietors of so many Highland estates had come to depend. With these same gentlemen now facing 'distress or rather ruin', as they complained in 1829, it was inevitable that the crofting townships which had been created to service the kelp business should themselves begin to be destroyed to make way for still more sheep-farms.[28]

On the South Uist and Benbecula properties belonging to Clanranald, whose agents had been so anxious to prevent emigration not very many years before, it was now thought 'absolutely necessary' to arrange matters 'so as to draw a revenue from the lands altogether independently of kelp'. That, of course, implied the 'parcelling out of the estate' among such sheep-farmers as were willing to pay the rents required of them. But what, then, was to become of South Uist and Benbecula crofters? The ideal solution, or so it seemed to Clanranald's agent on those islands, would be to ship 'at least 3,000 people to America'.[29]

Now there was not the faintest echo of the humanitarian rhetoric of 1803 to be heard from Highland landlords and their politician friends. Now the talk was all of estates which had become 'overburdened with a large mass of population'; of the need for government to 'assist in establishing a system of emigration on a great scale'; of the 'redundancy' of crofting. So it came about that in 1827, to the unrestrained delight of those interest-groups which had insisted on such measures in the first place, the restrictions imposed on the operators of emigrant ships by the Passenger Vessels Act of 1803 were removed completely.[30]

But there remained one insuperable difficulty in the way of tackling the estate management problems posed by what practically everyone in authority now considered to be the 'surplus population' of the Scottish Highlands. The nature of that difficulty is immediately apparent from the contents of the various 'petitions or memorials transmitted to the Colonial Department' which the House of Commons ordered to be printed in 1826 and 1827.

One of these, signed by 29 residents of the Skye parish of Bracadale, was summarised as follows by the civil servants who received it. 'These persons, who with their families amount to 229 persons, are desirous of obtaining a free passage to Canada . . . They and their fathers occupied small farms . . . but their landlord, having consolidated these farms, let them to two persons for sheepwalks and the petitioners are to quit their homes at Whitsunday 1826 . . . Deprived of their farms, they are unable to provide for themselves or to pay their passage to Canada.'[31]

The plea thus made on behalf of the Bracadale tenants of MacLeod of Dunvegan, just one of many Highland landlords then engaged in a new round of clearances, was repeated by some fifty 'inhabitants' of Glen Garry. 'The petitioners have been deprived of the farms they held in consequence of the land being occupied by extensive sheep graziers . . . They are desirous of emigrating to Upper Canada, but have, owing to their wretched condition, no means of paying their passage.' The other Glengarry on the St Lawrence, it seems likely, in view of the British government's reluctance to put up the necessary cash, was never reached by those poor people.

There remained in the Scottish Highlands of the 1820s very few representatives of the tacksman class which had been so prominent in earlier emigrations to North America. But even if men like Archibald MacMillan of Murlaggan had been available to see to the task of hiring and provisioning the necessary ships, no emigration of the older type could have been financed by those still wishing to make the Atlantic crossing. Highlanders were now experiencing poverty much more profound, widespread and unyielding than any which had gone before in a region not exactly famed for its prosperity. Thrown back, as a result of the kelp boom having ended so precipitately, on the resources of crofts which had been deliberately designed to be agriculturally unviable, the mass of the Highland population were subsisting on a diet consisting mainly of potatoes. Their rents were generally in arrears. Their poor and skinny cattle were practically unmarketable. And the few other assets remaining at their disposal were of equally little account. If people so situated were ever to get to North America, it was obvious both to themselves and others, this could only be accomplished by some much cheaper means than had existed previously.

The Quebec city waterfront, just below the old walled town where Sergeant James Thompson and other survivors of the battle of 13 September 1759 found it so difficult to get shelter during the ensuing winter, is mostly given over nowadays to yachts, cruise liners and other traffic of that sort. Tourists who have taken the funicular railway down the cliff-face from Terrasse Dufferin to Rue Petit Champlain find little of interest here and tend not to linger on riverside wharves where the only vessel moving, very often, is the ferry to Levis on the St Lawrence's south bank.

In the first half of the nineteenth century, however, this was a place of furious activity. 'Were you ever in Quebec,' asks a sea-shanty of that time, 'loading timber on the deck?' And there were plenty of sailors who could have answered that question in the affirmative. This was where Glengarry County rivermen, along with the many others who engaged in that same dangerous business, brought those clumsy rafts of timber which they had steered carefully downstream from the Ottawa River's junction with the St Lawrence. This was where there waited the sea-going ships which conveyed that timber to its final destination on the Thames, the Mersey or the Clyde. And a very sorry lot of craft those were.

One of the most elementary rules concerning nineteenth-century maritime commerce was that the most valuable cargoes were always carried in the soundest ships – with Britain's East India Company, for example, transporting its silks and tea and spices from Asia to Europe in vessels which were commonly reckoned to be the pride of their age. This rule's converse was that those materials which were of a comparatively low value in relation to their weight and bulk should be reserved for ships which were approaching the end of their useful lives. One such material was coal. Another was North American timber which, despite its making a vital contribution to the United Kingdom's economic well-being, necessarily fetched a much lower price, on a ton-for-ton basis, than any other commodity carried in quantity across the Atlantic. Timber, of course, was also unlike tea, silk and cotton in that it did not need to be protected from seawater. It could be carried, in other words, in ships which leaked.[32]

In any early summer month in any year between the 1790s and the 1850s, when standards in such matters at last started to improve, Quebec's harbour area consequently contained some of the most run-down, decrepit, disreputable and jerry-built shipping in all the world. Some of these vessels had been constructed in New Brunswick for the trade in which they were engaged, but constructed from local pine,

spruce and even birch – inferior timbers which most shipbuilders of the
time would not have allowed into their yards. Others, as the contemporary saying went, had 'come down' to the business. Once they had been
trim, smart, clean and carefully rigged. Now their masts had frequently
been chopped off short to ease the strain on their hulls. Now their hulls
were themselves so rickety and undependable that, once the holds of such
ships had been filled with raw timber and their hatches battened down,
a series of chains was run down their sides, under their keels and back
across their decks. This process, known as 'swifting', was undertaken
with a view to preventing the rotting framework of such vessels finally
splitting apart. It was a technique which did not always work.

A timber ship was generally uninsured and often uninsurable. But
because it was invariably fit for no other traffic, it could be bought so
cheaply as to ensure that the proceeds of just two or three successful
Atlantic crossings would more than clear the purchase price. After that,
assuming the vessel in question was not wrecked, almost all its earnings
could be counted as pure profit by its owners.

Certainly there was not a lot of money spent on crews or skippers.
The timber trade, one Canadian legislature reported, was characterised
by 'indifferent ships, recklessly navigated'. It could not have been otherwise. No sailor who valued his life and who could get any better posting
was likely to sign up for a stint on those crazily patched-together vessels
which came upriver to Quebec each May or June when the St Lawrence
ice had broken. The timber ship, therefore, was the last refuge of irresponsible, drunken, unreliable officers and men who could obtain no
alternative employment.[33]

Losses, in such circumstances, were commonplace and only became
newsworthy when they resulted in some more than usually gory episode
such as that involving the wreck of the *Frances Mary* in 1826. Their
vessel having been reduced to a mastless hulk by ocean storms, the surviving crew of this particularly ill-fated timber ship were eventually discovered by their Royal Navy rescuers to have kept themselves alive for
several weeks by eating the corpses of other sailors who had already died
from hunger and exposure.

Catastrophes of the *Frances Mary* type were made more frequent
by the practice of loading a ship's decks, as well as its holds, with timber.
This added to the instability and unmanoeuvrability of vessels which
were already verging on being totally unseaworthy. But it also widened
profit margins. And these profit margins, as the various Scottish and
English companies which dominated the transatlantic timber trade were
all too well aware, were bound to be made much healthier still if there
could be found some means of minimising the possibility of having to
send vessels in ballast all the way to the St Lawrence. How were the relevant shipowners to obtain westward-bound cargoes which, like eastward-bound timber, need not be kept in the snug and watertight

conditions demanded by the shippers of those manufactured goods which constituted the bulk of British exports to North America? There was, it soon appeared, a simple answer to this question. All that was required to enable the typical timber ship to obtain some financial return on its voyage outward from the British Isles was for such a ship to take on board some small proportion of those people wishing to emigrate from places like the Scottish Highlands.

Highland emigrants had always run some risk at sea. Of the two hundred or so people who embarked on the brig *Nancy*, which sailed from the Dornoch Firth in September 1773, for example, only about a hundred stepped ashore, nearly three months later, in New York. The remainder, including all but one of fifty-one children under the age of four, had died in the course of a voyage made at an especially hazardous time of year on a ship where passengers were expected to get by on 'corrupted' water and musty, rotting oatmeal said to be 'hardly fit for swine'.[34]

This was exceptional, however. Its being so was due in large part to the fact that those tacksmen who were in charge of many earlier emigrant parties often went to enormous lengths to maintain the health of the people in their care. The painstaking preparations made by Archibald MacMillan of Murlaggan prior to his setting sail for Glengarry County are a case in point. Equally telling are the views of another tacksman, John MacDonald of Glenaladale, who organised his own emigration to Prince Edward Island from Moidart and South Uist in 1772.

Ensuring the availability of a 'full allowance of water' was 'rather more necessary' than stocking up on other provisions, MacDonald commented. And it was essential that 'the distribution of the water should be immediately put under regulation from the moment of going on board'. Infectious disease, of course, was to be avoided at all costs: 'The health and cleanliness of the passengers should be looked after for as long a time as possible before embarking.' Congestion had always to be kept in check and care needed to be taken to see that passengers exercised regularly in the fresh air: 'The ship should not be overcrowded with numbers and in all good weather they should be much on deck to ventilate below.'[35]

Virtually nothing of MacDonald's conscientious approach, it goes without saying, was to be observed in the conduct of the men responsible for the temporary conversion of timber-carrying cargo ships into passenger vessels capable of conveying emigrants to North America.

Such conversions began with the installation of a lower deck in holds still reeking of the Canadian lumber with which they had previously been crammed. Here, in a space which was usually so confined as to make it difficult for an adult to stand up straight, there were then constructed two tiers of roughly built wooden berths, one such tier running along each side of the vessel, with a third being placed amidships on occasion. Each of the dozens of berths which were thus provided measured some six feet by six. Each of those berths – the higher one some 24 or 30 inches above the lower – was intended to hold a minimum of four people, with emigrants of both sexes and all ages being bundled together in conditions which are utterly beyond our modern imagining.[36]

'The accommodation on board was very rough,' it was reported of one emigrant ship putting out from Uig in Skye. 'The whole lower decks were cleared and two rows of sleeping berths were erected on each side of the ship. The centre was piled with boxes, bags, chests, etc. Into this den – for it could not be called anything else – were huddled some 200 or 300 men, women and children.'[37]

Emigrants provided their own food and, since a westward voyage by sailing ship on the Atlantic, being undertaken against the prevailing winds, could vary between one month and three months in length, supplies could very easily give out. Fresh water was the responsibility of the ship's company. It was seldom good and often scarce. Cooking was done on stoves on the upper deck when the weather was fair. In bad weather, which could last for several weeks at a stretch, there were neither hot food nor hot drinks to be had.

Privacy was always at a premium. Males and females were obliged to 'relieve nature', as contemporaries delicately put it, in full view of one another. And since such sanitary facilities as existed were rudimentary, consisting for the most part of wooden buckets, the lower deck, in heavy seas, was invariably awash with urine, faeces and, of course, vomit – for seasickness was the emigrant's most constant source of misery. Even for the occupant of a private cabin on the better class of passenger ship, remarked the American novelist, Herman Melville, whose experience of these matters derived from his own years as a sailor, seasickness was a dreadful scourge. 'How, then, with the friendless emigrants, stowed away like bales of cotton and packed like slaves in a slave ship; confined in a place that, during storm time, must be closed against both light and air; who can do no cooking, nor warm so much as a cup of water; for the drenching seas would instantly flood the fire in their exposed galley on deck? We had not been at sea one week, when to hold your head down the hatchway was like holding it down a suddenly opened cesspool.'[38]

Melville's comparison between emigrants and slaves was no facile one. There were those, in fact, who believed an African slave to have a better chance of surviving an Atlantic voyage than most European emigrants – if only because emigrants paid their fares prior to embarkation while slaves, in contrast, were worth nothing to slave traders unless delivered safely in America. To have a slave die was to incur a real financial loss. To have emigrants die meant little to masters and crews who received no real monetary benefit from the emigration business and who were known to work out their own frustrations on their passengers – the latter being sometimes kicked, cuffed, beaten or deluged in icy seawater by some set of drunken and semi-mutinous sailors.[39]

There were always fortunate emigrants, of course. 'We had a most pleasant passage from Greenock to Montreal,' recalled Martin Donald MacLeod who emigrated from Skye to Ontario in 1845. 'We never had a reef tied. Indeed we carried royals all the way. A lighted candle could have been carried on the deck until we saw land . . . The master was particularly civil and we were as comfortable as we could desire.'[40]

That was not the common experience, however. Most emigrant ships encountered gales which quickly turned them into hell-holes of the sort described by Herman Melville. And when their hatches were battened down and emigrants left to fend for themselves in the stinking, heaving, crashing, terrifying darkness of the holds to which they were confined on occasion for weeks at a time, it was inevitable that children, in particular, died of the dehydration which followed on prolonged seasickness; inevitable, too, that infectious disease should take hold and spread. So it came about that death rates of around 10 per cent were not uncommon on emigrant ships, with mortality reaching 40 per cent or more on some voyages.[41]

This carnage could have been prevented, to some extent at least, by effective action on the part of the relevant British authorities. But governmental control of the emigrant traffic, for all that it had been attempted by ministers like Charles Hope when such ministers wanted to keep Highlanders in Scotland, was not a popular cause in an era now given over politically to runaway free enterprise and also given over, more and more, to the concept of unburdening the United Kingdom of its poor by means described as 'shovelling out paupers'. The ruling orders who had once opposed emigration were now in favour of it. Regulation of those ships which engaged in the emigrant and timber trades consequently remained dilatory and perfunctory until the 1850s and 1860s when faster, more reliable, more comfortable steamships had, in any case, begun to supplant the primitive and semi-derelict vessels of earlier decades. And because little or nothing had been done officially to prevent such occurrences, timber ships went with gruesome regularity to the bottom – 34 such vessels being wrecked in 1834 alone and many hundreds of emigrants being drowned as a result.[42]

But running the undoubted risks of an Atlantic passage was infinitely preferable, or so many Scottish Highlanders believed, to remaining in a country governed by men who clearly had no further use for them. 'At this time,' a visitor to the Highland port of Cromarty wrote in 1825, 'there were only two vessels in the harbour. One of these was a brig to carry emigrants to America. The baggage of the wanderers was piled in heaps on the quay. These men were natives of a district of Sutherland, one and all quitting their fatherland to seek an asylum in that of a stranger. Infancy, youth, manhood and old age; the patriarch of the tribe and his unweaned grandchild were there, prepared for the voyage . . . Driven from the huts that had sheltered their fathers for generations, the victims of . . . prejudice and that rage for speculative improvement which threatens to depopulate the Highlands, they had resolved on repairing in a body to the untrodden wilds of the new continent.'[43]

To David Stewart of Garth, the old soldier who had so comprehensively chronicled the career of the many Highland regiments which had fought in the French and Indian War, the American Revolutionary War and the war waged against Jacobin France, the evictions then occurring constantly in localities like Sutherland seemed an unforgivable betrayal of men who had bravely served the state which was now conspiring in the destruction of their communities. The Sutherland people were forever being accused of all sorts of crimes and misdemeanours by their landlords, Stewart noted. But if they were 'so degenerate' as was alleged, how was it that they had been 'found to be so virtuous and regular' when in the army? Most British regiments witnessed floggings almost daily. But 'one thousand men of Sutherland', as David Stewart pointed out, 'have been embodied four and five years together at different periods, from 1759 to 1763, from 1779 to 1783 and from 1793 to 1798, without an instance of military punishment'.[44]

Stewart's 'high-spirited and loyal people', however, appeared a mere 'parcel of beggars with no stock but cunning and laziness' to Patrick Sellar, the man immediately responsible for many of the clearances which David Stewart so deplored. Told in 1816 that a number of Sutherland tenants were thinking about leaving for North America, Sellar commented that 'it would be a most happy thing if they did . . . They are just in that state of society for a savage country'. And it was with capitalist entrepreneurs like Patrick Sellar, not with old-fashioned humanitarians like David Stewart, that the future of the Highlands clearly rested.[45]

'It must be admitted,' the authors of an official report concluded in 1837, 'that few cases could arise to which the remedy of emigration on a great scale would appear more appropriate than that of the Hebrides.' Such emigration was, in fact, continuing apace; some 1,300 people leaving Skye for North America in 1826 and 1827; more than 1,000 leaving Mull in those same years; 600 departing from North Uist in 1828; between 600 and 800 sailing from Harris; still more going from several other islands. 'The clans who, by heredity, were noble and splendid, true to their chief, to their king and their church, are now being exiled from their kingdom.' So runs a Gaelic poem composed by one of the Highlanders who made the crossing to Prince Edward Island at about this time. There was 'no advantage' in remaining in Scotland 'where the glens were being filled with sheep and the folk driven from their homes' as a result of the 'hostility of the merciless landlords, hard-hearted, importunate men'.[46]

Many such departures, as that Prince Edward Island poet claimed, were the direct result of clearance and eviction. And in a complete reversal of the position which they had adopted in the kelping heyday of twenty or thirty years earlier, landlords now considered it worth their while to meet the passage costs of those of their former tenants who could not find even the few pounds charged by the firms operating the timber ships to which Highlanders more and more looked for their means of escape to North America. When the owner of the island of Rum decided in 1826 to have his property cleared entirely of its people, he spent more than five pounds a head on shipping them to Nova Scotia. This was no charitable gesture, however, more a sound investment. Rum's evicted tenants had paid a total annual rent of some £300, not all of it collectable. The single sheep-farmer who took their place paid nearly three times more.[47]

The Scottish Highland emigrants of the 1820s and 1830s, enduring as best they could the drawn-out weeks which each of them spent aboard the fetid vessels transporting them across the Atlantic, were very differently situated from their eighteenth-century predecessors. None of them now arrived in North America, as Crevecoeur's Andrew the Hebridean and his many counterparts had done, with money in their pockets. They came both penniless and in rags from places where, since the folding of the trade in kelp, whole populations had been left quite destitute.

In Barra, the island from which Andrew had emigrated some sixty years before, 'the poverty of the people', according to one local priest, was 'now beyond description'. In 1827 a number of islanders had entered into financial arrangements with various shipping agents who, having taken these people's deposits, had failed to provide the promised passages. 'It was too late to commence sowing their seed and upon their friends they must live . . . The consequence was that people were actually starving, fainting away in different parts of the island.' Whole families, as far removed as it was possible to be from the comfortable and relatively trouble-free existence which had long ago been secured in North America by those people who had left Barra in Andrew the Hebridean's time, were said now by their clergy to be eking out a precarious existence on shellfish scavenged from the shore. And while this was still exceptional, it was not long to remain so, many more such gruesome scenes soon being enacted right across the Scottish Highlands.[48]

Some thirty or forty miles down the St Lawrence from Quebec City is a set of islands which, when first glimpsed as you head upstream, have something of the look of those other islands to be found in the like of Loch Awe, Loch Maree or Loch Lomond – being similarly tree-covered and low-lying. This riverine archipelago, together with the tidal marshes around nearby mainland towns like Montmagny and Berthier-sur-Mer, has been for thousands of years one of the stopping-off points favoured by the great snowgoose as that most magnificent of birds journeys between its Arctic breeding areas and its wintering grounds around the

Cape Fear River estuary and other coastal regions of North Carolina and New Jersey.

It was because of their association with *les oies blanches*, the snowgeese, that two of these St Lawrence islands became known to this locality's French settlers as Grosse Ile aux Oies and Petite Ile aux Oies, the former being abbreviated in time to Grosse Ile. Although Grosse Ile, despite its name, is certainly not the biggest island in these parts, it is undoubtedly the one to which there attaches the most history. For it was on Grosse Ile, in the 1830s and 1840s, that the Canadian colonial authorities established what they called a quarantine station. Here, as a result, the passengers carried by the timber ships which arrived each year in the St Lawrence from Britain were compulsorily disembarked. Here each man, woman and child was rigorously inspected by medical teams whose job it was to discover any trace of those infectious and frequently deadly diseases from which the people of Quebec, Montreal and other upriver communities were understandably anxious to protect themselves.[49]

Grosse Ile, now that it has been returned largely to *les oies blanches*, is a very peaceful place, all oak and maple, birch and pine. Beside the island's harbour, in the shade provided by the towering remnants of the disinfection building, you can quietly sit and gaze downriver to the spot where the emigrant ships of 150 years ago first hove into view – announcing their presence, if the breeze was from the east, as much by their gruesome stench as by any exchange of signals with the shore.

Grosse Ile then, of course, looked nothing like Grosse Ile today. 'Bad as it was on board,' one Scots emigrant, Hugh Johnson, was afterwards to recall of his reaching the island on a vessel which was rotten with smallpox, 'it became infinitely worse when we reached quarantine. On our arrival at the dock, ropes were stretched across the deck so as to leave a passage in the middle. A doctor was stationed on each side of this passage and only one person was allowed to go through at a time. All those who showed any symptoms of the disease were forced into quarantine . . . . I am an old man now, but not for a moment have I forgotten the scene as parents left children, brothers were parted from sisters, or wives and husbands were separated, not knowing whether they should ever meet again.'[50]

Hugh Johnson was one of a quarter of a million emigrants to make the Atlantic crossing in 1847, one of the 100,000 or so who landed in British North America rather than the United States. Of that latter number, some 5,300 got no further than Grosse Ile where they lie buried in those mass graves whose hummock-like shapes are still to be seen among the trees on the slopes above the little inlet which, ever since the 1840s, has been known simply as Cholera Bay. What had made the occupants of this Cholera Bay cemetery so tragically vulnerable to illness, Dr George Douglas, medical supervisor at Grosse Ile, was asked by a British parliamentary select committee. 'In the first instance,' he replied, 'the distress and the state of starvation in which the people embarked.'[51]

This was a time when the potato crop – on which the crofting population of the Scottish Highlands, just like the very similarly situated population of Ireland, had come to depend for the bulk of their food intake – failed entirely, not for one year, not for two years, but for several years in succession. A people who, a century before, had posed both a political and military threat to the United Kingdom's very existence were now reduced to the depths of dependency, despair and degradation; looking forward, very often, to nothing more than their next meagre ration of meal from one or other of the famine-relief organisations which were all that stood between many Highlanders and a squalid death from hunger.

'At the appointed time and place,' one visitor to Skye recorded of just one of many distributions of charitable aid, 'the poor creatures troop down in hundreds, wretched and thin, starved and wan. Some have clothing, some almost none, and some are a mass of rags. Old and young, feeble and infirm, they take their stations and await their turn. Not a murmur, not a clamour, not a word. But they wept aloud as they told of their miseries.'[52]

A clerical deputation reported from another Skye community that its homes were 'the very pictures of destitution and hopeless suffering'. What the deputation called 'a low typhus fever' had afflicted several families, causing additional anguish and distress. 'In one most deplorable case, the whole of the family of seven persons had been laid down . . . The eldest of the children, a son about nineteen years of age, had died just when his mother was beginning to get on foot. No one would enter the house with the coffin for the son's remains. It was left at the outside of the door and the enfeebled parent and a little girl, the only other member of the family on foot, were obliged to drag the body to the door and put it into the coffin there, whence it was carried by the neighbours, with fear and alarm, to its last resting place.'[53]

The typhus which wreaked such havoc among that island family and which so terrified the remainder of their community was also one of the principal causes of the thousands of deaths among the Irish and Scottish Highland emigrants now pouring into North America. At sea, of course, there could be no escaping from infection. 'The fear of death, when it takes possession of a crowd on board ship,' remarked one skipper of the period, 'is beyond the power of words to describe. Silence is the prevailing note. The boldest holds his breath.' Many, however, held their breath in vain.[54]

'This is a complaint which comes on when many persons are crowded together in a small space,' it was observed of typhus by the Society for the Propagation of Christian Knowledge in the society's

Medical Hints for Emigrants. 'Recollect that this, like all fevers, is a complaint that will last its own time; that there is no such thing as cutting it short; and that the game you have to play is to get the patient to *live on* till the fever leaves him.' Such advice was certainly well meant. In the conditions prevailing on a typically pestilential and congested emigrant ship, however, it was not exactly helpful. Both at sea and on Grosse Ile, deaths continued unabated, if not from typhus, then from measles, small-pox, cholera or some other such infection.[55]

Grosse Ile that summer of 1847, when Hugh Johnson arrived from Scotland, seemed at times a sort of charnel-house. The island's shed-like hospital buildings having long since overflowed, most of the 20,000 or more victims of typhus then reckoned to be here were accommodated in eight marquees and 266 bell tents which had been provided by the army. Others were forced to sleep in the open and, with the approach of the North American fall, some began to die of cold as well as of their illnesses. At times Grosse Ile, for all the heroic efforts made by George Douglas and his team, was bordering on chaos. Here and there were 'piles upon piles of unsightly coffins'. Burials went on constantly. Visitors struggled to describe what they had seen. He had never 'witnessed such a melancholy mass of suffering humanity', remarked one man from Montreal. 'After passing through nearly two thousand adults . . . you come to two or three hundred orphans, some only fifteen or twenty days old and many of them taken from the side, and some from the breast, of a dead mother.'[56]

Of the several hundred such orphans taken into care in 1847 by *La Société Charitable des Dames Catholiques de Québec*, the overwhelming majority, this being an explicitly Catholic charity, were Irish. The long list of parentless children to pass through the society's hands, however, contains the names of Ellen and Anne MacRae who had arrived in the St Lawrence on the *Eliza* and who were admitted to the orphanage maintained by the Société Charitable in Quebec City on 18 October. In the space reserved by this list's original compilers for an orphan's father's Christian name there is entered, in the case of Ellen and Anne, 'Farre' – as near as a French-speaking nurse or assistant was able to get, it seems likely, to the Scottish Highland *Fearchar* or Farquhar. This Farquhar's wife is entered as Margaret, the family's native parish of Lochalsh becomes Loughelsh and their county of origin – probably because neither Anne nor Ellen were familiar with the term Ross-shire – is left blank. Ellen, aged twelve, was adopted by a Québecois family. Anne, aged ten, was eventually found a home in the United States. What happened eventually to those Lochalsh sisters there is no way of knowing. But it is highly improbable that they were ever to see one another again.[57]

Historians have from time to time advanced the thesis – first propounded, of course, by nineteenth-century landlords – that the wholesale Highland emigrations of the 1840s and 1850s were in the best long-term interest of the emigrants involved. Such historians, perhaps, should be brought to Grosse Ile, sat down in the cemetery above Cholera Bay and asked how they would set about justifying their opinions to Ellen and Anne MacRae. The sheer horror of the plight in which these two small girls found themselves here in 1847 can hardly now be comprehended. Their mother was dead. Their father was dead. They were newly arrived in a strange country. Coming from what was then a wholly Gaelic-speaking area, they knew neither of this country's languages, understanding no French and at best, it is almost certain, only a word or two of English. Soon they were to be separated by many hundreds of miles. But having thus got rid of Anne and Ellen, to say nothing of their parents, a Lochalsh landowner had helped relieve his estate of its surplus population, thereby making that estate a more attractive prospect to sheep-farmers. And this, to those who counted then politically in Scotland, was really all that mattered.

Canadians generally felt considerable sympathy for Highland refugees from famine and clearance. Orphans like Ellen and Anne MacRae were consequently adopted rather than simply abandoned to an institutional upbringing. Substantial finance, from both private and governmental sources, was devoted to various measures designed to ease the predicament in which so many new arrivals from Scotland now found themselves. Alongside such generosity, however, there was growing anger. By the early 1850s, it is clear, colonial opinion was outraged and infuriated by the way in which North American susceptibilities were being wholly disregarded by the landlords responsible for funding so many of the emigrations of the famine period.

'We have been pained beyond measure for some time past,' an Ontario newspaper editorialised in October 1851, 'to witness in our streets so many unfortunate Highland emigrants, apparently destitute of any means of subsistence, and many of them sick from want.' These people had been conveyed to Canada at the expense of the Scottish landed gentleman on whose properties they had previously lived, this newspaper continued. 'There will be many to sound the fulsome noise of flattery in the ear of the generous landlord who has spent so much to assist the emigration of his poor tenants. They will give him the misnomer of *benefactor*, and for what? Because he has rid his estates of the encumbrance of a pauper population. Emigrants of the poorer class who arrive here from the Western Highlands of Scotland are often so situated that their emigration is more cruel than banishment . . . They are reduced to the necessity of begging.'[58]

The particular landlord whom this newspaper leader-writer had in mind was Colonel John Gordon who, some ten years earlier, had purchased the islands of Benbecula, South Uist and Barra from their former owners – those owners, Clanranald and MacNeil of Barra, having gone bankrupt in the wake of the kelping collapse. Reputedly one of the richest men in Scotland, Gordon had attracted a great deal of censure from the government officials sent to the Highlands in 1846 and 1847 to assist with the distribution of famine-relief supplies. Despite his wealth, these men insisted, John Gordon had refused to assist his starving tenants. And from the colonel's Hebridean properties, among the most attractive scenically of all of Scotland's islands, there consequently emanated reports of particular hunger and hardship. 'The scene of wretchedness which we witnessed as we entered on the estate of Colonel Gordon was deplorable, nay heart-rending,' Norman MacLeod, a Church of Scotland clergyman, wrote in 1847. 'On the beach the whole population of the country seemed to be met, gathering the precious cockles . . . I never witnessed such countenances – starvation on many faces – the children with their melancholy looks, big-looking knees, shrivelled legs, hollow eyes, swollen-like bellies – God help them, I never did witness such wretchedness!'[59]

Gordon's response to this calamity was simply to order eviction and deportation on an unprecedented scale and in circumstances of extraordinary brutality. From Andrew the Hebridean's island of Barra, it was reported, families ejected from their homes in the spring of 1850 had contrived 'to erect tents by means of blankets raised upon sticks, while some of them took refuge in caves and in their boats. From these places also they were subsequently warned to remove and shortly afterwards . . . their tents were demolished and their boats broken up.' Some such unfortunates eventually found their way to Edinburgh where the city authorities made arrangements for them to be 'served with an allowance of bread to prevent them from starving'. Others, on reaching Glasgow, were sent immediately to the Town Hospital where their clothes were found to be so verminous that they were promptly burned.[60]

Asked what he proposed to do to help these castaways, Gordon, in a letter which found its way into the newspapers, answered, 'Nothing.' But it may have been because of the controversy thus generated in Scotland in 1850 that the colonel took care to have the following year's crop of dispossessed families shipped directly from his island properties to North America – chartering the *Brooksby*, the *Montezuma*, the *Perthshire*, the *Admiral* and the *Liskeard* for the purpose of conveying some 1,700 people from Barra, South Uist and Benbecula to the St Lawrence.[61]

Gordon's objective was quite simply to rid the more fertile parts of his estate, particularly the superb grazings on his property's Atlantic coastline, of as many as possible of their occupants. In this he succeeded, the localities thus depopulated being at once converted into some of the most attractive sheep-farms in the Hebrides. But not all the colonel's deportees went willingly. Several individuals from among the 1851 contingent, as is confirmed by an extensive range of contemporary testimony, had to be hunted down and handcuffed before they could be got aboard the little flotilla which Gordon had arranged to have stationed that year in the South Uist port of Lochboisdale.[62]

A South Uist woman, Catherine MacPhee, who lived in the crofting township of Iochdar, was afterwards to give some indication of the impact made on her community by these events. She had seen 'the townships swept and the big holdings made of them', Catherine MacPhee commented in her native Gaelic, 'the people being driven out of the countryside to the streets of Glasgow and to the wilds of Canada, such of them as did not die of hunger and plague and smallpox while going across the ocean'. She had seen 'the women putting the children in the carts which were being sent from Benbecula and the Iochdar to Lochboisdale, while their husbands lay bound in the pen and were weeping beside them, without power to give them a helping hand, though the women themselves were crying aloud and their little children wailing like to break their hearts'. She had seen 'the big strong men, the champions of the countryside, the stalwarts of the world, being bound on Lochboisdale quay and cast into the ship as would be done to a batch of horses or cattle . . . the bailiffs and the ground-officers and the constables and the policemen gathered behind them in pursuit of them. The God of life and He only knows all the loathsome work of men on that day.'[63]

Now it was the turn of the colonial authorities to care for Gordon's cast-offs. 'The fifteen hundred souls whom Colonel Gordon has sent to Quebec this season have all been supported for the past week at the expense of the colony,' the *Quebec Times* complained in the autumn of 1851. 'And on their arrival at Toronto and Hamilton the greater number have been dependent on the charity of the benevolent for a morcel of bread. Four hundred are in the river at present and will arrive in a day or two, making a total of nearly two thousand of Colonel Gordon's tenants . . . whom the province will have to support.'[64]

That these destitute people had managed to get as far as Toronto and Hamilton was due entirely to the intervention of Alexander Buchanan who was then in charge of immigration matters in the St Lawrence area and who had arranged forward transport at public expense. Buchanan, who had been dealing with immigration into Canada from both Scotland and Ireland all through the famine period and who was consequently difficult to shock, was both appalled and angered by the condition of this latest group of Scottish Highlanders. 'These parties presented every appearance of poverty,' he observed. 'And from their statement, which was confirmed by the masters of the several vessels, were without the means of leaving the ships or of procuring a day's subsistence for their helpless families on landing.'[65]

George Douglas, writing from Grosse Ile, was equally forthright: 'I never during my long experience at the station saw a body of emigrants so destitute of clothing and bedding,' the doctor reported. The wife of the master of the *Admiral*, who happened to have been accompanying her husband on this occasion, 'was busily employed all the voyage in converting empty bread bags, old canvas and blankets into coverings for them'.

Buchanan, meanwhile, was endeavouring to extract from John Gordon – who was to be revealed on his death in 1858 as having been that rarest of mid-nineteenth-century individuals, a sterling millionaire – the considerable sums which it had cost to get the Barra, South Uist and Benbecula people taken from Quebec to Upper Canada. Gordon, Buchanan noted tiredly at the end of 1851, had 'refused to pay this charge'.

It remained only for this most punctilious of imperial civil servants to draw the attention of Scotland's landed proprietors to the obvious defect in those assisted emigration schemes which were claimed by their promoters to be undertaken always with the best interests of emigrants in view. 'The mere transfer of an indigent tenantry, without an alteration in any respect in their condition, gives no reasonable ground for expecting their subsequent successful progress,' Alexander Buchanan commented. It was as good a conclusion as any to draw from events which had led so many impoverished Scottish Highlanders to be deposited in North America. But it was one, needless to say, to which John Gordon and his fellow landlords paid not the slightest heed.

CHAPTER SIX

Many Men Have Loved the Island of Cape Breton

LIKE ITS MORE FAMOUS Australian counterpart, which was established at about the same time and named after the same colonial secretary in distant London, the Cape Breton Island town of Sydney owes its position to its harbour. But this Sydney Harbour is a lot less bustling than its Pacific counterpart. On an otherwise deserted quay, where the bollards look to have been unused for quite some time, an elderly man is finding it peaceful enough to be getting in some fishing. Nothing other than a gull or two is moving on the water. The oceangoing freighters which once docked in this vicinity have departed for more cargo-rich localities. And such passenger traffic as reaches Cape Breton Island from Europe nowadays does not get here by ship.

It was not always so. When, in September 1827, there dropped anchor here the brig *Stephen Wright*, several weeks out of Tobermory and carrying 170 passengers from the Isle of Mull and other parts of the Scottish Highlands, it was with the weariness of a man accustomed to dealing with the less attractive consequences of the emigration business that Thomas Crawley, one of several colonial officials then resident in Sydney, reported the vessel's arrival to his superiors. 'Another load of poor emigrants is arrived in our harbour,' Crawley wrote. 'We know little of them yet except that they brought with them some bad cases of malignant smallpox. Four are dead. Three more, I understand, are dying, and happy shall we be if the contagion does not spread over the city.'[1]

A constable had been stationed on the *Stephen Wright*, Crawley continued, in an attempt to keep out of Sydney the forty or so smallpox sufferers known to be aboard the brig. But what was to happen eventually to these unfortunates it was impossible to say. 'The master of the vessel, who is an obstinate, brutish fellow, declares he will do nothing towards the relief or recovery of his unhappy living cargo and, in pursuance of that determination, perversely refuses to let air into the hold of the vessel where it must necessarily be pestilential.'

For all their ghastliness, such happenings were very much routine in early nineteenth-century Sydney, a place which seems at times to have been virtually overwhelmed by those penniless Highlanders deposited here by the many westward-bound timber ships which skirted Cape Breton Island on their way to the St Lawrence. 'In the course of the present year,' the town's magistrates noted in 1828, 'upwards of 2,100 persons have come into this district from the western part of Scotland, many of whom, on their landing, were quite destitute of food and also of the means of procuring it'. Sydney was again thought to be at risk from smallpox. And 'great numbers' of newly disembarked Highlanders had been reduced to 'begging from door to door'.[2]

The longer-term impact of this Highland incursion is obvious in Cape Breton still: in the island's flourishing folk music; in the extent to which its numerous tourists are directed towards stores selling tartan knick-knacks; even in the physical appearance of those many Cape Bretoners who, if you were not strolling in the streets of Sydney or Baddeck, you would suspect that you had met at one time or another in a place like Harris, Lewis, Uist, Skye, Lochaber or Tiree. Here, as in North Carolina, the visitor is greeted with a *Ceud Mile Failte*. And if that visitor does not readily come across much information as to how so many Highland Scots first got to be here, then that is understandable enough. Who wants horror stories to intrude on their vacation?

Cape Breton Island has been longer known to Europeans than almost any other part of North America. Visited probably by the Vikings and reached again in 1497, it seems likely, by the Anglo-Venetian navigator John Cabot, the island became in the sixteenth century a busy forward base for the French, English, Portuguese and Spanish fishermen who came to these parts to exploit the Grand Banks cod shoals which Cabot described as having 'sometimes stayed his ships'. Along with the adjacent mainland, from which it is separated by the Strait of Canso, Cape Breton was claimed briefly in the 1620s by a Scottish government then trying to establish its own transatlantic empire in those territories to which Edinburgh politicians gave the name of Nova Scotia. Garrisoned subsequently by the French, the island passed finally into British hands following the surrender of Fortress Louisbourg to the besieging Fraser's Highlanders and their comrades in the summer of 1758. No veterans of that campaign were to make their homes here, however, and most of the many other Scottish Highlanders who came to North America in the

1760s and 1770s were likewise to bypass Cape Breton in favour of more southerly destinations in the Mohawk Valley and the Cape Fear River district.[3]

But Cape Breton had its enthusiasts even then. 'Nature has blessed few countries with so many advantages as this island,' the former soldier Samuel Holland observed in 1787 when completing an official survey. Among many 'inducements' to the rapid settlement of this new colony, or so Holland continued, were 'the conveniency and number of its ports, the general fertility of the soil, the quantity of timber, the many rivers, rivulets, creeks, lakes . . . abounding with fish'.[4]

Cape Breton is undoubtedly attractive. Here, as in the Scottish Highlands, land, sea, hill and sky have got themselves arranged in such a way as to ensure that, once you have had the chance to look around, some small, or maybe not so small, impression of the place will go on lingering for a long time in your mind. But you cannot, as folk say so often in both Cape Breton and the northern part of Scotland, live very well on scenery.

Set against the more prosaic realities of an island where no more than a quarter of the total land area can be said to have any agricultural value, where cold, snowy winters are followed by cool and often foggy springs and where inland localities have only about sixty frost-free days on average each year, Samuel Holland's comments take on something of the air of boosterism run riot. A few of those loyalists who left the United States in the 1780s came here. But only a few. At the start of the nineteenth century, the total population of Cape Breton Island – possessing then a mere six miles of reasonable road and given over still to native forests of spruce, fir, birch and pine – is generally reckoned to have been a mere 2,500. Of that number, it seems probable, no more than two or three hundred were Scottish Highlanders.[5]

There were more Highlanders in Cape Breton's general vicinity. The extensive emigrations of the 1770s had brought several hundred people from the West Highlands to Prince Edward Island in the Gulf of St Lawrence and to Pictou on the Nova Scotian mainland. And some families from among these groups had afterwards made their way to Cape Breton. But it was not until August 1802, when a ship carrying 299 emigrants arrived in Sydney from Scotland, that there began the Highland influx which was largely responsible for taking Cape Breton Island's population to 55,000 by the 1850s – when people of Highland extraction are estimated to have outnumbered all other Cape Bretoners by at least two to one.

It was indicative of what was subsequently to transpire that the colonial authorities in Sydney had to advance funds to members of this 1802 party to ensure that they survived the rigours of a Cape Breton winter. Each man got 40 shillings, each woman 30 shillings, with older and younger children being eligible for 20 shillings and 15 shillings respectively. These sums, to be repaid either in cash or in the form of so many days' labour on public-road construction projects, were the first of many such calls which Scottish Highlanders were to make on the public finances of Cape Breton Island and the wider colony of Nova Scotia during the first half of the nineteenth century.[6]

The comparatively small number of emigrants who got to Cape Breton in the period following the Passenger Vessels Act of 1803 were exceptional in this regard. The price of an Atlantic passage then being comparatively high, and their landlords still being anxious to keep as many Highlanders as possible in the Highlands, these early settlers tended to be drawn from families of some small property and position. In this category were the 382 people who arrived in Sydney from Barra in 1817 on the *Hope* and the *William Tell*. A family group consisting of two adults, two older and two younger children would have had to find 44 guineas prior to embarking on one or other of these ships. Since this was no small amount at that time, the *Hope* and *William Tell* emigrants were clearly in the tradition of those comparatively prosperous Highlanders who, in the 1760s and 1770s, had come to the conclusion that they were likely to do rather better for themselves in North America than in Scotland.[7]

The thousands of Highlanders who came to Cape Breton in the 1820s and ensuing decades were very differently situated. Victims for the most part of the steadily worsening economic and social crisis which affected so much of the Scottish Highlands in the wake of the kelp industry's collapse, many of them had been physically ejected from their former homes. Some of them reached North America principally because their landlords found it expedient to transport them overseas. Others got here only as a result of the cheap passages which could now be obtained by folk sufficiently desperate to be out of Scotland as to risk spending several miserable and highly dangerous weeks in the hold of a timber ship.

Nor did these people's troubles end with the Atlantic crossing. Because Cape Breton was the earliest landfall made by ships heading ultimately for the St Lawrence and Quebec, aspiring emigrants could get here more economically than they could travel to any other part of North America. And because Cape Breton's coastline, rather like that of the Scottish Highlands, is replete with sheltered coves and inlets, it was possible for those less scrupulous skippers who were common in the timber trade to put their passengers ashore in remote and unregulated harbours in order to avoid the delays and complexities which would have been encountered at more formal ports of entry to North America. 'Several vessels arrive annually and land their passengers on the western shore of this island,' customs officers complained from Sydney, 'the masters neglecting to make any report of the number.'[8]

A substantial proportion of these unrecorded and unregistered immigrants were doubtless among the 'poor creatures from the Highlands and Islands of Scotland' whom a Cape Breton surgeon described as regularly meeting 'famine, disease and death on the shores of Cape Breton'. Many of the two hundred or so emigrants who left Scotland in the summer of 1827 on the *Harmony* were among those to perish in this way. At least thirteen of them died in the course of the voyage. Another twenty-two died following their being deposited in some uninhabited spot on Cape Breton Island. Five more were found to be dead when this most inappropriately named vessel was finally obliged by bad weather to put into Sydney.[9]

The *Harmony* having anchored off Cape Breton's principal administrative centre, something at least was learned of the misfortunes of its passengers. But most such happenings went unreported, with unknown numbers of men, women and children from the Scottish Highlands seeing no more of the New World than those tree-fringed beaches where they were abandoned to their fate.

'My great-grandmother was pregnant with my grandmother coming across,' one modern Cape Bretoner has recalled of his Moidart family's arrival in North America. 'They landed here in the fall of 1834 ... They didn't know where they were, just told to get off ... My grandmother would be the seventh child and she was born shortly after they arrived. And her mother told the story about them coming across on the boat, you know, there was squalor and filth and sickness and dying and fighting ... They were dumped right on the ocean. They had no shelter. Just told to get off, that's all. With their trunk and bedding. They had to go into the woods to cut down a lean-to. And they stayed there for the winter. And my grandmother was born in that shack.'[10]

Nothing, it seemed, could stop the 'dreadful inundation' which the Cape Breton authorities believed, with no small justification, was turning their island into 'a refuge for the poor' and, in the process, draining away tax revenues which were being diverted from other purposes in order to provide a modicum of care for the many Highlanders who were being 'thrown on shore incapable of procuring their own subsistence'. Shipload after shipload came from Scotland every year. And since, by about 1830, the more attractive and more fertile 'frontlands' on Cape Breton's many lakesides and in the island's river valleys had generally been occupied, later arrivals frequently found themselves with no choice but to settle on the altogether less attractive 'backlands' where it was much more difficult, indeed virtually impossible, to establish a viable farm.[11]

Nor was it now so easy to acquire a freehold as it had been in the 1820s when the outright possession of a 200-acre 'lot' of crown land could be obtained, in effect, for a single payment of about five pounds – a figure equivalent to the rent which the typical Highland landlord was then charging annually for the occupancy of a croft of maybe half a dozen acres. In 1827, with the influx of people from Scotland approaching its peak, the Colonial Office in London began to insist that crown land in Nova Scotia must fetch some two shillings and sixpence an acre – thus quintupling the price of the standard 200-acre holding. Settlers, admittedly, were permitted to make payment for their land in four equal instalments over a period of one year. Even this concession was withdrawn in 1837, however, with emigrants now being instructed to make full payment for crown land within a fortnight of taking possession of it.[12]

The inevitable outcome, as observed by Cape Breton Island's understandably harassed surveyor-general, was that new arrivals simply squatted on such land as had not already been clearly allocated to others. 'People learn to look upon the orders of the government as mere matters of form and conclude that they may do as they please, and that the surest way of obtaining land is to take it, without the delay of asking leave, and to plunder it at pleasure.'[13]

Even when an emigrant family managed to acquire a farm, other problems quickly crowded in on them. 'In every work he has to perform,' the Earl of Selkirk wrote in 1805 when reflecting on the difficulties confronting the typical Scottish Highland immigrant in North America, 'he is unpractised and has all the awkwardness of a novice.' A cabin had to be constructed before the onset of winter weather which – anywhere north of the Cape Fear River area – was necessarily much more severe than anything ever experienced in Scotland. And in undertaking this most urgent task, it was essential that the settler, who might never before have set his hand to an axe, let alone brought down a tree, avoid disabling injury. 'If, however, he escapes this disaster and proceeds with industry to clear his land, this work, on which all his hopes are founded, is so new to him, that it must be expected to advance with a discouraging degree of slowness . . . He will probably, as the reward of a great deal of severe labour, have but a small plot of land cleared in the course of many months, perhaps not the fourth part of what a man accustomed to the business might have accomplished with less exertion. To cut down the trees is but half the work . . . The seasons of sowing, and many details in the management of unknown kinds of grain, are all to be learnt. Thus, independently of the accidents . . . to which all are subject, and over and above the danger of losing his seedtime altogether, by not having his land ready, the new settler has to add many chances that, from his own ignorance and mismanagement, his crop may totally fail.'[14]

The more than usually disorganised state of Cape Breton Island, combined with its scarcity of even passably productive land and combined, too, with there now being so few financial and other resources at the disposal of most Scottish Highland emigrants, made it inevitable that hazards of the type identifed by Selkirk were more evident here than anywhere else in North America. In Cape Breton in the 1820s and the 1830s there was precious little possibility of an emigrant readily making good in the manner celebrated by Hector St John de Crevecoeur's parable of Andrew the Hebridean. Here, in contrast, there was every likelihood of Highlanders finding themselves every bit as sparsely provided for as they had been at home.

Reports emanating from Cape Breton in March 1834, for example, were sufficiently alarming to result in a newspaper in the Nova Scotia capital of Halifax highlighting 'unparalleled distress' among 'the new settlers on the backlands near Baddeck and Middle River . . . We have been informed that it is positively affirmed that in one settlement about forty families . . . of whom 130 are children, are for the most part reduced to one meal per day, and this consisting wholly of potatoes of miserable quality.'[15]

The correspondence of Cape Breton Island clergymen contains considerable testimony to the same effect. One churchman commented: 'I have baptized where neither father, mother or children could venture out in their tattered rags. I have seen dwellings where six or eight of a family lived for five weeks on the milk of a cow, without any other food.' Another minister wrote: 'There are children in abundance who, covered with rags, lie stretched all night alongside the fire on the floor from having no bed clothes to cover them, and a person starts up every other hour to throw a log on the fire.'[16]

Those families who had managed to get hold of frontland farms naturally fared best. Around Mabou, Lake Ainslie, Broad Cove and Margaree – still among the most distinctively Scottish Highland localities in Cape Breton and populated mainly by people whose origins were in Mull, Coll, Tiree, Muck, South Uist, Moidart, Arisaig and Lochaber – the typical frontland holding consisted, by about 1850, of some forty acres of cleared and improved land. Sales of livestock and livestock products brought in a modest cash income. Firewood and timber were extracted from those parts of the holding which was still under forest. Game was usually plentiful and there was imported flour, sugar, molasses and tobacco to be had in most households.[17]

Both in this vicinity and elsewhere, however, backland farmers were struggling on plots which, as far as their agricultural potential was concerned, were no very great improvement on the crofts which Highland landlords had been so anxious to create at the height of the kelp boom. On most backland holdings, only ten or twenty acres had been cleared of trees by mid-century. This was insufficient, as a result of the essential infertility of the glacial soils which underlay the native forest, to support more than one or two milk cows, two or three beef cattle and maybe half a dozen sheep. Being remote from markets and having little or nothing to sell, the backland farmer enjoyed no cash income of the kind earned by his frontland counterpart. His house was invariably of a poorer, less finished, more shack-like type. His agricultural implements were more

Strath of Kildonan   *(Scottish Highland Photo Library)*

Jacobite Memorial, Glenfinnan   (*National Trust for Scotland*)

West Loch Tarbert   (*Scottish Highland Photo Library*)

Glen Coe   *(William Hunter)*

Loch Arkaig   *(William Hunter)*

Knoydart from Skye   (*Cailean Maclean*)

Uist   (*Cailean Maclean*)

Glen Garry   *(William Hunter)*

Memorial stone, Culloden Moor   *(National Trust for Scotland)*

Cille Choraill   *(Cailean Maclean)*

Ruined house   *(Cailean Maclean)*

Island beach   *(Cailean Maclean)*

Atlantic coast   *(Scottish Highland Photo Library)*

Strathspey   *(Scottish Highland Photo Library)*

primitive. With his wife and children, he subsisted, for the most part, on the one crop which, whether on a Cape Breton backland farm or on a Highland croft, could be grown in sufficient quantity to meet a family's food requirements. In painstakingly created clearances in the North American forest, for reasons similar to those which had brought about an identical situation in the more northerly and westerly parts of Scotland, an entire population had come to be reliant, very largely, on potatoes.

The blight which wiped out the potato harvest in the Scottish Highlands in 1846 reached Cape Breton Island the previous summer. Its impact was the same here as in Scotland. Families sold their few cattle and sheep and, when the little cash thus realised ran out, turned to a variety of more or less desperate expedients – such as mortgaging their land and, in the end, searching the woods for the eggs of wild birds and scavenging the beaches for shellfish.[18]

On this side of the Atlantic Ocean, as on the other, the blight returned, year after year, right through the 1840s. And here, as in the crofting areas which so many Cape Bretoners had so recently left, those famine years were characterised by exceptionally bad weather. One week into April 1847 there were 'three feet of snow on the ground' in various parts of Cape Breton – with some backland districts still having more than two feet lying a month later. 'Poverty, wretchedness and misery have spread through the Island of Cape Breton . . . to an alarming degree', it was reported officially, with more remote communities said to be experiencing 'starvation' and 'indescribable' suffering.[19]

At St Ann's Harbour, some twenty miles east of Sydney, a Presbyterian minister, Norman MacLeod, who had himself emigrated from the West Highlands to Cape Breton in 1817, recorded at this time: 'The general destitution has made it impossible, even for the most saving, to shut their ears and eyes from the alarming claims and craving of those around them, running continually from door to door, with the ghastly features of death staring in their very faces.' It was, perhaps, the crowning irony of the Scottish Highland emigrant experience in this northeastern corner of North America that several hundred people, having already made the voyage here from Scotland, should now, at Norman MacLeod's urging and partly in response to the conditions he described, leave Cape Breton Island for other still more distant British possessions in the Pacific – taking ship, first of all, for Australia and travelling on, a year or two later, to the Waipu district of New Zealand.[20]

The fields once cultivated by Norman MacLeod – who was himself to lead his congregation on their onward emigration from North America to Waipu – are occupied today by Cape Breton Island's Gaelic College. Here they offer summer courses in Nova Scotia's Scottish heritage. Here, too, they can sell you practically any tartan that you care to name, this being a popular stopping-off point with tourists travelling on the highway which leads south from Sydney through Baddeck to Whycogomagh and the junction with the more westerly route to Mabou, Inverness, Dunvegan, Gillisdale and Margaree.

These are pleasant enough localities nowadays. Around Baddeck, where you look across the narrow waters of St Patrick's Channel to the tree-covered hills which rise behind McIvor's Point and Washabuck, you might imagine yourself to be in one of the less wind-scoured corners of the Scottish Highlands. The views from the Mabou Road – as it heads through Stewartdale and Skye Glen, offering you the possibility, in the passing, of taking in Glencoe Mills and Mull River – are equally benign. This is a country of numerous homesteads, grassy clearings, occasional wayside stores and, at very frequent intervals, neat, carefully painted churches.

But to families fresh off a timber ship from Scotland, at a time when this was still a thinly populated frontier region, these were strange and sometimes even frightening places; places full of unfamiliar threats and hazards; places which demanded skills no emigrant could possibly possess. 'The new settler,' commented the Earl of Selkirk on the basis of the visits which he made in 1803 and 1804 to several Highland communities in North America, 'is unacquainted with the methods by which a practised woodsman can find his way through the trackless forest. Every time he leaves his hut he is exposed to the danger of being bewildered and lost.' The more experienced pioneer took care to leave conspicuous blaze marks on the trees when venturing into uncleared woodland. But even when the head of a settler household had learned the importance of blazing a trail in this fashion, Selkirk observed, 'still he can feel no confidence that his children will have the same caution and must still shudder when he thinks of the howling wilderness that surrounds him'.[21]

Something of the sense of dread which could so readily be inspired by wild country is evident in one of the first Gaelic songs to be composed in the New World. 'We are now in America,' that song runs, 'in the shade of the never-ending forest . . . We have become Indians surely enough. Skulking under trees, not one of us will be left alive, with wolves and beasts howling in every direction.' These particular apprehensions, as it happens, were experienced in North Carolina. But Cape Breton Island, where the natural environment was generally harsher than anything likely to be met with in the Cape Fear River country, was equally capable of engendering feelings of disillusionment among its early Highland settlers.[22]

John MacDonald, *Iain Sealgair*, who came to Mabou from Brae Lochaber in 1834, was especially disenchanted with what he found – his *Oran do dh'America*, Song for America, hauntingly expressing its composer's longing to be out of this 'land of snows and sere grasses'. So little is Mabou to be recommended, MacDonald feels, that he wishes now that he had died in Scotland where he would have been interred 'on the heights' above Glen Spean in the churchyard of Cille Choraill, the traditional burial-place of his West Highland clan. 'Alas, Lord, that I am not among them as I ardently long to be,' Iain Sealgair, John the Hunter, says finally of those of his kinsfolk who have the good fortune to be lying forever in Cille Choraill's 'sunny, smooth enclosure . . . the most beautiful graveyard that I ever knew'.[23]

To sense something of the feelings which this Brae Lochaber exile was attempting to recapture in his verse, it is necessary only to visit the particular spot in Scotland to which Iain Sealgair was referring – preferably on one of those May evenings when the Glen Spean birchwoods have just come into leaf and when the yellowish light from the westering sun is picking out every stone and every boulder on the surrounding hillsides. At such a time in such a place, with all its psychologically vital sets of linkages to those forebears who necessarily loom large in any kinship-orientated social system of the traditional Scottish Highland type, it is easy to understand why those Gaelic verses written in Mabou came out the way they did. Nor have emotions of the sort expressed so well by Iain Sealgair vanished wholly from Cape Breton even yet. It is a measure of Mabou people's continuing affection for the Scottish locality from which their families have been separated now for nearly two hundred years that when, in the 1980s, a fund was launched in the Highlands with a view to reroofing the ancient church of Cille Choraill – which owes its name to the Gaelic-speaking monk reputed to have brought Christianity to Brae Lochaber twelve or thirteen centuries ago – no small amount of dollars were contributed to that fund by families living in this part of North America.

To wish to maintain one's links with Scotland, however, is not the same thing as to wish one had never left. And it is indicative of the extent to which John MacDonald's evident dislike of Cape Breton Island was at odds with the opinions of many of his contemporaries that his *Oran do dh'America*, on its beginning to circulate among the new settler's Mabou neighbours, at once evoked a stinging riposte from another Brae Lochaber emigrant, Allan MacDonald, cousin to the homesick Iain Sealgair.

He, too, had known 'conditions over there in cold Scotland', Allan observes caustically in his native Gaelic. He consequently considers it 'no great loss' to be so far away from his homeland. 'A true cause of sorrow is the harsh treatment endured by the poor people there.' The Highland nobility are treating crofters like slaves, Allan MacDonald tells his kinsman. 'The land you left is a land without kindness, a land without respect for tenants.' While it was natural to be 'sorrowful' on leaving Lochaber, it was wrong to be critical of North America where Highlanders were 'respected men' who enjoyed 'a right to free land'. Cape Breton Island, Allan MacDonald insists, is a better place than

Scotland. It would be well, therefore, if his cousin were less 'loud and boastful' about the country he has left and more understanding of his good fortune in being now in North America. 'It is not fitting to dispraise the land of promise.'[24]

In Nova Scotia, then, as in North Carolina, the Mohawk Valley or Glengarry County, a dominant theme of the many songs composed by Scottish Highland pioneers is this emigrant people's powerful feeling of having managed to gain here, on the western side of the Atlantic, the ability to determine their own destinies in a manner which was simply not conceivable in their country of origin. And in the few surviving letters posted back to Scotland by these emigrants there can be found no small amount of additional testimony to the sheer strength of this sense of having suddenly escaped oppression. 'Thank God, I am well pleased for coming to this country,' one Cape Bretoner wrote in 1830 to relatives still living in the Isle of Lewis. His land was 'free from all burdens whatso-ever', this man continued, and he was able to go about his business entirely at his 'pleasure'. In Cape Breton, in contrast to Scotland, 'no soul living forces me to do a turn against my will, no laird, no factor, having no rent, nor any toilsome work but I do myself'.[25]

Not even the famine conditions prevailing in much of the Cape Breton backlands in the 1840s were to alter such opinions. However bad things might be here, most Highland settlers evidently felt, they were a considerable improvement on what was customary in Scotland. 'Even the log hut, in the depths of the forest, is a palace compared with some of the turf cabins of Sutherland and the Hebrides,' one commentator noted in 1869. And what was true of housing was true of much else also – the few individuals who had the chance in the later part of the nineteenth century to make direct comparisons between Nova Scotian circum-stances, on the one hand, and conditions in Scotland's crofting localities, on the other, being in no doubt as to where the balance of overall advan-tage lay.[26]

John Sinclair, who was himself the son of Highland emigrants, spent some time in Scotland around 1880 and returned to his native Nova Scotia convinced that its inhabitants were 'a great deal better off' than those Scottish Highlanders who had 'remained in that country of landlords and rents'. Alexander MacKenzie, a Highland author and journalist who visited this part of North America at the same time, came to an identical conclusion. Nova Scotia farmers were 'not wealthy', MacKenzie acknowledged. 'But they have as much bread, potatoes, meat, butter, cheese . . . as anyone needs to have . . . Add to all these home comforts . . . the independence enjoyed by a fine race of men living unmolested by laird or factor, on their freehold possessions, and what more can be wished for?'[27]

MacKenzie, it should be noted, was very actively involved in the political campaign then developing in Scotland to obtain for the crofting population legal rights which, when they were embodied finally in the Crofters Act of 1886, made it impossible for Highlanders to be evicted any longer by their landlords. He took a particular pleasure, therefore, in underlining Nova Scotia's lack of an estate-owning aristocracy – as did that other Scottish land reformer, John Murdoch, who also spent some time in North America in the early 1880s and who was equally delighted to report from Ontario that people there 'laugh with scorn at the wretched system of landlordism and flunkeyism' which Scottish Highlanders at home, as opposed to Scottish Highlanders overseas, were still having to endure.[28]

But the Nova Scotian farmer of Highland extraction required no prompting from itinerant Scotsmen to make him properly aware of what his people had gained by settling in places like Mabou. 'It was not worth much as farms went,' such a man was in the habit of remarking of his little piece of North America. 'But it was his.' That was what mattered above all other things – that and the immense effort which had gone into carving even the most modest of agricultural enterprises out of old-growth forest.[29]

The earliest crops of grain and potatoes to be grown on the typical Cape Breton farm were planted in little fields still bristling with tree-stumps which were sometimes several feet across and which could not be removed until their roots had rotted. But secure in the knowledge that this land, unlike the croft on which he might well have lived in Scotland, could not be taken from him, the Cape Bretoner immediately set about making improvements of a sort his crofting counterparts could not even contemplate prior to the British parliament conceding the security of tenure so forcefully demanded by men like John Murdoch and Alexander MacKenzie. Year after year, decade after decade, the arable acreage of the Cape Breton farm was determinedly expanded. More cattle, sheep and horses were acquired. Barns and cowsheds were erected. And as living standards gradually rose during the second half of the nineteenth century, the roughly constructed log cabins of the pioneering period gave way to rather more comfortable houses of the type which are still characteristic both of Mabou and of much of the rest of the Cape Breton Island countryside – these square-built, white-painted, two-storey, timber-framed and clapboard-covered homes you see when driving along highways where each and every mailbox bears a Scottish Highland name.

'The largest and principal room was the kitchen and in it centred all family and most social activities,' one Nova Scotian writer, Neil MacNeil, recalled of his upbringing in such a home at the beginning of the twentieth century. 'A huge, black, crude, wood-burning iron stove on legs, with an ungainly oven perched upon it, dominated the kitchen and served for cooking the meals for the family and the feed for the stock, and for heating the home. There was always a steaming and whistling iron kettle sitting on the stove and a stack of cut firewood placed beside it. On winter nights the family sat around the stove, the men placing their stockinged feet upon it, so that the women had to step over or around them to place pots on the stove or pans in the oven.' To move even a few paces from this stove and its surrounding clutter, Neil MacNeil's reminiscences make clear, was immediately to be reminded of the bone-chilling temperatures prevailing outside. Windows were nailed permanently shut in an attempt to keep out the bitterly cold north-westerlies which came hurtling off the pack ice in the Gulf of St Lawrence. But still the household water froze in the buckets used to bring it from the nearby well. And sometimes the snow was so deep as to isolate one community from the other for several weeks, even months, at a time.[30]

In just such Nova Scotia kitchens, right through the nineteenth century and well into the twentieth, there were sung the songs and recited the stories which the original emigrants had brought with them from Scotland. 'Over and over again he told us of the virtues of the Scots,' Neil MacNeil recalled of his grandfather's contribution to the conversation round the family stove. 'He repeated the legends of our people. He extolled Scottish triumphs, which were many, and explained away Scottish failings, which were few.' And all this, Neil MacNeil's account suggests, the old man did in exactly the same words as he might have used had his people never left their native Barra: 'For Gaelic was the language of grandfather's household as it was of the countryside.'[31]

'Gaelic was the first language that I spoke for there was no English used in the home,' one of modern Cape Breton's best-known storytellers, Joe Neil MacNeil, recalled in the 1980s. It was in the predominantly Gaelic setting of the Middle Cape community where he was raised in the first and second decades of the twentieth century that Joe Neil MacNeil – a carpenter, plumber, sawmill-operator, mechanic and electrician as well as a highly skilled exponent of one of his people's oldest art forms – acquired his quite enormous repertoire of traditional tales; tales of the sort which, through innumerable generations, had been handed down in the Celtic world from one set of narrators to the next; tales which, in many instances, had first been brought to Scotland by those Gaelic-speaking emigrants who moved from Ireland to Argyll at about the time the Roman Empire was beginning to collapse in Western Europe.[32]

As happened also in the Cape Fear River country, in Glengarry County, in Prince Edward Island and in the various other North American localities where Highland emigrants first settled, the language in which Joe Neil MacNeil's stories were invariably told has been inexorably displaced by English. There remain now in Cape Breton Island, which contained many thousands of Gaelic-speakers as recently as the 1930s, only a few hundred individuals who are fluent in the language spoken in the holds of the timber ships which brought their ancestors here almost two hundred years ago. Which is not to say, of course, that every other aspect of the original emigrant population's cultural inheritance is similarly disappearing.

To read the meticulously crafted fiction of a contemporary Cape Bretoner like Alistair MacLeod, one of Canada's most universally praised writers, is to be constantly aware of the extent to which his literary world is one that draws no sharp distinction between the Scottish and North American components of the Highland experience. The one, for Alistair MacLeod at least, is simply an extension of the other – the act of emigration denoting no sharp break with what had gone before. 'My grandmother,' runs one of many MacLeod passages in which this sense of continuity is implicit, 'gets up and goes for her violin which hangs on a peg inside her bedroom door. It is a very old violin and came from the Scotland of her ancestors, from the crumbled foundations that now dot and haunt Lochaber's shores. She plays two Gaelic airs – *Gun Bhris Mo Chridh' On Dh'Fhalbh Thu* and *Cha Till Mi Tuille*. Her hands have suffered stiffness and the lonely laments waver and hesitate as do the trembling fingers upon the four taut strings. She is very moved by the ancient music and there are tears within her eyes.'[33]

The sounds which float across the hundreds of people who cluster round a little concert platform in the corner of a field this Sunday afternoon are very much the sounds of Scotland. A man sings, in Gaelic, alone and unaccompanied in the traditional manner. There are pipers and drummers to be heard. Soon clapping hands and stomping feet greet fiddlers playing Highland airs in a distinctively Highland style. There are especially loud cheers for a local folk group who, you notice, take some care to plug their new recording of a song which celebrates, in Gaelic once again, the merits of an island which, or so the song claims, is one of the most favoured spots in all the world.

But the island which these singers have in mind is not part of the Hebrides. The summer sun possesses here a strength it never gains in Scotland. The nearby stretch of water is the Bras d'Or Lake and not the Minch. The cars and station wagons parked in long lines on the grass mostly carry Nova Scotia license plates. The shouting sellers of hotdogs, popsicles, cotton candy and Mickey Mouse balloons are as North American as the warm, forest-scented breeze which now and then comes swirling down from the surrounding hillsides.

This Big Pond music festival is very much a Cape Breton Island event. While some songs sung on such occasions have implicit in them still a hankering for the Scottish Highlands, these are not the songs, you quickly sense, which tug most strongly at the audience's emotions. The sentiments which really matter here have more to do with this small part of modern Canada than with the faraway country to which so many of today's Canadians can trace their family origins.

'S e Ceap Breatunn tir mo ghraidh, runs a song made in this island

by Dan Alec MacDonald of Framboise, *Tir nam craobh 's nam beanntan ard; 'S e Ceap Breatunn tir mo ghraidh, Tir a's aillidh leinn air thalamh*. Cape Breton is the land of my love, the song says, the land of trees and mountains high; Cape Breton is the land of my love, the loveliest land on earth, in its people's opinion.[34]

For all that it is concerned with Cape Breton Island rather than with Lewis, Harris, Uist, Barra, Tiree, Knoydart or Glen Garry, the visitor from Scotland finds Dan Alec MacDonald's song peculiarly familiar. That is appropriate. In no way is this song indicative of Cape Bretoners of Highland extraction having turned their back on their collective cultural inheritance. It is representative rather of the extent to which, in the course of the past two centuries, that inheritance has been adapted to a new, and wholly North American, purpose.

An intensely strong attachment to place and to locality – of the sort one senses in Dan Alec MacDonald's tribute to Cape Breton – is one of the most persistent elements in the culture developed, over the larger part of two millennia, by Scotland's Gaelic-speaking people. It is to be found in those medieval verses in which Deirdre of the Sorrows – heroine of a Gaelic saga which was itself a thousand years old when it inspired this piece of fourteenth-century poetry – remembers her Highland glen of steep-ridged peaks and pools and dappled deer and rowans and hawks and round-faced otters. It is evident in the work of those eighteenth-century bards, *Alasdair MacMhaigstir Alasdair* and *Donnachadh Ban Mac an t-Saoir*; Alasdair, who served as an officer in the Jacobite army of 1745, writing powerfully about the landscapes of his native Ardnamurchan; Donnachadh Ban, a deer stalker as well as a soldier in the Black Watch, dwelling evocatively on his memories of the high hills around Tyndrum and Bridge of Orchy. It is a constant theme in the twentieth-century poetry of *Somhairle Mac Gill-Eain*, Sorley MacLean, whose writings describe in the most intricate detail so many of the natural features of Raasay, the little island to which he belongs. And it is this same feeling for particular, intimately known locations – not in Scotland now but in Cape Breton – which is to be heard, in North American English as well as Gaelic, from several of the singers at this August concert in Big Pond.[35]

'The American agriculturalists seem to have little local attachment,' a traveller in the United States observed in 1835. 'A New Englander or Virginian, though proud of his state, will move off to Missouri or Illinois, and leave the home of his childhood, without any visible effort or symptom of regret, if by so doing he can make ten dollars where he before made eight.' But there was one set of American farmers to whom his comments most emphatically did not apply, this traveller continued. Somewhere in the United States he had stumbled across one of the several places which became home to eighteenth-century emigrants from the Scottish Highlands. Its people, in sharp contrast to their perennially restless neighbours, were 'as unwilling to quit that spot as they were to leave their original country'.[36]

Something of this same bond between community and locality is to be seen in the 'down home' verses composed in the years around 1900 by the North Carolina poet, John Charles McNeill – both of whose grandfathers were Gaelic-speaking Highlanders. Something of it is to be glimpsed also in contemporary country music. Such music, for all its commercialisation, is rooted in cultural characteristics which run very deep in the American South. And it is at least an arguable proposition that these characteristics – 'the intimate friendship with nature, the tender feeling for all the aspects of earth and sky, the almost passionate attachment to particular places' – owe at least a little to the long standing Scottish Highland influence on localities like North Carolina and Tennessee.[37]

Clearer still is the case of Glengarry County. 'For Glengarrians, and particularly Glengarrians of Scottish descent, and many of those descended from them,' comment two of the county's modern historians, Royce MacGillivray and Ewan Ross, 'Glengarry has traditionally seemed a special, almost a holy, place.' And what applies to Glengarry County is felt by many commentators to apply equally to Cape Breton Island. 'Committed to their sense of place and their personal relationships,' Kenneth Donovan remarks in the course of his introduction to a recent collection of essays on Cape Breton history, 'many Cape Bretoners have sacrificed the affluent incomes of more wealthy regions of the country to remain on the island.'[38]

Ever since the 1840s, however, there have been Cape Bretoners who felt themselves to have no alternative but to go elsewhere. Hence the extent to which the Gaelic songs inspired by this North American island, like so many of those other Gaelic songs intended to pay tribute to some part of the Highlands, were conceived and shaped in exile. What had sapped his joy and spirit, insisted Alexander MacDonald in the nineteenth century, was that he had turned his back on his Cape Breton community. 'In my bed when I awake, mourning for the land that I left, I imagine that my eyes see every hill and pond in Mabou.' The anonymous composer of *Duanag a California*, Song for California, dating from the 1920s, expressed very similar sentiments. Cape Breton was his 'own country', this man insisted. 'You would find none better under the sun.' And for all that he had benefited financially from his migration, he was by no means convinced that he had made the right decision: 'I would prefer to be among Gaels with their humanity and warmth . . . I dream of home when awake and when asleep; I often think, when morning comes, that I hear the rush of the river.'[39]

While the sound of a Cape Breton stream is certainly much to be preferred to the din of traffic in San Francisco or Los Angeles, the pressures which resulted in movement from the island to more prosperous parts of North America were gradually becoming irresistible. It was all very well for the author of this Song for California to 'advise any young man who has even a small bit of land to work it eight hours a day' rather than abandon his Cape Breton Island home. The fact of the matter was that the overwhelming majority of the farms created so laboriously here in the period following the initial Highland influx were simply incapable of providing a family with anything approximating to an adequate standard of life. In Cape Breton Island, as in the Scottish crofting areas from which so many Cape Bretoners had originally come, it was generally essential to supplement the produce of the land with income from some other source.

Those crofters who were not actually removed from the Highlands during the first half of the nineteenth century were obliged, in the decades following the kelp industry's demise, to diversify into a whole range of alternative occupations. Some became fishermen as well as agriculturalists. Others went each year to Scotland's more productive farming districts where they took temporary jobs as farm labourers. There were wages to be earned on the sporting estates which became a more and more important aspect of the Highland scene as the nineteenth century advanced. There was work to be had in shipping, on the railways, in the postal service, in local boatyards, in the hotels which were built to cater for the steadily expanding tourist business. And when all such sources of additional income failed, as they did very often, both in the nineteenth century and in the twentieth, there was, of course, the possibility of leaving the Highlands altogether. Hence the tendency for people from crofting communities to take themselves to industrial cities like Glasgow or to those other still more distant places where many thousands of young men and women from a crofting background went in search of the employment they could not obtain at home.

The Cape Breton Island experience was more or less identical. There was a little money to be made from lumbering on the Glengarry County pattern. There were rather better opportunities in the fishing industry. For a time in the 1850s and 1860s, just prior to Cape Breton's nascent shipbuilding business being overwhelmed as a result of the universal switch from sail to steam, there were carpenters and other craftsmen needed in those island yards which supplied brigs, brigantines and barques to the Atlantic trade. But for many Cape Bretoners of Highland extraction, as for many of their crofting counterparts back in Scotland, it was necessary to look much further afield for the means to personal advancement. When, in 1884, a visitor to the island asked a farm girl where a particular road eventually led, he is reputed to have been given this reply: 'It goes to the Strait of Canso, see, and on to Montana – that's where my brother John is working on a ranch – and I don't know where else it goes.' Insofar as it provided Cape Bretoners with the most obvious route to improved prospects, that road went, in fact, to practically every part of both the United States and Canada.[40]

Scotland's crofting counties attained their highest population in the early 1840s. Rural Cape Breton's demographic maximum was reached some four decades later. Both localities were then locked into the same debilitating downward spiral. In 1869 'the inhabitants of Cape Breton' were reported to be 'flocking' to the United States. Ten years afterwards the regular departure of a US-bound steamship had been transformed into a 'weekly leavetaking', with an additional 9,000 or so Cape Bretoners emigrating in the course of the 1880s alone. These people were moving out, one correspondent remarked in a letter to an island news-paper, for the 'same reason . . . that the Scotchman and Irishman have left their native shores'. They were trying to 'procure a better living for themselves and their families'.[41]

In Glengarry County, which had 22,447 inhabitants in 1891 and only 18,666 in 1931, the farms of the settlement period were similarly failing to provide for families descended from those Scottish Highlanders who had emigrated there a century before. Of the six children from one such family, it was reported around 1900, only one remained in Glengarry. Two were in Michigan and the others were in Chicago, Indiana and California. Cape Bretoners, too, were scattered right across the North American continent. But by far the biggest concentration of them, in the decades prior to the First World War, was to be found in Boston – the New England city which occupied the same sort of position in Cape Breton at that time as Glasgow was then occupying in the life of Scotland's crofting communities.[42]

Baile nam Beans, city of beans, one Gaelic-speaking Cape Bretoner called Boston, this rapidly expanding centre where his living quarters consisted of 'a tiny room in a garret'. Few such criticisms of Boston were voiced in the hearing of relatives still resident in Cape Breton, however. Those exiles who came back for a week or two most summers to the family homestead in Big Pond or Margaree – in much the same way as their distant cousins temporarily abandoned Glasgow's overcrowded tenements each July or August in order to renew their connections with the croft on which they had been brought up – naturally preferred to gloss over the disadvantages of an urban existence and to linger instead on those features of city life which compared favourably with conditions in Cape Breton. 'Until last year he thought indoor plumbing was his intestines,' it was said caustically of one of those 'vacation Americans' whose newly acquired airs and graces were clearly hard for stay-at-homes to take. 'He never had that goddam accent in Mabou,' it was remarked of another man back 'for the hay'. But no such comments could disguise the extent to which those Cape Bretoners who wished to get on in the world now felt that they had no choice but to begin by heading south across the Strait of Canso.[43]

It was for reasons of this sort that farms created with such effort in the pioneering period were increasingly abandoned as the twentieth century advanced. You see such farms here and there across Cape Breton Island; houses and barns tilted all awry as their timber framing slowly rots; access roads grassing over; fields gone entirely under spruce trees.

To be shown a typically wooded Cape Breton hillside by an old man who tells you how, as a boy, he helped to take several wagonloads of hay from that same piece of ground is as intensely depressing an experience as to see a previously well-worked crofting township back in Scotland given over more and more to weeds and rushes. But those of us who have never had to get by on the meagre product of an unforgiving piece of land – whether in the Highlands or Cape Breton Island – are in no position to call into question the motives of those who felt it both right and expedient to give up that sort of struggle.

'The days of a crofter living off his land are past and not all the romantics in the Lowlands will make them return,' a group of Scottish trade unionists observed of the Highlands in the early 1950s. 'It is from this understanding that the problem of depopulation can best be approached. People leave the Highlands because a reasonable living cannot be made in them. This may appear rather an obvious truth, but it cannot be overemphasised. It is often said that the reasons for depopulation are the lure of the city lights, the poor housing, the lack of electric light or the poor transport. It is true that the lack of these things may drive people to the towns. But the lack itself is only a symptom of the main cause – poverty.'[44]

Much the same might have been said of the Cape Breton countryside. There were those among the island's population who managed both to earn wages elsewhere in North America and to retain their hold on their island farms – prominent among them the Cape Bretoners who travelled thousands of miles by train from Nova Scotia to Manitoba, Saskatchewan and Alberta each summer from the 1890s until the 1920s in order to supply those relatively underpopulated prairie provinces with the labour needed to get in their annual crop of wheat. But 'hitting the harvest' in this way was never going to result in individuals radically transforming their financial prospects. More ambitious Cape Bretoners, therefore, remained inclined to leave the island permanently – the Pacific seal-hunters, Alex and Dan MacLean, transformed by Jack London into the heroes of his 1904 novel, *The Sea Wolf*, being merely an extreme example of a process which was taking many Cape Breton Highlanders as far from their new homeland as that homeland is itself from Scotland.[45]

Some such emigrants, having eventually made good, came back. So it was in the case of Hugh Campbell who moved to Boston from Whycogomagh in Cape Breton as early as 1845 and who then trekked from one side of America to the other in the hope of striking it rich in the course of the Californian gold rush of 1849. The Whycogomagh man, whose parents had emigrated to Cape Breton Island from Argyll, was not among those to make his fortune that year. But being clearly smitten now with gold fever, he next took ship across the Pacific to the latest set of diggings in Australia. There Campbell was at last successful. With several thousand dollars in his pocket, he sailed, by way of South Africa, for Scotland where he paid a call on his West Highland relatives before completing his round-the-world journeyings by returning finally to Nova Scotia.[46]

This was unusual, however. Much more common, once the island had acquired the educational facilities which had inevitably been lacking in the pioneer period, were those individuals for whom a country school in the Cape Breton backwoods was a springboard to a career in one or other of the professions. As was equally the case in the Scottish Highlands, where academic attainment also tended to be a prelude to migration, the man or woman who showed some aptitude for learning – and there were Cape Breton couples who managed to send several of their offspring to college or university – almost invariably took up residence in a distant city. That was better, the parents of these departed young folk maybe felt, than having their children gravitate to the one line of work which Cape Breton Island, for a time, provided in abundance. This line of work was mining.

It was one of the misfortunes of nineteenth-century Highlanders that the few natural resources to which they had ready access, whether in Scotland or North America, were so frequently exploited largely for the benefit of others – the essential role of Highlanders in the development of these resources being simply to provide an unfailing supply of cheap labour. It was bad enough that the kelp industry had been managed in such a way as to leave crofters impoverished, one visitor to the Hebrides commented in the 1840s. But worse still was the fact that the 'solid advantages' which had been 'opened up' to the crofting population's landlords by the demand for seaweed-based alkalis had been 'bartered for the merest baubles', being squandered on 'residences, dress, furniture, equipages, pleasures and styles of living' rather than invested in such a way as to provide localities like Skye or Uist with the means of advancing economically. A raw material which was essential to the expansion of the wider British economy had been extracted for a period of years from the Scottish Highlands, in other words, by means which, apart from enabling landowners to indulge themselves more than they might otherwise have done, had resulted in the region gaining no long-term benefit. And what one nineteenth-century observer felt to hold true of the trade in Highland kelp, interestingly enough, another believed to be the case with regard to the export of Canadian timber.[47]

'A stranger would naturally suppose that such a trade must produce great riches to the country,' Peter Fisher, New Brunswick's first historian, remarked of the lumber business in 1825. But anyone holding such expectations, Fisher continued, would be 'disappointed' and 'astonished' by what was actually taking place. 'The persons principally engaged in shipping the timber have been strangers who have taken no interest in the welfare of the country, but have merely occupied a spot to make what they could in the shortest possible time. Some of these have done well and others have had to quit the trade; but whether they won or lost, the capital of the country has been wasted, and no improvement of any consequence made to compensate for it, or to secure a source of trade to the inhabitants when the lumber shall fail.'[48]

The 'strangers' to whom Peter Fisher referred were, of course, the representatives of those companies which habitually turned to places like Glengarry County to find the workforce needed to make it possible for Britain to be supplied so readily with Canadian timber. For all that the Glengarry men took a proper pride in their work, and for all that they were certainly treated less harshly than their kelping counterparts in Scotland, it is nevertheless the case that, as Fisher suggested, the Canadian lumberjack tended to do a lot less well out of the nineteenth-century timber business than the Liverpool, Glasgow and other firms which had such a tight grip on the industry's finances.

Peter Fisher's critique of the manner in which his country's natural assets were habitually treated has a particular relevance to Cape Breton Island. There never was much worthwhile lumber here, admittedly. But there was coal – and in enormous quantities. Worked in a desultory way as early as the eighteenth century, the deposits in the general vicinity of Sydney began to be exploited on a large scale in the 1870s and 1880s. Soon Cape Breton was accounting for a third of the Canadian Confederation's total coal production. Soon, too, steelworks were constructed to apply Cape Breton coal to smelting iron ore shipped here across the Cabot Strait from Newfoundland. But that was as far as Cape Breton Island ever got in acquiring a genuinely industrialised economy. Whether or not it had anything to do with Cape Breton's coal and steel enterprises being always in the ownership of financial interests in Britain, the United States or Central Canada – and Peter Fisher would certainly have known what conclusion to draw from that fact – it is certainly the case that no significant downstream manufacturing ever developed here. A Yorkshire mining engineer, Francis Gray, who emigrated to Cape Breton Island at the start of the twentieth century, put his finger neatly on what, from the local point of view, had gone so sadly wrong. 'Nova Scotia has achieved the status of a mining camp,' Gray commented, 'whereas its full status should be that of a metropolis of industry.'[49]

Today most of the Sydney area's mines and their associated industries have long since closed. Although various federal and provincial agencies have been battling now for decades to improve the region's prospects, Sydney and its various satellite towns exhibit all the dismal characteristics of places finding it next best thing to impossible to get a battered industrial economy back on to its feet. In a recently compiled league table of living standards in one hundred of Canada's urban districts, this particular locality came in last. And while Cape Breton Island – as long as it possesses both a beautiful countryside and an extraordinarily rich human culture – will always be attractive to its inhabitants, it is an easy thing to feel, on visiting the former mining community of Glace Bay, just a few miles east of Sydney, that the many people here whose roots are in the Highlands have had an exceptionally raw deal from history. For a single family to have laboured in the kelp industry, to have been evicted from a croft, to have made the ocean crossing in an emigrant ship, to have hacked a farm out of virgin forest, to have found it impossible to make a living on that farm, to have gone into coal-mining, to have endured that industry's grim casualty toll and to have seen, at the end of all of this, the mines shut down is, whatever way you look at it, to have endured an awful lot in the space of half a dozen generations.[50]

No doubt because it was cheaper to build in North American timber than in Lanarkshire stone, the homes which a corporation like the Dominion Coal Company constructed for its workforce are a little bit more spacious than their counterparts in Scotland's former mining and steelmaking centres. The proximity of the Atlantic Ocean also gives to Glace Bay a more open, fresher feel than you get in Motherwell or Wishaw. But this Cape Breton community nevertheless possesses something of that air of dereliction you find also in those faraway West Central Scotland towns which have similarly had their coal seams abandoned and their industrial plants declared outmoded, obsolete, redundant.

Here, when this was still a new town in the years around 1900, there came thousands of the younger members of Cape Breton Island's Scottish Highland farming families. 'Call any man *Mac* on the streets of Glace Bay,' one visitor noted in 1925, 'and if he doesn't answer his neighbour will.' So numerous, in fact, were the various MacDonalds, MacNeils and MacLeods in such communities that one had to be distinguished from the other, on the mine payroll and in the town records as well as in daily conversation, by their nicknames. Mention Jack MacLean and you might have meant any one of several individuals. But Jack the Bottomer, a man who loaded tubs at the shaft foot, and Jack the Face, who worked far forward in the mine were much more readily recognisable. Black Sandy, Red Sandy, Little Sandy, Sandy the Boxer and Sandy Cape North would otherwise have all been Sandy MacDonald. So would Sandy Big Pay who, by the time the coal company had made its various deductions, was left one week with just two cents in his wage packet.[51]

Some part at least of Cape Breton's Highland culture now made the transition to these mining towns. When a man was called Jack Sandy's this was to give him, in English, the patronymic which he would have had in his father's Gaelic. When one of that man's workmates was known as Alec Ossian MacDonald this was by way of indicating that he was as good a storyteller as the saga poet whose name has been familiar to Gaelic-speakers for perhaps two thousand years. Another such narrator of Scottish Highland tales, John Joe Red Angus MacNeil, was employed to fill the gaps between the newest Hollywood films at the Glace Bay moviehouse. And every now and then, in bar-rooms, on street corners, on a fine day at the Lingan and Dominion beach, a crowd of hundreds, even thousands, might well gather to hear Dawn Fraser read aloud his latest poem.

Oswald Donald Fraser this Cape Bretoner was christened at Antigonish in 1888. But Oswald being 'a hell of a name to tag on a wee helpless Scotchman', Fraser chose to be known all his life as Dawn: at school; in New Brunswick lumber and construction camps; while on the tramp down in New England; in the Canadian army during the First World War; above all, through the 1920s, as a salesman and shopkeeper in Glace Bay.[52]

O nach bochd do Ghaideal fhallain fuireach anns an aite seo, one Glace Bay resident wrote in his native language at this time. 'Oh isn't it a shame for a healthy Gael to be living in this place, a slave under the heels of tyrants, when he could be happy on a handsome, spreading farm with milk-cows, white sheep, hens, horses . . . and clean work on the surface of the earth, rather than in the black pit of misery.' It was Dawn Fraser's self-appointed, almost bardic, task to articulate in English, and thereby give a wider currency to, resentments of this sort – his lament for the death of an unemployed Newfoundlander, a man by the name of Eddie Crimmins, giving something of an insight both into this Cape Bretoner's writing style and his political philosophy.[53]

> His name was Eddie Crimmins
> And he came from Port aux Basques.
> Besides a chance to live and work,
> He had nothing much to ask . . .
> And yet he starved, he starved, I tell you,
> Back in nineteen twenty-four,
> And before he died he suffered
> As many have before.
> When the mines closed down that winter
> He had nothing left to eat,
> And he starved, he starved, I tell you,
> On your dirty, damnèd street.

As these lines more than amply indicate, Dawn Fraser's poetry drew its inspiration from a long series of bitter struggles between Cape Breton miners and their employers. Strikes in the Sydney coalfield were frequent, protracted and sometimes violent, with the coal company's own police force, the civil police and the Canadian military being deployed, from time to time, against the strikers. But Glace Bay in the 1920s, when these troubles were at their height, was not a place which was readily cowed – even when its streets were occupied by troops armed with machine-guns. 'The miners of Cape Breton are not slave-spirited,' the *Maritime Labor Leader* proclaimed in 1922. 'They come from fighting Scottish ancestors, where the clan spirit was strong, where the burnt cross dipped in blood was carried by the runner and roused the clansmen to the fray.'[54]

This is, to say the least, not the sort of political context in which one normally comes across North Americans referring to their Highland roots. But it is a theme, significantly enough, which has been taken up by modern historians of the Cape Breton mining industry. 'Most of the mines were controlled by outside interests,' writes Del Muise. 'The workforce was predominantly native-born and first-generation urban proletariat. These people took with them to their new environment many of the cultural and kinship relationships that had helped them to survive dispossession in Scotland and resettlement in Cape Breton. To their new masters they soon began to show a close solidarity that was untypical . . . of Canada . . . The sources of this strength lay in the process of migration and the clannishness of these men and women who made up the new society.'[55]

For much of the twentieth century's first three decades, many Cape Breton miners identified politically with that most formidable of North American labour activists, James Bryson McLachlan, leading representative in the Sydney area of the United Mine Workers of America. McLachlan, who came to Cape Breton Island from a Scottish mining district where his attitudes had resulted in his losing his job, stood for election on several occasions to both the Nova Scotia House of Assembly and the Canadian House of Commons – under a socialist banner, to begin with, and afterwards, in the 1920s, on behalf of the Communist Party of Canada.[56]

Although the UMWA man's mining supporters were consistently outvoted in these contests, there was thus initiated in Cape Breton a lingering tradition of political radicalism. It was no coincidence that it was here in the 1960s and the 1970s that the New Democratic Party – then emerging as a leftward-leaning alternative to the Conservatives and Liberals who have dominated this country's politics for more than a century – scored its only electoral successes in the eastern part of Canada. And it was appropriate, perhaps, that when a song recorded by a Canadian singer of Cape Breton and Barra ancestry, Rita MacNeil, became an international hit in 1990, the song in question, *Working Man*, should have been a commemoration of the coal-mining life.

* * *

'Whenever I stop to think about it,' one of modern Canada's more significant novelists, Hugh MacLennan, wrote in the 1950s, 'the knowledge that I am three-quarters Scotch, and Highland at that, seems like a kind of doom from which I am too Scotch even to think of praying for deliverance. I can thank my father for this last-ditch neurosis. He was entirely Scotch; he was a living specimen of a most curious heritage. In spite of his medical knowledge, which was large; in spite of his quick nervous vitality and tireless energy, he was never able to lay to rest the beasties which went bump in his mind at three o'clock in the morning. It mattered nothing that he was a third-generation Canadian who had never seen the Highlands before he visited them on leave in the First World War. He never needed to go there to understand whence he came or what he was. He was neither a Scot nor was he Scottish; he never used those genteel appellations which now are supposed to be *de rigueur*. He was simply Scotch. All the perplexity and doggedness of the race was in him, its loneliness, tenderness and affection, its deceptive vitality, its quick flashes of violence, its dog-whistle sensitivity to sounds to which Anglo-Saxons are stone deaf, its incapacity to tell its heart to foreigners save in terms foreigners do not comprehend, its resigned indifference to whether they comprehend or not. *It's not easy being Scotch*, he told me once. To which I suppose another Scotchman might say, *It wasn't meant to be.*'[57]

Hugh MacLennan was born in Glace Bay in March 1907, 'during a blizzard', he wrote years afterwards, 'that shook my father's house as a north-easterly gale drove the Atlantic thundering against the rocky shores of Cape Breton Island'. That house, like practically everything else in Glace Bay, belonged to a coal company – Sam MacLennan, the novelist's Scotch father, being a doctor in that company's employment.[58]

Sam's own father, Duncan, was a tailor in Cape Breton. And Duncan's father, Neil, was one of the many people to come to the island from Kintail in the West Highlands, sailing here on an emigrant ship from Applecross in 1832. It was that ancestry, no doubt, which gave Hugh MacLennan what one critic has called his 'sense of belonging to a wronged people' – a sense reinforced by the fact that the writer's mother, whose name before her marriage was Katherine MacQuarrie, was also descended, on her father's side, from Cape Breton Island's Scottish Highland settlers.[59]

'We're a dispersed people doomed to fight for lost causes,' remarks a character in one of MacLennan's early novels, *Each Man's Son*, a story set in the Cape Breton mining town of the novelist's childhood. 'The houses had all been painted the same fierce shade of iron-oxide red when they were built by the coal company.' The population – consisting of folk 'who had been driven from the outdoors into the pits' – is largely of Highland extraction. 'The women were always on the steps on a fine evening . . . some of the older ones speaking in Gaelic, the others in English with a strong Gaelic accent.'[60]

'Continents are much alike,' MacLennan wrote in his preface to *Each Man's Son*, 'and a man can no more love a continent than he can love a hundred million people. But all the islands of the world are different. They are small enough to be known, they are vulnerable, and men come to feel about them as they do about women. Many men have loved the island of Cape Breton.'[61]

Scottish Highlanders had been in this part of North America 'long enough', MacLennan continued, 'to transfer to Cape Breton the same passionate loyalty their ancestors had felt for the hills of home'. But their feeling for Cape Breton, MacLennan acknowledged, had not been sufficient to keep its people there. Angus Murray, the army doctor who is among the central characters of another Hugh MacLennan novel, *Barometer Rising*, set in Halifax during the First World War, is one of those who have left the island. 'He remembered a day,' MacLennan wrote of Murray, 'when he had arrived home for Christmas after his first term in college. There was no road to his father's valley in these days; it had been necessary to go from Sydney by a small coaster which brought mail and provisions to the Cape Breton outports twice weekly. He had left the ship at the jetty and walked the river road three miles to his father's house . . . His father had taken him out to the barn to cut a sirloin off the frozen carcase of beef that hung there for the winter, and he could still remember the whiteness of the old man's moustache, his soft voice asking questions about college and the life in the city, his gruff manner as he tried to conceal his pride in the fact that his son Angus had the brains to secure a better life than had been possible for his parents.'[62]

That is a scene with which – in their more sentimental moments anyway – enormous numbers of Cape Bretoners could identify, enormous numbers of Scots also; those teachers and engineers and medical men and clerics and journalists and executives whose lives began on Highland crofts or Nova Scotia farms. 'Murray had returned to the little valley . . . in 1914,' MacLennan went on. 'The house had not been painted in twenty years and a stranger lived in it, the land was untidy and one of the barns was not being used, and when he walked up the slope from the river he saw the fences running into a stand of young spruce, and realised that nearly fifty acres of his father's clearings had already reverted to forest.'

In Cape Breton Island, as in the Scottish Highlands, then, the fact that a landscape looks to be both wild and uninhabited does not mean that such a landscape has never been populated. He had not seen such 'sweeps of emptiness' outside the Canadian Arctic, Hugh MacLennan wrote on his return from a visit he once made to his great-grandfather's Kintail. 'But this Highland emptiness, only a few hundred miles above the massed population of England, is a far different thing from the emptiness of our own North West Territories. Above the sixtieth parallel in Canada you feel that nobody but God has ever been there before you, but in a deserted Highland glen you feel that everyone who ever mattered is dead and gone.'[63]

The plane which takes Hugh MacLennan back from Europe is due to land at Gander in Newfoundland but is diverted southwards because of bad weather. A few minutes later, MacLennan writes, 'the sun broke dazzlingly through the window into the cabin. I looked out and there, in a semi-circle of sunshine, the only sunshine apparently in the whole northern hemisphere at that particular moment, lay Cape Breton Island. The plane sloped down to eight thousand feet and I saw beside the Bras d'Or Lake the tiny speck which was the house where my mother and sister at that very moment lay asleep.'[64]

That same day, MacLennan eats lunch in Montreal. The man next to him at the restaurant counter wants to know where he has been and MacLennan tells him he has been in the Scottish Highlands. 'It must have been nice,' the man says. 'It was,' MacLennan answers. 'But it's also nice to be home.' Then this Cape Bretoner asks both himself and his readers: 'Am I wrong, or is it true that it is only now, after so many years of not knowing who we were or wanted to be, that we Canadians of Scotch descent are truly at home in the northern half of North America?'

CHAPTER SEVEN

Lords of the Lakes and the Forests

TAKE ONE OF THOSE globes which were once standard pieces of equipment in any schoolroom, place a finger just above the little town of Stornoway on the eastern coast of the Hebridean island of Lewis and rotate the globe in an anticlockwise direction. The line of latitude thus traced westwards passes 300 miles to the south of Iceland and 100 miles to the south of Cape Farewell in Greenland. It crosses the North American coast some 900 miles to the north of Cape Breton at a spot not far below the entrance to the Hudson Strait which separates Labrador from Baffin Island. Then, having swept some 600 miles overland without encountering a single human habitation, this same line of latitude bisects Hudson Bay, coming ashore at a spot a little to the north of York Factory which, for some two centuries, was the principal North American base of that most renowned of all fur-trading corporations, the Hudson's Bay Company. Moving westwards again for another 600 or 700 miles, across the northernmost regions of the Canadian provinces of Manitoba and Saskatchewan, you come eventually to the 200-mile-long Lake Athabasca, its westernmost end projecting into the north-eastern corner of Alberta. Here, not far from the place where the Slave River exits northwards from the lake and on exactly the same latitude as Stornoway, is Fort Chipewyan, selected as his centre of operations, in the years around 1790, by an especially ambitious fur trader whose name was Alexander MacKenzie.

MacKenzie, who had been born in Stornoway in 1764, was twenty-three years old when he first made his way into the Athabasca country which, in the 1780s, was just beginning to yield a particularly rich crop of furs. But already his life had been more than usually eventful. Alexander's father, Kenneth MacKenzie, who tenanted a farm, or tack, at Melbost, a mile or two to the east of modern Stornoway's airport, belonged to one of those relatively well-to-do families whose social position was seriously threatened by the many changes which occurred in the Scottish Highlands in the period following the Battle of Culloden. It was to men of Kenneth MacKenzie's type – men who were having both their financial position and their social status undermined by rent increases of the kind which were being enforced energetically in Lewis in the early 1770s – that pro-emigration pamphleteers like Scotus Americanus principally addressed their tracts. Whether or not such works made their way into Kenneth MacKenzie's Lewis home, the Melbost tacksman, a number of whose relatives had already taken themselves across the Atlantic, certainly proved as susceptible to the idea of emigration as others of his time and class. In 1774, having been left in sole charge of his several children as a result of his wife's early death, Kenneth MacKenzie did what so many other Highland tacksmen were then doing. He sailed for North America.[1]

It was Kenneth MacKenzie's intention to settle in upcountry New York. As happened to those MacDonell tacksmen who arrived in the colony at the same time, however, MacKenzie quickly became embroiled in the Revolutionary War, fighting on the loyalist side in one of Sir John Johnson's units and dying of disease while still a serving officer. Alexander, who was a boy of ten on his arrival in America, had meanwhile been entrusted to the care of two aunts who had taken him first to the Mohawk Valley and afterwards to Canada. There the womenfolk joined Alexander's uncle, John MacKenzie, who had also been a loyalist officer and who had been granted, as a result, a tract of farmland in Glengarry County. As for the young Alexander, after a year or two's schooling in Montreal he was taken on as a clerk by one of that city's fur-trading firms – a firm which, as it happened, was soon to ally itself with the much larger fur-trading consortium known as the North West Company.

It was as a full partner in the North West Company that Alexander MacKenzie was posted to Athabasca in the summer of 1787, travelling by canoe from Montreal on the rivers and lakes which provided North America's fur traders with their means of communication. Lake Athabasca is considerably further from Montreal than Moscow or Istanbul are from Edinburgh. But such is the extent of the waterways of which he was able to take advantage that only twice in the course of his initial venture into the North American interior was it necessary for Alexander MacKenzie's canoe to be carried more than a relatively short distance overland. The first of these two major portages – some nine miles in length – was made a little to the west of Lake Superior on the watershed which separates those rivers which drain into the Atlantic by way of the St Lawrence from those other rivers, like the Red and the Saskatchewan, which flow ultimately into Hudson Bay. His second such overland traverse – of about twelve miles – was the one which took MacKenzie across the further watershed beyond which the land slopes towards the Arctic Ocean, still more than a thousand miles to the north.[2]

This was the so-called Methy Portage which ends, or so it was reported in 1844 by a Royal Artillery surveyor, John Henry Lefroy, on a steep bluff high above the Clearwater River. The Clearwater is a west-ward-flowing tributary of the northward-flowing Athabasca, a river which eventually empties itself into the lake of the same name. From his vantage-point on the slopes above the first of these two great water-courses, Lefroy wrote, he found himself looking out across 'a wide and regular valley, of great depth, stretching for a distance of thirty miles to the west. The sun was just setting as I arrived there, the light gleaming from the nearer foliage and filling the distance with golden haze . . . The Clearwater River winds through the midst, sometimes expanding into a placid little lake, then diminishing to a thread of light, barely caught among the trees. Upon the whole, I have seen few views more beautiful.'[3]

The territory to which the Clearwater and the Athabasca give access is an enormous one. Today the drainage basin of which these two rivers form part is known to be exceeded in size in all the Americas only by the basins of the Amazon and the Mississippi. Its area is greater than that of Western Europe. It stretches across three time zones and its prin-cipal river – the one which now bears Alexander MacKenzie's name – is longer than the Volga.[4]

The Methy Portage safely behind him, MacKenzie came at last to Lake Athabasca, getting there in mid-October 1787, just as winter was beginning. Here he established the trading post which – because this was the name of the locality's native people – became known as Fort Chipewyan. And here MacKenzie wintered in the company of a veteran fur trader called Peter Pond.

Pond, who had been born in Connecticut in 1740 and who had served alongside British regiments like Fraser's Highlanders in the course of the French and Indian War, had made his way into the Athabasca country in 1778, subsequently shipping back to Montreal beaver pelts of a uniformly higher quality than the city's fur-trading houses had ever before handled. Now Pond – at 47 an old man by fur-trade standards – was about to retire to the United States. But in the course of the winter which he and Alexander MacKenzie devoted to gathering in still more pelts from the Indian trappers and hunters in their vicinity, Pond managed to ensure that his suspicions about the geography of the Athabasca country would be acted upon by the young Highlander who was to take over from him as the North West Company's principal repre-sentative in the region. That Lake Athabasca was drained by the Slave

River which flowed, in turn, into the huge body of water known as the Great Slave Lake, Alexander MacKenzie already knew. What he heard from Peter Pond during the bitterly cold and snowy months the two men spent together was something else entirely. By way of a still unexplored river flowing from the Great Slave Lake, Pond suggested, it might take a canoe party no more than half a dozen days to reach the Pacific Ocean.[5]

For nearly three hundred years, ever since the pioneering voyages of Christopher Columbus and John Cabot had established that the continent of North America barred the westward route from Europe to Asia, men had been looking for a way across or around the enormous landmass which is occupied today by the United States and Canada. No such way had ever been found. Now Alexander MacKenzie made up his mind to be its discoverer. This would be no easy task. 'I had to encounter perils by land and perils by water,' MacKenzie wrote later of his explorations. 'The toil of our navigation was incessant and oftentimes extreme.' But the possibility of his being unable to attain his objective was not one which this tall, fair-haired Highlander was ever prepared to consider for any length of time. 'Being endowed by nature,' as he once commented, 'with an inquisitive mind and enterprising spirit, possessing also a constitution and frame of body equal to the most arduous undertakings,' Alexander MacKenzie clearly thought himself perfectly capable of succeeding where so many had previously failed.[6]

The summer of 1788 was spent conveying the winter's harvest of furs eastwards to the point, not far from the western end of Lake Superior, at which these furs were transferred to other North West Company canoe parties which had set out from Montreal at about the same time as MacKenzie was leaving the Athabasca country. But the following summer, so Peter Pond's successor in that quarter now began to make clear to his North West Company associates, he intended to be heading west instead of east.

As in most such instances of human endeavour, Alexander MacKenzie's motives were nothing if not mixed. He was driven partly, one might safely guess, by a simple urge to see what lay beyond the next bend in the river, the next lake, the next ridge. But he was impelled onwards also by a commercial and strategic vision almost global in its scope. The North West Company, despite its very brief existence and its comparative lack of political and financial clout in London, was already shipping more furs to Britain than the much longer-established Hudson's Bay Company. But MacKenzie wanted to open up the Pacific, as well as the Atlantic, to North American trade. If furs from the Athabasca country could be got as readily to the continent's western rim as they could be got to the St Lawrence, then those furs could be transported directly to the lucrative Chinese market which had previously been dominated by Russian traders operating out of Siberia but which was now, as Alexander MacKenzie seems to have known or suspected, increasingly in need of new sources of supply.

To most people of MacKenzie's time and later, the term Canada implied no more than it had meant since the French had first applied this Iroquois word to their settlements on the St Lawrence. Canada was still the relatively confined locality to the north and east of the Great Lakes. But in Alexander MacKenzie's mind, as he assessed what he had heard from Peter Pond and learned what he could of the geography of the Pacific, the concept of an altogether different Canada was beginning to take shape. This would be a Canada of continental scope and international significance; a Canada looking west as well as east; a Canada dealing with Asia as well as with Europe. No such Canada, of course, would take shape politically until long after Alexander MacKenzie's death. But his exploratory journeys would go no small way to making the modern country possible.

The opening entry in the journal which Alexander MacKenzie kept by him during the first of his excursions into the North American wilds is dated Wednesday, 3 June 1789. 'We embarked at nine o'clock in the morning at Fort Chipewyan,' it begins. There follow details of MacKenzie's party which consisted of the four Québecois voyageurs, François Barrieu, Charles Ducette, Joseph Landry and Pierre Delorme, the wives of two of these voyageurs, John Steinbruick, a German whose presence in the Athabasca country has not been explained, a Chipewyan Indian known as English Chief and various other Chipewyans, both men and women, whose names seem never to have been recorded. Into this party's four canoes there had been loaded guns, ammunition, tents, food, fishing nets, blankets, trade goods and the all-important navigational instruments which MacKenzie was to use to determine his progress towards the sea.[7]

It is suggestive of the climate in this part of North America that, though it was barely a fortnight short of midsummer when Alexander MacKenzie's trip commenced, the explorer's party left Fort Chipewyan in a snowstorm. Nor did the weather improve greatly in the days ahead. The snow was succeeded by rain which 'came on so hard', MacKenzie recorded, 'that we were obliged to land and unload to prevent our goods getting wet'. Drenched, frozen and tormented by 'muskettows', 'gnatts' and other insects, the expedition reached the Great Slave Lake towards the end of its first week – only to find this expanse of water still so choked with winter ice as to make it difficult to discover the outlet leading to the river which Peter Pond had said would turn out to link the Great Slave Lake with the Pacific.[8]

Not until 29 June, almost four weeks out from Fort Chipewyan, did Alexander MacKenzie finally find himself afloat on the spectacular watercourse which is his principal commemoration on the map of modern Canada. At first the river tended towards the west which, of course, was the direction in which MacKenzie wished to go. Before more than three or four days had passed, however, it was beginning to be apparent that Peter Pond had hopelessly miscalculated. Stretching right across the western horizon were the Rocky Mountains – 'the tops of them hid in the clouds', as MacKenzie noted ruefully. There could be no easily navigable route to the Pacific in that direction.[9]

Now the great river was more and more carrying the canoe-borne party northwards or north-westwards at a rate of as much as a hundred miles a day. On 3 July, in an attempt to spy out the nature of the terrain around them, Alexander MacKenzie and two of his Québecois voyageurs came ashore to climb a hill. But the resulting view was curtailed by other summits. All that was to be seen, the Highlander observed, were 'numbers of small lakes upon which we could perceive many swans. The country appeared very thinly wooded, a few trees of the pine and birch, very small in size. We were obliged to shorten our stay here on account of the swarms of muskettoes that attacked us and were the only inhabitants of the place.'[10]

Several more days passed. Occasionally the channel was obstructed by sandbars, by driftwood, by great mounds of ice swept downstream by the current. Occasionally there were rapids which MacKenzie described as seething with a noise like a kettle and which Hugh MacLennan, who made this same journey on a river tugboat in the 1950s, was to find peculiarly disconcerting. 'They swirl at depth and at a speed sometimes as high as twelve knots,' MacLennan wrote of those Mackenzie River rapids, 'and when you look at them the whole surface of the river seems to be quivering.'[11]

MacKenzie portaged his canoes around the most savage of these obstacles. But he and his voyageurs chose to shoot the majority of the rapids they encountered, MacKenzie becoming all the while increasingly concerned as to where the river was taking him. Those permanently snowbound outliers of the Rockies which were afterwards named the Mackenzie Mountains – 'running to the northward as far as we could see' – were now a constant presence on the Highlander's left as he gazed anxiously downriver. 'I am much at a loss here how to act,' he wrote on 10 July, 'being certain that my going farther in this direction will not answer the purpose of which the voyage was intended, as it is evident that these waters must empty themselves into the Northern Ocean.' The next day's entry in MacKenzie's journal contained one more piece of evidence as to how far he was beyond the sphere of European influence: 'I sat up last night to observe at what time the sun would set, but found that he did not set at all.' Forest had given way to tundra, Indian encampments to those of the Inuit or, as men of MacKenzie's background then called this northern people, Esquimaux. The fur trader's travels, it was clear, had now taken him beyond the Arctic Circle.[12]

On 10 July MacKenzie assured his Chipewyan companions that, irrespective of where their party might then be, he would turn southwards again at the end of one more week. But this was a promise which the explorer was to have no need to keep. Some three days later and another two hundred miles or so to the north, the character of the river changed dramatically. Where there had been one channel there were now several. MacKenzie got a glimpse of creatures which he reckoned to be whales and that evening the party's campsite was almost inundated by an incoming tide. Alexander MacKenzie had not reached the Pacific, but he had certainly reached the sea. 'This morning,' he now wrote, 'I fixed a post close by our campment on which I engraved the latitude of the place, my own name and the number of men with me and the time we had been here.' It was 14 July 1789, the day, as it happened, on which the Bastille fell to the Parisian crowds who were just then precipitating the French Revolution. Alexander MacKenzie had covered some 1,075 miles in a fortnight. He had travelled more than 1,500 miles from Fort Chipewyan, some 4,000 miles from Montreal – the latter distance being greater, by many hundreds of miles, than the length of the sea crossing from Scotland to the St Lawrence. It was time to start for home.[13]

The downstream voyage from the Great Slave Lake to the Arctic Ocean had taken thirteen or fourteen days. It was not the least of Alexander MacKenzie's many achievements that the upstream journey, undertaken in the teeth of swift currents which were now as much of a hindrance as they had previously been a help, was accomplished in only thirty-two days. There was an urgent need for haste. It was now well into August and the short northern summer was drawing to a close. The imminent freeze-up would make river travel impossible and MacKenzie, with the Great Slave Lake and the Slave River still to master, had no desire to overwinter in the wilderness. On 11 September his journal recorded hard frost and an 'appearance of snow'. But this was less alarming than it might have been, for next day he was back in Fort Chipewyan.[14]

From a purely commercial perspective, the Mackenzie River was of little immediate interest. It did not provide a means of getting to the Pacific. It gave access to no new fur-bearing areas – most of its course lying outside the forest regions favoured by the beavers on whose pelts the North West Company primarily depended. Alexander MacKenzie was consequently unsurprised by the fact that his explorations were scarcely mentioned by his Montreal-based partners when he travelled east to meet them in the summer of 1790. 'My expedition was hardly spoken of, but that is what I expected,' he reported to his cousin, Roderick MacKenzie, then working with him in the Athabasca country.[15]

But the young man from Lewis had not yet given up on his ambition of getting clear across the North American continent. For all that it had yielded much new geographical knowledge, his great voyage, he felt, had shown him to be 'deficient in the sciences of astronomy and navigation'. He was, MacKenzie admitted, unable to fix his position as accurately as he would have wished. It was with a view to acquiring the necessary skills, and with a view clearly to preparing himself for another attempt on the Pacific, that he now crossed the Atlantic to spend the winter of 1791–92 in London.[16]

By the fall of 1792, having again made the long journey from Montreal, MacKenzie was back at Fort Chipewyan. In order to give himself something of a head start in the spring, however, he had made up his mind to winter that year further to the west. So now he headed some three hundred miles up the Peace River, which joins the Slave not far from Lake Athabasca, with a view to making a temporary headquarters just to the east of the Rockies and several hundred miles to the south of even the upper reaches of the Mackenzie River.

MacKenzie's principal collaborator in this new venture was another young fur trader of Scottish Highland extraction, Alexander MacKay, whose father had served with the 78th Highlanders at Louisbourg and Quebec and who had afterwards made his home in the Mohawk Valley where Alexander had been born in 1770. The MacKay family, like so many others of similar background, had made the hazardous trek from the Mohawk country to Glengarry County with the coming of American independence and the young Alexander, along with his two brothers, had eventually become clerks – as Alexander MacKenzie himself had previously done – in one or other of the Montreal trading houses which together constituted the North West Company.[17]

MacKenzie and MacKay resumed their westward push on 9 May 1793 – through hill landscapes, as the Lewisman observed, of quite amazing grandeur. They were accompanied by two Indian guides and by six voyageurs, two of whom were among those who had earlier been with MacKenzie to the Arctic. The little party's plan, in principle, was simplicity itself. They would ascend the Peace or such of its tributaries as seemed likely to take them furthest into the mountains. They would cross the continental watershed, carrying their canoes, and search out, on the far side of the Rockies, a navigable and westward-flowing stream. They would then sail down that stream to the ocean.

As things turned out, there was very little portaging required to get from the Peace River system to the Fraser River which reaches the sea at Vancouver and which was afterwards to be explored by that other North West Company trader whose name it bears. But MacKenzie – knowing nothing of the Fraser but being aware, as a result of information gleaned from the results of maritime exploration in the Pacific, of the existence of the Columbia River whose lower reaches now form the border between Oregon and Washington State – came to the erroneous conclusion that the Fraser River was likely to take him as far south as the Mackenzie River had earlier taken him north. He consequently abandoned this particular torrent and struck out again into the further mountain ranges to the west. Here Alexander MacKenzie and Alexander MacKay, along with their Québecois and Indian companions, eventually

picked up the Bella Coola River which the exploration party now followed to the sea.

Even today, when it takes two or three days of steady driving to
make the trip on the Trans-Canada Highway from Calgary to Banff and
on by way of the Kicking Horse Pass to Kamloops, Hope and Vancouver,
it is impossible not to be awed by the quite tremendous scale of
Alexander MacKenzie's accomplishment. The country here is of a vast-
ness which is difficult for a visiting Scot to comprehend. One range of
inaccessible-seeming, snowy, glacier-festooned peaks follows always on
another. The roaring rivers, their waters stained a grey-green colour by
glacial silt, look less like a means of communication than a series of insuperable obstacles to human travel. The forest, should you venture even
a couple of hundred yards from the road, has an impenetrable, slightly
frightening feel to it. And always there is about the landscape that sense
of sheer immensity which, to the European mind, is both fascinating and
intimidating. You look at the map and think that, if such a thing were
possible, you could abandon your car at this or that spot and walk northwards, southwards, westwards for hundreds upon hundreds of miles
without stumbling across much in the way of evidence that humanity has
ever exercised any worthwhile influence on this continent. You consider
the implications of the fact that you could lose virtually the whole of
Scotland in a single Rocky Mountain valley. You wonder how it felt to
be Alexander MacKenzie on that summer morning just over two
hundred years ago when this Highlander, still in his twenties but already
understanding more about the geography of the western part of North
America than any other man alive, realised that his canoe was floating in
saltwater.

For all that he had been groping more or less blindly westwards
since leaving the Peace country, MacKenzie had travelled some 1,200
miles in only seventy-four days, 960 of those miles on streams and rivers,
the remaining 240 on foot. It would take him only thirty-three days to
get back to Fort Chipewyan. He would return there from the Pacific, as
he had previously returned from the Arctic, having lost no member of his
party and having fired no shot in anger. He had, as he would have known
better than anyone, pioneered no very practicable route by which the
North West Company might develop links with China. But he had staked
a claim, which his North West Company colleagues and successors afterwards enforced strongly, to a Canadian presence on the Pacific Ocean.
And it was by way of making just this point that Alexander MacKenzie,
in a mixture of vermilion and beargrease, now inscribed on a rock at
Bella Coola, some three hundred miles to the north of modern
Vancouver, the words which still stand as a memorial to this most
remarkable Scottish Highlander. 'Alexander Mackenzie,' he wrote.
'From Canada by Land. 22 July 1793.'[18]

* * *

Montreal, now one of North America's leading commercial centres, its skyline dominated by the stalagmite-like cluster of highrise buildings projecting from the city's business district, was still a small town in Alexander MacKenzie's time. And Lachine, which has since become a bustling, expensive, riverside suburb on Montreal's western boundary, was then a wholly separate village located just a mile or two upstream from the St Lawrence River rapids which had foiled Jacques Cartier's sixteenth-century attempt to do what MacKenzie was eventually to accomplish – find a North American route to the Pacific.

Above Lachine the St Lawrence, which is joined in this vicinity by the Ottawa River, once more widens. The resulting body of water, stretching away to the south-west, is known as Lac St Louis. Today it is popular with the owners of the many yachts and cruisers moored in the various marinas strung out along the riverfront. You do not need to take to the water to appreciate modern Lachine, however. This is now a most attractive spot from any standpoint; a place of parks and cycleways and restaurants; one of the localities where Montrealers clearly like to spend their summer Sunday afternoons.

But in May 1798, or so one gathers from the account provided by an 18-year-old Royal Engineers lieutenant then on his way to supervise the construction of a military strongpoint in the Great Lakes region, Lachine still possessed something of the character of a frontier outpost. The road taken by the carriage conveying George Landmann from Montreal 'scarcely deserved such a name', in this young officer's opinion: 'It was at first rough enough, but on advancing it entered a wood where everyone followed his own fancy. The surface was covered . . . thickly with stones, each of them large enough to upset any kind of vehicle, and these were partly standing in water so that in proceeding it would not infrequently happen that in turning this way to avoid one of these masses you plunged the wheel of your carriage on the other side into a deep hole in the ground concealed by water.'[19]

But Landmann, despite the inadequacies of a track which has long since disappeared beneath a plethora of streets and highways, was by no means travelling alone. Lachine, on that May morning, was the setting for a carnival-like festival in which many Montrealers – of whom there were then 9,000 or so in total – eagerly participated. Winter, with its deep snows and penetrating frosts, had not long ended. The winners of the annual lottery as to when the ice would break on the St Lawrence had just collected their prize money. Now it was time to be off to Lachine to watch the North West Company's canoe brigades launch their annual forays into the interior from a spot where there is still preserved one of the fur-trading concern's stonebuilt warehouses.

Accompanying Landmann from Montreal to Lachine, where they no doubt intended to cast a supervisory eye over proceedings, were several of the North West Company's senior representatives. These men, the lieutenant reported, were 'natives of the Highlands of Scotland so that I was the only *foreigner* among them'. And it was clearly with a growing feeling of participating in an alien ritual that George Landmann – invited to a nearby house where 'an abundant luncheon was waiting' – found himself drawn into the lavish celebrations which habitually surrounded the North West Company's commencement of its trading season.

'We sat down,' the young man subsequently remembered, 'and, without loss of time, expedited the lunch intended to supersede a dinner, during which time the bottle had freely circulated, raising the old Highland drinking propensity, so that there was no stopping it.' From every quarter came 'Highland speeches and sayings, Highland reminiscences and Highland farewells'. What Landmann called 'the doch and dorich', the Gaelic toast proposed to departing friends, was to be heard 'over and over again'. Such was the 'extraordinary energy' with which these proceedings were 'kept up', the army officer confessed, 'that by six or seven o'clock, I had, in common with many of the others, fallen from my seat'.

Eventually, two men only remained sitting at the table on which the meal of several hours before had been served. One of the two was Alexander MacKenzie. The other was William MacGillivray who shared rooms in Montreal with the now famed explorer and who, like MacKenzie, was a partner in the North West Company. 'MacKenzie now proposed to drink to our memory and then to give the war-whoop over us, fallen foes or friends, all nevertheless on the floor, and in attempting to push the bottle to MacGillivray, at the opposite end of the table, he slid off his chair and could not recover his seat, whilst MacGillivray, in extending himself over the table in the hope of seizing the bottle which MacKenzie had attempted to push to him, also in like manner began to slide on one side and fell helpless on the floor.'

Now it was time for George Landmann to take his leave of these gloriously inebriated Highland traders and somehow make his way down to the waterside where there waited an altogether different set of people – their native language French instead of the Gaelic favoured, in his more sentimental moments anyway, by a fur-trade *bourgeois*, or boss, like Alexander MacKenzie or William MacGillivray. 'No men in the world are more severely worked than these Canadian voyageurs,' Landmann wrote of the Québecois on whom the North West Company ultimately depended. 'I have known them to work in a canoe for twenty-four hours out of twenty-four and go at that rate during a fortnight or three weeks without a day of rest or a diminution of labour.' The typical voyageur's only means of easing his toil, the army officer continued, was to reach for his pipe or to strike up one of those airs traditionally associated with the fur trade. 'They smoke almost incessantly and sing peculiar songs which are the same as their fathers and grandfathers, and probably their great-grandfathers, sang before them. The time is about that of our military quick marches and is marked by the movement of their paddles. They rest from five to ten minutes every two hours when they refill their pipes. It is more common for them to describe distances by so many pipes than in any other way.'[20]

As George Landmann commented, these Québecois canoemen belonged to families long connected with the fur trade. Their predecessors, who had left France to settle along the banks of the St Lawrence in the seventeenth century, were among the first Europeans to venture beyond the Great Lakes. Although subject since the 1760s to British rule rather than to the governance of the French aristocrats who had previously administered the countryside around Montreal and Quebec, the population from which the North West Company drew its French-speaking workforce retained many of the characteristics delineated in a report written in 1737 by one of the colonial officials sent here from Paris. 'They love distinctions and attentions, pride themselves on their bravery and are extremely sensitive to slights and punishments,' this man commented of Quebec's settlers. They were also, he added, perhaps a little superfluously in view of the distances which individual Québecois had already journeyed in search of furs, greatly given to 'hunting and exploring'.[21]

'They are short, thickset and active, and never tire,' a visiting American commented of the Canadian – or, as a later generation would have put it, French-Canadian – voyageurs he met on coming north in 1826. 'A Canadian,' this traveller went on 'if born to be a labourer, deems himself to be very unfortunate if he should chance to grow over five feet five, or six, inches – and if he should reach five feet ten, or eleven, it forever excludes him from the privilege of becoming a voyageur. There is no room for the legs of such people in canoes. But if he shall stop growing at five feet four inches, and be gifted with a good voice and lungs that never tire, he is considered as having been born under a most favourable star.'[22]

Perhaps. The Québecois voyageur, like the Glengarry County lumberjack, was certainly proud of his abilities. But both were involved in singularly dangerous and disabling trades. Practically every portage on the river routes linking Lachine with Lake Superior, the Red River, Athabasca and the Pacific had its quota of little wooden crosses marking the last resting-place of voyageurs who had died from injury, from drowning or, in all too many instances, from the sheer strain of carrying a one-and-a-half or two hundredweight load of furs or trade goods around one more waterfall, one more set of rapids. What primarily impelled French-Canadians into the fur trade was exactly what drove their Glengarry counterparts into lumbering – the difficulty of making a good living from a St Lawrence Valley farm. And just as the Glengarry man's undoubted skill with an axe did not preclude his exploitation by nineteenth-century lumber companies, neither did the voyageur's unrivalled proficiency as a riverman prevent the fruits of his labours accruing primarily to the merchants in whose interest the fur trade out of Montreal and the St Lawrence was invariably managed.

Those merchants were in the business of trying to satisfy an almost inexhaustible demand for the beaver pelts required for the manufacture of the fine felt which supplied successive generations of Europeans, from the time of William Shakespeare to the era of Charles Dickens, with their hats. Once the controlling luminaries of this trade – a trade which was the key to such wealth as eighteenth-century Montreal possessed – had been French. In the years following the British conquest of New France, however, they were mostly Scottish Highlanders.

Most of the traffic approaching Inverness by way of the Great Glen follows the modern highway through Drumnadrochit on the northern shore of Loch Ness. But there is an alternative, much less frequented, route to the south of the loch. To take it, you leave the main road at Fort Augustus and head south-eastwards through Glendoebeg until, just above Loch nan Eun, you find yourself, from an altitude of some 1,300 feet, looking down into the wide and nowadays well-wooded valley of Stratherrick.

The road here is unusually straight by Highland standards, striking across the hillside with an almost total disregard for natural features of the sort which would normally produce in the north of Scotland a protracted series of sharp bends. This is because the highway in question is one of the type which James Wolfe spent so many unhappy months constructing in the period following the last Jacobite rebellion. Like others of its sort, this road was built with a view to facilitating the rapid movement of the troops whose task it was to pacify the clans. It was consequently better made than the general run of Highland thoroughfares.

Prince Charles Edward Stuart came here to Stratherrick on the afternoon of 16 April 1746, fleeing with two or three guides and companions from the carnage of Culloden, a few miles to the east, where the Duke of Cumberland's redcoats were still busy with the bloody job of finishing off the Highland wounded. That evening at Gorthleck, on the north shore of Loch Mhor, a narrow stretch of water in the middle part of Stratherrick, the prince met the elderly Lord Lovat who was soon to pay with his life for having thrown in his lot with the Jacobite cause. Lovat was asked if Charles Edward Stuart should now put himself at the head of a guerilla campaign in order to maintain some sort of armed resistance to Cumberland and, still more, to Cumberland's father, King George II. The alternative was that the Jacobite prince should strike westwards through the mountains as a prelude to making his escape to France. This was what Lovat is reported to have advised. A political schemer of longstanding, he no doubt knew as well as anyone when some particular game should finally be given up. And though even Lovat was to find it impossible on this occasion to retrieve his own position, his son, Simon Fraser, was eventually – as already mentioned – to discover in America the means of restoring the Lovat family's fortunes. Here in Stratherrick, one of the several Fraser estates to be confiscated by a vengeful Hanoverian régime, Simon enlisted several hundred of the soldiers who, at Louisbourg and Quebec, would do so much to restore the Lovat name to favour.[23]

Among the men thus recruited to the 78th Highlanders was John MacTavish who had fought on the Jacobite side at Culloden and whose family occupied the tack of Garthbeg at the southern end of Loch Mhor. MacTavish, who held the rank of lieutenant, served in North America for the duration of the French and Indian War, getting back to Scotland in 1763. Garthbeg, to which this veteran soldier now returned, is a pleasant spot. Just behind its stonebuilt farmhouse are the rocky slopes of Carn na Glaice Moire. In front are fertile fields which slope gently down to the sheltered waters of Loch Mhor. But John MacTavish had seen enough of Britain's transatlantic colonies to suspect, as so many other tacksmen of the time suspected, that these colonies might offer rather better prospects than even the more attractively situated parts of the Scottish Highlands. When one of his fellow-officers, Hugh Fraser, declared his intention both to marry Elizabeth, one of MacTavish's daughters, and to settle with her in the Mohawk Valley, the Garthsbeg tacksman arranged for his son, Simon, then a boy of thirteen, to accompany the emigrant couple. So it came about that Simon MacTavish, instead of becoming a Stratherrick farmer, found himself apprenticed into the North American fur trade.[24]

The young Simon's initial base was Albany which had been familiar to so many Highland military men in the course of the campaign against New France and which was the commercial centre in easiest reach of the various Highland communities in the Mohawk country. But MacTavish, yet another of those New York loyalists set adrift by the Revolutionary War, moved north in the later 1770s, settling finally in Montreal where, during the 1780s, he became that city's leading businessman and, as such, the driving force behind the formation of the North West Company.

A variety of freelance traders – Englishmen and New Englanders as well as Scots – had been endeavouring ever since the 1760s, and with varying degrees of success, to reconstitute in their own interest the fur-trading empire which New France had maintained in the territories around and beyond the Great Lakes. MacTavish's vital contribution to this effort was to provide these previously disunited entrepreneurs both with decisive leadership and with a sense of common purpose.[25]

It was possibly by way of emphasising his determination to be seen as the foremost inheritor of the commercial power exercised by French-ruled Montreal that Simon MacTavish, on marrying at the comparatively late age of forty-three, chose as his wife Marie Marguerite Chaboillez. Marie Marguerite's father, Charles Jean Baptiste Chaboillez, who had himself been born in the western interior, belonged to a family which had been involved in the fur business for the better part of a century. Simon MacTavish, it seems likely, saw no small advantage to himself in thus entering into a formal alliance with his principal Québecois predecessors in the trade.[26]

But it was to the Scottish Highlands, and primarily to his own connections there, that Simon MacTavish looked for most of the associates he needed to help consolidate and perpetuate his grip on the furs which then constituted North America's most lucrative resource. Eventually the North West Company – which was not so much a tight-knit corporation of the modern type as a voluntary partnership among a number of powerful individuals – was to contain in its higher reaches at least fourteen of its founder's relatives. In the importance which he thus attached to kinship, it is not too fanciful to discern something of the continuing influence on Simon MacTavish of the clan-orientated community into which he had been born. The extent of this influence is emphasised by the especially close nature of the family link between MacTavish and the man who would one day be his heir and successor. This was William MacGillivray whom George Landmann had so spectacularly encountered at Lachine in the course of the festivities surrounding the 1798 departure of the North West Company's westbound canoe fleet.[27]

One of Simon MacTavish's sisters, Elizabeth, had married a man who expected her immediately to emigrate to North America and to assist him set up home in the Mohawk Valley. Another MacTavish sister, Ann, in contrast, travelled no more than six or seven miles from her Garthbeg birthplace on marrying Donald MacGillivray who belonged, like Ann's own father, to one of the many traditionally Jacobite families then to be found in this part of the Highlands. MacGillivray's tack was situated on the upper reaches of the River Farigaig which straddles the boundary between Stratherrick and Strathnairn. The land hereabouts is comparatively poor and both Ann and Donald, who had a dozen children, must have felt no small sense of relief when Simon MacTavish, while on a visit to Scotland in 1776, offered to take financial responsibilty for the education and upbringing of his nephew, William, then a boy of eleven or twelve. Eight years later, William MacGillivray, already destined for rapid promotion in the fur trade, was overwintering far to the west of Lake Superior at the start of a career which was to culminate in his taking over the bulk of his uncle's business interests on the latter's death in 1804.[28]

William's younger brothers, Duncan and Simon, were each to be drawn into the North West Company. So was another young Highlander of very similar pedigree, John MacDonald, whose people came originally from the Braes of Lochaber and who was pugnaciously given to asserting his descent from the medieval Lords of the Isles. MacDonald's grand-father was yet another veteran of the Battle of Culloden. The fur trader's father, for his part, had seen active service in one of the other Highland regiments which accompanied the 78th to North America in the 1750s. And John himself, or so he said, had inclined also to a military career. But being afflicted from childhood with a withered arm, a characteristic which led to his being dubbed *Le Bras Croché* by the voyageurs with whom he worked, John MacDonald became instead a partner in the North West Company. There, in order to differentiate himself from the many other MacDonalds involved in the organisation, Le Bras Croché – on the grounds that his father, on retiring from the army, had purchased a small property in that part of Perthshire – took to insisting on the tacks-man-like title of MacDonald of Garth.[29]

The fact that William MacGillivray's second wife was John Mac-Donald's sister is one more piece of testimony to the North West Company's tendency to be both a business concern and an enormously extended family of the traditional Scottish Highland type. There is much more evidence to the same effect. Thus Roderick MacKenzie, another of the company's many partners, was not merely Alexander MacKenzie's cousin. He was also the brother-in-law of Simon MacTavish's wife – having married, as MacTavish himself had done, into the Chaboillez family of Montreal. So matters continued as long as the North West Company existed. Simon Fraser, who was to follow in Alexander Mac-Kenzie's footsteps to the Rockies and beyond, was Simon MacTavish's kinsman. So was John Fraser, one of the company's London agents. So, too, was John George MacTavish, a notable fur trader in his own right.[30]

Around this MacTavish dynasty, in the manner of those 'septs' so beloved of Scotland's clan historians, there clustered a number of par-tially separate groupings. One of them centred on Norman MacLeod who came originally from Duirinish in Skye and who entered the fur trade by way of service with Fraser's Highlanders and a subsequent sojourn in the Mohawk Valley. MacLeod was eventually to be instru-mental in having his nephew, Alexander MacLeod, follow him into the North West Company. Plenty other fur traders of Highland extraction were similarly to ease their kinsmen into the business – an especially striking example of the practice being provided by the history of the North West Company post at Fort Tamiskaming in Quebec. Aeneas Cameron from Glen Livet took charge here in 1793. In time, Aeneas was succeeded by his nephew, Angus Cameron, who, in turn, was followed by *his* nephew, James Cameron – with James giving way finally to his cousin, Charles Stuart.[31]

Simon MacTavish and William MacGillivray were both to equip themselves with the expected status symbols of their time. Each of them took the trouble to acquire Scottish coats-of-arms. And MacGillivray went so far as to buy a small Highland estate. But the North West

Company's ability to gain direct access to a British prime minister – as demonstrated, for example, in the course of a trip made by MacTavish to London in 1790 – owed nothing to such foibles. It depended entirely on these Scottish Highlanders having made themselves the men who mattered most in Montreal.[32]

'MacTavish,' the Earl of Selkirk noted while spending some time in the city in 1804, 'is entirely unequalled here in acuteness and reach of thought.' *Le Marquis*, the North West Company's prime mover was called by Montrealers. This, perhaps, was something of an ironic tribute – Simon MacTavish's purchase of a former French seigneury and his lavish spending on his house in St Jean-Baptiste Street having had the possibly intended effect of stirring up no small amount of jealousy among his fellow citizens. But there was no denying that the MacTavish home, presided over by Marie Marguerite who was described by an especially awestruck visitor as 'one of the most beautiful women I have ever met', had become Montreal's premier private residence; an appropriate setting for the innumerable balls, suppers and dinners to which the North West Company man invited his friends, his colleagues and such few British dignitaries as ventured then to Canada; a forerunner, in its way, of those still more ostentatious piles which would afterwards be built elsewhere on this continent by business magnates even more successful than Le Marquis.[33]

In their less sedate moments, the Nor'Westers, the name generally given to the fur trading company's mostly Highland personnel, were likely to gather at Montreal's Beaver Club where they dined on such frontier delicacies as venison steaks, roasted beaver tails and pickled buffalo tongues. Here William MacGillivray, whose musical abilities seem almost to have equalled his business skills, was heard by one club guest to sing 'a wild voyageur song, *Le Premier Jour de Mai*, playing the spirited tune on the piano at the same time with one hand'. MacGillivray, this account continues, 'sang as only true voyageurs can do, imitating the action of the paddle, and in their high, resounding, and yet musical, tones. His practised voice enabled him to give us the various swells and falls of sound upon the waters, driven about by the winds, dispersed and softened in the wide expanses, or brought close again to the ear by narrowing rocks. He finished, as is usual, with the piercing Indian shriek.'[34]

George Landmann of the Royal Engineers, a man who could be relied upon to seek out any available entertainment, was inevitably to find his way to the Beaver Club on more than one occasion. 'In those days we dined at four o'clock,' he recalled in later life, 'and after taking a satisfactory quantity of wine, the married men . . . retired, leaving about a dozen to drink to their health. We now began in right earnest and in true Highland style, and by four o'clock in the morning, the whole of us had arrived at such a state of perfection that we could all give the warwhoop as well as MacGillivray, we could all sing admirably, we could all drink like fishes and we all thought we could dance on the table without disturbing a single decanter, glass or plate . . . But on making the experiment we discovered it was a complete delusion and, ultimately, we broke all the plates, glasses, bottles . . . and the table also.'[35]

It was at this stage in the Beaver Club's proceedings that the Nor'Westers – now, in spirit at any rate, well afloat on the Ottawa or Saskatchewan Rivers – were liable to turn what remained of their dining table upside down as a prelude to a frenzied re-enactment of their rapid-shooting feats. Piling into the make-believe canoe with which they had thus provided themselves, and grabbing pokers, walking sticks and the like to serve as paddles, the partners of the North West Company – their voices raised, no doubt, in that 'most strange . . . *mélange* of Gaelic, English, French and half a dozen Indian dialects' which was uniquely characteristic of the fur trade – set sail for the oblivion in which all such revelries invariably ended.[36]

From Hillcrest Park, high above the Northern Ontario city of Thunder Bay, Lake Superior seems as vast as any ocean, its waters, broken only by the lumpy silhouettes of the Welcome Islands, stretching away eastwards into the gathering darkness of a winter's evening. Street-lights are flickering into life in the town centre down below. Lights are coming on also in the railway marshalling yards, around the docks, in the vicinity of the huge grain silos by the lakeside and on the freighter moored a mile or so offshore. Thunder Bay, those scenes suggest, is not the sort of place much given to the pomp and pageantry you commonly encounter in North America's more historic centres. But the various transportation businesses which have done so much to shape this city are, in their own unglamorous fashion, much more suggestive of Thunder Bay's beginnings than any piece of tourist-orientated costume drama could ever hope to be.

These towering waterfront silos, like the long lines of railway company freight cars all around them, were built to contain wheat brought here from the prairies for export to Europe – by way of Lake Superior, Lake Huron, Lake Erie, Lake Ontario and the St Lawrence. It is, of course, an arguable proposition that Canada generally has not been well served by its having been traditionally reliant on exports of this type. Few countries have stayed very rich for very long by simply selling raw materials. Because of the town's pivotal position on the country's transcontinental communications system, however, the Canadian commodities trade has certainly benefited Thunder Bay. Nor is this something new. If you head south from Hillcrest Park, swapping that residential district's spacious avenues for the more congested streets which back on to the railway, you can find, if well directed, a stone monument to the men who first realised, nearly two hundred years ago, that a sheltered harbour at the western end of Lake Superior was exactly what they needed to facilitate their breakneck exploitation of one of the earliest of North American natural resources to find a global market. These men – commemorated also in numerous Thunder Bay street names – were the Scottish Highlanders who ran the North West Company.

The strongly stockaded and well-planned outpost which the Nor'Westers constructed here – on a site now lost to view beneath successive layers of development and redevelopment – was known, to begin with, as Fort Kaministiquia. Afterwards, by way of honouring the most senior of the many MacGillivrays now involved in the fur trade, it was renamed Fort William. What did not change, for as long at least as the North West Company itself endured, was this Lake Superior outpost's vital function. Fort William existed only for the purpose of enabling its founding organisation to export huge quantities of furs from the enormous territories to which this carefully chosen location, in the period just after 1800, gave as speedy and efficient access as could then be got.

Two streams of travellers met at this spot every summer. From the east in their *canots du maître*, comparatively large craft capable of carrying a three- or four-ton cargo and manned by crews of between eight and ten, came those men who had left Lachine in May and who had made their way to Fort William by way of the Ottawa River, Lake Nipissing, the French River, Georgian Bay, the North Channel and Lake Superior. From the west, in their much lighter *canots du nord*, came those traders who had overwintered in places like Athabasca and the Peace country and whose route took them along the Churchill and Saskatchewan Rivers, across Lake Winnipeg and on to Fort William by way of Lake of the Woods and Rainy Lake.

Eastbound cargoes consisted of the furs which had been purchased from the native peoples of the interior in the course of the previous winter. Westbound loads were made up of the various commodities – everything from copper kettles, cloth and ammunition to beads, tobacco and hard liquor – which would fuel the next season's bartering. It was Simon MacTavish's great achievement to have devised the means of financing a business which required substantial sums to be laid out on such trade goods far in advance of the returns eventually generated by the sale of the furs thus gathered in. It was William MacGillivray's equal accomplishment to keep the North West Company in existence during a period which required him, from the advance headquarters which he established most summers at Fort William, to exercise some central control over trading operations which came to extend all the way from Montreal to Oregon.

It took the better part of six weeks for MacGillivray and his subordinates to get to Fort William from Lachine along a route which, though it did not involve any very long portages, included no fewer than thirty-six unloadings and reloadings of each and every canoe. All the numerous items carried in those lightweight birchbark vessels – of the sort which Canada's French settlers had begun to adopt from their Indian neighbours nearly two hundred years before – were packed carefully into bundles, or 'pieces', weighing some ninety pounds each. To carry two of those at a time while portaging was standard voyageur practice. And among the North West Company's Québecois workforce were men whose boast it was that they could manage three, maybe four, pieces on even the roughest, most treacherous and most insect-infested riverside terrain.

Sometimes there were accidents. 'One of the canoes imprudently advanced too near the fall to load,' Duncan MacGillivray wrote of one such mishap at an especially notorious series of rapids and whirlpools on the Winnipeg River. 'After the goods were debarked, the upper end through some negligence was suddenly carried out by the current with the steersman suspended after it, and the foreman, attempting to retain his end, was also carried away . . . They were hurled down through three successive cascades, the canoe several times overwhelmed with water and threatened every moment with being dashed to pieces on the rocks . . . At length the current drove it to shore, with the men still hanging on. Though they at first seemed insensible, after a little assistance they recovered and before night renewed their labours as if nothing had happened to them.'[37]

Not all such episodes ended quite so happily. But by one means or another, year after year, most of the Nor'Westers managed to win through to Fort William. Here traders from the interior exchanged news and gossip, as well as canoe cargoes, with their colleagues from back east. Here men who spent much of their lives almost entirely by themselves took this once-a-year chance to let rip – spending days and nights in eating, drinking, dancing, brawling, womanising. Here the North West Company's Montreal-based business managers – led by Simon MacTavish in the early days and by William MacGillivray in the years following his uncle's death – debated company strategy with their 'wintering partners' fresh in from the west.

As many as 3,000 people might be resident in Fort William each July. And they were accommodated, as visitors to the place reported with evident surprise, in rather more style than it was normal to find so far beyond the limits of permanent settlement. 'The buildings at Fort William,' commented Ross Cox who passed this way in 1817, 'consist of a large house in which the dining hall is situated and in which the gentleman in charge resides; the council house; a range of snug buildings for the accommodation of the people from the interior; a large counting house; the doctor's residence; extensive stores for the merchandise and furs; a forge; various workshops with apartments for the mechanics, a number of whom are always stationed there. There is also a prison for refractory voyageurs. The whole is surrounded by wooden fortifications, flanked by bastions, and is sufficiently strong to withstand any attack from the natives. Outside the fort is a shipyard in which the company's vessels on the lake are built and repaired. The kitchen garden is well stocked and there are extensive fields of Indian corn and potatoes. There are also several head of cattle, with sheep, hogs, poultry . . . and a few horses for domestic use.'[38]

The 'dining hall' mentioned by Cox was Fort William's architectural centrepiece. Described on one occasion as a 'noble apartment . . . sufficiently spacious to entertain two hundred', it was equipped – as any such building had to be in this part of North America prior to the advent of central heating – with enormous fireplaces. Above one of these was placed a bust of Simon MacTavish. Nearby hung portraits of other eminent Nor'Westers. Pride of place was reserved, however, for an enormous map prepared by David Thompson, one more of the company's partners and a man who was both a skilled surveyor and a noted western explorer in his own right. Entitled 'The North West Territory of the Province of Canada', Thompson's cartographic masterpiece was a fitting summation of what the Nor'Westers had contributed to the development of North America. 'This map,' read the inscription at its foot, 'made for the North West Company in 1813 and 1814 and delivered to the Honourable William MacGillivray . . . embraces the region lying between 45 and 60 degrees North Longtitude and 84 and 124 degrees West Latitude, comprising the surveys and discoveries of 20 years.' Not coincidentally, the area thus delineated encompasses the greater part of modern Canada.[39]

With the painstaking care habitually lavished on such projects by twentieth-century North Americans, Fort William has been reconstructed in recent years on the western outskirts of the modern Thunder Bay. Here, looking much as they would have done in 1815 or thereabouts, are all those features which so much impressed men like Ross Cox. Just inside the fort's perimeter palisade are the sheds where company canoes were both built and maintained. Nearby are the workshops occupied by the post's armourer, cooper, blacksmith, tinsmith, tailor and carpenter. Behind the stores where trade goods are prepared and packaged for westward shipment is the all-important counting house. A powder magazine stands in one corner, a hospital in another. Just off the fort's extensive central square is a warehouse containing a generous sample of the 300,000 or so furs which the North West Company handles here in a typical trading season. Beaver pelts, the staple commodity of the trade, inevitably predominate. But arctic fox, wolf, bobcat, lynx, muskrat, coyote, black bear, raccoon, mink, wolverine and marten are also represented. With difficulty, you hoist a standard 90-pound bale of such furs on your back and try to imagine how it might have felt to run – for no portaging voyageur ever walked – along a rough and slippery riverside path with one or two more bales of this sort added to the first.

There was nothing of the make-and-mend about Fort William. Everything was in its place and every man – no woman merited consideration here – was equally in his. The fort's great hall made this point perfectly. From their table just below their founder's bust, the North West Company's top-hatted and dark-coated partners looked out – and in some sense, no doubt, looked down as well – on their employees. The latter, meantime, took their seats in accordance with the dictates of a strictly defined hierarchy. Senior clerks and apprentices, some of them aspiring to an eventual partnership themselves, might dine within a yard or two of the top table. Such voyageurs as were permitted to eat here – and most of them were kept and fed beyond the fort grounds proper – took care, for their part, to keep as far as they could get from any bourgeois.

Opposite the great hall's open shelves – where the North West Company kept both its English porcelain and its Irish crystal – there hung, according at least to the people responsible for this huge building's meticulous reconstruction, a print based on Benjamin West's pageant-like painting of the moment when, despite the death of General James Wolfe, it became apparent that the forces of New France had been defeated on the Plains of Abraham. Other imperial icons were to be found in Fort William's great hall also – a portrait of Lord Nelson, hero of Trafalgar, for example. But the Benjamin West print, you sense, would have been especially important to the North West Company. It would have served to remind many of the organisation's leading figures of just how far and fast their families had risen since their fathers or grandfathers first came to North America as officers of the 78th Highlanders.

The North West Company's elaborate rituals inevitably grated on contemporary nerves. It comes as no surprise, then, to find the nineteenth-century American author Washington Irving, in a book he wrote about the fur trade, poking just a little fun at the pretensions of those men he memorably labelled 'hyperborean nabobs'. 'They ascended the rivers in great state,' Irving commented of the journey made each year to their Lake Superior stronghold by the North West Company's more prominent partners. 'They were wrapped in rich furs, their huge canoes freighted with every convenience and luxury and manned by Canadian voyageurs as obedient as Highland clansmen. They carried up with them cooks and bakers, together with delicacies of every kind and an abundance of choice wines for the banquets which attended this great convocation.'[40]

As his account of the North West Company clearly demonstrates, Washington Irving had read Walter Scott's several novels about the Scottish Highlands and had consequently absorbed something of Scott's detailed understanding of what it meant to belong to a society organised around clans and clanship. It was this that enabled the American to make his highly perceptive connection between the North West Company's sometimes ostentatious mode of operation and the Highland origins of so many of the company's leading personnel. Not only were the Nor'Westers clearly given, as Irving commented, to indulging in 'revels' which were not at all dissimilar to 'some of the old feasts described in Highland castles'. The way they went about their business had about it something of the brashness and bravado which had been so characteristic of the Scottish Highlands in the era preceding the British government's forcible imposition of its own, quite different, standards on the region. The buccaneering methods which, as will shortly be seen, the North West Company tended to employ in its dealings with its Hudson's Bay Company rivals become more readily comprehensible when one reflects on the fact that Simon MacTavish's Stratherrick father had once ridden into Inverness with some twenty armed men and coolly set about abducting one of the Highland capital's principal residents.[41]

In moving from the eighteenth-century Scottish Highlands to eighteenth-century North America, the North West Company's founder, in a sense, had simply swapped one semi-lawless frontier for another. And neither Simon MacTavish nor his colleagues, in making this transition, saw any reason to set aside those cultural and historical traditions which made them the sort of men they were. It is by no means accidental that, as well as a beaver and a fur-trade canoe, the North West Company's characteristically grandiose coat-of-arms features a Hebridean galley of the sort deployed by the Lordship of the Isles when that fifteenth-century and wholly Gaelic-speaking principality wished to demonstrate its effective independence from all external authority. While much had changed – and generally changed for the worse – in the Highlands between the lordship's demise in 1493 and Alexander MacKenzie's Pacific excursion of exactly three hundred years later, the tacksmen and tacksmen's sons who figured so largely in the making of the North West Company undoubtedly succeeded in recreating, for a period at least, their own version of the virtual autonomy which their Scottish ancestors had once enjoyed.

The Nor'Westers might not actually have been descended, despite the claims made to the contrary by John MacDonald of Garth, from the Lords of the Isles. As David Thompson's map was intended to remind them when they gathered annually at Fort William, however, they were the effective masters of a realm many times larger than any ever ruled before by Highlanders. 'Lords of the lakes and the forests,' Washington Irving called them. And he may well have meant his phrase to have a slightly condescending ring to it. But Simon MacTavish and William MacGillivray, had they lived long enough to read them, would very probably have considered Irving's words to be a compliment.[42]

CHAPTER EIGHT

Even if the Emigrants Escape the Scalping Knife...

FROM THE LITTLE fishing port of Helmsdale, on Sutherland's North Sea coast, a narrow road leads westwards into the Strath of Kildonan. On the road's left are the dark, peaty waters of a first-rate salmon river. On its right are low and rounded hills. 'Nature had done everything to make Kildonan one of the sweetest spots in northern Scotland,' Donald Sage, a nineteenth-century clergyman, commented in the course of the memoirs he compiled towards the end of his long life. This judgment was no doubt coloured by nostalgia – Sage having grown up here in the 1790s. But even when you come visiting briefly on an after-noon of sudden, drenching showers – the sort of showers that soak you in a moment – it is not difficult to see how Kildonan might inspire espe-cially strong affection. The place was 'beautifully wooded', Donald Sage wrote, 'with the black willow, oak, aspen, alder, and wild gean, the mountain ash, or rowan, the black flowering-thorn and the birch tree'. And Kildonan is still like that, its trees perhaps less varied now, but with the sunlight – during those astonishingly brilliant moments you get on days of this sort in the Scottish Highlands – picking out the varied tex-tures of several of the species which Sage listed. What has vanished since Donald Sage's boyhood, what was to disappear from much of Sutherland in his lifetime, is any worthwhile remnant of the many farming commu-nities he also remembered: Kilphedir with its mill; Torrish 'where the houses or cottages of the tenantry were built closely together'; Kilearnan, Dalhalmy, Balvalaich and several more such settlements. 'The townships ... which once teemed with life are now desolate and silent; and the only traces visible of the vanished, happy population are, here and there, a half-buried hearthstone, or a moss-grown graveyard.'[1]

The day is Sunday. But the doors of Kildonan Church – where Alexander Sage, Donald's father, was installed as minister in 1787 – are firmly locked. So are the churchyard gates. To gain access to the spot where the elder Sage is buried, you have to clamber carefully over a slippery stone wall.

Something of the nature of the transformation which overtook the Strath of Kildonan some ten years before Alexander Sage's death in 1824 can be deduced from his churchyard's tombstones. Those which are of nineteenth-century vintage tend to be commemorative of south country farmers and their shepherds. It is to older, sometimes fallen-over, invariably less legible, slabs of rock that you mostly have to turn for some small trace of the Gunns, MacKays, Sutherlands and Bannermans who, when Alexander Sage first came here, had been inhabiting this place for as long as it made sense for anyone to remember. But it is one of this latter group, for all that he was interred several thousand miles from here, who has finally acquired the most prominent of all the Kildonan graveyard's many memorials. This takes the form of a slate-grey plaque fixed to the eastward-facing gable of what was once Alexander Sage's church. 'In memory of George Bannerman,' it reads, 'great-grandfather of the Right Honourable John G. Diefenbaker, PC, QC, MP, Prime Minister of Canada, 1957–1963.'

On one of the trips he made here, Diefenbaker was shown the remnants of the house once occupied by this George Bannerman, his mother's father's father. On another visit, made more formal by his then being Canada's serving premier, he attended Sunday service down in Helmsdale. 'Of course our retinue was fairly large what with our staff and the pressmen,' John G. Diefenbaker afterwards recalled. But the Helmsdale minister, thinking maybe of Scottish Presbyterianism's longstanding reluctance to admit that any one person is more important than another in the sight of God, made 'no reference' to the eminent North Americans who had been added temporarily to his congregation – until, having reached 'the last minute or so' of his sermon, he remarked, to Diefenbaker's obvious delight, that the Highlands are 'forever in the hearts' of everyone descended from their people.[2]

George Bannerman, his great-grandson commented, had been one among many victims of the clearances which occurred here more than 180 years ago. 'The Countess of Sutherland,' the Canadian prime minister continued, 'had decided that she needed the land for her own purposes.'

What those purposes were is made explicit in another modern Canadian's account of the events which were to propel George Bannerman and many of his Strath of Kildonan neighbours across the Atlantic. 'In those days a darkness fell over all the lands and the crofts of

Sutherland,' Morag Gunn, heroine of Margaret Laurence's outstanding and enduringly controversial novel, *The Diviners*, is told by Christie Logan, town scavenger in the fictional Manitoban town of Manawakan and the man who raises Morag following the deaths of both her mother and her Sutherland-descended father. 'The Bitch-Duchess was living then,' Christie goes on to tell this child whose search for her own origins will one day lead her to the Scottish Highlands, 'and it was she who cast a darkness over the land, and sowed the darkness and reaped gold, for her heart was cold as the gold coins, and she loved no creature alive but only the gold. And her tacksmen rode through the countryside, setting fire to the crofts and turning out the people from their homes which they had lived in since the beginning of all time. And it was old men and old women with thin shanks and men in their prime and women with the child inside them and a great scattering of small children, like, and all of them was driven away from the lands of their fathers and on to the wild rocks of the shore, then, to fish if they could and pry the shellfish off the rocks there, for food . . . *All the lands of Sutherland will be raising the sheep*, says the she-devil, *for they'll pay better than folk.*'[3]

She was a significant figure in the United Kingdom of her day, this Bitch-Duchess of Margaret Laurence's novel, this Countess of John G. Diefenbaker's memoirs. In 1785 she married George Granville Leveson-Gower who, two or three years into the nineteenth century, inherited both his father's wealth and his father's title of Marquess of Stafford. Although her marriage was typical of the means by which Scotland's relatively impoverished aristocrats were then seeking to bolster their fortunes, Elizabeth, Countess of Sutherland, did considerably better than most of her counterparts. She began with very little in the way of ready cash. But the 800,000 Highland acres she brought to her marital partnership, when allied to the millions of pounds deriving from Leveson-Gower's huge financial stake in England's industrial revolution, were to ensure that the Duke and Duchess of Sutherland, as the marquess and the countess eventually became, were reckoned by contemporaries to be among the richest and most prestigious members of Britain's landowning élite. It was in order to live up to this status as much as to enhance it, perhaps, that Sutherland's leading family now set out to reorganise – or, in the jargon of the time, improve – their enormous Scottish property.

Among the men employed to give effect to the resulting grand design – which involved turning over the Sutherland interior to sheep-farmers and settling the consequently displaced population on coastal crofts of the type already standard elsewhere – were two Morayshire businessmen, William Young and Patrick Sellar. Tacksmen, Margaret Laurence called this duo. More properly they were estate managers or factors. What is more important than their designations, however, is the fact that both these men, and especially Sellar, as Laurence well understood, were to become firmly identified with some of the most contentious episodes in all of Scotland's history.

Young responded to Sutherland with an enthusiasm scarcely less than Donald Sage's. 'A beautiful strath,' he called Kildonan – but one, he added more prosaically, and more ominously, which might readily be 'adapted' to the 'sheep-farming system'. For advice as to how such adaption might best be effected, the Sutherland estate manager turned to Thomas Gillespie who, as mentioned previously, had pioneered sheep rearing in Glen Garry. To Gillespie, accustomed as he was to the much harsher terrain of the West Highlands, the Strath of Kildonan must have seemed every bit as attractive as it did to William Young. It was in the confident hope of similarly impressing others that advertisements were now placed in Scottish newspapers with a view to drawing the 'attention of sheep-farmers' to the 'several excellent tracts of land' shortly to be made available in Sutherland.[4]

To make way for the sheep-farms thus to be created in the Strath of Kildonan, of course, it was necessary to evict the several hundred people living there. This Sellar and Young proposed to accomplish in the spring of 1813. In January of that year, however, it began to be clear that Kildonan's inhabitants were not about to acquiesce meekly in their own removal. Several estate employees, valuers and others then engaged in mapping a prospective sheep-farm at Suisgill, some three miles beyond Alexander Sage's church, were understandably alarmed to find themselves confronting, one winter's morning, a number of Kildonan tenants who had all too evidently decided to make a stand on behalf of their endangered communities. 'The natives rose in a body,' a worried William Young reported, 'and chased the valuers off the ground and now threaten the lives of every man who dares to dispossess them.'[5]

Estate managers like Young were used to having their own way. Now, in Sutherland anyway, they faced rebellion on a growing scale. The men who took charge so dramatically at Suisgill were reportedly armed with bludgeons. 'If sheep were to be put upon the ground,' these men were alleged to have said, 'there should be blood . . . and not a little of it.' There were also rumours of a more general uprising being planned for all of Sutherland and talk to the effect that 'every shepherd's house in the county should be set on fire'. The implications of such unrest, the increasingly panicky authorities were quick to note, were all the more worrying in light of the fact that very many of Sutherland's menfolk had seen service with one or other of the Highland regiments raised in the course of Britain's still continuing war with Napoleonic France. 'They give out that they can muster 1,000 men, a great proportion of whom have been in the army,' George Cranstoun, Sheriff Substitute of Sutherland, wrote of the Kildonan people. 'They talk openly of resistance.'[6]

All this infuriated William Young and Patrick Sellar. The Kildonan tenants, according to Young, were simply savages, worse than American Indians, 'banditti' who had no conception of progress, men whose morals had been 'corrupted' by their alleged involvement in the illicit distillation of whisky. Sellar was equally irate. It was simply inconceivable to him that something so self-evidently right and proper as the expansion of sheep-farming should be impeded by 'insurgents' and 'aborigines'. And for all the Kildonan people's protestations that 'they were loyal men whose brothers and sons were now fighting Bonaparte', the British government was inevitably on the side of Young, Sellar and their aristocratic employers. In much the same spirit as they might have been deployed to deal with a tribal uprising on the North American frontier, therefore, troops were now sent to Sutherland to restore order and to bring the prospect of a wider insurrection to an end.[7]

Prior to the military's arrival, however, the Kildonan tenants, in a desperate attempt to get their case heard in London, had despatched their own emissary southwards. His name was William MacDonald. He was one of the many former soldiers then to be found in the Scottish Highlands and he had been given the task by the Kildonan people of seeking audiences both with the Marquess of Stafford, their absentee landlord, and the Duke of York, the British army's commander-in-chief.

MacDonald's instructions were to offer Stafford, on behalf of the strath's existing occupants, a higher rent for Kildonan than was being asked of prospective sheep-farmers by Sellar and Young. The Duke of York, meanwhile, was to be informed that the Kildonan people were willing to take the lead in raising a regiment of 700 men for service either in Europe or North America – where a new war had recently broken out between Britain and the United States – provided only that the 'fathers and mothers and wives and children' of these men were guaranteed possession of their 'native home'. The Sutherland estate management team, needless to say, took prompt steps to ensure that MacDonald, whom William Young was also trying to have deprived of his army pension, never got to see either the Marquess of Stafford or the Duke of York. By one means or another, however, the old soldier was put in touch with a quite different member of the British aristocracy – one whose attitude to Scottish Highlanders was altogether more positive than that of practically any other representative of his class. This was Thomas Douglas, Earl of Selkirk.[8]

Selkirk, who inherited his earldom in 1799, was born on the Douglas family's Wigtownshire estate and educated in Edinburgh. There his student friends included Walter Scott whose novels were to do so much to shape the world's image of the Scottish Highlands. And it may well be that something of Scott's romantic interest in clans and clanship rubbed off on the future Lord Selkirk. 'Without any immediate or local connexion with the Highlands,' he was one day to write, 'I was led, very early in life, to take a warm interest in the fate of my countrymen in that part of the kingdom. During the course of my academical studies, my curiosity was strongly excited by representations I had heard of the antient state of society, and the striking peculiarity of manners, still remaining among them, and in the year 1792 I was prompted to take an extensive tour through their wild region and to explore many of its remotest and most secluded valleys.'[9]

The north of Scotland in 1792 was by no means the idyllic backwater of the youthful Selkirk's imaginings. This was *bliadhna nan caoraich*, the year of the sheep, the name given by the region's Gaelic-speaking population to the tumultuous events surrounding the attempt made by the men of Easter Ross and neighbouring localities forcibly to expel the animals which were already beginning to displace so many Highlanders. Others of Selkirk's background attributed these disorders – which were eventually to be crushed, just like the later and very similar Kildonan protests, by the British army – to malign and seditious influences originating, or so it was suggested, in the work of the Jacobin revolutionaries then intent on overthrowing monarchical government in France. Selkirk was not so sure. His sympathies tended to be with the Jacobins – some of whom he encountered at first hand in Paris at about this time – and, still more unusually, with the common people of the Scottish Highlands. Selkirk consequently took to learning Gaelic, a language which others of his background now generally despised. He also began to consider what might most usefully be done to assist the victims of clearance and eviction.[10]

The transformations which had begun in the Highlands following the Battle of Culloden, Selkirk concluded, had already gone too far to be halted. Their more disruptive effects might still be mitigated, however. And the most practicable means of achieving such mitigation, or so the earl thought, was to be found in giving a wholly new impetus to those emigrations which, in the years around 1800, Highland landlords were still trying so hard to prevent. Hence Selkirk's remarkable book, *Observations on the Present State of the Highlands of Scotland*, which he published in 1805 and which was, among many other things, a devastating critique of the Passenger Vessels Act of 1803. Instead of falling in behind the landowning lobby's self-interested attempts to keep Highlanders at home, Selkirk argued, the British government should be seizing on this tremendous opportunity to establish in the colonies a set of people who were demonstrably well suited to the pioneering life and whose military antecedents were such as to give them an obvious role in foiling any attack by the United States on those North American territories which were still under imperial control.

As a result of his having read another publication of this period, *Voyages from Montreal through the Continent of North America to the Frozen and Pacific Oceans in 1789 and 1793*, Alexander MacKenzie's best-selling account of his various explorations, Selkirk was already beginning to conceive an ambition to found a new colony of Scottish Highlanders far to the west of the existing limits of settlement on the eastern fringes of the Great Lakes. That would not be readily accomplished. But there was much that could be attempted in the meantime by this tall, slim, red-haired, astonishingly energetic man whose most distinguishing and most attractive characteristic was always to be his reluctance to settle merely for the role of commentator and theoretician.

Selkirk began by arranging for a number of families from the Highlands to be settled during 1803 and 1804 in Prince Edward Island and at a place called Baldoon on the north shore of Lake Erie. Next he himself set out for North America; travelling extensively across the continent; gathering the facts, figures and impressions which were to be deployed to such good effect in the *Observations* of 1805; looking in on both Prince Edward Island and Baldoon; carefully assessing the overall involvement of Scottish Highlanders in the development of North America. Having visited the Hudson and Mohawk Valleys and spent some time in discussion with Simon MacTavish and other fur traders in Montreal, Selkirk made himself familiar finally with Glengarry County where – with consequences shortly to be seen – he was particularly impressed by a former soldier, Miles MacDonell. Miles, a teenage ensign on the loyalist side during the Revolutionary War and an officer in the Canadian militia, was one of the sons of the Knoydart tacksman, John MacDonell of Scotus, who had helped to lead to New York in 1773 the emigrant group who were afterwards to provide Glengarry County with its original Highland settlers. 'Very much a gentleman in manners and sentiments,' Selkirk wrote of this Glengarrian who had been born in Scotland in 1767 and to whom the visiting earl was one day to turn for assistance in progressing his colonisation schemes.[11]

Back in Britain and pondering how to gain access to those western territories of which he had now heard so much more from Simon MacTavish and his colleagues, Selkirk took time off in 1807 to marry Jean Wedderburn – whose attractions, it may not be overly cynical to postulate, included the fact that she was heiress to a substantial stockholding in the Hudson's Bay Company. Simon MacTavish's North West Company, to be sure, had been running rings around this most ponderous of imperial corporations since the 1780s – the Montreal men selling as much as five times more furs annually than their Hudson's Bay rivals and looking on with undisguised glee as Bay Company dividends tumbled catastrophically. Despite its having fallen on hard times, however, the Hudson's Bay Company retained the charter which its London founders had obtained from King Charles II in 1670. This charter made its possessors the 'lords and proprietors' of all the one-and-a-half million square miles of North America drained by watercourses flowing ultimately into Hudson Bay. Among those watercourses was one which Thomas Douglas had first read about in the chapters of Alexander

MacKenzie's book dealing with the canoe route from Montreal to Fort Chipewyan. The stream in question drains the prairies to the west of Lake Superior. It is called Red River.[12]

Within a year or two of his marriage, and with the active collaboration of his newly acquired brother-in-law, Andrew Wedderburn Colvile, a man whose considerable wealth stemmed from his extensive interests in West Indian sugar, the Earl of Selkirk had obtained a controlling position in the affairs of the Hudson's Bay Company. The wider business of the company was left to Colvile to put in order. Selkirk's principal interest was its landholdings or, more specifically, the possibility of his utilising those landholdings to acquire a territory large enough to accommodate the Scottish Highland colony towards which he had been striving for more than a decade. In 1811 the now middle-aged nobleman's persistence was at last rewarded. That year, in return for a nominal payment of ten shillings and Lord Selkirk's promise to supply its North American agents with both manpower and foodstuffs, the Hudson's Bay Company granted this Scottish earl effective jurisdiction over a 116,000 square mile slice of real estate centring on the Red River and including substantial segments of modern Minnesota and North Dakota in the United States as well as a large proportion of the modern Canadian province of Manitoba.[13]

Selkirk had finally acquired his colony. Next he needed colonists. The first of these, under the leadership of Miles MacDonell whom the earl had persuaded to become his principal representative at Red River, sailed for North America from Stornoway in the summer of 1811. A second small party left the following year. Already, however, it was evident to Selkirk that Red River, if it was to develop in the way that he envisaged, urgently required a much larger injection of manpower than he could readily recruit and despatch entirely on his own initiative. What the previously freelance earl now desired to have, in other words, was a measure of government backing. And when war broke out between the United States and Britain in 1812 – as a result of Royal Navy insistence on stopping and searching American ships bound for the parts of Europe then controlled by Napoleon – Lord Selkirk promptly grasped his opportunity. He personally would be prepared, Selkirk told the military authorities in London, to raise a Highland regiment for service against the United States which, by this time, had invaded Canada. He would attach but one condition to his offer, Selkirk added. His regiment must eventually be disbanded in North America and its soldiers, together with their wives and families, shipped meantime from Scotland at public expense, must afterwards be settled on the earl's territorial concession at Red River.

Government ministers were understandably reluctant to fall in immediately with Selkirk's proposals. But it was at this point in the early part of 1813, just when he was considering his next move, that the earl found himself presented with an apparent solution to his problems in the shape of William MacDonald, the envoy sent to London by the Kildonan people who, quite independently of Selkirk's manoeuvrings, were intent on offering their own regiment to the British army's high command – their condition being that, in return for providing several hundred troops, they should be given a guarantee that an immediate halt would be called to the Kildonan evictions planned by William Young and Patrick Sellar. Selkirk could not singlehandedly bring the Sutherland clearances to an end. But here, or so it seemed to him, was his chance to demonstrate once and for all the means by which the men, women and children being set adrift by landowners like the Countess of Sutherland and the Marquess of Stafford might be made to serve Britain's imperial purposes in North America. Carried away a little by his own enthusiasm, Selkirk promised MacDonald that, when the country's politicians finally commissioned him to raise his regiment, as he remained confident would happen soon, the men of Kildonan would at once be recruited to his colours and their wives, children and other relatives immediately conveyed to Red River.[14]

MacDonald promptly returned to Kildonan to identify families prepared to leave for North America on Selkirk's terms. This was no difficult task. Sellar and Young intended shortly to move the Kildonan folk to crofts then being created, some thirty or forty miles to the north, on one of the most exposed coasts in Scotland. To understand what this implied, it is necessary only to spend a day or so in Sutherland; for nobody who has ever walked Kildonan's comparatively sheltered fields, then gone on to visit the bleak and windswept shores where most of the strath's population were to be deposited, can have anything but sympathy for people peremptorily instructed to take themselves from the one place to the other. Practically any alternative would have appealed to the 'barbarous hordes' – the phrase, inevitably, is Patrick Sellars's – whose lives were now subject to such casual manipulation. It is not at all surprising, therefore, that William Young, by the spring of 1813, knew of no more than a dozen individuals who had agreed to take one of these newly available crofts. William MacDonald, meanwhile, had drawn up a list of several hundred people who were anxious to be off that summer to Red River.[15]

At this critical juncture, however, the Earl of Selkirk's plans began to go badly awry. Military commanders in London, it transpired, had no real interest in his proffered regiment. And in the absence of the official funding on which he had been relying when he first met William MacDonald and heard of the Kildonan population's plight, Selkirk could hold out to this population only a severely scaled-down version of his previous proposal. North America, a Kildonan poet had written more than forty years before, his Gaelic verses inspired by earlier emigrations from Sutherland to the Cape Fear region, was 'the land that will bring our children good'; a country wholly free of 'enslaving' landlords; a place to which the Good Lord was guiding Highlanders in exactly the same manner as He had once led the Israelites out of Egypt. But the Earl of Selkirk, it now transpired, was in no position to play Moses to more than a handful of the hundreds of people who wanted so desperately to take up his offer of an Atlantic passage.[16]

Only a small number of single men could be got to Red River that year, Selkirk explained to the Kildonan folk when he travelled north to meet them in the spring of 1813. In the event, however, and for no better reason, it seems likely, than his wishing to do his best for as many as possible of the people whom he had agreed to help, the earl was persuaded to find places also for several family groups.

Selkirk had earlier canvassed one of his Highland friends for the name of a 'gentleman of respectable character' who might be persuaded to 'go out' with the Kildonan emigrants. The earl had consequently been introduced to Archibald MacDonald whose father was tacksman at Leacantuim in Glen Coe. The Leacantuim family, like most of their Glen Coe neighbours, had participated in practically all the several Highland rebellions of the previous two centuries. But none of his forebears, it is safe to say, had faced challenges quite as demanding as those which were to confront the 21-year-old Archibald MacDonald as a result of his being put in charge of what turned out to be the most appalling journey ever undertaken by any of North America's many millions of European settlers.[17]

The Leacantuim tacksman's son took with him to Red River one of his own relatives, an Appin man called Donald Stewart. But the 94-strong party which mustered eventually under MacDonald's command at the Caithness port of Thurso, some forty miles from Kildonan, consisted otherwise of some of those Gunns, MacKays, Bannermans and others who, in the course of the previous winter, had received the one and only communication most of them ever got from the millionaire couple who were their landlords – this communication being, of course, a notice of eviction.

From Thurso, where their friends and neighbours from Sutherland had gathered to see them off, the Kildonan people were taken to Stromness in Orkney on the *Waterwitch*, a coasting vessel hired by Selkirk for this purpose. Kildonan having little tradition of seafaring and the waters between the Scottish mainland and the islands being notoriously rough, 'all on board', as was recalled by one of the young men making the trip, were 'prostrated' by this first encounter with the ocean. The young man in question, incidentally, was Donald Gunn and, despite his having a common Kildonan surname, he came from Halkirk in Caithness and was making for Orkney because he had got a job earlier that summer with the Hudson's Bay Company whose outward-bound convoys traditionally put in at Stromness prior to embarking on the Atlantic crossing. It was common enough for Hudson's Bay Company ships to take on young men of Donald Gunn's type at this little town of clustered homes and quays and warehouses. What was wholly novel – what was regarded, indeed, by more than one Hudson's Bay Company veteran as little short of crazy – was the notion of taking emigrants to North America by way of Arctic waters which, for all that they might provide the most direct route to Red River, had never been tackled by an emigrant ship prior to the Earl of Selkirk's involvement with the fur-trading corporation whose staff and seamen, often against their better judgment, now found themselves obliged to do the earl's will.[18]

Two Hudson's Bay ships were waiting at Stromness. Donald Gunn and his fellow employees were shepherded aboard the *Eddystone*. The Kildonan emigrants, for their part, joined the *Prince of Wales*. Escorted by the *Brazen*, a naval vessel intended to give protection against the American privateers then waging war on British maritime traffic in the Atlantic, the two company craft weighed anchor on 28 June 1813 and headed westwards, the hills of Sutherland sinking gradually below the horizon on the little flotilla's port side. Bad weather took its usual toll. 'Seasickness prostrated many to so great a degree that they could not think of anything but their own suffering,' Donald Gunn recalled. At last, some days after sighting Greenland far to starboard, the *Eddystone* and the *Prince of Wales*, their Royal Navy escort having long before departed on other duties, entered the comparatively sheltered, if ice-infested, waters of the Hudson Strait. Here, however, other dangers waited.[19]

'In our passage through the strait,' John West, an English clergy-man, was to write several years later of his own journey to Red River, 'our progress was impeded by vast fields of ice and icebergs . . . The scene was truly grand and impressive . . . There is a solemn and overwhelming sensation produced in the mind by these enormous masses of snow and ice, not to be conveyed in words. They floated by us from one to two hundred feet above the water . . . resembling huge mountains, with deep valleys between lofty clifts, passing in silent grandeur, except at intervals when . . . the crashing of the ice struck the ear like distant thunder.'[20]

The summer of 1813 saw even more ice than usual in Hudson Strait, making the going 'slow and difficult', in Donald Gunn's recollection. This was bad enough. What was much worse was the news that typhus had broken out on the *Prince of Wales*. 'Sunday, 15 August 1813,' the ship's captain now recorded in his log. 'This day have 19 passengers and eight seamen ill . . . The groans and cries of the sick on one side and the delirious on the other is dreadful beyond description.' Among those who were shortly to die without setting foot on North America was Archibald MacDonald's kinsman, Donald Stewart, and, most cruelly of all, William Laserre, the surgeon whom Selkirk had engaged in the vain hope of keeping his emigrants healthy. It was in a spirit of anything but optimism, therefore, that this latest contingent of Scottish Highlanders looked out on the continent to which they had pinned so many hopes. 'We beheld the low and uninteresting shore of Hudson Bay stretched before us,' Donald Gunn remembered, 'presenting its narrow border of yellow sand and dark blue swamp in the front, with its dark and dismal-looking line of tamarack in the background. The scenery appeared bleak and desolate beyond the power of description.'[21]

On the western edge of this enormous inland sea, which is as large in surface area as the Mediterranean but which has absolutely nothing else in common with that infinitely more accommodating stretch of water, the Hudson's Bay Company had maintained its principal North American base for almost 150 years before the Kildonan people's arrival. This base was York Factory. It was named after James, Duke of York, an early Hudson's Bay Company governor and the man who – in the wake of his being deposed in 1689 from the throne to which he had succeeded just four years earlier – was to become the first of those exiled Jacobite monarchs on whose behalf innumerable Highlanders were so readily to go to war. Geography had shaped York Factory more than history, however. The nineteenth-century Hudson's Bay Company clerk who called the trading post 'a monstrous blot on a swampy spot with a partial view of the frozen sea' got things just about right. This was as chill and miserable a locality as any in North America. James Isham, who over-wintered here in the eighteenth century, recorded grimly that there were periods when the ice grew so thick on the inside walls of the post's barrack-like living quarters that it had 'every day' to be 'cut away with hatchets'. Isham and his companions, confined to rooms which were permanently shuttered against the weather and heated – insofar as they were heated at all – by smoky stoves, went about all winter with faces 'as black as any chimbly sweeper's'. Outside, meanwhile, blizzard followed blizzard and the fahrenheit thermometer registered as much as eighty degrees of frost – with brandy, according to Isham, being reduced by the cold to the consistency of treacle.[22]

Hudson Bay, then, is no place to be other than in summer. Because it was impossible for them to reach Red River in advance of the frosts and snows which would soon make travel impossible, however, the Kildonan people were left with no option, when finally put ashore towards the end of August, other than to settle down here for the winter. Having already been directed away from York Factory, where they were told bluntly by the Hudson's Bay Company man in charge that neither he nor his staff could possibly provide for them, Archibald MacDonald and his party had next tried their luck at Fort Churchill, another Bay Company depot some two hundred miles further to the north. But Fort Churchill's personnel were no more welcoming than their York Factory counterparts. It would have been perfectly excusable, in such desperately depressing circumstances, if both the Kildonan people and their young and untried leader had there and then decided to give up.

This was when Archibald MacDonald more than proved his worth, however. Having set mothers and children to gather cranberries which would be used in the months ahead to ward off scurvy, MacDonald ordered his party's menfolk – their ranks already thinned by typhus – to start felling trees and building cabins. Three of those were more or less completed before the first snow fell at the beginning of October. And while the resulting encampment beside the now solidly frozen Churchill River offered precious little in the way of comfort, it served both to keep the remaining Highlanders alive and to attract the attention of the one Hudson's Bay Company man prepared to offer them assistance. This was Fort Churchill's resident surgeon, Abel Edwards, who reached the Kildonan people in time to insist on the 'absolute necessity' of their taking adequate precautions against the 'inclemencies' of a winter harsher by far than any previous set of emigrants from Scotland had encountered. Females were especially at risk from the intense cold, the surgeon clearly felt. 'Every woman to wear constantly three petticoats,' he instructed, 'one of which must be of cloth or thick flannel, also thick leggings.'[23]

Somehow the worst of the winter was endured. But a lot of travelling still lay ahead. That was why, just two or three days into April, though the sea ice had not yet begun to melt and though snow still lay thickly all around, Archibald MacDonald judged the time had come to strike out for York Factory in order to make as early as possible a start on the much longer onward journey to Red River. Sledges were built by William Lamont who, back in Kildonan, had been a miller and – since the two trades were frequently combined in the Highlands – very probably a carpenter or joiner also. Women and children, meanwhile, fashioned snowshoes, mocassins and mittens from such materials as they could lay their hands on. And the necessary guide having been provided by the now slightly more co-operative Hudson's Bay Company, the aspiring settlers finally began to move south – to the sound of the bagpipes brought here to Hudson Bay by a man called Robert Gunn. 'They took their departure by single files,' Archibald MacDonald wrote. 'The guide . . . took the lead, followed by the men and sleds, and they succeeded by the women . . . Single files would tend to make the track more firm and smooth that the women were enabled to walk in the snowshoes with greater facility, as they were by no means calculated for that arduous task.'[24]

'The idle and lazy alone think of emigration,' one estate manager had remarked of those Sutherland people who had elected to leave for North America rather than acquiesce in his plans for them. Now, however, the families who had thus been dismissed were being called upon to demonstrate qualities of tenacity, perseverance and courage beyond the imaginings of the men responsible for their expulsion from Kildonan. Morning after morning, MacDonald and his people were breaking trail when the day was only two hours old – getting in as many miles as they could before the rising sun, its light reflected from the ice-age landscape all around, brought on the misery of snowblindness. Several of the Kildonan people temporarily lost their sight all the same – John G. Diefenbaker's great-grandfather being among the victims. Others were afflicted, as Archibald MacDonald recorded, by 'a cursed distemper which we call the cramp'. This was a peculiarly agonising pain caused by the unaccustomed muscular stresses arising from having to walk mile after strength-sapping mile in clumsy, home-made snow-shoes.[25]

When, seven days out from the Churchill River, a young woman called Jean MacKay, suffering from both cramp and snowblindness, finally collapsed, MacDonald discovered her to be 'four months on in her pregnancy'. But still he pressed on, with the weather worsening once more and the sun blotted out by swirling snow which reduced visibility at times to less than twenty yards. Some slower members of the group were now deliberately left behind – so anxious was their leader to make contact with York Factory and to get its occupants to help him bring the Kildonan party through to shelter and safety. And at last this was accomplished. Thirteen days into their hellish trek, but with Robert Gunn still able to strike up an appropriate air on his pipes, the exhausted Highlanders at last encountered a detachment of Hudson's Bay Company men from York Factory.[26]

Still the Kildonan people's difficulties continued. At the end of a hard winter, and with both Hudson Strait and Hudson Bay likely to remain impassable to shipping for many more weeks, there were so few supplies to spare at York Factory that Archibald MacDonald found himself forced to reduce still further a daily food allocation which was already so small as to be bringing his party to the verge of starvation. But hunger, like the cold which went before it, was survived. And towards the end of May, with the days at last turning warmer, it became possible for the Kildonan emigrants, in boats borrowed from the Hudson's Bay Company, to start moving up the Hayes and Hill Rivers in the direction of Lake Winnipeg.

This final phase of one of the nineteenth century's more epic journeys took four weeks. It also involved a great deal of hard work. This was partly owing to the fact that the Hudson's Bay Company, unlike the Montreal-based Nor'Westers, made little or no use of birchbark canoes – preferring to rely on far heavier vessels modelled on the clinker-built and oar-powered craft used by the Orkney fishermen who provided the Bay Company with a large proportion of its staff. Although they could carry a much bigger load than canoes, these York boats, as they were known, were much harder to handle. It was difficult enough to row them upstream in the teeth of currents greatly strengthened by both rain and melting snow. It was more difficult still to get a York boat round a waterfall. No such vessel could possibly be carried. It had to be dragged – an operation made all the more unpleasant by the swarms of mosquitoes now being unleashed by the beginnings of a typically hot North American summer.

By one means or another, however, each set of rapids was surmounted safely. And in the wider, calmer waters to which the Hudson Bay river system eventually gives access – in Oxford Lake, Knee Lake, Playgreen Lake and, of course, Lake Winnipeg itself – the York boat came into its own. Now it was possible simply to set a sail, sit back and cruise before a breeze which grew a little warmer with every day that passed. Now North America began at last to be enjoyable.

A sense of matters finally improving must have remained with Archibald MacDonald and his little party as they reached the point where the Red River empties into Lake Winnipeg and realised that their destination – just below the eastward-flowing Assiniboine River's junction with the northward-flowing Red – was only hours away. 'As we proceeded,' another traveller of this period recalled of his own entry into the Red River, 'the banks were covered with oak, elm, ash, poplar and maple, and rose gradually higher as we approached the colony where the prairies, or open grassy plains, presented to the eye an agreeable contrast with the almost continuous forest of pine we were accustomed to on the route from York Factory.' Not since leaving their native strath, more than a year before, had the men of Kildonan glimpsed land which they could cultivate. Now every one of them was allocated a 100-acre lot. Now Archibald MacDonald, penning a despatch to Lord Selkirk, felt able to report of the Sutherland emigrants 'that they never were happier and more contented in Kildonan than they are here already'. If that was an exaggeration, it was, in the circumstances, a pardonable one. It was certainly not MacDonald's fault that these few untroubled weeks in the summer of 1814 were all too shortly to be followed by renewed catastrophe.[27]

At Lower Fort Garry, some twenty or thirty miles north of modern Winnipeg, the two York boats kept here by Parks Canada – the agency responsible for most of this country's historic sites – have been hauled from the nearby Red River for the winter. Tapering gracefully at both prow and stern, these vessels have the look not only of traditional Orkney fishing boats but also of the Viking longships from which all such Orcadian craft were ultimately descended. When under sail on Lake Winnipeg, then, a Hudson's Bay Company flotilla must have had something of the appearance of the Norse expeditions which had reached the eastern rim of North America several centuries earlier. But when you stand beside those Lower Fort Garry vessels today, you are impressed much less by their historical associations than by their sheer size and solidity. To portage a York boat around a set of rapids must indeed have been a muscle-tearing business.

Lower Fort Garry, which was afterwards to become the Hudson's Bay Company's Red River headquarters, did not exist when the Kildonan people came this way. But the Red River itself has not changed fundamentally in the intervening 180 years. It still meanders sluggishly towards Lake Winnipeg. Its banks are still tree-covered. And when you take the riverside dirt road southwards from the fort, it is possible even yet to form some impression of how this place would have appeared to those Sutherland folk who had endured so much to get here.

It is, admittedly, several weeks after freeze-up. The river ice, its rucked and broken surface glinting dully beneath a reddish-looking sun, is as far removed as it is possible to be from the blue waters which would have greeted the Kildonan party. It is also the case, inevitably, that Red River frontages now constitute the residential sites most eagerly sought after by Winnipeg's more affluent families – with the result that wilderness has long since given way to suburbs in this quarter. But the surrounding landscape's most essential characteristic remains as striking as ever to anyone coming here from Scotland. Absolutely nothing – not winter cold, not summer heat, not even its being gradually built over – can deflect a newly arrived visitor's attention from the almost unbelievable flatness of this part of Manitoba.

'After leaving the riverbank,' one Red River settler reported of his group's first encounter with their new homeland, 'we entered a fine plain, as level as a bowling green, covered with a fine sward of grass, knee high, with here and there a clump of wood as if planted for ornament by the hand of man.'[28]

This is prairie. In one direction, it stretches all the way to Texas. In another, it reaches to the foothills of the Rockies. And for about a hundred years now, this vast region has been the most productive agricultural area on earth. When the Sutherland emigrants first nosed their York boats into the Red River's lower reaches, however, the North American prairies were much as they had been for maybe six or seven millennia. Their grasses and their brightly coloured summer flowers – growing sometimes to a height of several feet and fuelling most falls wind-driven fires of frightening intensity – were home to a profusion of wildlife. They were home, most famously, to the enormous herds of bison, or buffalo, on which the Red River locality's native peoples – the Assiniboine, the Western Cree, the Saulteaux, the Ojibwa and the Sioux – traditionally depended for their food, their clothing and much else.

Although less directly relevant to the fur trade than the forest regions which were the principal source of beaver pelts, these natural grasslands in the vicinity of Red River were of no small importance to the North West Company traders who, long before the Earl of Selkirk's interest in the place became known, had firmly installed themselves here-abouts. Not only was Red River one of the principal staging posts on the canoe route from Montreal, by way of Fort William, to the Athabasca country and other scarcely less rich trapping grounds. The district was also a major source of a commodity which fuelled the fur trade in much the same way as petroleum fuels more modern communications systems. This commodity was pemmican. It was a dried and cured meat deriving from the numerous buffalo to be found around Red River. And it provided North West Company voyageurs – whose travels were far too demanding to leave any time for hunting – with the concentrated, high-nutrition diet these men needed to make possible their quite astonishing feats of endurance.

From the outset, therefore, the North West Company had regarded Selkirk's Red River venture with unconcealed suspicion. By moving the trading frontier ever further into the interior, Simon MacTavish and his colleagues had triumphantly outflanked their Hudson's Bay Company rivals – who had been content, for the most part, to confine themselves to dealing with such comparatively small numbers of Indian trappers as were prepared to take furs to York Factory. Now the Nor'Westers suspected Selkirk and the newly assertive Hudson's Bay Company – in which the earl, of course, had a controlling stake and from which he had obtained his Red River land grant – of attempting both to cut their canoe links with the west and to deprive them of essential pemmican.

As soon as Lord Selkirk began advertising for colonists in Scotland in 1811, therefore, Simon MacGillivray of the North West Company – whose private correspondence is insistent that the earl had, at all costs, to 'be driven to abandon' his settlement scheme – began supplying an Inverness newspaper with a series of bloodcurdling warnings as to what awaited anyone foolish enough to be enticed to Red River. Selkirk's prospective settlers, MacGillivray wrote anonymously, 'must first traverse the inhospitable regions in the vicinity of Hudson's Bay' where they were likely to 'perish . . . from excessive cold and want of food'. Even such individuals as might be lucky enough to win through to Red River would not find their troubles at an end, MacGillivray prognosticated gloomily. 'They will be surrounded by warlike natives who will consider them as intruders come to spoil their hunting ground, to drive away the wild animals and to destroy the Indians . . . Even if the emigrants escape the scalping knife, they will be subject to constant alarm and terror. Their habitations, their crops, their cattle will be destroyed and they will find it impossible to exist in the country.'[29]

Much of this prophecy, in the event, came true. But this was only partly owing to Simon MacGillivray's assessment of North American conditions being more accurate than Selkirk's. It had much more to do with the North West Company's own efforts to ensure that the settler community in the Red River country was beset with more than its fair share of troubles. In setting out to wreck Selkirk's prospective colony, moreover, the North West Company was able to call on allies who, in the last analysis, were willing to resort to force in order to preserve a mode of life which they valued every bit as much as the Kildonan emigrants had valued their own traditional way of living back in Sutherland.

The people who were thus to take the lead in what gradually developed into an all-out assault on the Red River settlement were not the Indians with whom Simon MacGillivray had tried to terrify his Scottish readers. They were rather the Metis, the mixed-blood population resulting originally from sexual contact – sometimes inside a form of marriage and sometimes not – between the Red River region's native peoples, on the one hand, and the fur trade's Scottish Highland and Québecois personnel, on the other. The Metis were quickly to develop their own distinctive lifestyle. And much the most vital element in this lifestyle was the highly dramatic but grimly dangerous buffalo hunt undertaken by this community's young men at those twice yearly intervals when the regular migrations of prairie bison herds brought those herds within striking distance of Red River.

'Imagine four hundred horsemen entering at full speed a herd of some thousands of buffalo,' one Red River resident wrote of such a Metis hunt. 'Riders in clouds of dust and volumes of smoke . . . crossing and recrossing each other in every direction. Shots on the right, on the left, behind, before, here, there, two, three, a dozen at a time, everywhere in close succession, at the same moment. Horses stumbling, riders falling, dead and wounded animals tumbling here and there, one over the other; and this zig-zag and bewildering melee continued for hours or more together in wild confusion.'[30]

The Metis – for reasons deriving from the riding and shooting skills which it demanded – were inclined to regard the buffalo hunt as an assertion of their Indian-influenced cultural identity as well as an important source of revenue. The Selkirk land concession consequently posed as potent a threat to this new prairie nation as it did to the commercial operations of the North West Company. The development of a farming economy in an area to which the Metis considered themselves to have just as good a claim as either the Earl of Selkirk or the Hudson's Bay Company was something to be resisted, or so the Metis thought at any rate, for reasons more or less identical to those which had driven the Kildonan folk to challenge the methods by which the Marquess of Stafford and the Countess of Sutherland were seeking to deprive so many Scottish families of their landholdings. What was at stake in the developing struggle for Red River, then, was what had been at stake also in the Strath of Kildonan – the control of territory. What differentiated this Red River conflict from the one which had gone before in Sutherland was that the dispossessed, in the shape of the Selkirk settlers, had all too readily been transformed, from a Metis standpoint anyway, into the dispossessors.

The mutual hostility which quickly developed between the Metis and the Kildonan Highlanders was to last a long time. As late as the 1970s, Margaret Laurence, her literary outlook influenced both by her own Scots antecedents and by her reading of Highland history, would attempt to resolve in *The Diviners* something of the consequent tensions in her account of the complex relationship between a twentieth-century Highlander-Canadian, Morag Gunn, and a twentieth-century Metis, Jules Tonnerre. But for all that Laurence's novel is as good an insight as one is likely to get into the tragedy inherent in the battle for Red River, the essential nature of that tragedy can be grasped from the simple fact that the central figure on the Metis side, during much of what now took place, was a man with a Scottish Highland name.

This was Cuthbert Grant who was born in the vicinity of Red River in 1793. Grant's mother, it seems, was of both Cree and French descent. His father, also Cuthbert Grant, was a Gaelic-speaking Highlander who came to North America from Strathspey and who went on to become one of the first North West Company traders to push into the Athabasca country. The elder Grant had been sufficiently attached to the boy to provide in his will for young Cuthbert's education, naming no less a person than William MacGillivray, soon to be the leading figure in the North West Company, as the lad's guardian. MacGillivray had accordingly arranged for Cuthbert to be sent away to school – in Montreal, say some accounts, in Scotland, say certain others – and it was not until around 1812 that Grant returned to the Red River district. He came back from the east, where he had entered North West Company employment, a highly articulate, fully literate and generally well-turned-out young man. But he also came back, as he made clear immediately, to live in the customary Metis manner – soon proving himself as good a shot and as talented a horseman as any of his compatriots.[31]

Cuthbert Grant's return to Red River coincided with the arrival there of the first party of settlers sent out by the Earl of Selkirk. This group, though they found the journey from Scotland no easier than the Kildonan people were to find it two years later, suffered no initial harassment from the resident population of Red River – not least because neither the Metis nor the North West Company seem to have expected the new colony to endure in the face of the many natural difficulties in the way of establishing an agricultural economy in such an isolated location. As it became increasingly obvious that the settlers were determined to persist, however, relations between the colonists and their neighbours began to deteriorate. They deteriorated further when Miles MacDonell, whom Selkirk had appointed governor of his enormous land concession, issued a proclamation which was intended to help secure the infant colony's food supplies by making it illegal to export pemmican from the Red River territory. This, of course, was interpreted both by the Metis and by the North West Company as a direct challenge to their position.

Something akin to actual warfare consequently began to be waged on the Selkirk settlement by Cuthbert Grant whose hostility to the Red River colony was much encouraged, needless to say, by his many friends and associates among the Nor'Westers.

The Kildonan Highlanders, then, were confronting not merely Highland-descended Metis like Grant. They were confronting also those other Highlanders who had created the North West Company and who regarded the Earl of Selkirk's entire colonising strategy as a means of re-establishing the Hudson's Bay Company's previous pre-eminence in the fur trade. He was on his way 'to commence open hostilities against the enemy in Red River', one Nor'Wester commented in the course of a letter written at about the time the Kildonan people were beginning to install themselves on their new farms. 'Nothing but the complete downfall of the colony will satisfy some,' this man added of the general North West Company attitude to Selkirk's plans. Such an outcome, he concluded, would be 'a most desirable object if it can be accomplished'.[32]

This letter's author was Alexander MacDonell – cousin to Selkirk's governor, Miles MacDonell, and one more of the many individuals who had come to North America from those Highland glens which Thomas Gillespie, the man who advised Patrick Sellar and William Young on how best to establish sheep-farming in Sutherland, had long since turned over to his own extensive flocks. Associated closely with Alexander MacDonell was Duncan Cameron who belonged originally to the same general locality, having been taken from his native Glen Nevis to New York by his parents in 1773 and having moved subsequently to Williamstown in Glengarry County. Cameron, on getting to Red River, sought simultaneously to befriend and frighten Selkirk's settlers. 'He began by prevailing upon several of the heads of families to visit him,' Archibald MacDonald reported. 'He treated them with the greatest attention; gave them dinners . . . and large allowance of liquors and even wine.' Always speaking to the Kildonan people in the Gaelic which was common both to the settlers and to most of the North West Company's senior representatives, Duncan Cameron sympathised with the new arrivals whose second winter in North America had proved little more enjoyable than their first, talked darkly of the risk of some sort of attack being made on their homesteads and began to hint discreetly at the possibility of his providing transport to take them to the comfort and safety to be found, so Cameron said, in Upper Canada.[33]

By the summer of 1815, when Cuthbert Grant and his Metis – driven beyond endurance by Miles MacDonell's extremely rash, if wholly unenforceable, pronouncement on the pemmican issue – began actively to harass the settlement, the prospect of a retreat eastwards was becoming steadily more enticing. 'The state of affairs this evening is miserable,' Archibald MacDonald wrote on 14 June. 'Our horses have been stolen and shot with arrows, our pigs worried by dogs, our cattle slaughtered.'

Metis horsemen were now riding freely through the settlement, firing their guns in the air, churning up the grain and other crops in the settler population's little fields, creating an atmosphere of terror and intimidation. Soon many of the more demoralised Red River colonists had accepted Duncan Cameron's now repeated offer of a free passage eastwards with one or other of the canoe brigades now heading for the annual Nor'Wester get-together at Fort William. The unfortunate Miles MacDonell having been compelled by Cameron to accompany these refugees, the few remaining settlers withdrew northwards in the general direction of York Factory. 'We have been driven from a country whose fertile soil, wholesome climate, natural productions and beautiful scenery promised to us and our children ages of happiness,' Archibald MacDonald commented of this, the second, enforced ejection experienced by his Kildonan charges on two different continents in the space of just two years. The Earl of Selkirk's latest experiment in colonisation looked to have been terminated before it had got properly under way.[34]

That matters did not end there was due, in the first instance, to one more of the many Highlanders who loom so large on both sides of the battle for Red River. This was a Perthshire man by the name of Colin Robertson, a big, burly individual whose guiding principle was summed up in his pithy injunction, 'When you're among wolves, howl!' Having run away from home in Scotland rather than complete his apprenticeship as a weaver, Robertson – who was also given in adversity to quoting Shakespeare – had somehow made his way to New York City where he worked briefly in a grocery store. Moving afterwards to Canada, he was taken on as a clerk by the North West Company. But that, too, had palled and by 1809, at about the time that Selkirk and his associates were taking over at the Hudson's Bay Company, Robertson was in London. There, in a gesture which is indicative of some deep disagreement between the former North West Company man and that concern's ruling partners, Colin Robertson offered his services to the Hudson's Bay Company's new directors. It was as their employee that he had been sent to Red River in 1815.[35]

Meeting the retreating colonists at a point towards the northern end of Lake Winnipeg, Robertson persuaded them to return with him to their abandoned settlement where, to everyone's surprise, the cereals which had been sown in the spring were discovered to be ripening satisfactorily under a Manitoban summer sun. Perhaps sixty of the Kildonan settlers were thus installed once more at Red River. There they were joined in the fall of 1815 by a new set of Sutherland families brought out by Robert Semple, a Boston-born businessman who had recently become Selkirk's latest protégé and who was delighted to observe, on sailing into the Red River from Lake Winnipeg in September, more than a dozen stacks of newly harvested grain standing out distinctly against a typically cloudless prairie sky. These few stacks, Semple noted proudly, were 'a sight perfectly novel in this country'.[36]

Moore's Creek, North Carolina   *(US National Parks Service)*

Louisbourg, Nova Scotia   *(Canadian Tourist Office)*

Margaree Meadows, Cape Breton   *(Wallace Ellison)*

Mabou Inlet, Cape Breton   *(Wallace Ellison)*

Red River cabin   *(Parks Canada)*

Quebec City and the St Lawrence River   *(Gouvernement du Quebec)*

Fraser Canyon, British Columbia   *(Peter Langer)*

Hill country in the Adirondacks, New York
(New York State Department of Economic Development)

Fort William, Thunder Bay   *(Canadian Tourist Office)*

Rocky Mountain lake   *(Alberta Tourism)*

McDonald Peak, Montana   *(William Munoz)*

Prairie wheatfields   *(Canadian Tourist Office)*

Farming country to the north of the Mohawk Valley
(New York State Department of Economic Development)

The several hundred bushels of wheat, barley and oats harvested in 1815 at Red River by men and women from Kildonan were both the first sign of North America's future role in world farming and a welcome indication that the Earl of Selkirk's choice of Red River as the setting for a Scottish Highland colony was less perverse than it had so far seemed. There had still to occur, however, one more violent episode.

Cuthbert Grant had now married a young Metis woman whose name, Elizabeth MacKay, shows her to have had a parentage very similar to his own. But he remained as opposed as ever to the Selkirk colonists: rallying his people in the spring of 1816 for a renewed campaign; writing that he intended to 'come off with flying colours' in any confrontation with the settlers; adding that he hoped never to 'see any of them again in the colonising way in Red River'. What Grant planned exactly is unclear. What actually happened is all too bloodily apparent. On 19 June 1816, seeing a Metis mounted column apparently reconnoitring the roughly constructed strongpoint which – in honour of their patron – the colonists had named Fort Douglas, Robert Semple led a party of armed volunteers to meet the approaching horsemen near a little woodland grove called Seven Oaks. The rival contingents attempted to encircle each other. Shooting started – from which side is still disputed. Soon Semple and nineteen other colonists were either dead or very badly wounded. For the loss of only one of his own men, Cuthbert Grant, for as long as it took the Earl of Selkirk to mobilise sufficient forces to keep the Metis threat at bay, had made himself the master of Red River.[37]

In a little park off modern Winnipeg's Tache Avenue is to be found the Manitoba Heritage Council plaque which marks the spot where Miles MacDonell formally took possession of the lands conveyed to Lord Selkirk by the Hudson's Bay Company. But of the actual settlement established hereabouts by the Kildonan people there is, of course, nothing to be seen – its riverside fields and log-built homes having long ago been lost to sight below the spreading streets of what, since the later decades of the nineteenth century, has been one of the Canadian Confederation's more important urban centres.

The name of Kildonan – which the Sutherland emigrants applied to their particular corner of North America – is still to be glimpsed as you drive downtown on Main Street. But the Selkirk settlement's only other surviving traces are those which have been found by Winnipeg archaeologists excavating city lots in the brief periods between the demolition of one building and the construction of its successor. The clay pipes, cloth fragments and bits of broken crockery recovered in the course of such digs are as close as it is possible to get nowadays to families who must sometimes have wondered if the crofts they had rejected might have been preferable, after all, to the terrible uncertainties of their first years at Red River.

It was in an attempt to minimise those uncertainties that the Earl of Selkirk came here in the summer of 1817 at the head of the force of Swiss and German mercenaries he personally led westwards in the aftermath of the Seven Oaks fighting. Tired of getting news of events at Red River some six to twelve months after they occurred, Selkirk had sailed for New York in the autumn of 1815, made his way up the Hudson Valley to Montreal, attempted to get the colonial authorities in Canada to impose order at Red River and, when they declined to become involved, took the law finally into his own hands. The soldiers whom Selkirk now employed had been brought to Canada in the course of the conflict which had provided the earl with the justification for the Highland regiment which he had been attempting to organise in 1813. With peace restored along the frontier between the United States and British North America, these troops were surplus to Britain's military requirements. Selkirk, before anyone could stop him, simply took them over, bundled them into canoes and, some two months after the events at Seven Oaks, landed this force of well-armed soldiers within easy striking distance of the North West Company post at Fort William. Finding several of the more senior Nor'Westers paying their customary summer visit to the fort, the earl – conducting himself now very much as his Douglas ancestors might have done in the course of their many medieval raids across the English border – promptly took these eminent Montrealers into custody on the grounds that they had conspired to bring about the destruction of his Red River colony.

The North West Company, of course, was much too powerful an organisation to be overthrown singlehandedly by Selkirk – whose activities at Fort William served simply to embroil him in a series of wholly unwinnable legal actions. But the earl's dramatic capture of its Lake Superior headquarters nevertheless turned out to mark the start of a rapidly deepening crisis in the affairs of the commercial concern which Simon MacTavish had so successfully established nearly forty years before. The Hudson's Bay Company, which Selkirk had helped to revitalise, was now challenging the Nor'Westers on a wider and wider front. Colin Robertson had gone on from Red River to lead a Bay Company detachment into the Athabasca country which the North West Company had long regarded as its exclusive preserve. Similar competition was becoming evident elsewhere. North West Company profits were falling steeply. The organisation's frontier traders were more and more at odds with its moneymen in Montreal. Soon the unthinkable was beginning to be thought. Their only sure way of surviving commercially, the North West Company's principal partners had concluded by 1820, lay in their seeking to amalgamate with the Hudson's Bay Company which those same Nor'Westers, in their heyday, had come close to forcing out of business.[38]

The resulting deal was concluded in March 1821. That summer

William MacGillivray, whom Simon MacTavish had first taken under his care in Scotland in 1776, left Fort William for the last time. He had been engaged there for several weeks, MacGillivray wrote, 'settling a most important business . . . the carrying into effect of the various deeds and covenants entered into on the part of the North West Company . . . with the Hudson's Bay Company. These arrangements are happily completed and I part with my old troops – to meet with them no more in discussions on the Indian trade.' MacGillivray had marked the occasion by making appropriate personal presents to several hardened veterans of the fur business – 'a handsome dagger to one, a pair of pistols to another'. And something of the old Nor'Wester brashness clearly lingered still. 'We have made no submission,' William MacGillivray insisted of his agreement with the long-detested Bay men. 'We met and negotiated on equal terms.'[39]

But something of significance was given up that summer all the same; something which Washington Irving was to hint at in the course of one of his several attempts to define what it was exactly that had made the North West Company so distinctive. 'The feudal state of Fort William is at an end,' Irving remarked. 'Its council chamber is silent and deserted; its banquet hall no longer echoes to the burst of loyalty or the *auld warld* ditty.' A frontier epoch shaped and dominated by Scottish Highlanders of William MacGillivray's type was inexorably passing away. The North West Company's founding father, Simon MacTavish, was long dead. MacGillivray himself, after that summer of 1821, would live for only four more years. Others of the company's leading men were withdrawing gradually from their trading posts. Duncan Cameron, John MacDonald of Garth and David Thompson were among the several eminent Nor'Westers who retired eventually to Glengarry County – where it is still possible to visit Thompson's home. As for Alexander MacKenzie, perhaps the most renowned of all the numerous Highlanders involved in developing the North American fur trade, he had earlier taken himself back to Scotland; buying the estate of Avoch in the Black Isle; being buried there in 1820 in a graveyard where casual visitors are today surprised to find a Canadian flag rooted permanently in a stone-walled enclosure from which your eye is unavoidably drawn across the Moray Firth to the hills above Culloden and Stratherrick.[40]

Standing by Alexander MacKenzie's grave and looking at that red and white maple-leaf emblem, it is impossible to do other than sympathise with William MacGillivray's own verdict on his company's loss of identity. 'The fur trade is forever lost to Canada,' the veteran Nor'Wester wrote in 1821. By this MacGillivray meant that his Montreal-based and Montreal-controlled concern had been forced to give way at last to a consortium managed entirely from London. It is in this sense that the demise of the North West Company can be portrayed as a victory for the selfsame British imperialism which, just a single human lifetime earlier, had brought about the ruin of the Highland clans from which the company was so directly derived. It was certainly with a view to making exactly this connection that a modern Canadian writer of Scottish Highland extraction, Hugh MacLennan, was to compose his own particular tribute to William MacGillivray, Simon MacTavish and their associates. There was much that was 'pathetically true to the Highlander's lifestyle', Hugh MacLennan commented, in the tangled story of the 'absorption' of the North West Company 'by calculating Anglo-Saxons whose greatness, I truly believe in my more Hebridean moods, has always consisted in their capacity to appropriate to themselves with a free conscience not only the labours of other men, but the credit won by other men's genius and courage'. It did not surprise Hugh MacLennan that practically every Canadian of his generation was familiar with the work of the Hudson's Bay Company, while of the North West Company, which had been largely responsible for ensuring that modern Canada extends from sea to sea, almost no Canadian knew anything worth knowing. It had been the Hudson's Bay Company's 'final success', MacLennan thought, that they had been able to round off their 1821 takeover by 'claiming most of the credit for what other men had done'.[41]

But if it is difficult to feel much sympathy for the Earl of Selkirk when in that Avoch cemetery, or when in the great hall at Fort William, come to that, the events surrounding the extinction of the North West Company seem less clear cut when viewed from downtown Winnipeg. Stroll from Main Street along Broadway prior to turning into the Manitoba Legislative Building. Look at this structure's utterly self-confident architecture. Consider its evocation, achieved through colour, tone and soaring vaulting, of prairie wheatfields ripening beneath a prairie sky. And when you have finished contemplating how Manitoba got to be the way it is, reflect for just a moment on Thomas Douglas, Earl of Selkirk, and his pigheaded determination to get the Kildonan people settled here. 'These Highlanders were magnificent human material,' Hugh MacLennan commented, 'and what was done to them when they were helpless was . . . disgraceful . . . They were enclosed so that landlords might turn the glens into sheep runs . . . For these reasons it is difficult for anyone of Scotch descent to sneer at Lord Selkirk, despite what his recklessness, and at times his arrogance, did to so many people.'[42]

Selkirk, like Alexander MacKenzie from whom the earl had first learned of the Red River country, died in the early part of 1820. He was ruined financially, largely discredited, his enduring vision of a flourishing colony here on the edge of the prairies commonly regarded as the foolish eccentricity of a hopelessly inept aristocrat with more cash to his name than good sense. But if this was ever a reasonable verdict, it is so no longer. The Canadian Kildonan, after all, has become an integral component of one of North America's more appealing cities. As for the Scottish Kildonan, which the Marquess of Stafford and the

Countess of Sutherland believed they had set on so sure an economic footing, it is today so empty, so deserted, so devoid of any sign of life that nobody finds it worth while to unlock its church door even on a Sunday.

CHAPTER NINE

Stand Fast, Craigellachie!

BECAUSE FEW PARTS of the Scottish Highlands are more than twenty or thirty miles from the sea, even the region's larger rivers, such as the Spey, do not begin to approximate to the size of those North American watercourses which drain territories as big as all of Western Europe. The Ottawa, which North West Company fur traders followed westwards from Lachine, is merely a tributary of the much more substantial St Lawrence. But it still seems enormous by Scottish standards; looking nothing like the comparatively narrow, noisy and fast-flowing Spey; consisting rather of an interlinked set of placid, lake-like stretches which are often long enough and wide enough to take on something of the character of a fair-sized Highland loch.

Only at the rapids which separate these calm and readily navigable pieces of water from each other does the Ottawa conform to the Scottish concept of a river. Its eastward-tending current, scarcely noticeable for much of the river's several hundred miles, begins to gather pace. Soon it is travelling faster than a man can run. Then, its velocity still increasing, the previously smooth surface of the river is suddenly ripped and torn by huge, white-crested waves which themselves dissolve, a few more yards downstream, into a broken, shapeless mass of roaring, rumbling water.

It is an exhilarating experience to sit on the shelving rocks at the spot which French-speaking traders christened Rapides des Chênes and watch the Ottawa hurtling towards the distant ocean. Men like William MacGillivray and Alexander MacKenzie came here each springtime in the years around 1800. It is easy to imagine them making this particular portage, their voices raised above the racket of the river as they issue the occasional instruction, in heavily accented French, to the teams of sweating voyageurs who are responsible for getting their canoes and trade goods safely into Lac des Chênes, the name given to the quieter waters above the rapids. It is equally easy to imagine the very different scene of twenty or thirty years later when Glengarry County rivermen, shouting to each other in the Gaelic which many of the Nor'Westers also used among themselves, regularly manoeuvred their timber consignments past this point in the course of those repeated journeys which began in Ottawa Valley forest shanties and ended on the Quebec City waterfront.

The lumber trade was eventually to result in the emergence of permanent riverside settlements along the Ottawa; untidy, casually laid-out, roughly built collections of sawmills, lodging places, warehouses, brothels, drinking dens and gambling halls. One such frontier community, initially called Bytown, began to take shape in the 1820s not far below the Rapides des Chênes. Some thirty years afterwards, when the newly united colonies of Lower and Upper Canada were in search of a common administrative centre, the choice – exercised finally, as it happens, by Queen Victoria – fell on Bytown for no better reason than its being a geographical and linguistic compromise between the rival claims of English-speaking Toronto and French-speaking Montreal. Thus it came about that Ottawa, as Bytown was now renamed, became eventually the capital of the still wider confederation which took shape in the wake of most of the other British North American colonies deciding to throw in their lot with the two Canadas.[1]

A little to the east of modern Ottawa's parliament buildings, where tourists gather to watch the ceremonial changing of the guard and to listen to a Canadian army pipe band properly resplendent in tartan of the type once worn by Fraser's Highlanders, you come across a statue of the politician who, more than any other, ensured that Canada eventually became the sort of country Alexander MacKenzie had envisaged: a transcontinental nation; a country incorporating all the vast territories between the original, much smaller, Canada and the Pacific Ocean. This statue shows a man in the heavy overcoat and stout boots which were necessary to survive a nineteenth-century Ottawa winter. His hair is long, his face – even allowing for the flattery of sculptors – is impressive. His name, as stated on a plinth which carries no subsidiary wording, was John A. Macdonald.

Some 3,500 miles east of Ottawa, on a hillside near the Sutherland village of Rogart, you find another memorial to the same man. This one takes the shape of a stone cairn. 'Sir John A. Macdonald,' reads its inscription. 'First Prime Minister of Canada. Father of Confederation.'

In the unsettled decades following the last Jacobite rebellion, this Sir John's paternal grandfather, John MacDonald, farmed the little patch of land now overlooked by that tall cairn which another Canadian premier of Sutherland ancestry, John G. Diefenbaker, unveiled in the 1960s. Behind are the rocky slopes of Creag na Dalach Moire. In front is the narrow valley of Strathoykel which, in 1792, provided more than a few recruits to the makeshift army which, as mentioned previously, assembled hereabouts in a desperate – and doomed – attempt to prevent large-scale sheep-farms supplanting smallholdings of the type occupied by John MacDonald. Perhaps MacDonald was one of the many Strathoykel tenants evicted at this time. Perhaps not. All that is known for certain is that he now moved – and the fact that he made such a transition so comparatively late in life is suggestive of a degree of compulsion having been involved – to the coastal town of Dornoch, bringing with him from Strathoykel his wife, Jean, and their several children.[2]

Among these children was a boy by the name of Hugh who had been born in 1782 and who was himself to move, as so many other landless and workless Highlanders were doing at this time, to Glasgow. There Hugh Macdonald – who, though amiable enough, appears to have been both an idler and a boozer – established a series of small businesses, all of which rapidly crashed. There, too, Macdonald married Helen Shaw, a woman of considerably greater energy and mettle than himself.

Like her husband, Helen was a Gaelic-speaking Highlander. Her own mother, Margaret Grant, had grown up in Strathspey, marrying initially a local man by the name of William Shaw and going on, following her first husband's death, to become the wife of another Shaw, this one called James. William Shaw and James Shaw – the latter of whom had fought on the Jacobite side at Culloden before going on, like so many other Highlanders of the period, to join the British army – were unrelated. But both belonged, as did various other Shaws, Gows and Smiths in this part of the Highlands, to what had long been known as Clan Chattan. This was a tribal grouping which, together with the neighbouring Clan Grant, had long dominated the territories extending northwards from Strathspey in the direction of Inverness. Clan Chattan's chiefs were MacIntoshes. Its great men included several by the name of MacGillivray. And as can be seen immediately from this rollcall of its component elements, Clan Chattan, in the eighteenth century, had become intimately involved with North America. John MacIntosh of the Georgia Highland Rangers belonged to a Clan Chattan family. The same was true of William MacGillivray of the North West Company. It was true also of a whole host of other fur traders as well as many of the officers and men serving with those several Highland regiments which were deployed in North America between the outbreak of the French and Indian War in the 1750s and the close, in the 1780s, of the subsequent armed struggle between Britain and its rebel colonists.[3]

Among the Strathspey soldiers who saw action in the course of this second conflict was a young man called Donald MacPherson who, at the Revolutionary War's end in 1783, came back to Scotland and settled in the vicinity of Dalnavert, a little township on the rising ground to the east of the River Spey, not far from the modern village of Kincraig. Dalnavert's principal family were the Shaws – among them Margaret Grant's first husband, William – who had once occupied much more extensive territories but who had been displaced, several generations back, by the Grants of Rothiemurchus. One of these Grants, Elizabeth by name, was to leave an account of the Shaw home at Dalnavert as it appeared to her at the start of the nineteenth century. The walls of the residence belonging to what she called 'the ruined clan' of Shaw, Elizabeth Grant remembered, were constructed largely of turf cut from the surrounding fields. Its windows 'were not made to open'. And 'the kitchen fireplace' consisted of nothing more elaborate than 'a stone on the floor and a hole in the roof'.[4]

The Revolutionary War veteran, Donald MacPherson, was no doubt familiar with this Strathspey house. MacPherson was to re-enter the army at the start, in the early 1790s, of Britain's latest war with France. Following a military career which ended in his attaining the rank of colonel and which brought him back to North America when Canada was invaded by the United States in 1812, he was finally to retire and settle down in the little town of Kingston at the eastern end of Lake Ontario. While in Strathspey, however, MacPherson had met and married Anna Shaw, daughter of that earlier marriage between Margaret Grant and William Shaw of Dalnavert and thus the half-sister of Helen Shaw who, around 1811, became engaged in Glasgow to the feckless, Strathoykel-born businessman, Hugh Macdonald. It was natural, therefore, that when Hugh and his wife, in the wake of one more of the former's financial failures, decided in 1820 to try their luck in North America, they should settle alongside Helen's half-sister in Kingston. To follow in the wake of one's relations, after all, had always been the favoured Highland way of emigrating.[5]

Hugh Macdonald did little better in Kingston than in Scotland. But Hugh's son, John Alexander, born in Glasgow in 1815 and only five when the Macdonald family disembarked from the ship which brought them from the Clyde to the St Lawrence, was arguably to make more impact on Canada than any other single individual; not because the legal career on which he started in 1835 proved particularly lucrative; nor because his various business speculations – which were not notably more successful than those undertaken by his father – brought him a fortune of the kind soon to be made by other Strathspey-connected Canadians; but because this Kingston lawyer chose, in his thirties, to go into politics, rapidly becoming the dominant personality in Canada's Conservative Party.

John A. Macdonald was not the stuff of which conventional Victorian heroes were made. Like his father, he drank rather more than was good for him. And the means by which he achieved his political objectives included bribery, corruption and chicanery on an occasionally lavish scale. But what redeems, and even renders admirable, this greatest of Canadian statesmen – who, right through his life, retained the 'heavy Scottish brogue' he had acquired from his parents – is the extent to which he was prepared to sacrifice practically everything on the altar of the cause that became with him a virtual obsession. This cause was nothing less than that of Canada itself. It was John A. Macdonald's tremendous achievement to bring into existence a nation which – for all that the pieces from which Macdonald constructed it have sometimes seemed inclined to fly apart again – has both survived and provided successive generations of Canadians with the means of conducting one of the world's more ambitious experiments in mutual co-existence.[6]

It was difficult enough to bring Atlantic colonies like Nova Scotia, New Brunswick and Prince Edward Island into a confederation which was clearly destined to be dominated economically and politically by the territories which now had their name applied to the whole of what had thus been created. It was much more difficult still to ensure that the new Canada also included all of the vast landmass which the Highlanders of the North West Company had done so much to explore and which this latest Highlander-Canadian, John A. Macdonald, his flamboyant and sometimes reckless style more than a little reminiscent of the operating methods favoured by the likes of Simon MacTavish and William MacGillivray, was determined to place under Ottawa's control.

For much of the nineteenth century the only settlement of any consequence west of the Great Lakes, east of the Rockies and north of the United States was Red River. And for much of the nineteenth century Red River's isolation remained almost as profound as it had been when the Kildonan people first made their way there from Hudsons Bay. 'There is a spot on this continent,' commented one American who spent some time in Red River in 1855, 'which travellers do not visit. Deserts, almost trackless, divide it from the habitations of men. To reach it, or once there to escape it, is an exploit of which one may almost boast. It is not even marked on the maps nor mentioned in the gazetteers.' But for all its remoteness, this American continued, Red River was nothing if not civilised. While there, he had danced, dined well, sampled the contents of several excellent wine cellars, come across a good library which included several recent novels by Dickens and Thackeray, seen more than one copy of the *Illustrated London News* and participated in 'intellectual conversation' every bit as stimulating, or so this visitor claimed, as any to be had in Washington.[7]

The many Highland families then living around Red River – those Sutherlands, Gillespies, MacKays, MacPhersons, Mathesons, MacBeaths, Campbells, Bethunes, Finlays, MacLeans, Johnstons, MacKinnons, MacDonalds, Murrays, Bannermans and others – had not found it easy to bring their community to this state of comparative comfort. Hostility between the Metis and the Highlanders – one of whom, Donald Murray, was afterwards to describe the Metis leader, Cuthbert Grant, as 'quite a friend of mine' – had eased steadily in the years following the Seven Oaks episode of 1816. But there remained no lack of other threats to the Red River settlement's existence. Fields were flooded in spring. Crops were devastated by grasshoppers in summer and threatened by prairie fires or early frosts most falls. Winter, in the words of one Red River resident, was a time of 'bleak and stormy winds . . . accompanied with deep snows and intense cold'. In January and February a fahrenheit thermometer might record as much as seventy degrees of frost. And it was at that time of year, of course, that wolves tended, as this same Red River settler commented, 'to be very annoying and destructive' of such sheep and cattle as the community had managed to accumulate.[8]

The Earl of Selkirk had promised his Kildonan emigrants that they would be provided by him with a Gaelic-speaking – and Presbyterian – minister. Indeed Donald Sage, a son of the Kildonan manse and afterwards a well-known Highland clergyman in his own right, had been engaged for just this task. But Sage, who made no mention of the affair in his extensive memoirs, seems to have reneged on the deal, leaving Red River to make do with one John West, appointed the community's chaplain by the Hudson's Bay Company. West, however, ministered in accordance with Church of England rites. 'And the Scotch,' as one of Red River's first historians remarked, 'could see no spirituality in such forms; besides which, the English language was to them a foreign tongue and they longed to hear their native Gaelic.' So it came about that, rather than rely on alien rituals, Red River's Highland settlers made one of their own number, James Sutherland, responsible for baptisms, marriages and other matters of that kind.[9]

These same Highlanders imported more than Scotland's predominant religion. Their agricultural techniques began as variants of those to which they had been accustomed in Sutherland – with the first Red River farms being laid out in much the same way as those which their occupants had previously worked in the Strath of Kildonan. Fields were small initially. Sheep and cattle were pastured on what amounted to a common grazing of the Highland type. There was, after all, no alternative pattern on which the Red River settlers might draw. But new circumstances clearly called for new methods. Adaption and innovation – of a sort which the men responsible for the Sutherland evictions were inclined to think Highlanders incapable – were consequently quick in coming. Soon pumpkins and melons were being grown in addition to barley, oats and potatoes. Soon wheat, which this part of North America would eventually produce in enormous quantities, began to be cultivated successfully – one visitor who reached Red River just before sunset on a cloudless day in early fall remarking on how each high stack of wheat sheaves sent 'its long eastward shadow over the closely shaven plain'.[10]

Red River wheat was harvested with the help of sickles brought from Scotland. Whether or not some Red River Highlander's baggage also included the hooked stick or *caman* used by players of the ancient Highland game of shinty is unclear. What is certain is that shinty or 'shinny', as it was commonly called in North America, was being played at Red River from the moment of the Kildonan people's arrival – just as it was played by other Highlanders in Glengarry County and the American South. What is equally evident is that shinny, in Red River as in Glengarry, rapidly made the transition from snowy fields to the much smoother, faster surface provided by frozen lakes and rivers. Not the least of the many still enduring contributions made by Scottish Highlanders to North American life, it thus seems likely, is the modern sport of ice hockey.[11]

Its farms may have been increasingly productive. Its homes may have contained examples of the latest literary fashions. One of its pastimes, in the shape of shinny on an icebound river, may have been destined to become part of the common heritage of the United States and Canada. Its population – consisting more and more of Metis families and of retired fur traders as well as of those folk whose family origins were in Kildonan – may have grown from the few hundred individuals of 1820 to the several thousand living here in the decade which saw John A. Macdonald preside over the beginnings of Canadian confederation. But Red River, more than fifty years after the Earl of Selkirk had committed himself to peopling the plains between the Great Lakes and the Rockies, remained almost as inaccessible as ever. From Canada's St Lawrence heartland, Red River had still to be reached by way of the canoe route which had been the North West Company's principal means of getting to the interior. Only from the south, where the steadily expanding American railroad network now made it easy to get as far as the Minnesota town of St Paul, some three or four hundred miles from Selkirk's colony, was Red River becoming noticeably more approachable. And this, from John A. Macdonald's perspective, was a most worrying development.

Even today – and especially perhaps if you are freshly come from a country characterised, for the most part, by smaller, more domesticated, landscapes – there is something awe-inspiring, even a little bit intimidating, about the sheer scale, the utterly unsheltered feel, of Manitoba and Saskatchewan. 'Having grown up in a little province by the sea,' Hugh MacLennan once observed, 'its experience to some extent recorded by the literatures of maritime peoples from the Greeks to the English, I was appalled when I first found myself on the prairie. It was as alien to me as the moon's surface. I wondered how anyone could endure life in a land which seemed to me so stark. Later on I realised that what I really feared here was the idea of my own littleness. Later still I realised that the prairie's monotony contains inner beauties and harmonies as subtle as those of a Bach fugue. But it is a challenge to the soul, just the same. It is also a challenge to the eye.'[12]

Even at the steady 100 kilometres an hour they allow you on the Trans-Canada Highway, the journey westwards from Winnipeg to Regina seems somehow to take place in slow motion. Like a little island glimpsed from an especially sluggish Hebridean ferry, a prairie town, dominated in every instance by its square-built grain silo, appears on the horizon, very gradually gets into closer focus, is beside you for a moment, then falls away slowly behind. Ten miles go by; one hundred; several hundred. You pass Portage-la-Prairie, MacGregor, Austin, Brandon, Kemnay, Oak Lake, Virden, Elkhorn. But the landscape has not altered to any meaningful degree.

Seeing this landscape for the first time is perhaps a bit like having lived in this most landlocked part of North America all your life and then deciding to take an ocean cruise. Just as nothing other than direct experience of it can quite explain the essence of the sea, no book, no film, no photograph can possibly prepare you for the prairie; for its skies, its clouds, its sunsets; for its ungraspable immenseness; for its frequently grim weather. The prairie climate, you very soon discover, is one which deals habitually in extremes.

'Few sights in Canada,' Hugh MacLennan wrote, 'are more peaceful than the mirroring of the pastel sky-hues on the Saskatchewan on a fine summer day; none more chilling than an eddy of snow in January when the thermometer stands at forty or fifty below and the ice is too hard for a curling stone. The winds here are visible: in summer you see them as a throbbing radiance along a sea of grass, in winter as a drifting lace of ice crystals along a sea of snow.'[13]

The saving grace of modern prairie travel – on days of windchill so intense you do not leave your car until you have carefully donned your gloves and pulled your anorak hood as tightly as you can about your face – are those roadside diners where, for what seems not more than a pittance by European standards, they fill you full of food and then, once they have properly established where you come from, go on to tell you all about some relative of theirs who emigrated here from Scotland.

The first time someone mentions this kind of connection, you are inclined to put the matter down entirely to coincidence. Not until the third or fourth time round do you begin to realise that prairie society is like no other which you have encountered. Here practically everyone you meet is the product of emigration; not emigration, as in North Carolina, Glengarry County or Cape Breton Island, which took place six, seven, eight, nine generations back; but emigration which a lot of prairie people have heard about directly from folk who were the first to settle and to farm this huge region.

It is less than two average lifetimes, after all, since the prairies were much as they had been been for countless centuries; great wildernesses given over mostly still to buffalo herds and to these few humans – Indians, in the first instance, Metis also by the nineteenth century – who lived by hunting them. As John A. Macdonald had become uncomfortably aware, however, this was a situation which could not endure much longer. America's westward expansion, though checked for a time by that nation's Civil War, was clearly unstoppable. And if nothing was done by his own country to prevent such an outcome, or so the Canadian prime minister believed, then it was very probable that American settlers would begin to move into those still largely empty areas over which Ottawa claimed authority. 'It is quite evident to me,' Macdonald wrote in 1870, 'that the United States government are resolved to do all they can, short of war, to get possession of the western territory and we must take immediate and vigorous steps to counteract them.'[14]

The Canadian confederation, though increasingly self-governing, remained, of course, a part of the British Empire. And John A. Macdonald was a loyal enough imperialist. But he was a Canadian also. And he simply did not trust London – whose politicians, Macdonald once commented, were 'so squeezable in nature' – to enforce a Canadian claim to the prairies. One London government, after all, had already surrendered to the US those territories which constitute the modern American states of Montana, Idaho, Oregon and Washington – despite these territories having been opened up largely by the North West Company. What was to prevent another London government adopting a similarly accommodating attitude with regard to further segments of a continent in which Britain had no very direct stake? Only his own conviction, John A. Macdonald seems sometimes to have felt, that Canada, just like its southern neighbour, could not properly fulfil its destiny unless it stretched from sea to sea.[15]

It was in order to sustain Canada's claims to transcontinental status that Macdonald had made such huge efforts to persuade British Columbia, thousands of miles from Ottawa and consisting then of nothing more than a scattering of tiny coastal settlements, to join his confederation. British Columbia provided Canada with a toehold on the Pacific. But if this connection was to be made both meaningful and permanent, two things had to happen. Communications between Ottawa and its western province – which, short of following the route taken by Alexander MacKenzie, could be reached from the east only by way of the enormously long sea voyage round Cape Horn – had to be dramatically improved. Some means also had to be found of populating, under Ottawa's auspices, those intervening areas which might otherwise be occupied by Americans rather than by Canadians. Both these objectives, John A. Macdonald had concluded by the end of the 1860s, could be attained only by Canada constructing its own coast-to-coast railway;

a railway which would connect British Columbia firmly with Canada's eastern provinces; a railway which would assert Canadian sovereignty over the prairies; a railway which would immediately facilitate the settlement of these same prairies by settlers whom the Ottawa government would help to recruit both in other parts of Canada and in Europe.

The great railway which – more than any Ottawa statue or Rogart cairn – is John A. Macdonald's real memorial began by practically undoing him politically. It was not until 1869, after all, that the United States, with its far greater resources, had managed to open a railroad to the Pacific. Now Canada, with its relatively tiny population, its lesser wealth and its untried government, was aspiring to construct a considerably longer length of track across much more intractable terrain. The railway project, said Macdonald's many rivals and opponents, was 'one of the most foolish things that could be imagined', 'a preposterous proposition', 'an act of insane recklessness'. It is not altogether surprising, therefore, that in 1873, amid a strong odour of scandal which had its origins in the highly dubious financial methods to which the prime minister resorted in his desperation to prove his critics wrong and to have his railway built, John A. Macdonald's Conservative government was spectacularly driven out of office.[16]

In 1878, however, Canada's Liberal Party having found the business of governing the country less straightforward than they expected, Macdonald's Tories were back in power, their leader as strongly committed as ever to his railway. And within a year or two the prime minister had found two men on whom he could rely to see his project through. One was Donald Smith, the Hudson's Bay Company's principal representative in Canada. The other was George Stephen, textile manufacturer, businessman and president of the Bank of Montreal.

Smith and Stephen were cousins. Like the prime minister with whom they were to co-operate so closely, they had been born in Scotland. And as was the case with Macdonald himself, both Smith and Stephen belonged to families whose roots were to be found ultimately in Strathspey.

Donald Smith, whose Clan Chattan forebears had used the name Gow, which itself derives from *gobha*, the Gaelic for a blacksmith, was born in the little town of Forres, some thirty miles to the east of Inverness in 1820. Forres lies outside the Highlands. But Donald Smith's parents had just moved there from the valley of the Spey where their people had been resident for generations. The little Donald's paternal great-grandfather, like John A. Macdonald's maternal grandfather, had been among the many Clan Chattan men to serve with the Jacobite army at Culloden. And Donald Smith's family, like Macdonald's own and like so many others in the eighteenth-century Scottish Highlands, had afterwards gone on to develop various links with North America. Among Donald Smith's more distant connections was the North West Company trader, Cuthbert

Grant, and, it follows, Cuthbert's son and namesake, the leader of the Red River Metis. Among the future railway king's closer relatives were those other Nor'Westers, Robert and John Stuart, whose sister, Barbara, was Donald Smith's mother. When, in 1838, the 18-year-old Donald Smith sailed himself for the St Lawrence, his passage into the Hudson's Bay Company, with which he was to be associated in one capacity or another until his death in 1914, was consequently eased by the introductory letter he carried from his Uncle John who, following the 1821 merger between the North West Company and North America's other great fur-trading concern, had eventually become one of the latter organisation's chief factors.[17]

Having started with a menial job in the former North West Company warehouse at Lachine, Donald Smith was eventually posted to the Goose Bay district of Labrador, as bleak and harsh a place as any to be found in North America. Not until 1869 did he finally emerge from the wilderness to take charge of Hudson's Bay Company operations in the Montreal area and to find himself promptly elevated by none other than John A. Macdonald to the position of Canadian government emissary charged with the task of bringing peace to Red River where the Metis, urged on now by Cuthbert Grant's spiritual successor, Louis Riel, were in open rebellion against John A. Macdonald's plan to impose direct rule from Ottawa on both Red River and the prairies.[18]

Macdonald's thinking, as it first affected Donald Smith, was very simple. Red River, until the 1867 agreement which resulted in the 200-year-old organisation transferring its landholdings to the Canadian confederation, had formally been a Hudson's Bay Company responsibility. Smith, as the company's nearest available representative of any seniority, seemed to the prime minister to be the obvious man to deal with problems in that quarter. And in this matter, as in so many others, Macdonald proved correct. Although the Metis uprising ended in bloodshed, there was much less violence than there might have been – Smith managing to mollify feeling in Red River by recommending that the Selkirk colony and the lands for several hundred miles around it, now to be known as Manitoba, should be given a degree of local autonomy by being elevated into a new Canadian province.

His prominent role in these latest Red River excitements made Donald Smith, previously not much more than an obscure fur trader, a nationally known figure in Canada. It also introduced him to the issue of prairie communications and to the investment opportunity presented in neighbouring Minnesota by what was known as the First Division of the St Paul and Pacific Railroad, a bankrupt – but, as Smith quickly grasped, potentially profitable – American company into which the Hudson's Bay Company man now began to buy his way in collaboration with his Montreal-based cousin, George Stephen.

Stephen, who grew up within four or five miles of the point, at

Craigellachie, where the Spey leaves the Highland hills for the Moray Firth lowlands and whose mother was a sister of Donald Smith's father, arrived in Canada in 1850 to become a clerk in a Montreal drapery business belonging to yet another of this extended family's North American members. Soon going into business on his own account, Stephen eventually emerged as the controlling genius of the highly successful Bank of Montreal. And having once agreed to put his financial skills at the disposal of Donald Smith in the matter of the St Paul and Pacific Railroad, a speculation which was to make both cousins very rich indeed, it was inevitable that this Montreal banker would become Smith's partner in the altogether bigger venture into which the two men were drawn by John A. Macdonald in 1880 – the venture soon to be universally known as the Canadian Pacific Railway.[19]

In one of the many passages in which he tried to express his own powerful vision of what it means to be a Canadian, Hugh MacLennan brought one of his fictional characters, a First World War soldier whose name, Neil Macrae, is suggestive of his Cape Breton Island and Scottish Highland origins, to Halifax, Nova Scotia, towards the close of 1917. 'He stopped at a corner to wait for a tram,' MacLennan wrote of this young man, 'and his eyes reached above the roofs to the sky. Stars were visible and a quarter moon. The sun had rolled on beyond Nova Scotia into the west. Now it was setting over Montreal and sending the shadow of the mountain deep into the valleys of Sherbrooke Street and Peel; it was turning the frozen St Lawrence crimson and lining it with the blue shadows of the trees and buildings along its banks, while all the time the deep water poured seaward under the ice, draining off the Great Lakes into the Atlantic. Now the prairies were endless plains of glittering, bluish snow over which the wind passed in a firm and continuous flux, packing the drifts down hard over the wheat seeds frozen into the alluvial earth. Now in the Rockies the peaks were gleaming obelisks in the mid-afternoon. The railway line, that tenuous thread which bound Canada to both the great oceans and made her a nation, lay with one end in the darkness of Nova Scotia and the other in the flush of a British Columbian noon.'[20]

It would be a wild exaggeration to claim Canada as a Scottish Highland creation. But this country undoubtedly provided Highlanders with the means of exercising talents which never could be unleashed in the confined and constraining circumstances of the eighteenth- and nineteenth-century Scottish Highlands. Highlanders had helped bring the northern part of North America under British jurisdiction in the 1750s. They had been prominent in the struggle to keep it British in the 1770s and 1780s. They had charted Canada's western hinterland, opened up its trade, carried its name to the Pacific and now, in the shape of men like John A. Macdonald and Donald Smith, Scottish Highlanders had given the Dominion of Canada the railway which, as Hugh MacLennan clearly saw, was the key to his nation's existence.

It is wholly typical of this long-standing Highland involvement in the task of advancing a Canadian national interest – an involvement, of course, which might plausibly be argued to extend all the way to Hugh MacLennan himself – that one of the first men to take seriously the possibility of what would one day be the CPR was Allan MacDonell, grandson of one of the Mohawk Valley loyalists who went on to settle Glengarry County and nephew of Miles MacDonell who, on behalf of the Earl of Selkirk, was given the responsibility of installing the Kildonan people at Red River. MacDonell, a Toronto engineer and financier, published his *Observations upon the Construction of a Railroad from Lake Superior to the Pacific* in 1851. And though the company which he formed to put his proposals into practice never got anywhere, MacDonell would live to see another Glengarry man, Roderick MacLennan, whose father had left Kintail in 1802, handle the actual building of some of the CPR's toughest sections. Nor was MacLennan, or Big Rory as he was known, the only Glengarry Highlander to have a stake in one of the most demanding construction jobs the world has ever seen. 'There is no county in Canada that has turned out so many successful railwaymen,' Big Rory claimed in 1886 of his own part of Ontario.[21]

Men like MacLennan and his navvies were the frontline troops in the CPR's battle with Canadian geography; driving the railway through the iron-hard rock to the north of Lake Superior; establishing workshops and other facilities in the vicinity of the former North West Company base at Fort William; pushing the CPR's steel tracks on to Red River and out across the prairies; somehow managing to get the railway over the Rockies at Kicking Horse Pass; finding a way through the several other mountain ranges between the Kicking Horse and the western sea; finally linking Halifax on the Atlantic with Vancouver, just under 3,000 miles away, on the Pacific.[22]

No less difficult to surmount were the many financial obstacles in the CPR's way. Smith and Stephen had driven a hard bargain with the Canadian government in 1880. They had persuaded John A. Macdonald to grant them millions of dollars in direct aid as well as millions of acres of good prairie land which the CPR's founders hoped ultimately to sell to the settlers whom the railway was intended in part to attract. But over and over again the CPR's money men had to return to Macdonald for further assistance. And over and over again it was necessary for George Stephen to utilise his banking contacts on the London money market in order to raise the loans required to purchase materials, meet transport costs, pay thousands of labourers and generally keep the CPR in being.

In 1884, at the point when the whole, gigantically expensive, enormously precarious, venture came closest to collapse, Stephen, once more in London, wished urgently to inform Donald Smith – who was, of course, in Canada – that their company, against all the odds, had survived to fight another day. It was a moment, according to Donald Creighton, the Canadian historian responsible for the defining biography of John A. Macdonald, when Stephen became suddenly and acutely aware of his origins. 'Once again,' Creighton wrote, 'the partnership of company and government, the partnership of Donald Smith, John A. Macdonald and himself had triumphed.' This partnership, Creighton continued, was more than a matter of political and financial convenience. 'They were all Scotsmen, all Highlanders, all, ultimately, sons of the same river valley.' And it was this river valley – the strath carved through the Highland hills by the waters of the Spey, the strath that had long been home both to Clan Chattan and Clan Grant – which now provided Stephen with the means of conveying to his cousin his strong sense of exultation at having somehow preserved their joint enterprise. 'He remembered the river itself,' Creighton commented of Stephen, 'winding onward, peat black between the high banks, and brown, like old ale, over the shallows. He remembered the great rock which had given the Clan Grant its rallying-place and its battle slogan. The rock of defiance. Craigellachie . . . He took a telegraph form, addressed it to Donald Smith in Montreal and wrote a message of three words only: *Stand fast, Craigellachie!*'[23]

And eventually the railway was complete; its last spike driven by Donald Smith himself at a spot in British Columbia's Selkirk Mountains; a spot whose only significance lay in the fact that it happened to be the meeting-place of tracks which had been driven from the west as well as from the east. The CPR established a station here but the station never became the focus of any kind of settlement and was afterwards closed. Now the place is glimpsed not so much by railway passengers, of whom there are not very many these days, as by motorists on the Trans-Canada Highway which today parallels the railway in these parts. Driving towards Vancouver, bemused by the splendour of the surrounding peaks, you come so suddenly on this historic location's roadside noticeboard that you have almost passed before the noticeboard's several Gaelic syllables have registered in your mind. Craigellachie.

In 1886, the year during which the CPR opened formally for business, John A. Macdonald came here; crossing the continental divide at the Kicking Horse Pass and travelling on through this spectacular hill country past the sharply pointed and glittering peak which nowadays carries his name; making at least part of the journey perched, for all his gathering old age, on the cowcatcher of his train's heavy locomotive. 'The barrier of those mountains had haunted his entire political life,' Hugh MacLennan commented of the – now knighted – prime minister's first and only transcontinental journey. 'On the conquest of them had depended his country's survival . . . On the day when Sir John first rode through, he must have felt like a man who has always been poor, always stretched to the limit, always been required to *prove* that his country had a right to exist, and then suddenly, beyond expectation, knows that at last both he and the country have not quite failed.'[24]

It was just under a century since Alexander MacKenzie had pushed through those same Rocky Mountains on his way to the Pacific, dreaming of at last establishing the existence of a North West Passage – even if an overland one – which would link Europe, by way of Canada, with China. Now the CPR's silk specials – express trains carrying textiles which had originated in places like Canton and Hong Kong and which were being speeded on their way to London – clattered regularly eastwards from Vancouver to Montreal and Halifax. It was as a result of such developments that Donald Smith would soon become one of the wealthiest men on earth. It was equally due to the great railway that Sir John A. Macdonald would be remembered by Canadians, for all their first prime minister's many faults and flaws, as his country's principal founder. And it was due finally to the CPR that thousands, indeed millions, of other immigrants – most of them as poor and lacking in obvious prospects as Smith and, still more, Macdonald had originally been – were provided with the means of settling the prairies through which the Canadian Pacific Railway passed.

From Lochmaddy, where the ferry from Skye reaches North Uist, the single-track road heads south-westwards across moorland of the sort which is all too common in the northern half of Scotland. You see some sheep. You notice the spots where islanders have come to cut the peat still used in these parts as domestic fuel. But otherwise there are scant signs of life and absolutely none of habitation – until, that is, the road begins to dip towards the Atlantic and you find yourself looking out on one of the world's most distinctive landscapes. Here, in an entirely unexpected contrast to what has gone before, are houses; dozens of houses; their shapes outlined, as a result of the low-lying nature of their surroundings, against an oceanic sky. Here, instead of the unproductive terrain through which you have been driving since leaving Lochmaddy, are wide, meadow-like expanses of well-grazed, close-cropped grass. Should you stop your car and step outside, you will be aware, in spring and summer, of the scent of flowers, the constant sound of birdsong. Here, you realise, is what it is that has ensured a substantial human presence in these islands since neolithic times.

This is *machair*. And, by environmental scientists anyway, that Gaelic word has become one of the few such terms to be adopted into English. It had to be. This being a uniquely Hebridean ecosystem, and the Hebrides having been occupied for very many centuries by Gaelic-speakers, no other language contains quite the right expression to convey the effect produced here by the sea upon the land.

Machair owes its existence to the dazzlingly white sand you find on the Atlantic coast of islands such as Harris, North Uist, Benbecula, South Uist, Barra, Tiree, Iona, Colonsay and Islay. That sand – which gives an almost tropical-looking turquoise colouration to the machair's many tidal inlets – consists of the wave-smashed, ground-down, pulverised remains of shells. It is consequently rich in alkalis. These neutralise and fertilise the peaty, and consequently acidic, soils across which this shell-sand is blown and scattered by the wind. The overall outcome, many thousands of years in the making, is an extraordinarily productive and appealing natural habitat – one which has been further enriched, rather than depleted, by traditional, unintensive agricultural techniques of the kind practised still by island crofters.

In the first half of the nineteenth century, of course, the qualities which make machair so attractive were also those which guaranteed that most of its occupants would be forcibly removed by landlords anxious to maximise the profits then to be made from sheep-farming. Take the causeway from North Uist to Benbecula. Keep on by way of Balivanich and Liniclate to the further causeway leading to South Uist. Then take the road which leads in the direction of Lochboisdale. The wide expanses of machair to be seen all around you in this quarter were the scene, in the years around 1850, of the clearances and evictions which culminated in John Gordon shipping to the St Lawrence those hundreds of families whose condition, on their arrival at his Grosse Ile quarantine station, so clearly shocked George Douglas.

But the huge farms which Gordon thus created, to his own considerable benefit, have long gone. Today – as can be seen from the sheer density of population in these parts – the Benbecula and South Uist machairs are once again in crofting occupation. That is one of the more obvious results of crofting protest of the sort which first occurred in the Scottish Highlands in the 1880s and which continued, in one form or another, for nearly forty years. This was a time of rent strikes, illegal land seizures, political campaigning; a time when one British government, by yielding to the crofting community's demand for security of tenure, at last outlawed eviction; a time when other British governments, by establishing state-funded boards and commissions whose task it was to buy sheep-farms and to return them to crofters, went some way to undoing what it was that men like John Gordon thought to have accomplished irreversibly.

One immediate outcome of the crofting population's new assertiveness was the arrival in Lochboisdale in 1883 of a royal commission whose job it was to inquire into crofting grievances. Here in South Uist, the commission discovered, memories of what had been done to islanders by John Gordon still loomed large. John MacKay had been in his forties when, as he put it, so many of his neighbours were 'driven and compelled to emigrate'. Now he was in his seventies. But he would never forget, this crofter insisted, what he had witnessed in the summer of

1851. 'I saw a policeman chasing a man down the machair towards Askernish, with a view to catch him, in order to send him on board an emigrant ship lying in Lochboisdale. I saw a man who lay down on his face and nose on a little island, hiding himself from the policeman, and the policeman getting a dog to search for this missing man in order to get him on board the emigrant ship.'[25]

These events, one group of South Uist crofters commented in the course of the written statement they submitted to the royal commission, had done nothing to enhance the possibility of their now going voluntarily overseas. 'We desire not to see revived the cruel and forced evictions, as carried out in 1849 and 1851, when many were bound hand and foot and packed off like cattle on board the vessel to America. The recollections of ill-treatment . . . towards many in these days operates unfavourably on the mind of the present generation towards emigration.'[26]

Why should they take themselves to Canada, these and other South Uist and Benbecula crofters asked members of the royal commission, when there was so much good land available at home? What they wanted, these crofters continued, was the redistribution among them of the many thousands of acres which John Gordon had cleared and which his daughter and successor, Lady Emily Gordon Cathcart, was as determined as ever to keep in the occupation of no more than about half a dozen sheep-farmers. The commission, however, was unwilling to oblige. No wholesale land reform of the type requested by crofters was recommended in its 1884 report. Instead a range of lesser remedial measures, or so the commission considered, might appropriately be accompanied by renewed 'encouragement of emigration'. Such emigration, it was further suggested, could readily be directed towards Canada where 'families might be advantageously settled on . . . homestead allotments of 160 acres in the North West Territories'.[27]

By the North West Territories, this British royal commission meant the prairies. And the 'homestead allotments' to which its report referred were, of course, the basic components from which John A. Macdonald hoped to create, between Red River and the Rockies, a zone of settlement sufficiently dense as to secure his government's claims on all that huge expanse of real estate.

Teams of Canadian surveyors had been hard at work on the prairies since the early 1870s; dividing the plains into segments measuring one square mile in extent; subdividing each of these units into eight of the 160-acre farms or sections which, as had been laid down by the Dominion Lands Act of 1872, were to be made available virtually free of charge to homesteaders. The ownership of many thousands of these lots, admittedly, had been transferred by John A. Macdonald to the CPR in the course of the Canadian prime minister's various negotiations with Donald Smith, George Stephen and their associates. But the CPR had its own vested interest in prairie settlement – the railway company's profitability being in direct relation to its success in generating custom for its services. It consequently made little practical difference to prospective settlers whether they were dealing with the CPR or with the Canadian government. The one was as anxious to woo emigrants as the other.[28]

Soon George Stephen had appointed the CPR's own London-based emigration agent, Alexander Begg, who – in the best traditions of North American boosterism – promptly set out to portray the prairies as some sort of earthly paradise. The Scottish Highlands, it goes practically without saying, were one of Begg's immediate targets. His posters, advertising 'free homes for all', were nailed to the walls of hotels, railway stations and other public places throughout the region. His representatives – equipped with new-fangled magic lanterns and with reams of CPR literature which Begg had taken care to have translated into Gaelic – lectured crofters on the huge advantages to be gained by making a fresh start in a new country. And among the many people who were persuaded to take Begg and the CPR at their word were no small number from South Uist and Benbecula.[29]

The notion that Canada might provide a convenient receptacle for Britain's poor was one that flourished most spectacularly at the time when Highland landlords like John Gordon were shipping their unwanted tenants to the St Lawrence. But this type of thinking enjoyed something of a renaissance in the later nineteenth century also; one of its proponents noting that 'the only remedy to overcrowded workhouses was mass evacuation of their inmates'; another writing of the urgent need to convey 'shiftless, purposeless, aimless' persons as soon as possible to Canada. Such views undoubtedly influenced the royal commission of enquiry into crofting matters. They equally clearly influenced the estate management policies pursued in South Uist and Benbecula by Lady Emily Gordon Cathcart – to whom the royal commission alluded more than once in the most complimentary terms.[30]

Crofting pressure on Lady Emily's sheep-farms was eventually to prove irresistible – several of these farms being forcibly occupied by crofters in 1885 and all of them being formally handed back to crofters some years later. At the start of the 1880s, however, it seemed possible to John Gordon's daughter that she might remove the crofting threat to her farms if she could but find some alternative means of easing congestion and overcrowding in the few South Uist and Benbecula crofting townships to have survived her father's clearances. Developments in Canada offered just such a means. Other members of Lady Emily's class – such as Baroness Burdett-Coutts who installed a group of impoverished Londoners on the Canadian prairies – were already helping to finance the emigration of families who could not otherwise have met the cost of an Atlantic passage. And Lady Emily – whose husband, Sir Reginald

Cathcart, was soon to join Donald Smith and George Stephen on the board of one of the several land companies spawned by the CPR – now resolved to do likewise. In the spring of 1883, the South Uist and Benbecula estate management having advanced much of the necessary funding, some fifty islanders were despatched to what is now Saskatchewan – with a further two hundred or so to follow in 1884.[31]

To find the area – along the north bank of Pipestone Creek – where most of Lady Emily's emigrants settled, you leave the Trans-Canada Highway at either Moosomin or Wapella. These are typical prairie towns: small, friendly, comfortable places; anything but affluent; their main streets bisected by the CPR tracks to which so many such communities owe their existence.

The great railway still looms large in this part of Saskatchewan. Step outside your motel room in the late evening, stand there in the snow and listen. The chances are that, even in the minute or two before the frost drives you back inside, you will hear the sound that is second only to the loon's cry in its capacity to evoke the sense of space you get in so much of North America. Carrying an enormous distance in this otherwise quiet night, there comes the deep, strangely growling, rising, falling note of a locomotive whistle.

Next morning, when about to leave Wapella on the die-straight dirt road leading to John Currie's farm, you experience something of the casual arrogance which has always caused Canadians to be more than a little bit ambivalent about the CPR. One of the 87 freight cars making up a Winnipeg-bound train is being detached and steered in the direction of a silo. For roughly fifteen minutes, while the three huge locomotives hauling this astonishingly long train shunt back and forward with this single wagon, it is impossible to get from one side of Wapella to the other.

He is eighty years old this John Currie, you discover over coffee in his cluttered farm kitchen. He was born on this section, where he has always lived, just thirty years after his father first came here from Eilean Flodda, a little scrap of land between North Uist and Benbecula. They were tough times the 1880s, so John reckons. And his father, homesteading here on the prairie when it was no easy thing to earn a dollar, always did resent the way that Lady Emily Gordon Cathcart's agents hounded him and others for every last cent which had been advanced to them. 'You understand they weren't given any money,' John Currie says. 'They were lent it. And they were surely made to pay it back.'

Leaving the Currie farm and boxing the compass the way you have to do when driving in rural Saskatchewan, by heading first due south, then due west, then due north on the icy dirt roads which follow section boundaries, you come eventually to St Andrew's Church, its tall steeple something of a landmark in these parts. The iron gates giving access to the church's graveyard were placed here quarter of a century back, you read, 'in memory of the Scottish pioneers from the islands of Benbecula and South Uist . . . who settled this area in 1883 and 1884'. Many of those pioneers now lie here – those MacPhees, MacDonalds, MacEachens, Curries, MacPhersons and MacKinnons whose graves, in several instances, are decorated with little bunches of cut flowers which seem exceptionally brightly coloured in this setting of dark tombstones and smooth, wind-packed snow.

The South Uist and Benbecula families who came here – to what was still known then as the North West Territories – did not come by themselves. The spring and summer of 1883 alone brought 133,000 emigrants to Canada, most of them bound ultimately for those prairie regions across which the CPR was now advancing at the astonishing rate of three or four miles every day. Winnipeg which, not very many years before, had simply been one of several villages in the vicinity of Selkirk's Red River colony, was now a booming city of more than 20,000 people; a place of frantic trade in property; its inhabitants suddenly feeling themselves to be at the very centre of that wider world from which they had so long been isolated. Brandon, about 130 miles to the west and a town which had been founded only in 1881, was equally given over to a speculative frenzy; proclaiming itself 'the next great city on the CPR'; its residents, most of them still living in tents, buying and selling their community's newly pegged-out street frontages at rates which eventually peaked at around $140 a foot.[32]

In a letter sent home to his brother in June 1883, William MacPherson, who came from Iochdar in South Uist, reported that it had taken a 'half day and night' to make the train journey from Winnipeg to Brandon. There this first detachment of Lady Emily Gordon Cathcart's emigrant party had waited for a fortnight while Donald MacDiarmid – who belonged to Aird in Benbecula and who, on Lady Emily's behalf, had made something of a reconnaissance of the Wapella and Moosomin area during 1882 – completed arrangements regarding the acquisition of appropriate sections close to Pipestone Creek.[33]

These sections were occupied by the Benbecula and South Uist people towards the end of May. It had taken 'a whole week' to get his things from Wapella to his new farm, William MacPherson told his brother. Then he and his immediate neighbour, a Benbecula man with whom MacPherson shared a single team of oxen, had immediately set to ploughing a piece of land big enough to provide them with the crops they would need to see their two families through the coming winter. Between them, William MacPherson noted carefully, he and his partner had sown or planted 24 bushels of potatoes, four bushels of oats and two of barley. 'Now I may tell you about the country,' continues this Iochdar man's letter. 'It is as beautiful a place as I have ever seen, and I think very healthy. It is not a bit hotter than at home. We have plenty of wood and water. We have fine weather, with heavy showers of rain . . . I know I will be a great deal better here in a few years than at home.'

Others were of a similar opinion. 'About this country,' commented John MacDonald from Liniclate, Benbecula, in the course of correspondence with relatives still in Scotland, 'you are not able to understand the beauty of the soil – all covered with long grass and every sort of flower. Small ponds are very numerous, surrounded with . . . small trees.' Game of every kind – rabbits, prairie hens, partridges and plover – was abundant. And a man might take as much of this natural harvest as he pleased – there being, in contrast to the Scottish Highlands, 'no game law in this country'.[34]

He considered himself to have come to 'a real good country', Lachlan MacPherson, another Liniclate man, reported in mid-August. 'The crop is looking awful good. I haven't seen better-looking corn and potatoes in my life. We are lifting the potatoes. They were only eight weeks in the ground and they are as big as I have seen in the old country two months after this, and as good. You won't believe the crop and the grass that is here . . . I have some grass from three to five feet high for cutting . . . There is no trouble whatever in the grass here. We have only to cut it, and to put it in the stack the day after, because the weather is always dry.'[35]

Ever since the beginnings of Scottish Highland settlement in places like Darien and the Cape Fear River country nearly 150 years before, letters of this type had caused a second wave of emigrants to follow the first. So it was on this occasion. A further forty or so families, again assisted financially by Lady Emily Gordon Cathcart and urged on their way by her estate managers, left South Uist and Benbecula for Moosomin in April 1884 – getting there, in this new era of steamships and railways, in no more than about three weeks. Already, however, the prairies were proving a less hospitable environment than the 1883 pioneers had thought. 'We will be praising Lady Gordon Cathcart forever for her kindness to us,' one of these earlier emigrants had written. That was certainly not to be the attitude of at least one member of the 1884 party.[36]

This was Archie Kenneth MacDonald whose father, a Tiree man, had managed an inn at Gramisdale, the spot where the modern causeway from North Uist reaches Benbecula, and who had come out to Moosomin with his widowed mother, his brother and his sister. A 'vicious plot' had been devised in order 'to lure people to this cold and forbidding land', Archie Kenneth complained in the course of a Gaelic song he composed in Saskatchewan. Among the conspirators was the Gordon Cathcart estate manager, a man whom Archie Kenneth thought in thrall to his employer: 'If Emily should request our crucifixion, that vulture would accede to it.' But others were equally guilty of having misled both himself and his fellow emigrants, Archie Kenneth MacDonald's song continues. Most notable among them were the many agents of the CPR – those 'thousand liars, well rewarded, who went about with books extolling the North West'. It would have been much better for him, Archie Kenneth concludes, had he remained in Benbecula.[37]

There was nothing that was unique about Archie Kenneth MacDonald's bitter disillusionment with the prairies. The fine weather which featured so largely in the correspondence of the 1883 emigrants quickly proved an aberration. The series of rainy years which had lasted since the mid-1870s, and which had given a degree of credibility to the common portrayal of the region as a 'land of milk and honey', gave way now to protracted drought. Ponds, marshes and creeks dried out. Animals died. Crops failed. The boom times were succeeded by depression. The emigrant flood was reduced to a trickle. And those settlers who were already installed on their prairie sections – where they mostly lived, for lack of any available alternative, in houses made from nothing more substantial than sods cut from their fields – began inevitably to blame the CPR for their plight; not for the summer's heat and dust and insects maybe; nor for the bitter winter winds; but certainly for having enticed them here under what looked increasingly like false pretences; and still more certainly for having subjected them to the high freight charges made possible as a result of John A. Macdonald, in his anxiety to have his railway built, having bestowed on Donald Smith and George Stephen what amounted to a transportation monopoly.[38]

The CPR was vilified in Gaelic by Archie Kenneth MacDonald. It was equally vilified in English by those other prairie settlers who – in the year which saw the launch in Scotland of the Highland Land League, the organisation which spearheaded the crofting community's battle for security of tenure – established the Farmers Protective Union of Manitoba to demand, among other concessions, an immediate end to the CPR's officially ordained privileges.[39]

Donald Smith and George Stephen, more unassailable now than even Highland landlords, were to survive all such assaults. And as the nineteenth century gave way to the twentieth, prairie society – which, as even the CPR's fiercest critics were forced to acknowledge, would scarcely have existed were it not for the great railway – began gradually to live up to the many propagandist claims made on its behalf. New strains of wheat, the beginnings of agricultural mechanisation and an improvement in the weather had combined by 1900 to make Manitoba and Saskatchewan what they have ever since remained, one of the world's more important farming regions. By 1914, the centenary of the Kildonan people's arrival at Red River, the prairies were at last as the Earl of Selkirk had so fervently wished them to be – thickly settled, relatively wealthy and certainly productive.

There was to be no precise prairie equivalent, however, of the Cape Fear country, Cape Breton Island or Glengarry County. Many people from the northern part of Scotland were certainly among the millions who, in the years between 1895 and 1914 stepped ashore at Halifax or Montreal, climbed into the waiting CPR carriages – their bunks and their benches made from nothing more yielding than wood – and headed for the Canadian North West. But these millions consisted of Scandinavians, Germans, Ukrainians, Hungarians, Jews and many others as well as Scottish Highlanders. This would give to prairie communities the cultural diversity which is still one of their outstanding attractions. But it would prevent what had been common further east – the emergence of extensive settlements consisting exclusively of people from the same Scottish Highland locality.[40]

Small groups of families from Lewis and Harris – emigrating under the auspices of a government-funded programme which was abandoned almost before it had properly begun – were to settle at Saltcoats in Saskatchewan and Killarney in Manitoba in 1888 and 1889. And in the years immediately following the First World War several shiploads of emigrants would once again leave Lewis, Harris, the Uists and Barra for the United States and Canada. But these ships, unlike their predecessors of a century before, contained few entire families. The older form of emigration from the Scottish Highlands, the sort of emigration which had begun in the 1730s and which had resulted in the transfer of whole communities of Highlanders to so many parts of North America, had now come to an end. People would continue to leave Scotland's northern counties – and the crofting areas of these counties, in particular. But the emigration which took place in the 1920s and which occurred again in the 1950s and the 1960s – the sort of emigration which has resulted in so many modern crofting households containing neatly framed photographs of those sons, daughters, brothers and sisters now living in Toronto or Chicago, Vancouver or Los Angeles – was something mostly undertaken by individuals only. And in the last twenty years or so – as economic conditions in the Scottish Highlands have at last begun to improve and the region's population, after its 150-year decline, has finally started to increase again – even this later type of emigration has very largely ceased.[41]

Just as emigrants tend to dwell in their letters home on the more positive features of their new lives, so more generalised accounts of emigration deal mostly with success; with the achievements of Crevecoeur's Andrew the Hebridean; with the accomplishments of men like Simon MacTavish, William MacGillivray, John A. Macdonald, Donald Smith. But there is, of course, another side to the emigration story. The mass graves on Grosse Ile are one especially graphic illustration of the fact that the journey from the Scottish Highlands to North America was not always a prelude to automatic betterment. Cape Breton Island's abandoned farms, like that locality's depressed and deprived mining towns, are another reminder of the same sobering truth. And as you very quickly gather from talking to their people, the Canadian prairies are not without their own considerable testimony to the extent to which North America, every bit as much as any other part of the world, can be a place of human suffering.

The hundreds of emigrants who left Lewis for the St Lawrence in 1923 did so, as so many others had done before, because neither their own island nor the wider Scottish Highlands had anything to offer them. Livestock prices had been falling steeply for several years. The herring fishery and the harris tweed industry, on which many islanders depended, were simultaneously in crisis. Exceptionally wet and stormy weather had made it impossible for crofters to get in their crops. 'The present year,' a schools medical officer reported from Lewis at this time, 'shows that more children are below the weight average than for many years . . . That is to say, their nutrition has been affected by the bad harvest, the loss of employment and failures of the tweed and fishing industries.' In what amounted to a programme of famine relief, charitable donations were sought for a fund established to enable Lewis crofters to buy seed potatoes and seed grain – while the British government, for its part, launched an emergency road construction programme in an attempt to provide islanders with at least a basic income.[42]

The following decade was to bring equally bleak conditions to much of the rest of northern Scotland. But nothing experienced then in the Highlands even began to approximate to the sheer horror of the 1930s in places like Manitoba and Saskatchewan. These were what prairie communities would afterwards call the dirty years: years of massive unemployment in Winnipeg and other prairie cities; years of misery for farmers confronted by shrinking markets, falling prices, rising debts and some of the worst weather ever encountered in this part of North America.

Few prairie winters are pleasant. Those of the 1930s commonly brought seventy or eighty degrees of frost. And this almost unbearable cold was followed, season after season, by equally unendurable summer heat. Billions of tons of prairie topsoil was reduced to dust which, when the winds came, drifted across the ground like snow, blocking roads and hanging thickly in the air. Such wheat as got anywhere near maturity was frequently destroyed by grasshopper swarms which were so chokingly dense at times as to paralyse the railways and to render automobiles inoperative. The entire region, as one newspaper correspondent discovered in 1934, had become 'a landscape of almost incredible desolation'. Mile after mile this man drove through Saskatchewan; through a countryside 'as lifeless as ashes'; through farming settlements where 'there was scarcely a thing growing to be seen'; through localities as desiccated now as any desert. 'Gaunt cattle and horses with little save their skins to cover their bones stalked about the denuded acres . . . When the miserable animals moved it seemed as if their frames rattled. The few people in evidence in the little towns appeared haggard and hopeless.'[43]

It was little wonder, in such circumstances, that some Scottish Highland emigrants now did what practically none of their predecessors had done since the time of Allan MacDonald of Kingsburgh. They came home; not impelled, as the returning loyalist tacksmen of the eighteenth century had been, by their politics; but simply driven by hardship to the unpalatable conclusion that, in the 1930s anyway, even an island croft was a better place to be than North America.

CHAPTER TEN

I Will Fight No More Forever

ABERDEEN, THE MOST northerly of Scotland's cities, is best known nowadays for its key role in the exploitation of Britain's offshore oilfields. Many multinational corporations – some of them, of course, American in origin – have their North Sea headquarters in the city. Its harbour, once given over largely to fishing boats, is filled with the barge-like ships which carry supplies to the drilling rigs and production platforms littering the stormy waters to the east. From Aberdeen Airport roughnecks, roustabouts and other exotically designated personnel are ferried to these same installations by helicopters whose din has become every bit as familiar hereabouts as the shriek of gulls or the sound of the Girdle Ness foghorn's regular confrontations with the North Sea's bleak haars or mists.

When one of Britain's earliest oil industry moguls visited Aberdeen in the autumn of 1906, however, it was not as a result of his having foreseen the city's future. Baron Strathcona of Glen Coe, Argyll, and of Mount Royal, Quebec, Canada – to give this elderly gentleman his full title – was already chairman of Burmah Oil. He was shortly to become chairman of the Anglo-Persian Oil Company which, in the fullness of time, would turn into British Petroleum, one of the world's most successful businesses. But he was better known in 1906 for his continuing connection with a very different consortium, namely the Canadian Pacific Railway. For this Lord Strathcona – a man as rich as it was then possible to be – was none other than Donald Smith who, as a teenager, had left Forres, about seventy miles north-west of Aberdeen, to join the Hudson's Bay Company.[1]

Strathcona, now in his eighties, had come to Aberdeen to throw a party. He was lord chancellor of the city's ancient university. And that university had just equipped itself with a new building, Marischal College, which – so Aberdonians insisted anyway – was the largest, tallest, most expensive granite structure in the world. Marischal College, it was duly decided by Aberdeen University's lord chancellor, a man much given in his old age to grandiloquence, should be inaugurated in some style. He would invite several thousand people to a celebratory dinner. He would meet the bill himself. He would hold his dinner in an enormous marquee constructed purely for this purpose. He would bring 650 waiters from London. He would provide 12,000 glasses and 25,000 plates. And he would ensure that his good friend, King Edward VII, would be among his guests.[2]

Strathcona, one of the railway baron's Canadian admirers wrote afterwards of this occasion, presided over Marischal College's formal opening in a manner entirely appropriate to his position. 'Some five feet nine of the toughest kind of human stuff . . . a very benevolent unassuming figure of a man; soft voice with just a lingering suspicion of the original caressing Highland drawl, persuasive and homely yet flowing and musically rounded speech, the express echo of sweet reasonableness, full of grace and simple courtesy; and then that unmistakable dome of mingled sagacity and power in the massive head, bearded and crowned with snow, with the strong straight nose, forehead broad rather than high, and the mild light of forward-looking, grey-blue eyes under the formidable penthouse of tremendously bushy leonine white eyebrows. A head for wise counsel and action, both cautious and bold.'[3]

Not everyone with whom Donald Smith had dealt in the course of his career in North America would have turned in quite so obsequious a sketch of him. But there was no denying his eminence: his seat in the House of Lords; his close links with leading politicians; his innumerable directorships; his homes in Winnipeg, Montreal, Nova Scotia, London and Essex; his ownership of the Hebridean island of Colonsay and the 64,000-acre Black Corries estate in the West Highlands.

The Black Corries property included Glen Coe. And Glen Coe – dubbed Strathcona by one or other of the many poets who have lingered on the locality's tragic associations – provided Donald Smith with his title as well as with the chance to play the Scottish landlord. The mansion which he built here on the rising ground above Invercoe has long since been converted into a hospital. But its grounds are still as Strathcona laid them out. Noticeboards invite the public to walk around the artificial loch which Strathcona's teams of gardeners and labourers so painstakingly created. North American trees grow on the loch's shores. And if you have had the luck to visit Lake Louise near Banff in Alberta – a spot to which the CPR was running tourist trains within a very few years of the

great railway's opening – you sense, as Strathcona intended, more than
a passing resemblance between this spot and that faraway corner of the
Rockies. Hills like Mam na Gualainn and Sgor na Ciche lack the altitude
of their Lake Louise counterparts. And not even Donald Smith could
provide Glen Coe with glaciers. But his money certainly made it possible
for Strathcona to manipulate landscape to some considerable effect. To
walk into Glen Coe proper from the neighbourhood of the leading CPR
man's former home is to have the peculiar sensation of having somehow
swapped Canada instantaneously for the Scottish Highlands.

There are few parts of these same Scottish Highlands which are
more suggestive of the region's history than Glen Coe. The Feinn or the
Fenians, those mythical warriors who feature in tales brought here from
Ireland by Gaelic-speaking migrants of some 1,500 years ago, are commemorated still in the names of Glen Coe's peaks. That is exactly as it
should be – the miraculous doings of Cu Chulain, Ossian, Deirdre and
their saga comrades having been celebrated, through a score of human
lifetimes, by the storytellers who once practised their art in Glen Coe's
scattered farms and townships. The name shared by most of the folk who
gathered here on winter evenings to listen to their people's legends was
MacDonald. And though their branch of this clan was neither the largest
nor the most powerful, it was particularly associated, rightly or wrongly,
with all those qualities which caused the inhabitants of the rest of Britain
both to fear and to loathe Highlanders. By most Lowland Scots the
MacDonalds of Glen Coe were thought rebellious, irreligious, lawless,
barbarous, murderous, uncouth, dirty and despicable. They were also –
being comparatively lacking in numbers – thought vulnerable. That was
why, in 1692, the Glen Coe MacDonalds were selected for special treatment by southern politicians who were increasingly anxious to impose
their own brand of civilisation on unruly, troublesome hill tribes of the
Glen Coe variety.

The chiefs of suspect clans, it was announced in 1691, were to be
required to swear, by the end of that year, an oath of loyalty to the
government of King William – the monarch who, not long before, had
been instrumental in deposing the last of those Stuart kings with whom
the Glen Coe MacDonalds, insofar as they followed anyone other than
their own leaders, were inclined to identify politically. By failing to reg-
ister his oath in time, the aged Alasdair MacDonald, chief of the Glen
Coe people, had provided the authorities with an eagerly welcomed
justification for action of a sort intended to teach Highlanders an altogether unforgettable lesson. A company of soldiers was sent immediately
to Glen Coe. And on 13 February 1692 their commanding officer
received instructions which he and his men were promptly to carry out.
'You are hereby ordered to fall upon the rebels, the MacDonalds of Glen
Coe,' these orders ran, 'and put all to the sword under seventy.'[4]

The ensuing slaughter, on a night of snow and bitter cold, was an early example of the tribal massacres that were frequently to follow the rise to global dominance of the political culture which made possible what was done to the Glen Coe MacDonalds. This Highland clan's elderly chieftain was killed as he struggled from his nightclothes. Other men were bayoneted in their beds. A boy of twelve or thirteen, clinging to a soldier's legs and begging hysterically for mercy, was silenced with a bullet. Women died in the flaming ruins of their cottages. Many of those who escaped to the mountains perished later from exposure. At Leacantuim, some two miles inland from the spot where Donald Smith would one day build his mansion, Archibald MacDonald, a man of eighty, was stunned by a soldier's musket-butt and left to burn to death when other troops fired his farmhouse.[5]

Something of what was destroyed in the course of that winter's night was afterwards recreated, of course. A new farmhouse was built at Leacantuim. And Angus MacDonald, one of its eighteenth-century occupants, was to serve with other, still recalcitrant, men of his clan in the army which Prince Charles Edward Stuart led into England in 1745. From the British government's perspective, however, that army's eventual defeat was to complete the process begun at Glen Coe in 1692. Clanship of the traditional sort was not to be re-established following Culloden. And with the dissolution of the social order they had done so much to maintain, Highlanders of the type who had provided Leacantuim with its tacksmen were more and more attracted – as this book has so often emphasised – by the notion of making a fresh start in North America. One such was Angus MacDonald's thirteenth son. His name was Archibald. He was very possibly descended from that other Archibald MacDonald who was killed at Leacantuim in 1692. He was certainly the man placed in charge of the Kildonan emigrants despatched to Red River in 1813 by Lord Selkirk.[6]

Glen Coe, which counts as wild terrain in Scotland, seems tame by the standards of the Fraser Canyon. Even on the sort of day which is as common at certain seasons in this part of British Columbia as in Scotland – a day of mist and intermittent rain – you can see, when the visibility every now and then improves, that this is a desperately daunting place. Its mountains are as sheer as mountains ever get. But what is much more frightening than the ice-streaked cliffs above the road are the practically vertical drops below it. Down there, visible on occasion, audible always, is the Fraser River. You stop your car. You stand in the damp by a chain-link safety fence and look down at one of the most ferocious stretches of white water in the world. What would it have been like, you wonder, to pass through there in an early nineteenth-century birchbark canoe?

'On all major rivers you expect the occasional turbulence,' Hugh MacLennan wrote following a visit here, 'and you assume that all mountain streams are cataracts. Rivers like the St Lawrence quickly calm down after their rapids and mountain streams like the Kicking Horse are shallow and short. But the Fraser is neither short nor shallow. It is nearly a hundred miles longer than the Rhine and it flows with cataract force for more than six hundred miles with only a few interludes of relative quiet. In a sense the Fraser does not flow at all: it seethes along with whirlpools so fierce that a log going down it may circle the same spot for days as though caught in a liquid merry-go-round. It roars like an ocean in storm, but ocean storms blow themselves out while the Fraser's roar is forever.'[7]

Simon Fraser, the man whose name this fearsome river bears, belonged to a family whose home in Strathglass, some twenty miles to the east of Inverness, was burned by the British army in the course of Culloden's brutal aftermath. For all its rebel antecedents, however, this same family, like so many others in the Highlands, was soon to have its representatives in the ranks of the 78th Highlanders. Two of Simon Fraser's uncles served with the regiment at Louisbourg and Quebec and one of them, John Fraser, afterwards settled permanently in Canada. Simon's father, too, was soon to make the transition to North America, being one of the emigrants who sailed to New York on the *Pearl* in 1773 with a view to settling in the general vicinity of the Mohawk Valley. Even before Simon's birth in 1776, however, his father, also Simon by name, had become embroiled in the Revolutionary War – following his MacDonell neighbours into the loyalist camp and dying in an American prison in 1779. That left Simon's mother, whose name before her marriage was Isabella Grant and who belonged originally to Strathspey, in the unenviable position of having to abandon her dead husband's farm and join the many other Highlanders then trying to make a second North American beginning in Glengarry County.[8]

What now followed was a wholly typical instance of the extent to which the principles underlying Highland clanship were applied in North American circumstances. The elder Simon Fraser was related in some way to Hugh Fraser who had served with the 78th Highlanders, who had come home to marry Elizabeth MacTavish – daughter of that other veteran of the 78th, John MacTavish of Garthbeg – and who had subsequently taken with him to America his wife's younger brother. Since this younger brother, Simon MacTavish, was in effective charge, by the 1790s, of the North West Company, and since that organisation's senior personnel already consisted very largely of his extended family, it is no surprise that the company found a post in 1792 for the orphan son of its principal partner's brother-in-law's kinsman. Nor is it any more surprising, given the extent to which the fur trade was now dominated by Scottish Highlanders, that Simon Fraser should have gone on to acquire a position of some importance in the North West Company, being entrusted by his colleagues in 1805 with the task of following up Alexander MacKenzie's pioneering journey to the Pacific.[9]

Accompanying Simon Fraser westward was another man of very similar pedigree. This was John Stuart who came from Strathspey and who very probably owed his position in the North West Company, as Fraser did himself, to relatives who had preceded him in the organisation. The most significant of these relatives, in Stuart's case, was his uncle, Cuthbert Grant, whose Metis son – John Stuart's cousin – was to loom so large in developments at Red River. Among the Metis leader's other Scottish cousins was John Stuart's sister, Barbara. It was by way of replicating his own introduction to the fur trade that John Stuart was one day to help Barbara's son, Donald, the future Lord Strathcona, to get a position with the Hudson's Bay Company.[10]

All of this was far in the future in 1806. Then the immediate task confronting Simon Fraser and John Stuart was to establish North West Company trading posts to the west of the continental divide in what is now British Columbia – a region which Fraser called New Caledonia because its mountain scenery evoked childhood memories of his mother's descriptions of the Scottish Highlands. Acquiring furs in this enormous region proved relatively easy. What was infinitely more complex was the task of getting these furs to prospective purchasers – Fraser having to transport each and every New Caledonian pelt over the Rockies and on across the prairies to Fort William, the Great Lakes and Montreal. The obvious way around this difficulty lay in finding a navigable river route from the British Columbia interior to a point on the Pacific coast from which furs could be shipped either to Europe or Asia by sea. It was with this objective in mind that, towards the end of May 1808, Simon Fraser and John Stuart, accompanied by a 22-strong party of voyageurs and Indians, set out on what was to become one of the greatest feats of exploration in the history of North America.[11]

It seems almost inconceivable now, when you stare at the river's ragged-edged waters and listen to its constant din, that anyone could ever have travelled down the Fraser in an undecked canoe of the type used by the North West Company without coming spectacularly to grief. And though Simon Fraser was not the sort of man who was normally given to revealing his emotions, the journal which he kept during his 36-day voyage to the sea contains several passages which convey something of his own evident fear that neither he nor his companions would survive those 'tremendous gulfs and whirlpools' which were 'ready at every moment to swallow a canoe with all its contents'.[12]

So swift is the river and so precipitous are its banks, that Fraser frequently found it quite impossible, once launched upon its furious waters, to do anything other than press on regardless. 'The current throughout the day ran with amazing velocity,' he wrote on 5 June, 'and ... our situation was really dangerous, being constantly between deep and high banks where there was no possibility of stopping the canoe, and even could it be stopped there would be no such thing as going up the hills, so that had we suddenly come upon a cascade or bad rapid, not to mention falls, it is more than likely that all of us would have perished.' Thus matters continued for more than a month. 'I have been for a long period among the Rocky Mountains,' Simon Fraser noted while in the vicinity of the particularly terrifying gorge now called Hell's Gate, 'but have never seen anything to equal this country . . . We had to pass where no human being should venture.'[13]

Not far below Hell's Gate is lower-lying country. Having won through safely to this point, Fraser, Stuart and their companions now found the going comparatively easy. By the start of July 1808 they had reached the Pacific in the vicinity of the modern city of Vancouver. The risks he had run to reach the sea were such, of course, as to make it obvious to Fraser that, whatever else he had accomplished, he had not discovered a westward export route for furs. It was to take a further descent of the Fraser River by two more Scottish Highlanders in 1828, however, finally to convince everyone associated with the fur trade that the Fraser River was quite incapable of being tranformed into a commercial thoroughfare.

'The banks now erected themselves into perpendicular mountains of rock from the water's edge,' one of these new explorers commented of his encounter with the Fraser, 'the tops enveloped in clouds and the lower parts dismal and rugged in the extreme; the descent of the stream very rapid; the reaches short and, at the close of many of them, the . . . waters, pent up, from twenty to thirty yards wide, running with immense velocity and momentarily threatening to sweep us to destruction.' The author of these words was George Simpson, most renowned of all the Hudson's Bay Company's many governors. His companion in this perilous undertaking was Archibald MacDonald from Leacantuim in Glen Coe.[14]

George Simpson, who was born in the vicinity of Ullapool towards the end of the eighteenth century, began life as the illegitimate son of a minor member of the Highland gentry – his father, also George by name, being connected, for instance, with Duncan Forbes of Culloden, one of the leading pro-Hanoverian figures in the region in the years immediately preceding Prince Charles Edward Stuart's rebellion. As was the custom among Scottish Highlanders of his background, whether at home in Scotland or on the North American frontier, the elder Simpson, for all that he entered no permanent relationship with his son's mother, made arrangements for the boy's education and upbringing. The younger George was consequently sent off to live with an aunt and uncle in the Easter Ross town of Dingwall – his father, meanwhile, continuing to reside in Ullapool where he appears to have been employed by the British Fisheries Society, a semi-official agency which was then attempting to transform this Wester Ross village into a major fishing port.[15]

From Dingwall George Simpson moved in time to London where

he was given a junior post in the sugar-broking firm operated by another kinsman, Geddes MacKenzie Simpson. This Scots-born businessman – who was related to the wife of Alexander MacKenzie of Mackenzie River fame and who was soon to go into partnership with Andrew Wedderburn Colvile, brother-in-law to Lord Selkirk and a central figure in the Selkirk family's successful infiltration of the Hudson's Bay Company – proved to be the young George's introduction to the fur trade. When, in the course of the prelude to the 1821 amalgamation of the North West Company and the Hudson's Bay Company, Colvile and his London business colleagues were looking round for a man who could be relied on to serve their purposes in North America, George Simpson, then in his mid-twenties, was both available and eager to better himself. Soon he was placed in charge of a fur-trading concern which, as a result of the Nor'Westers having at last come to an agreement with their Hudson's Bay rivals, was by far the largest and most powerful organisation of its kind in the world.[16]

The long-standing hostility between Hudson's Bay operatives and their Montreal-based competitors did not vanish with the North West Company's formal extinction, of course. When John MacDonald of Garth was invited to a banquet which Simpson gave in an attempt to promote better relations among the many former enemies who were now expected to share a common loyalty to the Hudson's Bay Company, MacDonald found himself sitting opposite a Bay man with whom he had actually fought a duel in the past. Exercising superhuman restraint, the veteran Nor'Wester confined himself to spitting on the floor rather than – as instinct dictated – on the other trader's plate. A precarious harmony was thus maintained. But the moment was suggestive of the tremendous organisational problems with which George Simpson had to cope.[17]

Simpson began by insisting on administrative efficiencies of the kind he had made his speciality in his uncle's London trading house. Both employee numbers and wages were slashed, the new boss – or the Big Bourgeois as he began to be called – unceremonially dispensing with hundreds of men who found themselves peremptorily dubbed 'old' and 'useless'. But Simpson, for all his ledger-bound view of the world, nevertheless preferred the North West Company's characteristic dash and daring to the more stolid approach favoured by the Hudson's Bay Company of earlier decades. His predecessors had been content to run their North American empire from behind a desk at York Factory. George Simpson, however, was constantly criss-crossing the continent in a purpose-built canoe and in the company of the bagpipe-playing personal servants whom he had asked his father to recruit for him back in the Scottish Highlands.[18]

These pipers, commented Hugh MacLennan in the course of his reflections on a nineteenth-century print which shows George Simpson being conveyed in splendour through the wilderness, were indicative of something much more deep-seated than the Hudson's Bay Company governor's undoubted business talents. 'In Simpson's canoe,' MacLennan pointed out, 'the paddlemen are seated as usual two abreast and the bowman and steersman are in their usual places. But directly behind Simpson, who wears a grim expression on one of the most haughty faces in Canadian history, are a pair of undersized, wild-looking characters blowing bagpipes. The presence of these pipers in Simpson's canoe gives the Big Bourgeois an extra dimension. People who worked for him knew that he was the toughest employer there ever was in a notoriously tough trade. He pinched pennies, he was ruthless, he squeezed out of his servants the last ounce of work, he paid them as little as he possibly could. One knows that Simpson understood the value of every square foot of every canoe . . . in the service of his company. And yet, there sits that pair of private pipers! The Scotch are a peculiar people and never more so than when they try to out-English the English in cold calculation after they have gone into business and made a success of it. But the old wildness never quite leaves the pure Scot. Behind the granite features of George Simpson, underneath his brutal surface callousness, the primitive heat burned, and hence that pair of pipers.'[19]

By no means the least of Simpson's travels were those that took him to what is now the north-western corner of the United States – the region occupied by Montana, Idaho, Oregon and Washington State. This was an area which, in the wake of Simon Fraser's 1808 assault on the Fraser River, was painstakingly explored by that other leading Nor'Wester, David Thompson, in a series of epic journeys which culminated in his reaching the mouth of the Columbia River in the summer of 1811. Thompson, whose surveying expertise reached its apogee in the map to which his North West Company partners gave pride of place in faraway Fort William, was just three months too late to claim the Columbia estuary for Britain – the rivermouth having been occupied since April 1811 by representatives of John Jacob Astor's American Fur Company. Astor, a German immigrant who was to New York what men like Simon MacTavish were to Montreal and who was anxious to secure the far western fur trade for the United States, had sent his own Columbia River brigade to the Pacific by way of Cape Horn – thus stealing something of a march on Thompson and his colleagues. On war breaking out between the US and Britain in 1812, however, Fort Astoria, as Astor's outpost was known, quickly fell into North West Company hands – not least because Astor employees like Duncan MacDougall, Alexander Ross and Alexander MacKay, all of whom were of Scottish Highland extraction, found it extremely easy to desert the American Fur Company and join their many compatriots among the Nor'Westers.[20]

Subsequent events would result in the Pacific North West, to give the region its modern name, being ruled eventually from Washington instead of London. But that was by no means a foregone conclusion in the 1820s. Then the Columbia River basin, or the Oregon Territory as the district was beginning to be known, constituted one of the more obviously glittering prizes which the Hudson's Bay Company had gained from its merger with the Nor'Westers. The Big Bourgeois naturally enough resolved to make the most of this particular inheritance. And among the men chosen to give effect to Simpson's designs for the Columbia River country was Archibald MacDonald who, following his Red River exploits, had joined the Hudson's Bay Company in the same year as George Simpson himself.

Several other Scottish Highlanders were also to serve the Hudson's Bay Company in the Oregon Territory. Prominent among them was the enormous, red-bearded and endlessly flamboyant Finan MacDonald, one of David Thompson's most trusted lieutenants and a man whose strength was such as to have enabled him to survive a barehanded encounter with a wounded bison bull. Finan the Buffalo, as this younger brother of John MacDonald of Garth was inevitably nicknamed, spent a number of years in the Pacific North West before retiring, in the manner of so many other Nor'Westers, to Glengarry County – there to recall how he had been, among other things, one of the first traders to penetrate the valley of the Snake River in what is now South Idaho. 'I got home safe from the Snake River cuntre,' the Gaelic-speaking MacDonald wrote in his somewhat erratic English at the end of what he clearly regarded as an especially arduous mission, 'and when that cuntre will see me again the beaver will have gould skin.'[21]

Equally close to Thompson at the time of his early ventures in the Columbia River region was James MacMillan who had been born in Glen Pean at the western end of Loch Arkaig some twenty years prior to the enforced removal of that district's population by Cameron of Lochiel. Thompson thought MacMillan to be a 'staunch and manly friend and fellow traveller'. And George Simpson, who tended to be much more critical of other people than the North West Company's principal mapmaker, was equally generous. 'A very steady, plain, blunt man, shrewd and sensible, of correct conduct and good character,' the Big Bourgeois noted of MacMillan who, because of his detailed knowledge of the area's watercourses, was appointed principal assistant to the Hudson's Bay Company governor for the duration of the latter's first trip across the Rockies.[22]

But it was on Archibald MacDonald, whom he posted to the Oregon Territory in 1821, that George Simpson was to rely increasingly in the course of his various forays to the Pacific North West. It was this Glen Coe tacksman's son who, as mentioned previously, was chosen to accompany Simpson during his 1828 descent of the Fraser River. And it was MacDonald who, that same year, captured something of the pageantry which invariably attended George Simpson's progress along the much more readily navigable Columbia. 'As we wafted along under easy sail,' wrote this man from Leacantuim, 'the Highland bagpipes in the governor's canoe were echoed by the bugle in mine; then these were laid aside . . . to give free scope to the vocal organs of about eighteen Canadians to chant one of those voyageur airs peculiar to them, and always so perfectly rendered.'[23]

From Trail, in modern British Columbia, to Kettle Falls, in the north-eastern corner of Washington State, a road now parallels the course of the Columbia River. Sometimes this road climbs high above the river valley floor. Then you can look down on the Columbia, so much less turbulent than the Fraser, sweeping seawards far below, its wide waters gleaming in the sun. You imagine how it would be to hear the sound of bagpipes from upstream and to see the great canoe containing the invariably top-hatted governor of the Hudson's Bay Company come smartly round one of the many bends which the Columbia River makes here among the surrounding hills.

If glimpsed in these parts in the early 1820s, say, such a canoe party might well have been making for the place, some fifty miles from Kettle Falls, where the southward-flowing Columbia is joined by the westward-flowing Spokane River. There George Simpson and his accompanying contingent of voyageurs would leave the Columbia for this new water-course, pushing up against its currents for another forty or fifty miles until, on a little neck of flat land inside one of the Spokane's many elbow-bends, they saw ahead of them the post called Spokane House. Here, on a site where modern archaeological investigations have turned up musket-balls, musket flints, iron nails and other bits and pieces dating from Spokane House's early nineteenth-century heyday, first the North West Company and then the Hudson's Bay Company maintained the stockaded stores and warehouses of a typical frontier trading centre.

This is nowadays a most attractive corner. Across the Spokane is a wooded hill. Nearer at hand, along the water's edge, where the canoes of fur-trade times would have been lifted from the river, are scattered clumps of pine trees interspersed with springy turf. Now and then you hear the calls and splashing sounds made by wild ducks. Otherwise the silence, on a sunny, windless morning, is complete.

It is easy to understand, on such a day, why Spokane House was so favourably regarded both by North West Company men and their Hudson's Bay Company successors. Some parts of the Columbia River territory had proved as dangerous as any locality previously encountered during the fur trade's centuries-long westward expansion – with even the redoubtable Finan MacDonald being obliged in 1823 to fight his way out of a confrontation with Blackfoot war parties which had made it their business to resist his incursion into the Snake River region. That episode – which resulted in some sixty-eight Indians being killed in skirmishes which also led to MacDonald's men sustaining half a dozen casualties –

had no counterpart in the more northerly sections of the Columbia country which, to a trader like Alexander Ross, clearly seemed something of a paradise on earth.[24]

'Spokane House was a retired spot,' Ross commented in the course of the reminiscences he compiled while living in retirement at Red River. 'No hostile natives were there to disquiet a great man. There the bourgeois who presided over the company's affairs resided and that made Spokane House the centre of attraction . . . At Spokane House, too, there were handsome buildings. There was a ballroom even, and no females in the land were so fair to look upon as the nymphs of Spokane. No damsels could dance so gracefully as they. None were so attractive.'[25]

John George MacTavish, one of the great Simon MacTavish's many fur-trading relatives, was primarily responsible for Spokane House's construction. George Simpson was an occasional visitor here. So was Archibald MacDonald who was afterwards to take charge of a newer, and ultimately more important, trading post some eighty miles to the north. This was Fort Colvile. The place owed its name to Andrew Wedderburn Colvile who, as noted earlier, had played such a critical role in the Hudson's Bay Company's regeneration. To visit its site, in a flat-floored valley enclosed by rounded hills, is to see at once why one more of the many Scottish Highlanders who lived in this corner of the modern United States during the first half of the nineteenth century should have reported that Fort Colvile was widely reckoned the 'prettiest spot . . . on the Columbia River'.[26]

The Highlander who thought so highly of this place where the little city of Colville now stands was Angus MacDonald, who in 1839, at the age of twenty-three, became one of the Hudson's Bay Company's apprentice clerks at the original fort. Angus, though he had been born in Torridon in Wester Ross, was the son of one of Archibald MacDonald's elder brothers. He consequently took some pride, as Archibald did also, in tracing his descent from those Glen Coe people who, over the centuries, had proved such a notable thorn in the flesh of the Scottish and British political establishments. Indeed, as surviving accounts of his general demeanour and attitudes make clear, there was about Angus MacDonald himself more than a hint of the rumbustious outlook of his Highland ancestors.[27]

'He was a rather good-looking man,' wrote one of MacDonald's fur-trading acquaintances, 'about six feet in height, straight and slim, but said to be wiry and strong. He had a dark complexion, with long jet-black hair, reaching to the shoulders, and a thick, long and very black beard and moustache. He wore a dressed deerskin shirt and pants, a regattor or roving shirt, and had a black silk handkerchief tied loosely around his neck. He had a black, piercing eye and a deep, sonorous, rather musical voice . . . He read a great deal and was well up in the politics of the day. He was a good French linguist, but his native language was the Gaelic of the Scotch Highlanders, and he was very fond of singing or chanting . . . Gaelic songs or verses improvised by himself.'[28]

But what particularly distinguished Angus MacDonald, his fur-trading colleague continued a little disapprovingly, was his intimate knowledge of the peoples who had long inhabited this part of North America: 'He was excessively fond of the life of the aborigine and would rather live in a tent, or lodge, than in a house built in accordance with civilised plans . . . He was fond of telling Indian stories and legends and would sometimes keep an audience spellbound when . . . telling some bloodcurdling Indian story in which he had borne a conspicuous part. He could talk several Indian languages and lived a long time among the . . . Indians.' Nor was this surprising. For in 1842, while stationed at Fort Hall in what is now Montana, Angus MacDonald had met and married Catherine, a woman belonging to the Nez Perce tribe whose lands extended right across the middle reaches of the Columbia River country.

To Patrick Sellar, seeking to justify the compulsory removal of so many families from Sutherland, it seemed axiomatic that the 'aborigines of Britain', otherwise the people of the Scottish Highlands, occupied much the same sort of position in the overall scheme of things as the 'aborigines of America' – by which Sellar meant, though it is unlikely that he had heard of this particular group, peoples like the Nez Perce. Both Highlanders and North American Indians, Sellar contended, 'live in turf cabins in common with the brutes'. Both, moreover, 'were shut out from the general stream of knowledge and cultivation flowing in upon the commonwealth of Europe from the remotest fountain of antiquity' – American Indians being so excluded by geography, Highlanders by their linguistic and cultural isolation. 'Their seclusion . . . from this grand fund of knowledge,' Sellar went on to observe of the Gaelic-speaking families he was so busily evicting, 'places them, with relation to the enlightened nations of Europe, in a position not very different from that betwixt the American colonists and the aborigines of that country'. It was consequently every bit as appropriate, from Patrick Sellar's point of view at any rate, for Highlanders to be ejected from their homes to make way for sheep-farmers like himself as it was for the Nez Perce and other tribes to be expelled from their ancestral lands in order to make these lands available for settlement by the sheep-farming fraternity's North American counterparts. Only by such drastic means, so Sellar argued, could the cause of civilisation be advanced.[29]

The prejudices to which Patrick Sellar thus appealed were of very ancient vintage. As long ago as the fourteenth century, for example, Scottish Highlanders were being distinguished from their Lowland neighbours in language of which Sellar would have wholeheartedly approved. Lowlanders, according to the Aberdeenshire chronicler John Fordun, writing in the 1380s, were 'domesticated and cultured, trustworthy, patient and urbane, decent in their attire, law-abiding, devout in religious observance'. Highlanders, in contrast, were a 'wild and untamed people, rough and unbending, given to robbery, ease-loving, of artful and impressionable temperament, comely in form but unsightly in dress'. Nor was there to be any lack of similar comment in the centuries that followed, southern governments regularly accusing Highlanders of 'barbarity and wickedness'; of 'bathing themselves in the blood of others'; of 'beastly cruelties'; and, on one especially comprehensive occasion, of the 'most detestable, damnable and odious murders, fires, ravishing of women, witchcraft and depredations'.[30]

North America's colonists were to describe that continent's native peoples in identical terms, calling Indians cruel, childish, degraded, dirty, diseased, drunken, faithless, insolent, lazy, lying, murderous, profligate, stupid, thieving, vindictive, savage and much else besides. And because all such abuse serves to dehumanise those to whom it is applied, the many people who dealt habitually in talk of this kind found it comparatively easy – whether in the case of the Glen Coe MacDonalds or in the innumerable instances of massacre and slaughter which disfigure the European record in America – to treat both Scottish Highlanders and Indians in ways which would not otherwise have been regarded as morally acceptable.[31]

None of this was to lead automatically to those Scottish Highlanders who came to North America during the eighteenth and nineteenth centuries feeling any very profound sense of solidarity with the various native peoples they encountered. Just now and then, admittedly, some flicker of mutual recognition seems to have occurred – not least on the occasion of kilted regiments first arriving in New York in the 1750s. 'When the Highlanders landed,' it was reported of this event, 'they were caressed by all ranks and orders of men, but more particularly by the Indians. On the march to Albany, the Indians flocked from all quarters to see the strangers who, they believed, were of the same extraction as themselves, and therefore received them as brothers.'[32]

Similar sentiments possibly underlay the high degree of trust which clearly existed, at the time of the Revolutionary War, between Highland loyalists like the Mohawk Valley guerilla fighter, John MacDonell, and the Iroquois braves with whom men of MacDonell's stamp co-operated so successfully. It was certainly no difficult thing for eighteenth-century Highlanders to adapt to Indian lifestyles which, during that period, were not so very different from their own. Among the more permanent products of such adaption – John MacDonell having abandoned Indian ways at the Revolutionary War's end – were the Creek chieftains William MacIntosh and Alexander MacGillivray. Both had Scottish Highland fathers and Indian mothers. Both chose an Indian destiny rather than a European one. And MacGillivray, in particular, became one of the most adept of eighteenth-century Indian leaders – deploying as many as 6,000 fighting men, negotiating personally with President George Washington and managing for many years to secure his Creek people's claims to independence from Britain, the United States and Spain.[33]

Most North American native peoples, however, would have been hard pressed to distinguish between the behaviour of Scottish Highlanders and the conduct of any other of the various types of European with whom they came in contact. North Carolina's Highland settlers happily took over the hunting grounds of the Tuscarora and the Cherokee. Emigrants to Cape Breton Island, many of them refugees from clearances of the sort organised by Patrick Sellar, showed not the slightest scruple about displacing the area's traditional inhabitants, the Micmac, from territories which the latter had occupied for much longer than there had been Gaelic-speaking Scots in Scotland. And for all that the Kildonan people's leaders freely acknowledged the material and other assistance they were given by the region's Saulteaux and Cree Indians on their first reaching Red River, the Saulteaux and the Cree were afterwards to have every cause to regret their openhandedness.[34]

'Before you whites came to trouble the ground,' Chief Peguis of the Saulteaux was famously to lament, 'our rivers were full of fish and woods of deer. Our creeks abounded with beavers and our plains were covered with buffalo. But now we are brought to poverty. Our beavers are gone forever; our buffalo are fled to the lands of our enemies. The number of our fish is diminishing. Our cats and our rats are few in number. The geese are afraid to pass over the smoke of our chimneys and we are left to starve while you whites are growing rich on the very dust of our fathers, troubling the plains with the plough, covering them with cows in the summer and in the winter feeding your cattle with hay from the very swamps whence our beavers have been driven.'[35]

As Peguis of the Saulteaux so evocatively proclaimed, the ecological impact of the European settlement of his continent was everywhere entirely negative. Despite their own Gaelic culture having always laid great stress on the significance of the natural world, Scottish Highlanders were well to the forefront of the steadily gathering assault on North America's natural resources. Glengarry County lumber gangs laid waste the forests. Fur traders from the north of Scotland contributed energetically to those processes which would result in at least 140 animal and bird species becoming extinct in North America in the five centuries following the pioneering voyages of men like Christopher Columbus and John Cabot.[36]

This is not to imply that Scottish Highland traders were uncultured. Not all of them were as well-read as Martin MacLeod – who noted, in the course of one wilderness trip, that he had 'passed the day reading Tacitus' and who is known to have overwintered, on another occasion, in the company of a seven-volume *Life of Sir Walter Scott*, Byron's collected poems and the plays of Shakespeare. But many North West

Company Highlanders, and Hudson's Bay Company Highlanders also, took no small pride in keeping abreast of what was going on in the wider world. Their tacksmen forebears, after all, were every bit as familiar with books as with broadswords. And the Scotland that they themselves had left – the Scotland of David Hume and Adam Smith – was at the centre of the cultural upsurge known as the Enlightenment.[37]

One outcome of Scotland's growing obsession with learning was the *Statistical Account* organised by Sir John Sinclair of Ulbster in the 1790s. This consisted of highly detailed analyses of the country's social, economic and demographic condition – these analyses being compiled by Church of Scotland clergymen on a parish-by-parish basis. It is indicative of the extent to which he and his partners kept in touch with intellectual developments back home that Roderick MacKenzie of the North West Company should have urged this fur-trading organisation's representatives in the field to undertake a similar exercise in respect of those Indian peoples with whom they were in contact. What he wanted to discover, MacGillivray informed his colleagues, was 'the origin and meaning of the names of tribes, whence they came, how far distant, in what direction, by what means, their ancient and present state of population, the cause of their increase and decrease, number of families, number of men, women and children in each family and the number of souls in all, their morals, principles, statutes, superstitions, idols, ceremonies, traditions, amusements, disposition, qualifications, occupations, government, police, regulations, manners, customs, industry, economy, food and manner of preparing it, habitations, utensils, vessels, dresses, ornaments, arms, instruments, manner of making war, tombs, monuments, advantages and disadvantages, means of improvement'.[38]

This early exercise in anthropology, it is almost needless to say, was never completed. And it may well be that MacKenzie's attitudes were less typical of the North West Company than those of the altogether harder-headed Duncan MacGillivray. 'With respect to the fur trade,' the Stratherrick-born MacGillivray commented caustically, 'whatever peculiarity each tribe of Indians may have, and however various their customs, manners and language may be, they are divided by the North West Company into two classes: those who have furs and those who have none.'[39]

Others were still more dismissive. George Simpson – who seems seldom to have used the word 'Indian' in his correspondence without annexing to it adjectives like 'false' and 'cowardly' – thought native peoples so given to 'insatiable rapacity' as to be undeserving of anything other than contempt. 'They must be ruled with a rod of iron to . . . keep them in a proper state of subordination.'[40]

None of this, however, could disguise the extent to which the fur trade rested on Indian endeavour. Neither Simpson nor his predecessors could have created their continent-wide communications network were it not for Indian inventions such as the birchbark canoe and the snow-shoe. And neither the North West Company nor the Hudson's Bay Company would have had many beaver pelts to sell in Europe were it not for the willingness of successive tribes to act as trappers in return for the manufactured goods – the pots, pans, metal needles, knives, guns, ammunition and other items of that kind – which native peoples obtained in return for such furs as they brought each year, through decade after decade, to posts of the Spokane House and Fort Colvile type.

Among the most corrosive and inexcusable aspects of the fur trade was the willingness of the North West Company, in particular, to swap alcohol for furs – the rawgut liquor in which many Scottish Highland traders dealt going a long way to destroy societies and cultures which had no historical experience of so addictive an intoxicant. 'The love of rum,' Duncan MacGillivray nastily observed of this commodity's key role in his own commercial transactions with different Indian peoples, 'is their first inducement to industry. They undergo every hardship and fatigue to procure a skinful of this delicious beverage. And when a nation becomes addicted to drinking, it affords a strong presumption that they will soon become excellent hunters.'[41]

Sexual relationships between traders and Indian women could be, and often were, equally exploitative – it being difficult to imagine that George Simpson, for example, harboured any very profound feelings for the many 'bits of brown' whom he bedded in the course of his travels. It would be wrong, however, to assume that Simpson's casual attitudes to such matters were shared universally. The connection between many Scottish Highland fur traders and their Indian partners was frequently long-lasting. And the relatively binding nature of such frontier arrange-ments was commonly underlined by their being inaugurated by that most distinctive of fur-trade ceremonies, the marriage *à la façon du pays*. This was the ritual, incorporating both European and Indian elements, devised to mark the commencement of a semi-permanent relationship which placed well-understood responsibilities and obligations on both parties to it.[42]

From a fur trader's perspective, of course, such partnerships served utilitarian as well as emotional purposes. His 'country wife' cooked his food, made his clothes, overhauled his canoe, mended his snowshoes, acted as his interpreter in business negotiations. But none of this pre-cluded the emergence of affections strong enough on both sides to tran-scend the many barriers which eighteenth- and nineteenth-century European society placed in the way of trans-racial relationships. 'Robertson brought his bit of brown with him to the settlement this spring in the hope that she would pick up a few English manners before visiting the civilised world,' George Simpson noted in 1831 of one former North West Company man who had newly moved to Red River with his Indian wife. 'But it would not do. I told him distinctly the thing was impossible, which mortified him exceedingly.' It was greatly to this man's moral credit – though not to his standing with his superiors – that, even in the face of such hostility, he stuck loyally by the woman with whom he had shared much of his life on the frontier. Many others did likewise – their sense of duty frequently extending to those mixed-blood children, not least Cuthbert Grant of Red River, who were provided by fur-trader fathers with the means of obtaining both an education and a job.[43]

When, following the death of the Chinook woman with whom he had become involved shortly after his arrival in the Columbia River country, Archibald MacDonald from Leacantuim took an English-born wife, the trader's mixed-blood son, Ranald, was raised alongside his other children. Sent east to be apprenticed to a bank in Ontario, the young man – one of the more fascinating products of cross-cultural contact between Indians and Highlanders in the Pacific North West – promptly ran away to sea. His lifelong penchant for 'wandering freedom', which he attributed both to his 'Indian mother' and to his 'Highland father of Glen Coe', resulted in Ranald MacDonald becoming one of the first foreigners to gain access to Japan. Later Ranald was to prospect for gold in both Australia and British Columbia before settling down to farming in the vicinity of Fort Colvile. There he was known to his cousin, Angus MacDonald, whose own marriage into the Nez Perce created yet another set of linkages between the Scottish Highlands and the world of the North American Indian.[44]

The process which was to ensure that the Oregon Territory would eventually be incorporated into the United States rather than the British Empire had its origins in the opening years of the nineteenth century when President Thomas Jefferson decided, shortly after the publication of Alexander MacKenzie's account of his great journeys, that Americans should quickly follow where this Scottish Highlander had led. In 1804 a US government expedition, officered by Meriwether Lewis and William Clark, was duly despatched to the Pacific. Slowly that expedition – which was much more heavily equipped than MacKenzie had ever been – made its way up the Missouri. The Rockies were crossed. Modern Montana was reached. Then, by way of the Lolo Pass, Lewis and Clark made their way into the valley of the Clearwater River, a tributary of the Columbia. Here, in September 1805, the Americans encountered a group of Indians whom they reckoned to be 'among the most amiable . . . we have seen'. These Indians, who made it their business immediately to care for the distant Jefferson's half-starved emissaries, were known to each other simply as Nimipu, the people. Because of their habit of wearing dentalium shells in their noses, however, French-speaking Iroquois traders had already christened them the *Nez Percé*. It is by this name – though long since shorn of its French pronunciation – that the Nimipu have ever since been known.[45]

Theirs was a singularly striking homeland. 'From the first breath of spring until midsummer,' an American writer has commented, 'the Nez Perce country is a blaze of colour. Blue windflowers, purple shooting stars, yellow bells, blue bells, blue and purple penstemon, blue and yellow lupin, yellow sunflowers and Indian paintbrush in various hues follow one another in wild profusion. Mingled with the flowers are many important food plants, the feathery-leaved cowish, the pink bitterroot and, above all, the camas, covering the open meadows with blue carpets until, at a distance, they resemble little lakes.'[46]

Here the Nimipu hunted such bison as came westwards across the continental divide from Montana. Here they fished the king salmon, the sockeye, the coho and the silver when each of these distinct species made its different runs up this mountain region's many rivers. Here, when winter snows descended on the high hill country, the Nimipu retreated to the shelter of lower-lying valleys where, around the fires which burned day and night in their longhouses, men, women and children listened once again – in much the same way as their Glen Coe counterparts had also done habitually at this darkest and coldest time of year – to the many tales told by the tribe's tradition-bearers.[47]

It was among the Nez Perce that Angus MacDonald, who clearly felt himself as much part of this people as it was possible for any European to be, spent the greater part of his life – recording, in the process, much that is invaluable about the way the Nez Perce lived. In the notebooks he kept for this purpose in his saddlebag, MacDonald jotted down as much as he could learn of Nez Perce history, legends and ritual. Sometimes, indeed, he participated in such ritual himself.[48]

So it was in the case of what MacDonald called the *San-ka-ha*. This, the Highlander explained, was a ceremony in which 'the red man' engaged before going off to battle. A great deal of 'wild' and 'pathetic' chanting was involved; a great deal of strong feeling also. 'To hear it sung by five or six hundred voices in a calm, starry night on the plains of Montana is a rare thing,' Angus MacDonald wrote of the San-ka-ha. 'In 1850, at a great gathering of Indians to dance to this staid, insisting strain, I stripped with the leading men, painted with vermilion the grooves and dimples of my upper body, mounted my black buffalo charger with my full eagle feather cap and cantered round and round with them, keeping time to the song.'[49]

There was, unfortunately, to be much need of ritual of this kind in the Nez Perce country in Angus MacDonald's lifetime. As prospectors, miners and farmers poured into the Oregon Territory in the wake of its formal annexation by the United States in the 1840s, so relations between the Nez Perce and the region's growing white population began to deteriorate steadily. Soon the Nez Perce were urged to move to one of the reservations on which the authorities in Washington now wished to settle Indian tribes. 'If they were to live in peace,' Chief Tuekakas of the Nez Perce was informed by the US government's representative in the region, 'it was necessary . . . that the Indians should have a country set apart for them, and in that country they must stay.' It was also necessary that Tuekakas, just like Alasdair MacDonald of Glen Coe two centuries before, should put his signature to a document which formally acknowledged other men's authority over his people. 'Take away your paper,' the Nez Perce chieftain's son was afterwards to recall his father saying to the government agent sent to put this proposal to him. 'I will not touch it with my hand.'[50]

Now what had been done to Angus MacDonald's Glen Coe ancestors was done to his wife's people also. Tuekakas having died in 1871, his son and successor, Hinmahtooyahlatkekht, whose name signified the sound of thunder in the mountains but who was known to the American authorities as Joseph, came under such pressure to evacuate his tribal lands in Oregon's Wallowa Valley that, for the first time in their history, the Nez Perce went to war with whites. In the company of other Nez Perce chieftains such as White Bird, Toohoolhoolzote and Looking Glass, Chief Joseph embarked on a guerilla campaign so successful as to enable him to inflict a number of defeats on the United States military at various points in the mountains of Idaho and Montana. But any such contest – involving just several hundred Indian families, on the one side, and one of the nineteenth-century world's emerging industrial powers, on the other – was bound to be unequal. 'I learned . . . that we were few,' Joseph himself remarked subsequently, 'while the white men were many, and that we could not hold our own with them. We were like deer. They were like grizzly bears. We had a small country. Their country was large. We were contented to let things remain as the Great Spirit Chief made them. They were not and would change the rivers and mountains if they did not suit them.'[51]

Defeat, in such circumstances, was inevitable. It was made all the more inevitable, and all the more total when it came, as a result of the Nez Perce having to involve their whole society in what gradually turned into a fighting retreat in the direction of Canada – where Chief Joseph and his people hoped to find some sort of sanctuary. What the Americans called the Nez Perce War involved only a handful of their mounted formations. The Indian bands against whom these US cavalry units were deployed, however, consisted of women, children and the elderly as well as warriors. When Colonel John Gibbon's troops descended on the Nez Perce at a place called Big Hole in Montana, therefore, it was not at all surprising that many non-combatants should be killed in the ensuing fighting.[52]

Big Hole, for all its horror, did not spell the end of Nez Perce resistance. Gibbon's attack on Chief Joseph's camp was eventually repulsed and the Americans once more defeated. The Nez Perce now moved into Yellowstone – which, not long before, had been declared the world's first national park. Then they backtracked toward the north, skilfully evading their pursuers, coming at last to Snake Creek in the Bear Paw Mountains. Here, not much more than forty miles from the safety represented by the Canadian border, the Nez Perce were again caught by the US cavalry. Here there was a further battle. And here, at the beginning of October 1877, with snow already falling and with ice already gripping the Montana rivers, Chief Joseph surrendered formally to General Oliver Otis Howard of the American army. 'Our chiefs are killed,' runs a contemporary account of what Chief Joseph now so memorably said. 'Looking Glass is dead. Toohoolhoolzote is dead. The old men are all dead . . . It is cold . . . The little children are freezing to death. My people, some of them, have run away to the hills, and have no blankets, no food. No one knows where they are . . . I want to have time to look for my children and see how many of them I can find. Maybe I shall find them among the dead . . . I am tired. My heart is sick and sad. From where the sun now stands I will fight no more forever.'[53]

Many months later, in the United States capital, this same Chief Joseph, Hinmahtooyahlatkekht, attempted to explain to a white audience what it was that had caused him so effectively to resist his people's expulsion from the Wallowa Valley. 'I took his hand in mine,' Joseph recalled of the moments preceding the death of his father, Tuekakas. 'He said, "My son, my body is returning to my mother earth and my spirit is going very soon to see the Great Spirit Chief. When I am gone, think of your country . . . Always remember that your father never sold his country. You must stop your ears whenever you are asked to sign a treaty selling your home . . . My son, never forget my dying words. This country holds your father's body. Never sell the bones of your father." I pressed my father's hand and told him that I would protect his grave with my life . . . I buried him in that beautiful valley of winding waters. I love that land more than all the rest of the world. A man who would not love his father's grave is worse than a wild animal.'[54]

The settlers who took the place of the Nez Perce in the Wallowa Valley were to rob this grave and give the skull of Tuekakas to a local dentist for display in his surgery. And for all that their own forebears would readily have understood Chief Joseph's affection for his people's place and his desperate desire to retain his hold on it, some of these settlers, it should possibly be noted, had Scottish Highland names. This was also true, however, of the man who, even before Chief Joseph spoke in Washington, had published in a Montana newspaper a series of articles which, as the paper's extraordinarily courageous editor put it, were intended to give 'the Nez Perce version of their troubles'. The author of these articles had followed to Canada the few Nimipu – members mostly of the band led by Chief White Bird – who had managed to escape the US army. There he talked at length with the Indian refugee contingent. There he heard much that was strangely reminiscent of what had once happened in Glen Coe.[55]

'On the night they camped at the battleground,' this enquirer now reported of what had been done to the Nez Perce at Big Hole, 'most of the warriors were up until a late hour engaged in their war dance. This caused a deep sleep to fall on them after they went to their lodges. Some of them slept so soundly they never awakened. The camp, not apprehending danger, was sleeping soundly, when suddenly the rifles of the soldiers belched forth their deadly fire. The camp was awakened to find their enemies plunging through it dealing death and destruction in every direction . . . Many women and children were killed before getting out of their beds. In one lodge there were five children. One soldier went into it and killed every one of them . . . About forty women and children were piled up in one little ravine where they had run for shelter. Many women, with from one to three children in their arms, were found dead in that ravine. Some of the children had their mother's breasts in their mouths.'[56]

The writer of these words knew the Nez Perce well. In fact, he was one of them himself. He was related, through his mother, to Chief Looking Glass who had died in the Bear Paw Mountains fighting. He was related also to Chief White Bird and to Chief Eagle-from-the-Light who, previous to White Bird taking over this position, had led the one Nez Perce band to get away to Canada. And this writer's own name? It was Duncan MacDonald. He was the eldest son of the now ageing fur trader who, years before, had married into the Nez Perce and whose own ancestry can be traced back to people who died around Leacantuim in February 1692.[57]

CHAPTER ELEVEN

The Power of Your Dreams

SOMETIMES IT SEEMS that there is no part of North America which does not have its connection with the Scottish Highlands. Eastwards from Spokane on Interstate 90 is Coeur d'Alene, a neat little resort town at the northern end of a mountain lake of the same name. Towards the town's western edge, on the site once occupied by Fort Sherman, one of the nineteenth-century US military's several strongpoints in this vicinity, is North Idaho College. Among the college's teachers is Jim McLeod whose great-great-great-great-grandfather, Malcolm MacLeod, held the rank of captain in Prince Charles Edward Stuart's army. Jim's people, he tells you, got to this part of the United States by way of Prince Edward Island – PEI folk frequently finding it as necessary as their Cape Breton Island neighbours to move elsewhere in search of employment. 'My grandfather came out to Montana around the turn of the century,' Jim explains. And it is to Montana that he is now planning a day-trip.

There is deep snow in Lookout Pass where the highway from Coeur d'Alene in Idaho to Missoula in Montana crosses the continental divide. The surrounding scenery is spectacular. But the talk, inevitably, is of the Scottish Highlands; of what it meant to Brock McLeod, Jim's college student son, to be taken recently to see the spot in Raasay, a small island off the eastern coast of Skye, where his MacLeod ancestors lived; of how Brock got the opportunity, when visiting Culloden, to stand in the place where his Jacobite great-great-great-great-great-grandfather would have stood some 250 years before.

On the outskirts of Missoula, the towering signs which you encounter on the approaches to any North American city – those lurid advertisements for MacDonald's, Burger King, Exxon, Conoco, the Holiday Inn, the Ponderosa and half a thousand other enterprises – seem especially incandescent below a dark and heavy sky. Here, some eighty years ago, there was raised the Presbyterian minister's son, Norman Maclean, whose book, *A River Runs Through It*, afterwards the basis of a Robert Redford film, has done so much to make Montana's hill terrain loom large in the modern American consciousness. 'In our family,' Maclean's book famously begins, 'there was no clear line between religion and fly fishing.' Nor was there any doubt as to this family's strong bond with the place where they had come to rest at the end of travels which, though they ended in Missoula, had earlier taken the Macleans – who came originally from the Isle of Mull – to Nova Scotia and Iowa. 'My father loved America so much,' Norman Maclean wrote, 'that, although he had a rather heavy Scotch burr when he came to this country, by the time I was born it was all gone. He regarded it as his American duty to get rid of it.'[1]

Another Missoula writer was the poet, Richard Hugo, a friend of Jim McLeod's and a man who, in the 1970s, made his own pilgrimage from the United States to the Scottish Highlands where he lived for some months in Uig, a village towards the northern tip of Skye. There this American put together his own account of the events which resulted in so many Highlanders being expelled from their homeland.[2]

Lord, it took no more than a wave of a glove,
a nod of the head over tea. People were torn from their crofts
and herded aboard, their land turned over to sheep.
They sailed. They wept.
The sea said nothing and said I'll get even.
Their last look at Skye lasted one hour. Then fog.
Think of their fear . . .
Think of loss that goes stormy knots beyond bitter
and think of some absentee landlord home in his tower
signing the order and waving off a third ale.

'The lovelier the land the worse the dispossession,' Richard Hugo wrote of the clearances which so emptied Skye. And if that is true of what was experienced by Scottish Highlanders, it is surely still more true of what was suffered by those people – the Nez Perce and their Flathead neighbours among many others – who were forcibly deprived of so much territory in the memorably beautiful tracts of mountain country which extend westwards, northwards, eastwards from Missoula.

Outside the redbrick church at St Ignatius Mission on Montana's Flathead Reservation, Jim McLeod is greeted by Tom Branson. Both of them, the thought occurs as they shake hands, this college teacher and this forester, are descended from men who stood in the bitter wind and cutting sleet that long-gone morning when the Duke of Cumberland's artillery broke finally the power of Scotland's clans. And both these men are Americans. But Jim is what our world calls white. And Tom – the great-great-great-great-grandson of a Jacobite soldier from Leacantuim and the great-great-grandson of a Hudson's Bay Company fur trader named Angus MacDonald – is what our world equally calls Indian. Or did until this world came up with the replacement term, native American. Which to use? 'Now don't you worry about all of that,' Beverly Branson, Tom's wife, remarks when you try to feel your way, a little clumsily maybe, towards the correct terminology.

At the nearby home of Tom Branson's great-uncle, Charlie MacDonald, aged ninety-four, Eileen Decker, Charlie's niece, carefully spreads across a table the contents of a wooden box. 'Most of these belonged to the old Scot,' Eileen says of the letters, photographs and other material thus revealed.

Here, where you are made so welcome by his descendants, this man who left the Highlands in the 1830s seems suddenly very close. Here is the ornate warrant appointing Angus MacDonald one of the Hudson's Bay Company's chief traders. Here are his annual statements of account. Here Joseph Alexander MacDonald, one of the old Scot's sons and Charlie MacDonald's father, is pictured playing the bagpipes which Angus took with him from Scotland. Here is Angus MacDonald's cousin, Ranald, photographed after that adventurer's return from Japan. Here is a letter from Archibald MacDonald, Ranald's father, Angus's uncle and the man, of course, who brought the Strath of Kildonan emigrants to Red River in 1814. Here Angus himself is pictured with two of his daughters, Margaret and Christina, whom Charlie MacDonald remembers as his aunts. Here is a letter, dated 20 July 1845, sent to Angus MacDonald from his sister Margaret – clearly a family name this – then living in Dingwall. 'My dear Angus,' the letter begins. 'There are not many things on earth that can afford so great pleasure than to hear of you living well.'

Outside it is snowing slightly. Inside Charlie is talking about his uncle, Duncan MacDonald, the man who wrote so forcefully, back in 1878, in the cause of the Nez Perce. 'He was real gruff when he talked,' Charlie says of Duncan. 'He had me kind of scared when I was a kid. He spoke French a lot, English too, Nez Perce, of course. And he spoke some Gaelic as well. The Gaelic he would have got from old Angus. I remember hearing him speak a bit of Gaelic. I guess I knew a word or two of Gaelic myself. But I've gotten so old I've forgotten all of that.'

Duncan lived to be eighty-five, Charlie goes on. 'He was an adventurous kind of guy. After Chief Joseph surrendered to the army in 1877, Duncan went right up to Canada with White Bird and the few other folk that made it to the border ahead of the soldiers. He got their story from them there, I guess.'

Now Tom Branson offers to show the way to the single timber building which is all that remains of Fort Connah, the Hudson's Bay Company post in Mission Valley, just a few miles beyond St Ignatius. This is where Angus MacDonald lived for many years. This is where he developed his own cattle-ranching business. This is where he was visited regularly by the Nez Perce chief, Eagle-from-the-Light, 'a close relative of my children', as Angus explained in one letter. 'From him I learned many items about the Nez Perce,' the old Scot added.[3]

Here Angus MacDonald did what he could to make the case for his wife's people during the months following their slaughter and defeat. 'It is the old drift,' Angus wrote of these events. 'The strong oppresses the weak and power is always power, right or wrong.' Praise and attention were being lavished on the American troops responsible for what had occurred at Big Hole, the now retired fur trader continued. Nothing, however, was being done for the Nez Perce. 'I see them out to meet the United States wounded . . . I see their . . . care for the soldiers of Big Uncle Sam, who is rich as he is silly . . . and strong as he is comfortable . . . I also see a little girl away in the grass, lying and moaning in her blood.'[4]

The place where these words were written was considered by Angus MacDonald to be 'one of the most beautiful valleys of America'. And even on a winter's day, with a chill wind blowing and the grass stripped of all colour by the frost, it is hard to disagree. Gently rolling buffalo country extends mile after mile, both north and south, along the line of Mission Valley. Eastwards the valley is walled off by the Mission Mountain Wilderness, a wilder version of Glen Coe's Aonach Eagach ridge, its summits dominated by McDonald Peak, named after Angus and, at just under 10,000 feet, the highest pinnacle hereabouts.[5]

Sometimes these scenes seemed, to Angus MacDonald, to be reminiscent of the Scottish Highlands. Sometimes there were other reminders also. 'The other night,' the fur trader and rancher wrote of an evening spent with his family at Fort Connah, 'whilst the wild Rocky Mountain winds played their own solemn, unrecorded ways over my humble roof, Maggie played *Old Hundred*, *Bonnie Doon* and *Annie Laurie*, and to be sure I felt the thing. The sight was strange to me to see the . . . daughter of old America and far back Scotland playing these splendid airs.'[6]

At the Scottish Cultural Centre in Vancouver, where the men and women of this Pacific city's Gaelic Choir are gathering for their weekly practice session, the music of Angus MacDonald's 'far back Scotland' is very much in evidence. Maureen Lyons, who comes originally from the Isle of Lewis, is in charge. There is discussion of how plans are coming along for the latest in Vancouver's steadily lengthening series of Gaelic festivals. Mention is made of several of the people who travelled from Scotland to attend the last such happening – the sort of get-together which, in Maureen's native language, is called a *mod*. Maureen names a number of individuals living in Skye, Dingwall and other parts of the Highlands. 'You'll be sure to give them our best wishes when you get back home,' she says.

They are all Canadians here; all proud to be so; harbouring no regrets about their being in North America. But their connection with the Scottish Highlands is important to them all the same. That this should be so is not at all surprising in the case of those first-generation emigrants – Maureen Lyons, Peggy MacKinnon, Murdo and Mary MacIver, Duncan and Donelle MacKenzie – to be met with at the Scottish Cultural Centre this evening. What would be less expected – if it were not for your having frequently come up against in North America those emotions which Hugh MacLennan had in mind when he wrote about 'the permanent Highland homesickness' – is the extent to which the Highlands remain meaningful to Vancouver Gaelic Choir members whose links with Scotland are far in the past.[7]

Maureen makes the necessary introductions. To Ishbel Cameron whose mother and father emigrated from Lochaber to British Columbia in the 1940s. To Bill MacDonald whose people left the Uists for Vancouver around 1910. To Brian Webster whose grandfather, Donald Sinclair, came out to Saskatchewan from Easter Ross in the 1890s. To Sharon Gunn whose folk emigrated from Sutherland to Nova Scotia around 1820. To Frank Ward whose Highland forebears, Shaws and MacCallums mostly, left the Argyll parishes of Southend and Kilmartin in the decade which brought Allan and Flora MacDonald of Kingsburgh to North Carolina.

You talk to Sharon Gunn whose Gaelic, Maureen comments, is as fluent as any to be heard in Scotland. She 'picked up' the language, Sharon says, from her Nova Scotia grandfather. And so committed is this Vancouver schoolteacher to maintaining her grip on her Highland origins that she took time to go to Glasgow University and take a degree in Celtic Studies.

Listening to Sharon, six or seven generations removed from the depopulated straths of Sutherland, still speaking the language of the Scottish Highlands, it is impossible to do other than recall Margaret Laurence's fictional creation, Morag Gunn; separated from Scotland by a similar span of time; managing somehow to acquire in Winnipeg a recording of Gaelic songs of the sort being sung tonight in Vancouver's Scottish Cultural Centre.

'She could not understand the words,' Laurence wrote of Morag, 'nor even distinguish between them, make any kind of pattern of them. Just a lot of garbled sounds to her. Yet she played the record often, as though if she listened to it enough, she would finally pierce the barrier of that ancient speech and have its meaning revealed to her.'[8]

Murdo MacIver, who comes from Arnol in Lewis and who acquired English as a second language, is recalling his arrival in Vancouver. In 1953 that was – about the same time, Duncan MacKenzie chips in, that he got here from Gairloch in Wester Ross. Murdo was a seaman by trade. Duncan was a joiner or, to use the North American term, a carpenter. Both of them, it now emerges, were helped into their first jobs hereabouts by other men they happened to meet whose family origins were also in the Scottish Highlands. It was following a church service this happened to him, Duncan tells you. It was in a shipping office in his case, Murdo remembers.

This is always how it has been on this continent, you remark. One or two Highlanders get themselves established; in North Carolina; in the Mohawk Valley; in Glengarry County; in the fur trade. Then others of their friends, their kin, their neighbours come along behind – the newer emigrants having their path smoothed by those who have preceded them.

Murdo agrees. He mentions Trail in the British Columbia interior, not very far from the point, just south of the modern US–Canada border, where the Hudson's Bay Company established their Fort Colvile outpost. He spent some time in Trail when he originally got here, Murdo says. That was because there were then a whole lot of people from his own crofting township of Arnol – by no means a big place – living in this one small Canadian town. 'They'd followed one another out there,' Murdo explains.

During his first evening in Trail, this Lewisman continues, he was questioned, interrogated more like, by a man he later discovered to be nearly ninety years of age; a man who grilled him about the doings of everyone back home in Arnol. 'When the old fellow finally left the house where I was being put up,' Murdo goes on, 'I asked who he was exactly. And when they told me, I just couldn't believe it. He was a man whose name I'd known all my life because, when I was a kid, I'd played often in the ruins of what had once been his home in Arnol. He'd left that home for Canada before the turn of the century. But there he was, still going strong, still as interested as ever in what might be happening in Lewis.'

Trail, when you visit the town in winter, seems half-buried in the snow which makes the surrounding Kootenai Mountains a good place to go ski-ing. Nowhere could be more unlike Arnol, one of many crofting townships strung out along the low-lying Atlantic coast of Lewis. But Trail, for reasons now hard to pin down, clearly became this island community's point of access to the New World. And the links thus made between Arnol and Trail will extend today – as a result of subsequent onward movement – to very many other parts of North America.

These links will neccessarily be more diffuse now than once they were. But Arnol's name, judging at any rate from the experience of the American writer, John McPhee, will still mean a great deal to those families who got to be where they are on this continent as a result of some

Arnol man or woman having decided – maybe a hundred or more years ago – to be up and off to another country.

His own great-grandfather, McPhee comments, left the Argyll island of Colonsay in the mid-nineteenth century to become eventually a miner in the United States. 'He went into the Ohio mines, and stayed there, and died in 1907,' John McPhee writes. 'He has about a hundred and thirty descendants who have sprayed out into the American interior, and they have included railroad engineers, railroad conductors, brakemen, firemen, steelworkers, teachers, football coaches, a chemist, a chemical engineer, a policeman, a grocer, salesmen, doctors, lawyers, druggists, janitors and postmen.'[9]

The one thing which connects these highly disparate North Americans, McPhee continues, is their Scottish Highland origin. 'It has always seemed extraordinary to me how the name of the island, Colonsay, seems to hang suspended in the minds not only of my immediate relatives but also of collateral clansmen in scattered parts of the United States and Canada . . . Just the name of the island seems to set off in virtually all these people, who now live anywhere between the oceans, some sort of atavistic vibration, and all they really have in common is the panoptic glaze that will appear in their eyes at the mention of the word *Colonsay*.'

There was, thought Hugh MacLennan, 'something Judaic in the Scotch of the north'; in their often enforced dispersal from their homeland; in their turning exile to advantage by learning to master 'the techniques and the culture of their conquerors'; in their always retaining, wherever they might find themselves and however strongly they might identify with their countries of adoption, a sense of belonging still to those faraway places whose names alone, as John McPhee so plainly recognises, possess, for folk of Highland origin, an almost talismanic power.[10]

This Scottish Highlander's North American journey, which began on a summer's day at Moore's Creek Bridge, ends in the early darkness of a winter's night in Stanley Park, Vancouver. On the tapedeck of the last of a long series of rented cars there is playing a song which has accompanied me across the continent. The song was written on a Winnipeg bus by Calum and Rory Macdonald from North Uist. It is sung by Runrig, the band to which Calum and Rory belong and the band which, for several years now, has helped to make the traditional culture and language of the Scottish Highlands seem meaningful and important to a new generation. The song is a tribute to North America's countless thousands of Gaelic-speaking immigrants from Scotland. 'You tamed this land by enterprise,' the song says, 'and by the power of your dreams.'[11]

The song stops. Across Burrard Inlet, a part of the Pacific, the lights of North Vancouver spread up a hillside towards a starry sky. I get out

251

of my car and stand there in the cold, looking back the way I have come. Between me and my home on the Isle of Skye, for which I will set out again tomorrow, is the full breadth both of North America and the Atlantic Ocean.

'In the evening,' James Boswell wrote on the occasion of his 1773 visit to the island where I now live, 'the company danced as usual. We performed, with much activity, a dance which, I suppose, the emigration from Skye has occasioned. They call it *America*. Each of the couples, after the common involutions and evolutions, successively whirls round in a circle, till all are in motion; and the dance seems intended to show how emigration catches, till a whole neighbourhood is set afloat.'

Getting back into my car, I listen once more to Runrig's music and think a bit about the places I have been, the people I have met, the history books, the novels and the poems I have read – all of them reflecting, one way or another, the enduring Scottish Highland impact on this continent. It is a long time since it started. But the dance they called America, I guess, continues still.

Notes

Chapter One: King George and Broadswords!

1. H.F. Rankin, *The Moore's Creek Bridge Campaign*, Philadelphia, 1986, 34. For the wider background to British strategy in the American Revolutionary War see, C. Hibbert, *Redcoats and Rebels: The War for America, 1770–1781*, London, 1990. My account of the Battle of Moore's Creek draws mainly on, N. Callahan, *Royal Raiders: The Tories of the American Revolution*, New York, 1963, 15–24; R.M. Calhoon, *The Loyalists in Revolutionary America, 1760–1781*, New York, 1973, 444–47; H.F. Rankin, *The North Carolina Continentals*, Chapel Hill, 1971, 28–54. See also, B.G. Moss, *Roster of the Loyalists in the Battle of Moore's Creek Bridge*, Blacksburg, 1992.

2. J.P. MacLean, *An Historical Account of the Settlement of Scotch Highlanders in America Prior to the Peace of 1783*, Glasgow, 1900, 134–36.

3. J. Boswell, *The Journal of a Tour to the Hebrides*, Penguin edition, London, 1984, 265.

4. S. Johnson, *A Journey to the Western Islands of Scotland*, Penguin edition, London, 1984, 80; Boswell, *Journal of a Tour to the Hebrides*, 265.

5. For the background to the North Carolina involvement of the Kingsburgh MacDonalds see, E.G. Vining, *Flora MacDonald: Her Life in the Highlands and America*, London, 1967. Also, H. Douglas, *Flora MacDonald: The Most Loyal Rebel*, Stroud, 1993.

6. J.A.G. Roussos, *The Argyll Colony: The Last Clan Gathering*, Fayetteville, 1992, 18–33, 54.

7. J.P. MacLean, *Scotch Highlanders*, 117; Ian G.C. Graham, *Colonists from Scotland*, Ithaca, 1956, 158.

8. MacLean, *Scotch Highlanders*, 126.

9. MacLean, *Scotch Highlanders*,

126–27; Graham, *Colonists from Scotland*, 159.

10. MacLean, *Scotch Highlanders*, 128–29; L. Lee, *The Lower Cape Fear in Colonial Days*, Chapel Hill, 1965, 266–67; E.W. and C.M. Andrews (eds), *Journal of a Lady of Quality, Being the Narrative of a Journey from Scotland to the West Indies, North Carolina and Portugal in the Years 1774 to 1776*, New Haven, 1939, 167.

11. MacLean, *Scotch Highlanders*, 130; Callahan, *Royal Raiders*, 17.

12. K.G. Davies (ed), *Documents of the American Revolution, 1770–1783*, Dublin, 21 volumes, XII, 116.

13. Moss, *Roster of the Loyalists*, 51; C. Moore, *The Loyalists: Revolution, Exile, Settlement*, Toronto, 1984, 52.

14. Moss, *Roster of the Loyalists*, 57; Moore, *The Loyalists*, 52.

Chapter Two: What, Then, is the American, this New Man?

1. For a comprehensive account of Darien's history see, B. Sullivan, *Early Days on the Georgia Tidewater: The Story of McIntosh County and Sapelo*, third edition, Darien, 1992.

2. P. Spalding, *Oglethorpe in America*, Chicago, 1977, 27; Graham, *Colonists from Scotland*, 107.

3. Spalding, *Oglethorpe in America*, 152.

4. K. Coleman, *Colonial Georgia: A History*, New York, 1976, 49; L.B. Schaitberger, *Scots of McIntosh*, Darien, 1986, 2–3.

5. Schaitberger, *Scots of McIntosh*, 5–9.

6. MacLean, *Scotch Highlanders*, 161; Schaitberger, *Scots of McIntosh*, 4.

7. A.M. Shaw, *Historical Memoirs of Clan MacIntosh*, London, 2 volumes, 1880, II, 515; I.F. Grant, *Along a Highland Road*, London, 1980, 74–76; B. Lenman, *The Jacobite Risings in Britain, 1689–1746*, London, 1980, 142.

8. L.E. Ivers, *British Drums on the Southern Frontier: The Military Colonization of Georgia, 1733–1749*, Chapel Hill, 1974, 100–01; H.H. Jackson and P. Spalding, *Forty Years of Diversity: Essays on Colonial Georgia*, Athens, 1984, 156–57.

9. Ivers, *Drums on the Southern Frontier*, xii, 198.

10. Coleman, *Colonial Georgia*, 49–50.

11. M. Magnusson and H. Palsson, *The Vinland Sagas: The Norse Discovery of America*, New York, 1966, 95.

12. Lee, *Lower Cape Fear*, 183–84; MacLean, *Scotch Highlanders*, 104–5.

13. D. Meyer, *The Highland Scots of North Carolina, 1732–1776*, Chapel Hill, 1961, 24; MacLean, *Scotch Highlanders*, 103; E Cregeen, 'The Changing Role of the House of Argyll in the Scottish Highlands', *in* N.T. Phillipson and R. Mitchison (eds), *Scotland in the Age of Improvement*, Edinburgh, 1970, 10–12; M.C. Storrie, *Islay: Biography of an Island*, Port Ellen, 1981, 61–63.

14. M.M. MacKay (ed), *The Rev Dr John Walker's Report on the Hebrides of 1764 and 1771*, Edinburgh, 1980, 97–98, 140, 153; J. Bardon, *A History of Ulster*, Belfast, 1992, 176–79.

15. Bardon, *History of Ulster*, 178–79; A. Murdoch, 'A Scottish Document Concerning Emigration to North Carolina in 1772', *North Carolina Historical Review*, LXVII, 1990, 438–39.

16. Andrews, *Journal of a Lady of Quality*, 145, 158; Vining, *Flora MacDonald*, 107–10.

17. Andrews, *Journal of a Lady of Quality*, 163.

18. For a general account of eighteenth-century conditions in the Cape Fear

country see, Meyer, *Highland Scots*, 1961. Also, Scotus Americanus, *Informations Concerning the Province of North Carolina*, reprinted in, W.K. Boyd (ed), *Some Eighteenth Century Tracts Concerning North Carolina*, Raleigh, 1927, 429–51.

19. H.E. Davis, *The Fledgling Province: Social and Cultural Life in Colonial Georgia, 1733–1776*, Chapel Hill, 1976, 13, 127; Meyer, *Highland Scots*, 108–9; MacLean, *Scotch Highlanders*, 160; Sullivan, *Early Days on the Georgia Tidewater*, 57.

20. J.M. Bumsted, *The People's Clearance: Highland Emigration to British North America, 1770–1815*, Edinburgh, 1982, 20.

21. Graham, *Colonists from Scotland*, 39.

22. Scotus Americanus, *Informations*, 429–51.

23. M. Fry, *The Dundas Despotism*, Edinburgh, 1992, 66–67.

24. Graham, *Colonists from Scotland*, 66.

25. Johnson, *Journey to the Western Islands*, 73.

26. Johnson, *Journey to the Western Islands*, 97.

27. Boswell, *Journal of a Tour to the Hebrides*, 327.

28. W. Matheson (ed), *The Songs of John MacCodrum*, Edinburgh, 1938, 199–203.

29. Scotus Americanus, *Informations*, 433.

30. Johnson, *Journey to the Western Islands*, 95.

31. A.J. Youngson, *After the Forty–Five: The Economic Impact on the Scottish Highlands*, Edinburgh, 1973, 12; Boswell, *Journal of a Tour to the Hebrides*, 248; I.F. Grant and H. Cheape, *Periods in Highland History*, London, 1987, 219; Bumsted, *People's Clearance*, 58.

32. R.J. Adam (ed), *John Home's Survey of Assynt*, Edinburgh, 1960, xxvi.

33. Scotus Americanus, *Informations*, 445–47; Murdoch, 'Document Concerning Emigration', 444–47.

34. Graham, *Colonists from Scotland*, 39; Meyer, *Highland Scots*, 126.

35. Graham, *Colonists from Scotland*, 40; J. Hector St John de Crevecoeur, *Letters from an American Farmer*, Penguin edition, London, 1986, 66–105.

36. Meyer, *Highland Scots*, 112; B. Bailyn, *Voyagers to the West: Emigration from Britain to America on the Eve of the Revolution*, London, 1987, 504.

37. H. Brogan, *History of the United States of America*, London, 1985, 15; Bailyn, *Voyagers to the West*, 111; H. MacPhee, 'The Trail of the Emigrants', *Transactions of the Gaelic Society of Inverness*, XLVI, 1969, 178; Murdoch, 'Document Concerning Emigration', 442. See also, D.H. Fischer, *Albion's Seed: Four British Folkways in America*, New York, 1989, 611.

38. M. MacDonell, *The Emigrant Experience: Songs of Highland Emigrants in North America*, Toronto, 1982, 36–37.

39. J. Raban, *Hunting Mr Heartbreak*, Picador edition, London, 1991, 302.

40. MacLean, *Scotch Highlanders*, 164, 171, 402–04; *Dictionary of American Biography*, XII, 69–70; Sullivan, *Early Days on the Georgia Tidewater*, 57–64.

41. Meyer, *Highland Scots*, 116, 157; Callahan, *Royal Raiders*, 18; MacLean, *Scotch Highlanders*, 121; Rankin, *North Carolina Continentals*, 40–42.

42. R. Middlekauf, *The Glorious Cause: The American Revolution, 1763–1789*, Oxford, 1982, 551; W. Brown, *The Good Americans: The Loyalists in the American Revolution*, New York, 1969, 47.

43. Graham, *Colonists from Scotland*, 151.

44. W.R. Brock, *Scotus Americanus*, Edinburgh, 1982, 84; Graham, *Colonists from Scotland*, 106; J.L. Campbell, *Songs Remembered in Exile*, Aberdeen, 1990, 2; W.S. Powell, *North Carolina: A History*, Chapel Hill, 1988, 39; G. McWhiney, *Cracker Culture: Celtic Ways in the Old South*, Tuscaloosa, 1988, 36.

45. T.R. and J.S. Buie, *The Family Buie: Scotland to North America*, Arlington, 1983, 19–22; McWhiney, *Cracker Culture*, 37.

46. Crevecoeur, *Letters from an American Farmer*, 70; Powell, *North Carolina*, 101; *Dictionary of American Biography*, III, 452–53.

Chapter Three: A Hardy and Intrepid Race of Men

1. J.T. Findlay, *Wolfe in Scotland*, London, 1928, 247.

2. L. Colley, *Britons: Forging the Nation, 1707–1837*, London, 1992, 13; Findlay, *Wolfe*, 246.

3. Findlay, *Wolfe*, 252.

4. J.R. Harper, *The Fraser Highlanders*, Montreal, 1979, 14.

5. B. Lenman, *The Jacobite Clans of the Great Glen, 1650–1784*, London, 1984, 179–80.

6. J. Prebble, *Mutiny*, Penguin edition, London, 1977, 13–87; Linda Colley, *Britons: Forging the Nation, 1707–1837*, London, 1992, 104.

7. H.H. Peckham, *The Colonial Wars, 1689–1762*, Chicago, 1964, 121–34; F Jennings, *Empire of Fortune: Crowns, Colonies and Tribes in the Seven Years War in America*, New York, 1988, 65–68.

8. J. Fenimore Cooper, *The Last of the Mohicans*, Panther edition, London, 1970, 11.

9. R. Hargreaves, *The Bloodybacks: The British Serviceman in North America and the Caribbean, 1655–1783*, London, 1968,

10. J. Black, *Pitt the Elder*, Cambridge, 1992, 126–80.

11. D. Stewart, *Sketches of the Highlanders of Scotland*, John Donald edition, 2 volumes, Edinburgh, 1977, II, 63.

12. Lenman, *Jacobite Clans*, 188.

13. Lenman, *Jacobite Risings*, 27.

14. Lenman, *Jacobite Clans*, 177–79.

15. J. Hunter, *Scottish Highlanders: A People and their Place*, Edinburgh, 1992, 145–155; S. Cairney, *The Killing of the Red Fox: An Investigation into the Appin Murder*, Moffat, 1989, 72–123.

16. The principal source of information about the regiment is, Harper, *Fraser Highlanders*, 1979.

17. Stewart, *Sketches*, I, 333.

18. Stewart, *Sketches*, I, v; II, 64.

19. Stewart, *Sketches*, I, 235–36.

20. T. Douglas, Earl of Selkirk, *Observations on the Present State of the Highlands of Scotland*, second edition, Edinburgh, 1806, 65.

21. Hibbert, *Redcoats and Rebels*, 84; Stewart, *Sketches*, I, 303.

22. Harper, *Fraser Highlanders*, 54.

23. Youngson, *After the Forty–Five*, 34; Harper, *Fraser Highlanders*, 19.

24. Harper, *Fraser Highlanders*, 20.

25. Harper, *Fraser Highlanders*, 18, 33, 54; Stewart, *Sketches*, II, 66.

26. Bumsted, *People's Clearance*, 103.

27. K.M. Strobeck, *Mohawk Valley Happenings*, Montgomery, 1990, 51; Jennings, *Empire of Fortune*, 312–16.

28. Strobeck, *Mohawk Valley Happenings*, 51.

29. Cooper, *Last of the Mohicans*, 12.

30. J. Fortier and O. Fitzgerald, *Fortress of Louisbourg*, Toronto, 1979; L.F. Hannon, *Forts of Canada*, Toronto, 1976.

31. Hannon, *Forts of Canada*, 30.

32. Harper, *Fraser Highlanders*, 48–49; Hargreaves, *Bloodybacks*, 145–46.

33. Hargreaves, *Bloodybacks*, 145–46.

34. Harper, *Fraser Highlanders*, 49.
35. Harper, *Fraser Highlanders*, 50; Hannon, *Forts of Canada*, 36; J.S. MacLennan, *Louisbourg: From its Foundation to its Fall, 1713–1758*, London, 1918, 249–52.
36. Stewart, *Sketches*, I, 320; Hannon, *Forts of Canada*, 36.
37. Stewart, *Sketches*, II, 68,
38. MacLennan, *Louisbourg*, 250–52; Stewart, *Sketches*, I, 310.
39. G. Donaldson, *Battle for a Continent: Quebec 1759*, Toronto, 1973, 78; Harper, *Fraser Highlanders*, 50; Jennings, *Empire of Fortune*, 220.
40. Peckham, *Colonial Wars*, 186.
41. J.A. Dickinson and B. Young, *A Short History of Quebec*, second edition, Toronto, 1993, 48; Jennings, *Empire of Fortune*, 419–23.
42. For a full account of the Quebec campaign see, C.P. Stacey, *Quebec, 1759: The Siege and the Battle*, Toronto, 1959; Donaldson, *Battle for a Contintent*, 1973.
43. Stewart, *Sketches*, I, 238; Harper, *Fraser Highlanders*, 98.
44. Lenman, *Jacobite Clans*, 189.
45. Lenman, *Jacobite Clans*, 197–98.
46. Harper, *Fraser Highlanders*, 97.
47. Harper, *Fraser Highlanders*, 98.

Chapter Four: To Found in the New Land a New Glengarry

1. Graham, *Colonists from Scotland*, 46–49; Harper, *Fraser Highlanders*, 17, 122–23; F.W.P. Bolger, *Canada's Smallest Province: A History of PEI*, Toronto, 1973, 39–41; G. Woodcock, *The Century That Made Us: Canada, 1814–1914*, Toronto, 1989, 175.
2. C. Hislop, *The Mohawk*, Syracuse, 1989, 20–116; J. Fenimore Cooper, *The Pioneers*, World's Classics edition, Oxford, 1991, 15.
3. Graham, *Colonists from Scotland*, 77–80.
4. E. Countryman, *A People in Revolution: The American Revolution and Political Society in New York, 1760–1790*, Baltimore, 1981, 117–18; M. Kammen, *Colonial New York: A History*, New York, 1975, 308–10; Jennings, *Empire of Fortune*, 75–77.
5. A.B. Lawson, 'The North West Company of Canada: The Highland Connection', *in*, L. MacLean (ed) *An Inverness Miscellany*, Inverness, 1987, 30; W.K. Lamb (ed), *The Letters and Journals of Simon Fraser, 1806–1808*, Toronto, 1960, 2–8.
6. M. McLean, *The People of Glengarry: Highlanders in Transition, 1745–1820*, Montreal, 1991, 87–88.
7. Bailyn, *Voyagers to America*, 582–83.
8. P.U. Bonomi, *A Factious People: Politics and Society in Colonial New York*, New York, 1971, 267–71; P. Ranlet, *The New York Loyalists*, Knoxville, 1986, 44; *Dictionary of American Biography*, XII, 21–22.
9. For details of the *Pearl* emigration see, McLean, *People of Glengarry*, 84–88.
10. McLean, *People of Glengarry*, 89; Colley, *Britons*, 140.
11. Meyer, *Highland Scots*, 150.
12. Moore, *The Loyalists*, 5–10.
13. Moore, *The Loyalists*, 50–52; *Dictionary of Canadian Biography*, IV, 503–04.
14. McLean, *People of Glengarry*, 93–94; R.S. Allen, *The Loyal Americans*, National Museums of Canada, 1983, 11; J.A. Macdonell, *Sketches Illustrating the Early Settlement and History of Glengarry in Canada*, Montreal, 1893, 22–23.
15. J. Prebble, *Culloden*, Penguin edition, London, 1967, 104; R.W. Munro, *Taming the Rough Bounds: Knoydart, 1745–1784*, Isle of Coll, 1984; N.H. MacDonald, *The Clan Ranald of Knoydart and Glengarry*,

Edinburgh, 1979, 83.

16. MacDonald, *Clan Ranald*, 79.

17. J.J. Talman (ed), *Loyalist Narratives from Upper Canada*, Toronto, 1946, 270–72; Moore, *The Loyalists*, 64–66, 130; *Dictionary of Canadian Biography*, V, 517–18; McLean, *People of Glengarry*, 95; B. Graymont, *The Iroquois in the American Revolution*, Syracuse, 1972, 203.

18. Macdonell, *Glengarry in Canada*, 25–26.

19. D. Dumbrille, *Braggart in my Step: More Stories of Glengarry*, Toronto, 1956, 2–3.

20. *The Glengarry News*, 25 August 1993.

21. D. Dumbrille, *Up and Down the Glens: The Story of Glengarry*, Toronto, 1954, 7; Macdonell, *Glengarry in Canada*, 124–25.

22. Selkirk, *Observations*, 170–74.

23. McLean, *People of Glengarry*, 74–77.

24. McLean, *People of Glengarry*, 102–09; *Dictionary of Canadian Biography*, V, 523–25.

25. MacDonell, *Emigrant Experience*, 131–37.

26. This and the following paragraphs draw on, Selkirk, *Observations*, 50–53.

27. McLean, *People of Glengarry*, 208.

28. Talman, *Loyalist Narratives*, 268.

29. W.F. Laughlan (ed), *James Hogg's Highland Tours*, Hawick, 1981, 69.

30. McLean, *People of Glengarry*, 125, 215.

31. Dumbrille, *Braggart in my Step*, 72–75.

32. McLean, *People of Glengarry*, 214–16; R. MacGillivray and E. Ross, *A History of Glengarry*, Belleville, 1979, 355.

33. *Dictionary of Canadian Biography*, V, 518.

34. Macdonell, *Glengarry in Canada*, 83.

35. E. Richards, *A History of the Highland Clearances: Agrarian*

Transformation and the Evictions, 1746–1886, London, 1982, 254.

36. MacDonell, *Emigrant Experience*, 140–45.

37. Macdonell, *Glengarry in Canada*, 62–63.

38. R. Connor, *The Man from Glengarry*, New Canadian Library edition, Toronto, 1993, 36.

39. R. Nash, *Wilderness and the American Mind*, third edition, Yale, 1982, 23–27; Brogan, *History of the United States*, 37.

40. For a comprehensive study of these developments see, A.M. Lower, *Great Britain's Woodyard: British America and the Timber Trade, 1763–1867*, Toronto, 1973.

41. H.I. Cowan, *British Emigration to British North America: The First Hundred Years*, revised edition, Toronto, 1961, 160; MacGillivray and Ross, *History of Glengarry*, 355; H. MacLennan, *Seven Rivers of Canada*, Toronto, 1977, 98.

42. This and succeeding paragraphs are based mainly on, MacGillivray and Ross, *History of Glengarry*, 446–56; Lower, *Great Britain's Woodyard*, 187–88; MacLennan, *Rivers of Canada*, 96–97.

43. MacGillivray and Ross, *History of Glengarry*, 445–48.

44. MacGillivray and Ross, *History of Glengarry*, 43; Connor, *Man from Glengarry*, 14–15.

45. Connor, *Man from Glengarry*, 9, 12, 15.

Chapter Five: Such of Them as Did Not Die While Going Across the Ocean

1. J. Loch, *An Account of the Improvements on the Estates of the Marquess of Stafford*, London, 1820, xvii.

2. E. Richards, *A History of the Highland Clearances: Emigration, Protest, Reasons*, London, 1985, 373–407.

3. Richards, *Highland Clearances: Agrarian Transformation*, 349.
4. J. Hunter, *The Making of the Crofting Community*, Edinburgh, 1976, 15–21.
5. W. MacGillivray, 'Report on the Hebrides', *Transactions of the Highland Society*, New Series, II, 1831, 301.
6. J. Hall, *Travels in Scotland by an Unusual Route*, 2 volumes, London, 1807, II, 548.
7. Hunter, *Crofting Community*, 20.
8. Selkirk, *Observations*, 4.
9. Bumsted, *People's Clearance*, 100.
10. Selkirk, *Observations*, 148.
11. Laughlan, *Hogg's Highland Tours*, 72.
12. Cameron to MacMillan, 1 July, 1803. Papers supplied to the author by Sir Donald Cameron of Lochiel.
13. McLean, *People of Glengarry*, 139–44; S. MacMillan, *The Emigration of the Lochaber MacMillans to Canada*, Paisley, 1958, 1–2.
14. Cameron to MacMillan, December 1804. Lochiel Papers.
15. S. MacMillan, *Bygone Lochaber*, Glasgow, 1971, 183.
16. Johnson, *Journey to the Western Islands*, 97; Selkirk, *Observations*, 124.
17. T. Telford, *A Survey and Report of the Coasts and Central Highlands of Scotland*, Parliamentary Papers, 1802–03, IV, 14–15.
18. Fry, *Dundas Despotism*, 247; Bumsted, *People's Clearance*, 131.
19. Bumsted, *People's Clearance*, 100, 122; Hunter, *Crofting Community*, 22–25.
20. McLean, *People of Glengarry*, 134, 145–46; Bumsted, *People's Clearance*, 143.
21. Hunter, *Crofting Community*, 25; Bumsted, *People's Clearance*, 145.
22. McLean, *People of Glengarry*, 131, 145.
23. Hunter, *Crofting Community*, 26–27.
24. MacMillan, *Bygone Lochaber*, 181; McLean, *People of Glengarry*, 145.
25. Somers, *Letters from the Highlands on the Famine of 1846*, Inverness, 1977, 124; Cameron to MacMillan, 23 March 1804. Lochiel Papers.
26. S. MacLean, *Ris a' Bhruthaich*, Stornoway, 1985, 58.
27. MacDonell, *Emigrant Experience*, 9.
28. Hunter, *Crofting Community*, 35.
29. Hunter, *Crofting Community*, 39.
30. *Reports from the Select Committee on Emigration*, Parliamentary Papers, 1841, VI, 1, 4, 217–18; Hunter, *Crofting Community*, 42; Cowan, *Emigration to British North America*, 147–48.
31. *Report from the Select Committee Appointed to Enquire into Emigration*, Parliamentary Papers, 1826, IV, 354–56.
32. Lower, *Great Britain's Woodyard*, 230–40.
33. Lower, *Great Britain's Woodyard*, 240.
34. Meyer, *Highland Scots*, 64–65.
35. Bumsted, *People's Clearance*, 59–60; Bolger, *Canada's Smallest Province*, 47.
36. This and subsequent paragraphs are based largely on, Cowan, *Emigration to British North America*, 146, 151; Lower, *Great Britain's Woodyard*, 242; T. Coleman, *Passage to America*, London, 1972, 20, 95, 111–17; O. MacDonagh, *A Pattern of Government Growth, 1800–60: The Passenger Acts and their Enforcement*, London, 1961, 49–51.
37. J. Mitchell, *Reminiscences of My Life in the Highlands*, 2 Volumes, Newton Abbott, 1971, 111–12.
38. Coleman, *Passage to America*, 20.
39. Coleman, *Passage to America*, 86; Lower, *Great Britain's Woodyard*, 242.
40. Coleman, *Passage to America*, 108.
41. MacDonagh, *Pattern of*

Government Growth, 50–51.

42. Lower, Great Britain's Woodyard, 243.

43. Richards, Highland Clearances: Agrarian Transformation, 366–67.

44. Stewart, Sketches, I, 167.

45. Stewart, Sketches, I, 165–66; Richards, Highland Clearances: Emigration, 397, 401.

46. Report on the Applicability of Emigration to the Relief of the Distress in the Highlands, Parliamentary Papers, 1837, XXVII, 1; Hunter, Crofting Community, 41, 47; MacDonell, Emigrant Experience, 127.

47. Hunter, Crofting Community, 46.

48. Campbell, Songs Remembered in Exile, 71–72.

49. M. O'Gallagher, Grosse Ile: Gateway to Canada, 1832–1937, Quebec, 1984, 15–26.

50. E.C. Guillet, The Great Migration: The Atlantic Crossing by Sailing Ship Since 1770, London, 1937, 149–50; Coleman, Passage to America, 140–50.

51. First Report of the Select Committee on Emigrant Ships, Parliamentary Papers, 1854, XIII, 152.

52. Lady MacCaskill, Twelve Days in Skye, second edition, London, 1852, 32.

53. Hunter, Crofting Community, 54–55.

54. D. Craig, On the Crofters' Trail: In Search of the Clearance Highlanders, London, 1990, 106.

55. Coleman, Passage to America, 140.

56. Guillet, Great Migration, 149–50; Coleman, Passage to America, 140–50.

57. O'Gallagher, Grosse Ile, 56–57, 130.

58. J.M. Gibbon, Scots in Canada, London, 1911, 132.

59. J.N. MacLeod, Memorials of the Rev Norman MacLeod, Edinburgh, 1898, 221–22.

60. Richards, Highland Clearances: Agrarian Transformation, 409–19.

61. Richards, Highland Clearances: Agrarian Transformation, 411.

62. Richards, Highland Clearances: Agrarian Transformation, 413–18; Hunter, Crofting Community, 81–82.

63. A. Carmichael, Carmina Gadelica, 6 volumes, Edinburgh, 1928–71, III, 351.

64. Gibbon, Scots in Canada, 131.

65. This and subsequent paragraphs are based on, Papers Relative to Emigration to the North American Colonies, Parliamentary Papers, 1852, XXXIII, 7–19.

Chapter Six: Many Men Have Loved the Island of Cape Breton

1. D.C. Harvey, 'Scottish Immigration to Cape Breton', in D. MacGillivray and B. Tennyson (eds), Cape Breton Historical Essays, Sydney, 1980, 36.

2. Harvey, 'Scottish Immigration', 37.

3. K. McNaught, The Penguin History of Canada, London, 1988, 9, 20–21.

4. C.W. Dunn, Highland Settler: A Portrait of the Scottish Gael in Nova Scotia, Toronto, 1953, 18; Bolger, Canada's Smallest Province, 34–35.

5. Scottish Highland settlement in Cape Breton Island is examined in, D. Campbell and R.A. MacLean, Beyond the Atlantic Roar: A Study of the Nova Scotia Scots, Carleton Library edition, Ottawa, 1975; S. Hornsby, 'Scottish Emigration and Settlement in Early Nineteenth Century Cape Breton', in K. Donovan (ed), The Island: New Perspectives on Cape Breton's History, 1713–1990, Sydney, 1990.

6. Harvey, 'Scottish Immigration', 33.

7. Hornsby, 'Scottish Emigration', 54.

8. Campbell and MacLean, Beyond the Atlantic Roar, 67.

9. Richards, Highland Clearances: Emigration, 232; Dunn, Highland Settler, 20.

10. Craig, *On the Crofters' Trail*, 104–5.
11. Hornsby, 'Scottish Emigration', 56; Cowan, *Emigration to British North America*, 212.
12. Hornsby, 'Scottish Emigration', 57–58.
13. Hornsby, 'Scottish Emigration', 58.
14. Selkirk, *Observations*, 190–92.
15. Harvey, 'Scottish Immigration', 38.
16. Campbell and MacLean, *Beyond the Atlantic Roar*, 73; G.G. Patterson, *History of Victoria County*, Sydney, 1978, 83.
17. This and ensuing paragraphs are based on, Campbell and MacLean, *Beyond the Atlantic Roar*, 66; Hornsby, 'Scottish Emigration', 60–67.
18. For details of the famine in Cape Breton see, S. Hornsby, *Nineteenth-Century Cape Breton: A Historical Geography*, Toronto, 1992, 111–16.
19. Hornsby, *Nineteenth-Century Cape Breton*, 113–16.
20. F. McPherson, *Watchman against the World: The Remarkable Journey of Norman McLeod and his People from Scotland to Cape Breton Island to New Zealand*, Breton Books edition, Wreck Cove, 1993, 130. See also, N. Robinson, *Lion of Scotland*, Auckland, 1974.
21. Selkirk, *Observations*, 190.
22. Dunn, *Highland Settler*, 27–28; MacDonell, *Emigrant Experience*, 42–43.
23. MacDonell, *Emigrant Experience*, 80–87.
24. MacDonell, *Emigrant Experience*, 88–93.
25. Hornsby, 'Emigration', 62–63.
26. Campbell and MacLean, *Beyond the Atlantic Roar*, 23.
27. Campbell and MacLean, *Beyond the Atlantic Roar*, 83, 184.
28. J. Hunter (ed), *For the People's Cause: From the Writings of John Murdoch*, Edinburgh, 1986, 176.
29. N. MacNeil, *The Highland Heart in Nova Scotia*, Toronto, 1958, 52.
30. MacNeil, *Highland Heart*, 21–22. See also, C.L. MacMillan, *Memoirs of a Cape Breton Doctor*, Book Room edition, Halifax, 1992.
31. MacNeil, *Highland Heart*, 4–5.
32. J.J. MacNeil, *Sgeul gu Latha, Tales until Dawn: The World of a Cape Breton Storyteller*, translated and edited by John Shaw, Edinburgh, 1987, xvii–xxii, 3–7.
33. A. MacLeod, *The Lost Salt Gift of Blood*, Flamingo edition, London, 1993, 190.
34. Dunn, *Highland Settler*, 148.
35. Deirdre's lament for her Scottish glen can be found in, K. Jackson (ed), *A Celtic Miscellany*, Penguin edition, London, 1971, 72. Further detail on Alasdair MacMhaighstir Alasdair and Donnachadh Ban Mac an t–Saoir is provided in, D. Thomson, *An Introduction to Gaelic Poetry*, London, 1974. Sorley MacLean's poetry is available in, S. MacLean, *From Wood to Ridge: Collected Poems in Gaelic and English*, Manchester, 1990.
36. Graham, *Colonists from Scotland*, 106.
37. J.C. McNeill, *The Pocket John Charles McNeill*, Laurinburg, 1990, 1–14; G. McWhiney and P.D. Jamieson, *Attack and Die: Civil War Military Tactics and the Southern Heritage*, Alabama, 1982, 173.
38. MacGillivray and Ross, *History of Glengarry*, 646; K. Donovan, 'Reflections on Cape Breton Island Culture', *in* K. Donovan (ed), *The Island: New Perspectives on Cape Breton's History, 1713–1990*, Sydney, 1990, 1.
39. MacDonell, *Emigrant Experience*, 168–73, 176–79.
40. Campbell and MacLean, *Beyond the Atlantic Roar*, 185.
41. Hornsby, *Nineteenth-Century Cape Breton*, 186–90; Campbell and

MacLean, *Beyond the Atlantic Roar*, 100.

42. MacGillivray and Ross, *History of Glengarry*, 134, 517.

43. MacDonell, *Emigrant Experience*, 168–69; Campbell and MacLean, *Beyond the Atlantic Roar*, 109.

44. J. Hunter, *The Claim of Crofting: The Scottish Highlands and Islands, 1930–1990*, Edinburgh, 1991, 38.

45. A.A. MacKenzie, 'Cape Breton and the Western Harvest Excursions, 1890–1928', *in* K. Donovan, *Cape Breton at 200: Historical Essays in Honour of the Island's Bicentennial, 1785–1985*, Sydney, 1985, 71–73; J. London, *The Sea Wolf*, World's Classics edition, Oxford, 1992, Appendix 2, 337–40. My attention was drawn to this Jack London connection by Frances MacEachen.

46. Hornsby, *Nineteenth-Century Cape Breton*, 197.

47. R. Somers, *Letters from the Highlands on the Famine of 1846*, Inverness, 1977, 103.

48. Lower, *Great Britain's Woodyard*, 32–33.

49. D. Frank, 'The Cape Breton Coal Industry and the Rise and Fall of the British Empire Steel Corporation', *in* MacGillivray and Tennyson, *Historical Essays*, 112. For further information on the Cape Breton coal industry, see the relevant contributions to, Donovan, *Cape Breton at 200*.

50. Donovan, 'Cape Breton Island Culture', 1.

51. This and the following paragraph are based on, D. Frank, 'Tradition and Culture in the Cape Breton Mining Community in the Early Twentieth Century', *in* Donovan, *Cape Breton at 200*, 211–12.

52. D. Fraser, *Echoes from Labour's Wars*, with an Introduction by D. Frank and D. MacGillivray, Wreck Cove, 1992, ix–xii.

53. Dunn, *Highland Settler*, 131; Fraser, *Echoes from Labour's Wars*, 3.

54. Donovan, 'Tradition and Culture', 206.

55. D. Muise, 'The Making of an Industrial Community', *in* MacGillivray and Tennyson, *Historical Essays*, 81. Further details can be found in, P. MacEwan, *Miners and Steelworkers: Labour in Cape Breton*, Toronto, 1976.

56. D. Frank, 'Working-Class Politics: The Election of J.B. McLachlan, 1916–1935', *in* Donovan, *The Island*, 187–89. See also, D. Frank and D. MacGillivray (eds), *George MacEachern: An Autobiography*, Sydney, 1987.

57. H. MacLennan, *Scotchman's Return and Other Essays*, Toronto, 1960, 1–2.

58. T.D. MacLulich, *Hugh MacLennan*, Boston, 1983, 3.

59. MacLulich, *MacLennan*, 3; E. Cameron, *Hugh MacLennan: A Writer's Life*, Toronto, 1981.

60. H. MacLennan, *Each Man's Son*, Laurentian Library edition, Toronto, 1971, 8, 15–16, 67.

61. MacLennan, *Each Man's Son*, vii, ix.

62. H. MacLennan, *Barometer Rising*, New Canadian Library edition, Toronto, 1958, 206–07.

63. MacLennan, *Scotchman's Return*, 7.

64. MacLennan, *Scotchman's Return*, 11–12.

Chapter Seven: Lords of the Lakes and the Forests

1. R. Daniells, *Alexander MacKenzie and the North West*, London, 1969, 46–49; W. Kaye Lamb (ed), *The Journals and Letters of Sir Alexander MacKenzie*, Cambridge, 1970, 1–2; Prebble, *Mutiny*, 11–12.

2. E.W. Morse, *Fur Trade Routes of Canada*, Toronto, 1979, 27.

3. P.C. Newman, *Caesars of the Wilderness: The Story of the Hudson's Bay Company*, Penguin edition, London, 1988, 53.

4. Newman, *Caesars of the Wilderness*, 51.

5. C.M. Gates (ed), *Five Fur Traders of the Northwest*, Minnesota, 1933, 13–14. There are many accounts of MacKenzie's journeys. I have drawn particularly on, Lamb, *Journals and Letters*; Daniells, *Alexander MacKenzie*; Newman, *Caesars of the Wilderness*.

6. A. MacKenzie, *Voyages from Montreal through the Continent of North America to the Frozen and Pacific Oceans in 1789 and 1793*, with an Introduction by W.L. Grant, Toronto, 2 volumes, 1911, I, viii, xi.

7. M.W. Campbell, *The North West Company*, revised edition, Toronto, 1983, 63; MacLennan, *Seven Rivers of Canada*, 57.

8. Daniells, *Alexander MacKenzie*, 61–64.

9. Daniells, *Alexander MacKenzie*, 72.

10. Daniells, *Alexander MacKenzie*, 73.

11. MacLennan, *Seven Rivers of Canada*, 57.

12. Daniells, *Alexander MacKenzie*, 76.

13. Daniells, *Alexander MacKenzie*, 78–79; Campbell, *North West Company*, 64–65; Lamb, *Journals and Letters*, 15–16.

14. Daniells, *Alexander MacKenzie*, 80–89.

15. Campbell, *North West Company*, 67.

16. Lamb, *Journals and Letters*, 18–20.

17. *Dictionary of Canadian Biography*, V, 532–33.

18. Lamb, *Journals and Letters*, 22; Newman, *Caesars of the Wilderness*, 67–68.

19. M.W. Campbell, *McGillivray: Lord of the Northwest*, Toronto, 1962, 93–95; Daniells, *Alexander MacKenzie*, 166–67.

20. Daniells, *Alexander MacKenzie*, 24.

21. McNaught, *History of Canada*, 31.

22. MacLennan, *Seven Rivers of Canada*, 25.

23. Frank McLynn, *Charles Edward Stuart: A Tragedy in Many Acts*, London, 1988, 258–62.

24. *Dictionary of Canadian Biography*, V, 560–61; Campbell, *McGillivray*, 14–15.

25. For more detailed accounts of the North West Company see, Campbell, *North West Company*; Newman, *Caesars of the Wilderness*.

26. W.S. Wallace, *Documents Relating to the North West Company*, Champlain Society, Toronto, 1934, 432.

27. Newman, *Caesars of the Wilderness*, 9.

28. Campbell, *McGillivray*, 13–17.

29. A.S. Morton (ed), *The Journal of Duncan McGillivray of the North West Company, 1794–5*, Toronto, 1929, xliv; *Dictionary of Canadian Biography*, IX, 482.

30. These and further relationships can be traced in, *Dictionary of Canadian Biography*; Campbell, *North West Company*; Wallace, *Documents Relating to the North West Company*.

31. Wallace, *Documents Relating to the North West Company*, 480–82; Newman, *Caesars of the Wilderness*, 9; *Dictionary of Canadian Biography*, VI, 110–11.

32. Campbell, *McGillivray*, 113, 253–56. See also, E.F. Bradford, *MacTavish of Dunardry*, Whitby, 1991.

33. Newman, *Caesars of the Wilderness*, 10; Campbell, *North West Company*, 74–77.

34. Campbell, *McGillivray*, 210.

35. Newman, *Caesars of the Wilderness*, 14–16.

36. R. Cox, *Adventures on the Columbia River*, 2 volumes, London, 1831, I, 349.

37. Campbell, *North West Company*, 43.

38. Wallace, *Documents Relating to the North West Company*, 1; Cox, *Adventures on the Columbia River*, II, 290–91.

39. Campbell, *North West Company*, 194.

40. Newman, *Caesars of the Wilderness*, 17; W. Irving, *Astoria: Adventures in the Pacific Northwest*, KPI edition, London, 1987, 8–11.

41. Irving, *Astoria*, 11; A.B. Lawson, *A Country Called Stratherrick*, Inverness, 1987, 32–33; Lawson, 'North West Company', 32. See also, E. Wagenknecht, *Washington Irving: Moderation Displayed*, New York, 1962.

42. Irving, *Astoria*, 11.

Chapter Eight: Even if the Emigrants Escape the Scalping Knife . . .

1. D. Sage, *Memorabilia Domestica: Parish Life in the North of Scotland*, second edition, Wick, 1899, 58–75.

2. J.G. Diefenbaker, *One Canada*, Toronto, 1975, 3–4.

3. M. Laurence, *The Diviners*, New Canadian Library edition, Toronto, 1993, 58–59.

4. R.J. Adam (ed), *Papers on Sutherland Estate Management, 1802–1816*, 2 volumes, Edinburgh, 1972, I, 31–34; Richards, *Highland Clearances: Agrarian Transformation*, 293–98.

5. Richards, *Highland Clearances: Agrarian Transformation*, 299.

6. Richards, *Highland Clearances: Agrarian Transformation*, 299–302; K.J. Logue, *Popular Disturbances in Scotland, 1780–1815*, Edinburgh, 1979, 66–69.

7. Richards, *Highland Clearances: Agrarian Transformation*, 301–2; Adam, *Sutherland Estate Management*, II, 180–87; Logue, *Popular Disturbances*, 71.

8. Adam, *Sutherland Estate Management*, II, 185; Bumsted, *People's Clearance*, 209.

9. Selkirk, *Observations*, 1–2.

10. J.M. Bumsted (ed), *The Collected Writings of Lord Selkirk, 1799–1809*, Winnipeg, 1984, 11–20; J.M. Gray, *Lord Selkirk of Red River*, 11–17; Richards, *Highland Clearances: Agrarian Transformation*, 249–81.

11. Bumsted, *Writings of Lord Selkirk, 1799–1809*, 29–42; Gray, *Selkirk*, 29–32; *Dictionary of Canadian Biography*, VI, 440–44.

12. Campbell, *North West Company*, 200; G. Friesen, *The Canadian Prairies: A History*, Toronto, 1984, 62.

13. Gray, *Selkirk*, 62.

14. J.M. Bumsted (ed), *The Collected Writings of Lord Selkirk, 1810–1820*, Winnipeg, 1987, xxvi–xxvii; Bumsted, *People's Clearance*, 210.

15. *Dictionary of Canadian Biography*, VI, 463–64; Adam, *Sutherland Estate Management*, I, 156; II, 192.

16. Bumsted, *Writings of Lord Selkirk, 1810–1820*, xxvii–xxviii; I. Grimble, 'Emigration in the time of Rob Donn, 1714–1778', *Scottish Studies*, VIII, 1963, 139–41.

17. J.M. Cole, *Exile in the Wilderness: The Biography of Chief Factor Archibald McDonald, 1790–1853*, Toronto, 1979, 5–7.

18. D. Gunn, *Manitoba from the Earliest Settlement to 1835*, Ottawa, 1880, 91; *Dictionary of Canadian Biography*, 324.

19. Gunn, *Manitoba*, 92–94.

20. J. West, *The Substance of a Journey during a Residence at the Red River Colony*, second edition, London, 1828, 6–7.

21. Gunn, *Manitoba*, 96; Cole, *Exile in the Wilderness*, 13.

22. Newman, *Company of Adventurers: The Story of the Hudson's Bay Company*, Penguin edition, London, 1987, xxx; G.

Woodcock, *A Social History of Canada*, London, 1989, 130.

23. Cole, *Exile in the Wilderness*, 14–19.

24. Cole, *Exile in the Wilderness*, 23–25; Bumsted, *Writings of Lord Selkirk, 1810–1820*, xxxiii.

25. J. Prebble, *The Highland Clearances*, Penguin edition, London, 1969, 115; Cole, *Exile in the Wilderness*, 23–27.

26. Cole, *Exile in the Wilderness*, 27–31.

27. West, *Substance of a Journey*, 21; Cole, *Exile in the Wilderness*, 37–42.

28. R. Guinn, *The Red–Assiniboine Junction: A Land Use and Structural History, 1770–1980*, Ottawa, 1980, 27.

29. Campbell, *North West Company*, 203; Newman, *Caesars of the Wilderness*, 149.

30. F. Pannekoek, *The Fur Trade and Western Canadian Society, 1670–1870*, Ottawa, 1987, 20.

31. M.A. MacLeod and W.L. Morton, *Cuthbert Grant of Grantown: Warden of the Plains of Red River*, Toronto, 1963, 1–18; *Dictionary of Canadian Biography*, VII, 341–44; D. Purich, *The Metis*, Toronto, 1988, 35–38.

32. Cole, *Exile in the Wilderness*, 44.

33. *Dictionary of Canadian Biography*, VI, 445–46; VII, 137–39; Cole, *Exile in the Wilderness*, 44–45; A. Ross, *The Red River Settlement*, London, 1856, 33; Lawson, 'North West Company', 37.

34. Bumsted, *Writings of Lord Selkirk, 1810–1820*, xliv; Cole, *Exile in the Wilderness*, 51–57.

35. *Dictionary of Canadian Biography*, VII, 748–50.

36. W.L. Morton, *Manitoba: A History*, Toronto, 1957, 52.

37. Friesen, *Canadian Prairies*, 77–79.

38. Detailed accounts of the amalgamation of the North West Company with the Hudson's Bay Company can be found in, Newman, *Caesars of the Wilderness*; Campbell, *North West Company*.

39. Campbell, *North West Company*, 273–75.

40. Campbell, *North West Company*, 278; MacGillivray and Ross, *History of Glengarry*, 48–49.

41. H. MacLennan, 'Foreword', *in* Campbell, *North West Company*.

42. MacLennan, *Seven Rivers of Canada*, 116–17.

Chapter Nine: Stand Fast, Craigellachie!

1. J.H. Taylor, *Ottawa: An Illustrated History*, Toronto, 1986, 17–75; McNaught, *History of Canada*, 121.

2. D. Creighton, *John A. Macdonald: The Young Politician*, Toronto, 1952, 4; Prebble, *Highland Clearances*, 34–41.

3. Creighton, *Young Politician*, 3–4; J.C. Shaw, *A History of Clan Shaw*, Chichester, 1983, 42–44. See also, C.F. MacKintosh, *The Minor Septs of Clan Chattan*, Glasgow, 1898.

4. E. Grant, *Memoirs of a Highland Lady*, Canongate Classics edition, Edinburgh, 1992, 256–57.

5. Creighton, *Young Politician*, 3–7.

6. McNaught, *History of Canada*, 188. See also, Creighton, *Young Politician*; D. Creighton, *John A. Macdonald: The Old Chieftain*, Toronto, 1955.

7. MacLennan, *Seven Rivers of Canada*, 119.

8. A. Ross, *The Red River Settlement*, London, 1856, 14–15; Newman, *Caesars of the Wilderness*, 156; C.N. Bell, *The Selkirk Settlement*, London, 1887, 37.

9. Ross, *Red River Settlement*, 30–31, 54; W.L. Morton, *Manitoba: A History*, 56.

10. Morton, *Manitoba*, 64–65, 84–87; W.J. Healy, *Women of Red River*, 1923, 55–56.

11. M.A. MacLeod, *Red River's Festive Season*, Winnipeg, 1962, 5; Connor, *Glengarry School Days*, 272–73; G. Redmond, *The Sporting Scots of Nineteenth-Century Canada*, Toronto, 1982, 248, 266; Fischer, *Albion's Seed*, 739; R. Hutchinson, *Camanachd: The Story of Shinty*, Edinburgh, 1989, 92–100.

12. MacLennan, *Seven Rivers of Canada*, 105.

13. MacLennan, *Seven Rivers of Canada*, 126.

14. P.B. Waite, *Macdonald: His Life and World*, Toronto, 1975, 79.

15. McNaught, *History of Canada*, 149.

16. P. Berton, *The National Dream: The Great Railway, 1871–1881*, Penguin edition, Toronto, 1989, 6–7.

17. B. Willson, *The Life of Lord Strathcona*, Toronto, 1915, 3–7; J. MacNaughton, *Lord Strathcona*, Toronto, 1926, 15–23.

18. Smith's career has been most recently recounted in, P. Newman, *Merchant Princes: Company of Adventurers*, Penguin edition, Toronto, 1991, 3–227.

19. H. Gilbert, 'Mount Stephen: A Study in Environments', *Northern Scotland*, I, 1972, 177–79; W.K. Lamb, *History of the Canadian Pacific Railway*, 58–71,

20. MacLennan, *Barometer Rising*, 79.

21. *Dictionary of Canadian Biography*, XI, 552–55; Berton, *National Dream*, 16–19; R. MacGillivray and E. Ross, *History of Glengarry*, 191, 649; D.G. Anderson, 'Big Rory MacLennan', *Glengarry Historical Society Newsletter*, September 1993, 1.

22. The CPR story is best followed in, Lamb, *Canadian Pacific Railway*; Berton, *National Dream*; P. Berton, *The Last Spike: The Great Railway, 1881–1885*, Penguin edition, Toronto, 1989.

23. Creighton, *Old Chieftain*, 397–98.

24. MacLennan, *Seven Rivers of Canada*, 32.

25. *Royal Commission of Inquiry into the Condition of the Crofters and Cottars of the Highlands and Islands of Scotland, Report and Evidence*, Parliamentary Publication, London, 1884, Evidence, 698.

26. *Royal Commission on Crofters and Cottars*, Evidence, 779.

27. *Royal Commission on Crofters and Cottars*, Report, 97–108.

28. Friesen, *Canadian Prairies*, 181–183; N. MacDonald, *Canada: Immigration and Colonization, 1841–1903*, Aberdeen, 1966, 173–74.

29. Berton, *Last Spike*, 287–88; MacDonald, *Immigration and Colonization*, 168–71.

30. MacDonald, *Immigration and Colonization*, 93–94.

31. Hunter, *Crofting Community*, 148; MacDonald, *Immigration and Colonization*, 247; G. MacEwan, *Between the Red and the Rockies*, Toronto, 1952, 88; *Royal Commission on Crofters and Cottars*, Report, 105; *Centenary History of the Scottish Settlement at Wapella*, Wapella, 1983, 19.

32. Berton, *Last Spike*, 35–40, 66–96, 133; Friesen, *Canadian Prairies*, 206–07.

33. *Royal Commission on Crofters and Cottars*, Report, Appendix A, XXXII, 125–26; J.N. MacKinnon, *A Short History of the Pioneer Scotch Settlers of St Andrews*, Saskatchewan, 1921, 3; *Scottish Settlement at Wapella*, 19, 26–28.

34. *Royal Commission on Crofters and Cottars*, Report, Appendix A, XXXII, 128; MacKinnon, *Pioneer Scotch Settlers*, 4.

35. *Royal Commission on Crofters and Cottars*, Report, Appendix A, XXXII, 129; MacKinnon, *Pioneer Scotch Settlers*, 4.

36. *Scottish Settlement at Wapella*,

29–36; *Royal Commission on Crofters and Cottars*, Report, Appendix A, XXXII, 127.

37. MacDonell, *Emigrant Experience*, 150–55; MacPhee, 'Trail of the Emigrants', 213–16. MacDonell attributes this song to Donald MacKinnon. MacPhee, following a Benbecula informant, the late Donald A. MacEachen, attributes it to Archie Kenneth MacDonald. I prefer the latter attribution because Archie Kenneth's father was my great–great–grandmother's brother. See, Hunter, *Scottish Highlanders*, 174–78.

38. Berton, *Last Spike*, 27–28; MacDonald, *Immigration and Colonization*, 171–72; Friesen, *Canadian Prairies*, 222.

39. Morton, *Manitoba*, 211–12.

40. Friesen, *Canadian Prairies*, 242–44, 262–63; MacDonald, *Immigration and Colonization*, 197–234. See also, P. Berton, *The Promised Land: Settling the West, 1896–1914*, Penguin edition, Toronto, 1990.

41. *Reports of Her Majesty's Commissioners appointed to carry out a scheme of Colonisation in Canada of Crofters and Cottars from the Western Highlands and Islands*, Parliamentary Publications, London, 1890–1906; K. Stuart, 'The Scottish Crofter Colony, Saltcoats, 1889–1904', *Saskatchewan History*, XXIV, 1971, 42–50. See also, J. Wilkie, *Metagama: Journey from Lewis to the New World*, Edinburgh, 1987.

42. Hunter, *Crofting Community*, 205–6; Wilkie, *Metagama*, 65. See also, Hunter, *Claim of Crofting*, 30–47.

43. J. Gray, *The Winter Years*, MacMillan Paperback edition, Toronto, 1990, 105–18; E. McCourt, *Saskatchewan*, Toronto, 1968, 5–6.

Chapter Ten: I Will Fight No More Forever

1. J. MacNaughton, *Lord Strathcona*, Toronto, 1926, 1–6; A. Sampson, *The Seven Sisters: The Great Oil Companies and the World They Made*, Coronet edition, London, 1976, 68–71.

2. MacNaughton, *Strathcona*, 110; Newman, *Merchant Princes*, 192.

3. MacNaughton, *Strathcona*, 3–4.

4. J. Prebble, *Glencoe*, Penguin edition, London, 1968, 203.

5. Prebble, *Glencoe*, 211–22; P. Hopkins, *Glencoe and the End of the Highland War*, Edinburgh, 1986, 336.

6. Cole, *Exile in the Wilderness*, 6–7.

7. MacLennan, *Seven Rivers of Canada*, 142.

8. Lamb, *Journals of Simon Fraser*, 2–8; Campbell, *North West Company*, 171.

9. Lamb, *Journals of Simon Fraser*, 7–8; Lawson, 'North West Company', 34; *Dictionary of Canadian Biography*, VII, 837–38.

10. *Dictionary of Canadian Biography*, VII, 837–38; Lawson, 'North West Company', 34.

11. Campbell, *North West Company*, 171–73; Lamb, *Journals of Simon Fraser*, 15–16, 28.

12. Lamb, *Journals of Simon Fraser*, 24.

13. Lamb, *Journals of Simon Fraser*, 24–27.

14. Cole, *Exile in the Wilderness*, 141.

15. J.S. Galbraith, *The Little Emperor: Governor Simpson of the Hudson's Bay Company*, Toronto, 1976, 11–15; J. Dunlop, *The British Fisheries Society, 1786–1893*, Edinburgh, 1978, 146–48.

16. Galbraith, *Little Emperor*, 16–32; Newman, *Caesars of the Wilderness*, 194–95.

17. Galbraith, *Little Emperor*, 55; Friesen, *Canadian Prairies*, 86.

18. Galbraith, *Little Emperor*, 60–61, 89–96.

19. MacLennan, *Seven Rivers of Canada*, 24.
20. C.A. Schwantes, *The Pacific Northwest*, Lincoln, 1989, 56–59; Campbell, *North West Company*, 184–195; Newman, *Caesars of the Wilderness*, 98–107; *Dictionary of Canadian Biography*, V, 532–33; VIII, 765–68; Cole, *Exile in the Wilderness*, 87.
21. Newman, *Caesars of the Wilderness*, 278.
22. Galbraith, *Little Emperor*, 76; *Dictionary of Canadian Biography*, VIII, 583–84.
23. Cole, *Exile in the Wilderness*, 93–99; Newman, *Caesars of the Wilderness*, 232.
24. Newman, *Caesars of the Wilderness*, 278.
25. A. Ross, *Fur Hunters of the Far West*, Chicago, 1924, 126–27.
26. Campbell, *North West Company*, 239–40; Cole, *Exile in the Wilderness*, 179; F.W. Howay, W.S. Lewis and J.A. Meyers (eds), 'Angus MacDonald: A Few Items of the West', *Washington State Historical Quarterly*, XI, 1917, 196.
27. A.J. Partoll, 'Angus MacDonald: Frontier Fur Trader', *Pacific Northwest Quarterly*, XLII, 1951, 138–40.
28. Partoll, 'Angus MacDonald', 139–43.
29. Adam, *Sutherland Estate Management*, I, 175–76.
30. R. Nicholson, *Scotland: The Later Middle Ages*, Mercat Press edition, Edinburgh, 1989, 206; W.C. MacKenzie, *History of the Outer Hebrides*, Paisley, 1903, 187–96; Grant and Cheape, *Periods in Highland History*, 165.
31. Brogan, *History of the United States*, 55–56.
32. Stewart, *Sketches*, I, 296.
33. T. Morgan, *Wilderness at Dawn: The Settling of the North American Continent*, New York, 1993, 438–447; R.S. Cotterill, *The Southern Indians*, Norman, 1954, 41–99; *Dictionary of American Biography*, XII, 70–71.
34. Cole, *Exile in the Wilderness*, 45; *Dictionary of Canadian Biography*, IX, 626. See also, T. Perdue, *Native Carolinians: The Indians of North Carolina*, Raleigh, 1985; L.F.S. Upton, *Micmacs and Colonists: Indian–White Relations in the Maritimes, 1713–1867*, Vancouver, 1979.
35. Woodcock, *Social History of Canada*, 271.
36. K. Sale, *The Conquest of Paradise: Christopher Columbus and the Columbian Legacy*, Papermac edition, London, 1992, 363.
37. L.O. Saum, *The Fur Trader and the Indian*, Seattle, 1965, 7–8.
38. Saum, *Trader and Indian*, 21.
39. R. Mitchison, *Agricultural Sir John: The Life of Sir John Sinclair of Ulbster, 1754–1835*, London, 1962, 120–136; Saum, *Trader and Indian*, 46.
40. Galbraith, *Little Emperor*, 62–63.
41. Newman, *Caesars of the Wilderness*, 113.
42. S. Kirk, *Many Tender Ties: Women in Fur Trade Society in Western Canada, 1760–1870*, Winnipeg, 1980, 4–5.
43. J.S.H. Brown, *Strangers in Blood: Fur Trade Company Families in Indian Country*, Vancouver, 1980, 81–84; Friesen, *Canadian Prairies*, 67–69; Galbraith, *Little Emperor*, 71.
44. See, W.S. Lewis and N. Murakami (eds), *Ranald MacDonald: The Narrative of his Life, 1824–1894*, Portland, 1990.
45. W. Goetzmann, *New Lands, New Men: America in the Second Great Age of Discovery*, Penguin edition, London, 1987, 110–15; J. Hook, *Chief Joseph: Guardian of the Nez Perce*, Poole, 1989, 6–9; D. Brown, *Bury My Heart At Wounded Knee: An Indian History of the American*

West, Picador edition, London, 1975, 251.

46. M.D. Beal, *I Will Fight No More Forever: Chief Joseph and the Nez Perce War*, Seattle, 1966, 6–7.
47. D. Lavender, *Let Me Be Free: The Nez Perce Tragedy*, Anchor Books edition, New York, 1993, 8–16.
48. Partoll, 'Angus MacDonald', 143.
49. Howay, Lewis and Meyers, 'Angus MacDonald', 191–92.
50. L. Laughy (ed), *In Pursuit of the Nez Perce*, Wrangell, 1993, 281.
51. Laughy, *Pursuit of the Nez Perce*, 285.
52. Lavender, *Let Me Be Free*, 280–91; C.E. Trafzer, *The Nez Perce*, New York, 1992, 82–84.
53. Lavender, *Let Me Be Free*, 306–326.
54. Laughy, *Pursuit of the Nez Perce*, 283–84.
55. Laughy, *Pursuit of the Nez Perce*, 213–14; Lavender, *Let Me Be Free*, 5–7.
56. Laughy, *Pursuit of the Nez Perce*, 260–62.
57. Lavender, *Let Me Be Free*, 228; Laughy, *Pursuit of the Nez Perce*, 213; R. Cordier, 'My Son, My Son: Angus MacDonald and Fort Connah', *The Dovetail Magazine*, I, 1973, 19.

Chapter Eleven: The Power of Your Dreams

1. N. Maclean, *A River Runs Through It*, Chicago, 1976, 1, 27; R. McFarland and H. Nichols (eds), *Norman Maclean*, Lewiston, 1988, 11.
2. R. Hugo, *Making Certain It Goes On: Collected Poems*, New York, 1991, 387–88.
3. Cordier, 'My Son, My Son', 21.
4. Cordier, 'My Son, My Son', 21–22.
5. Howay, Lewis and Meyers, 'Angus MacDonald', 191–92.
6. Cordier, 'My Son, My Son', 23.
7. MacLennan, *Seven Rivers of Canada*, 116.
8. Laurence, *The Diviners*, 263–64.
9. J. McPhee, *The Crofter and the Laird*, Noonday Press edition, New York, 1992, 8–10.
10. MacLennan, *Seven Rivers of Canada*, 116–17.
11. C. Macdonald and R. Macdonald, 'Rocket to the Moon', as recorded on *The Cutter and the Clan*, Ridge Records, 1987; T. Morton, *Going Home: The Runrig Story*, Edinburgh, 1991, 124.

Bibliography

Adam, R.J. (ed), *John Home's Survey of Assynt*, Edinburgh, 1960.

Adam, R.J. (ed), *Papers on Sutherland Estate Management*, 2 volumes, Edinburgh, 1972.

Adams, Howard, *Prison of Grass: Canada from a Native Point of View*, Saskatoon, 1989.

Allen, Robert S., *The Loyal Americans*, Ottawa, 1983.

Anderson, David G., 'Big Rory MacLennan', *Glengarry Historical Society Newsletter*, September 1993.

Andrews, E.W. and C.M. (eds), *Journal of a Lady of Quality, Being the Narrative of a Journey from Scotland to the West Indies, North Carolina and Portugal in the years 1774 to 1776*, New Haven, 1939.

Bailyn, Bernard, *The Peopling of British North America*, London, 1987.

Bailyn, Bernard, *Voyagers to the West: Emigration from Britain to America on the Eve of the Revolution*, London, 1987.

Bailyn, Bernard, and Morgan, P.D. (eds), *Strangers within the Realm: Cultural Margins of the First British Empire*, Chapel Hill, 1991.

Bardon, Jonathan, *A History of Ulster*, Belfast, 1992.

Beal, Merrill, D., *I Will Fight No More For Ever: Chief Joseph and the Nez Perce War*, Seattle, 1966.

Bell, Charles N., *The Selkirk Settlement*, Winnipeg, 1887.

Bennett, Margaret, *The Last Stronghold: The Scottish Gaelic Traditions of Newfoundland*, Edinburgh, 1989.

Bergman, Sharon and McAlear, J.F., *The Fabulous Flathead: The Story of the Development of Montana's Flathead Indian Reservation*, Polson, 1988.

Berton, Pierre, *The National Dream: The Great Railway, 1871–1881*, Penguin edition, Toronto, 1989.

Berton, Pierre, *The Last Spike: The Great Railway, 1881–1885*, Penguin edition, Toronto, 1989.

BIBLIOGRAPHY

Berton, Pierre, *The Promised Land: Settling the West, 1896–1914*, Penguin edition, Toronto, 1990.

Black, Jeremy, *Pitt the Elder*, Cambridge, 1992.

Bolger, Francis W.P., *Canada's Smallest Province: A History of PEI*, Toronto, 1973.

Bonomi, Patricia U., *A Factious People: Politics and Society in Colonial New York*, New York, 1971.

Boswell, James, *The Journal of a Tour to the Hebrides*, Penguin edition, London, 1984.

Bradford, E.F., *MacTavish of Dunardry*, Whitby, 1991.

Brock, William R., *Scotus Americanus*, Edinburgh, 1982.

Brogan, Hugh, *History of the United States of America*, London, 1985.

Brown, Dee, *Bury My Heart At Wounded Knee: An Indian History of the American West*, Picador edition, London, 1975.

Brown, Jennifer S.H., *Strangers in Blood: Fur Trade Company Families in Indian Country*, Vancouver, 1980.

Brown, Wallace, *The Good Americans: The Loyalists in the American Revolution*, New York, 1969.

Bruckner, P.A., and Frank, D. (eds), *The Acadiensis Reader: Atlantic Canada Before Confederation*, Fredericton, 1990.

Bryce, George, *The Scotsman in Canada: Western Canada*, London, 1911.

Buie, T.R., and Buie, J. Scott, *The Family Buie: Scotland to North America*, Arlington, 1983.

Bumsted, J.M., *The People's Clearance: Highland Emigration to British North America, 1770–1815*, Edinburgh, 1982.

Bumsted, J.M., *The Scots in Canada*, Ottawa, 1982.

Bumsted, J.M. (ed), *The Collected Writings of Lord Selkirk, 1799–1809*, Winnipeg, 1984.

Bumsted, J.M. (ed), *The Collected Writings of Lord Selkirk, 1810–1820*, Winnipeg, 1987.

Bumsted, J.M., *Land, Settlement and Politics on Eighteenth-Century Prince Edward Island*, Kingston, 1987.

Bumsted, J.M., *The Peoples of Canada: A Pre-Confederation History*, Toronto, 1992.

Cage, R.A., *The Scots Abroad: Labour, Capital, Enterprise, 1750–1914*, London, 1985.

Calhoon, Robert McCluer, *The Loyalists in Revolutionary America, 1760–1781*, New York, 1973.

Callahan, North, *Royal Raiders: The Tories of the American Revolution*, New York, 1963.

Cameron, Elspeth (ed), *The Other Side of Hugh MacLennan: Selected Essays Old and New*, Toronto, 1978.

Cameron, Elspeth, *Hugh MacLennan: A Writer's Life*, Toronto, 1981.

Cameron, Elspeth (ed), *Hugh MacLennan: 1982*, Toronto, 1982.

Campbell, D., and MacLean, R.A., *Beyond the Atlantic Roar: A Study of the Nova Scotia Scots*, Carleton Library edition, Ottawa, 1975.

Campbell, John L., *Canna: The Story of a Hebridean Island*, Oxford, 1984.

Campbell, John L., *Songs Remembered in Exile*, Aberdeen, 1990.

Campbell, Marjorie W., *McGillivray: Lord of the Northwest*, Toronto, 1962.

Campbell, Marjorie W., *The North West Company*, revised edition, Vancouver, 1983.

Campbell, Wilfred, *The Scotsman in Canada: Eastern Canada*, London, 1911.

Carmichael, A., *Carmina Gadelica*, 6 volumes, Edinburgh, 1928–71.

Carney, Seamus, *The Killing of the Red Fox: An Investigation into the Appin Murder*, Moffat, 1989.

Centenary History of the Scottish Settlement at Wapella, Wapella, 1983.

Cline, Gloria G., *Peter Skene Ogden and the Hudson's Bay Company*, Norman, 1974.

Cole, Jean M., *Exile in the Wilderness: The Biography of Chief Factor Archibald McDonald, 1790–1853*, Toronto, 1979.

Coleman, Kenneth, *Colonial Georgia: A History*, New York, 1976.

Coleman, Terry, *Passage to America*, London, 1972.

Colley, Linda, *Britons: Forging the Nation, 1707–1837*, London, 1992.

Connor, Ralph, *Glengarry School Days*, New Canadian Library edition, Toronto, 1975.

Connor, Ralph, *The Man from Glengarry*, New Canadian Library edition, Toronto, 1993.

Cooper, J. Fenimore, *The Last of the Mohicans*, Panther edition, London, 1970.

Cooper, J. Fenimore, *The Pioneers*, World's Classics edition, Oxford, 1991.

Cordier, Rick, 'My Son, My Son: Angus MacDonald and Fort Connah', *The Dovetail Magazine*, I, 1973.

Corkran, David H., *The Creek Frontier, 1540–1783*, Norman, 1967.

Cotterill, R.S., *The Southern Indians*, Norman, 1954.

Countryman, Edward, *A People in Revolution: The American Revolution and Political Society in New York, 1760–1790*, Baltimore, 1981.

Countryman, Edward, *The American Revolution*, Penguin edition, London, 1987.

Cowan, Helen I., *British Emigration to British North America: The First Hundred Years*, revised edition, Toronto, 1961.

Cox, Ross, *Adventures on the Columbia River*, 2 volumes, London, 1831.

Craig, David, *On the Crofters' Trail: In Search of the Clearance Highlanders*, London, 1990.

Creighton, Donald, *John A. Macdonald: The Young Politician*, Toronto, 1952.

Creighton, Donald, *John A. Macdonald: The Old Chieftain*, Toronto, 1955.

Crevecoeur, J. Hector St John de, *Letters from an American Farmer*, Penguin edition, London, 1986.

Daniells, Roy, *Alexander Mackenzie and the North West*, London, 1969.

Davies, K.G., *Documents of the American Revolution, 1770–1783*, 21 volumes, Dublin, 1972–1981.

Davis, Harold E., *The Fledgling Province: Social and Cultural Life in Colonial Georgia, 1733–1776*, Chapel Hill, 1976.

DeMond, Robert O., *The Loyalists in North Carolina During the Revolution*, Hamden, 1964.

Devine, T.M., *The Great Highland Famine*, Edinburgh, 1988.

Devine, T.M. (ed), *Scottish Emigration and Scottish Society*, Edinburgh, 1992.

Devine, T.M., and Mitchison, R. (eds), *People and Society in Scotland, 1760–1830*, Edinburgh, 1988.

Dickinson, John A., and Young, Brian, *A Short History of Quebec*, second edition, Toronto, 1993.

Dickson, R.J., *Ulster Emigration to Colonial America, 1718–1775*, London, 1966.

Dictionary of American Biography, 20 volumes, New York, 1928–1936.

Dictionary of Canadian Biography, 12 volumes, Toronto, 1966–1990.

Diefenbaker, John G., *One Canada*, Toronto, 1975.

Donaldson, Gordon, *The Scots Overseas*, London, 1966.

BIBLIOGRAPHY

Donaldson, Gordon, *Battle for a Continent: Quebec 1759*, Toronto, 1973.

Donovan, Kenneth (ed), *Cape Breton at 200: Historical Essays in Honour of the Island's Bicentennial, 1785–1985*, Sydney, 1985.

Donovan, Kenneth (ed), *The Island: New Perspectives on Cape Breton's History, 1713–1990*, Sydney, 1990.

Douglas, Hugh, *Flora MacDonald: The Most Loyal Rebel*, Stroud, 1993.

Douglas, Thomas, Earl of Selkirk, *Observations on the Present State of the Highlands of Scotland*, second edition, Edinburgh, 1806.

Dumbrille, Dorothy, *Up and Down the Glens: The Story of Glengarry*, Toronto, 1954.

Dumbrille, Dorothy, *Braggart in my Step: More Stories of Glengarry*, Toronto, 1956.

Dunn, Charles W., *Highland Settler: A Portrait of the Scottish Gael in Nova Scotia*, Toronto, 1953.

Dunlop, Jean, *The British Fisheries Society, 1786–1893*, Edinburgh, 1978.

Dunlop, William, *Statistical Sketches of Upper Canada for the Benefit of Emigrants*, London, 1832.

England, Robert, *The Colonization of Western Canada*, London, 1936.

Findlay, J.T., *Wolfe in Scotland*, London, 1928.

Fischer, David H., *Albion's Seed: Four British Folkways in America*, New York, 1989.

Flexner, James T., *Mohawk Baronet: A Biography of Sir William Johnson*, Syracuse, 1989.

Fortier, J., and Fitzgerald, O., *Fortress of Louisbourg*, Toronto, 1979.

Frank, David, and MacGillivray, Donald (eds), *George MacEachern: An Autobiography*, Sydney, 1987.

Fraser, Dawn, *Echoes from Labor's Wars*, Breton Books edition, Wreck Cove, 1992.

Friesen, Gerald, *The Canadian Prairies: A History*, Toronto, 1984.

Fry, Michael, *The Dundas Despotism*, Edinburgh, 1992.

Fyfe, J.G. (ed), *Memoirs of the Life and Gallant Exploits of the Old Highlander Sergeant Donald MacLeod*, London, 1933.

Galbraith, John K., *Made to Last*, London, 1964.

Galbraith, John S., *The Little Emperor: Governor Simpson of the Hudson's Bay Company*, Toronto, 1976.

Gates, Charles M. (ed), *Five Fur Traders of the Northwest*, Minnesota, 1933.

Gibbon, John M., *Scots in Canada*, London, 1911.

Gilbert, Heather, 'Mount Stephen: A Study in Environments', *Northern Scotland*, I, 1972.

Goetsch, Paul (ed), *Hugh MacLennan*, Toronto, 1973.

Goetzmann, William, *New Lands, New Men: America in the Second Great Age of Discovery*, Penguin edition, London, 1987.

Goldring, Philip, 'Lewis and the Hudson's Bay Company in the Nineteenth Century', *Scottish Studies*, XXIV, 1980.

Graham, Ian C.G., *Colonists from Scotland: Emigration to North America, 1707–1783*, Ithaca, 1956.

Grant, Elizabeth, *Memoirs of a Highland Lady*, Canongate Classics edition, Edinburgh, 1992.

Grant, Isobel F., *Along a Highland Road*, London, 1980.

Grant, Isobel F., *Everyday Life on an Old Highland Farm*, London, 1981.

Grant, Isobel F., and Cheape, Hugh, *Periods in Highland History*, London, 1987.

Gray, James, *The Winter Years*, MacMillan Paperback edition, Toronto, 1990.

Gray, John M., *Lord Selkirk of Red River*, London, 1963.

Graymont, Barbara, *The Iroquois in the American Revolution*, Syracuse, 1972.

Grimble, Ian, 'Emigration in the time of Rob Donn, 1714–1778', *Scottish Studies*, VII, 1963.

Grove, Frederick P., *Over Prairie Trails*, New Canadian Library edition, Toronto, 1957.

Guillet, Edwin C., *The Great Migration: The Atlantic Crossing by Sailing Ship since 1770*, London, 1937.

Guinn, Rodger, *The Red-Assiniboine Junction: A Land Use and Structural History, 1770–1980*, Ottawa, 1980.

Gunn, Donald, *Manitoba from the Earliest Settlement to 1835*, Ottawa, 1880.

Hall, J., *Travels in the Highlands by an Unusual Route*, 2 volumes, London, 1807.

Handlin, Oscar, *The Uprooted*, second edition, Toronto, 1973.

Hannon, Leslie F., *Forts of Canada*, Toronto, 1976.

Hargreaves, Reginald, *The Bloodybacks: The British Serviceman in North America and the Caribbean, 1655–1783*, London, 1968.

Harper, J.R., *The Fraser Highlanders*, Montreal, 1979.

Harper, Marjory, *Emigration from Northeast Scotland*, 2 volumes, Aberdeen, 1988.

Haws, Charles H., *Scots in the Old Dominion, 1685–1800*, Edinburgh, 1980.

Healy, W.J., *Women of Red River*, Winnipeg, 1923.

Hewitson, Jim, *Tam Blake and Co: The Story of the Scots in America*, Edinburgh, 1993.

Hibbert, Christopher, *Redcoats and Rebels: The War for America, 1770–1781*, London, 1991.

Hill, Douglas, *The Scots to Canada*, London, 1972.

Hislop, Codman, *The Mohawk*, Syracuse, 1989.

Hook, Jason, *Chief Joseph: Guardian of the Nez Perce*, Poole, 1989.

Hopkins, Paul, *Glencoe and the End of the Highland War*, Edinburgh, 1986.

Hornsby, Stephen, *Nineteenth-Century Cape Breton: A Historical Geography*, Toronto, 1992.

Howay, F.W., Lewis, W.S., and Meyers, J.A. (eds), 'Angus McDonald: A Few Items of the West', *Washington State Historical Quarterly*, XI, 1917.

Hugo, Richard, *Making Certain It Goes On: Collected Poems*, Norton Paperback edition, New York, 1991.

Hunter, James, *The Making of the Crofting Community*, Edinburgh, 1976.

Hunter, James (ed), *For the People's Cause: From the Writings of John Murdoch*, Edinburgh, 1986.

Hunter, James, *Skye: The Island*, Edinburgh, 1986.

Hunter, James, *The Claim of Crofting: The Scottish Highlands and Islands, 1930–1990*, Edinburgh, 1991.

Hunter, James, *Scottish Highlanders: A People and their Place*, Edinburgh, 1992.

Hutchinson, Roger, *Camanachd: The Story of Shinty*, Edinburgh, 1989.

Innis, Harold A., *The Fur Trade in Canada*, Toronto, 1956.

Insh, George P., *Scottish Colonial Schemes, 1620–1686*, Glasgow, 1922.

Irving, Washington, *Astoria: Adventure in the Pacific Northwest*, KPI edition, London, 1987.

Ivers, Larry E., *British Drums on the Southern Frontier: The Military Colonization of Georgia, 1733–1749*, Chapel Hill, 1974.

Jackson, Harvey H., and Spalding, Phiziny (eds), *Forty Years of Diversity: Essays on Colonial Georgia*, Athens, 1984.

Jackson, Kenneth, *A Celtic Miscellany*, Penguin edition, London, 1971.

Jennings, Francis, *Empire of Fortune: Crowns, Colonies and Tribes in the Seven*

Years War in America, New York, 1988.

Johnson, Samuel, *A Journey to the Western Islands of Scotland*, Penguin edition, London, 1984.

Johnston, H.J.M., *British Emigration Policy, 1815–1830*, Oxford, 1972.

Josephy, Alvin M., *The Nez Perce Indians and the Opening of the Northwest*, New Haven, 1971.

Kammen, Michael, *Colonial New York: A History*, New York, 1975.

Kirk, Sylvia van, *Many Tender Ties: Women in Fur Trade Society in Western Canada, 1670–1870*, Winnipeg, 1980.

Lamb, W. Kaye (ed), *The Letters and Journals of Simon Fraser, 1806–1808*, Toronto, 1960.

Lamb, W. Kaye (ed), *The Journals and Letters of Sir Alexander Mackenzie*, Cambridge, 1970.

Lamb, W. Kaye, *History of the Canadian Pacific Railway*, New York, 1977.

Laughy, Linwood (ed), *In Pursuit of the Nez Perce*, Wrangell, 1993.

Lauglan, W.F. (ed), *James Hogg's Highland Tours*, Hawick, 1981.

Laurence, Margaret, *The Diviners*, New Canadian Library edition, Toronto, 1993.

Lavender, David (ed), *The Oregon Journals of David Douglas, 1825–1827*, 2 volumes, Ashland, 1972.

Lavender, David, *Let Me Be Free: The Nez Perce Tragedy*, Anchor Books edition, New York, 1993.

Lawson, Alan B., *A Country Called Stratherrick*, Inverness, 1987.

Lawson, Alan B., 'The North West Company of Canada: The Highland Connection', in L. MacLean (ed), *An Inverness Miscellany*, Inverness, 1987.

Lee, Lawrence, *The Lower Cape Fear in Colonial Days*, Chapel Hill, 1965.

Lenman, Bruce, *The Jacobite Risings in Britain, 1689–1746*, London, 1980.

Lenman, Bruce, *The Jacobite Clans of the Great Glen, 1650–1784*, London, 1984.

Le Roy, Bruce, *Lairds, Bards and Mariners: The Scot in Northwest America*, Seattle, 1978.

Lewis, William S., and Murakami, Naojiri (eds), *Ranald MacDonald: The Narrative of his Life, 1824–1894*, Portland, 1990.

Loch, James, *An Account of the Improvements on the Estates of the Marquess of Stafford*, London, 1820.

Logan, G. Murray, *Scottish Highlanders and the American Revolution*, Halifax, 1976.

Logue, Kenneth J., *Popular Disturbances in Scotland, 1780–1815*, Edinburgh, 1979.

London, Jack, *The Sea Wolf*, World's Classics edition, Oxford, 1992.

Lopez, Barry, *Arctic Dreams*, Picador edition, London, 1987.

Lotz, Jim, *Understanding Canada*, Toronto, 1977.

Lotz, Jim, and Lotz, Pat, *Cape Breton Island*, Newton Abbott, 1974.

Lower, Arthur M., *Great Britain's Woodyard: British America and the Timber Trade, 1763–1867*, Toronto, 1973.

MacCaskill, Lady, *Twelve Days in Skye*, second edition, London, 1852.

McCourt, Edward, *Saskatchewan*, Toronto, 1968.

MacCulloch, Donald B., *Romantic Lochaber, Arisaig and Morar*, Edinburgh, 1971.

MacDonagh, Oliver, *A Pattern of Government Growth, 1800–1860: The Passenger Acts and their Enforcement*, London, 1961.

MacDonald, Allan R., *The Truth about Flora MacDonald*, Inverness, 1938.

MacDonald, Norman, *Canada: Immigration and Settlement, 1763–1841*, London, 1939.

MacDonald, Norman, *Canada: Immigration and Colonization, 1841–1903*, Aberdeen, 1966.

MacDonald, Norman H., *The Clan Ranald of Knoydart and Glengarry*, Edinburgh, 1979.

Macdonell, J.A., *Sketches of Glengarry in Canada*, Montreal, 1893.

MacDonell, Margaret, *The Emigrant Experience: Songs of Highland Emigrants in North America*, Toronto, 1982.

MacEwan, Grant, *Between the Red and the Rockies*, Toronto, 1952.

MacEwan, Paul, *Miners and Steelworkers: Labour in Cape Breton*, Toronto, 1976.

McFarland, Ron, and Nichols, Hugh (eds), *Norman Maclean*, Lewiston, 1988.

MacGillivray, Don, and Tennyson, Brian (eds), *Cape Breton Historical Essays*, Sydney, 1980.

MacGillivray, Robert, and MacGillivray, George B., *A History of the Clan MacGillivray*, Thunder Bay, 1974.

MacGillivray, Royce, and Ross, Ewan, *A History of Glengarry*, Belleville, 1979.

MacGillivray, W., 'Report on the Hebrides', *Transactions of the Highland Society*, New Series, II, 1831.

MacGregor, Alexander, *The Life of Flora MacDonald*, Inverness, 1882.

MacKay, Donald, *Scotland Farewell: The People of the Hector*, Toronto, 1980.

MacKay, Margaret M. (ed), *The Rev Dr John Walker's Reports on the Hebrides of 1764 and 1771*, Edinburgh, 1980.

MacKenzie, Alexander, *Voyages from Montreal through the Continent of North America to the Frozen and Pacific Oceans in 1789 and 1793*, Introduced by W.L. Grant, 2 volumes, Toronto, 1911.

MacKenzie, W.C., *History of the Outer Hebrides*, Paisley, 1903.

MacKinnon, James N., *A Short History of the Pioneer Scotch Settlers of St Andrews*, Saskatchewan, 1921.

MacKintosh, Charles Fraser, *The Minor Septs of Clan Chattan*, Glasgow, 1898.

MacLean, J.P., *An Historical Account of the Settlements of Scotch Highlanders in America Prior to the Peace of 1783*, Glasgow, 1900.

McLean, Marianne, *The People of Glengarry: Highlanders in Transition, 1745–1820*, Montreal, 1991.

Maclean, Norman, *A River Runs Through It and Other Stories*, Chicago, 1976.

MacLean, Sorley, *Ris a' Bhruthaich*, Stornoway, 1985.

MacLean, Sorley, *From Wood to Ridge: Collected Poems in Gaelic and English*, Manchester, 1990.

MacLennan, Hugh, *Barometer Rising*, New Canadian Library edition, Toronto, 1958.

MacLennan, Hugh, *Scotchman's Return and Other Essays*, Toronto, 1960.

MacLennan, Hugh, *Each Man's Son*, Laurentian Library edition, Toronto, 1971.

MacLennan, Hugh, *Seven Rivers of Canada*, Toronto, 1977.

MacLennan, J.S., *Louisbourg: From its Foundation to its Fall, 1713–1758*, London, 1918.

MacLeod, Alistair, *The Lost Salt Gift of Blood*, Flamingo edition, London, 1993.

MacLeod, J.N., *Memorials of the Rev Norman MacLeod*, Edinburgh, 1898.

MacLeod, Margaret A., *Red River's Festive Season*, Winnipeg, 1962.

MacLeod, Margaret A., and Morton, W.L., *Cuthbert Grant of Grantown: Warden of the Plains of Red River*, Toronto, 1963.

MacLulich, T.D., *Hugh MacLennan*, Boston, 1983.

McLynn, Frank, *Charles Edward Stuart: A Tragedy in Many Acts*, London, 1988.

BIBLIOGRAPHY

MacMillan, Somerled, *The Emigration of the Lochaber MacMillans to Canada in 1802*, Paisley, 1958.

MacMillan, Somerled, *Bygone Lochaber*, Glasgow, 1971.

McNaught, Kenneth, *The Penguin History of Canada*, London, 1988.

MacNaughton, John, *Lord Strathcona*, Toronto, 1926.

MacNeil, Joe Neil, *Sgeul gu Latha, Tales until Dawn: The World of a Cape Breton Storyteller*, translated and edited by John Shaw, Edinburgh, 1987.

MacNeil, Neil, *The Highland Heart of Nova Scotia*, Toronto, 1958.

McNeill, John Charles, *The Pocket John Charles McNeill*, Laurinburg, 1990.

MacNutt, W.S., *The Atlantic Provinces: The Emergence of a Colonial Society, 1712–1857*, London, 1965.

MacPhail, Margaret, *Loch Bras d'Or*, Windsor, 1970.

MacPhee, Hugh, 'The Trail of the Emigrants', *Transactions of the Gaelic Society of Inverness*, XLVI, 1968–69.

McPhee, John, *The Crofter and the Laird*, Noonday edition, New York, 1992.

McPherson, Flora, *Watchman against the World: The Remarkable Journey of Norman McLeod*, Breton Books edition, Wreck Cove, 1993.

McWhiney, Grady, *Cracker Culture: Celtic Ways in the Old South*, Tuscaloosa, 1988.

McWhiney, Grady, and Jamieson, Perry D., *Attack and Die: Civil War Military Tactics and the Southern Heritage*, Alabama, 1982.

Magnusson, Magnus, and Palsson, Herman, *The Vinland Sagas: The Norse Discovery of America*, New York, 1966.

Malone, Michael P., and Roeder, Richard B., *Montana: A History of Two Centuries*, Seattle, 1976.

Matheson, William (ed), *The Songs of John MacCodrum*, Edinburgh, 1938.

Mathiesen, Peter, *In the Spirit of Crazy Horse*, Penguin edition, New York, 1992.

Meek, Donald E., 'Scottish Highlanders, North American Indians and the SSPCK: Some Cultural Perspectives', *Records of the Scottish Church History Society*, XXIII, 1989.

Memorandum of Arrangements Entered into with the Canadian Government for the Purpose of Starting a Colonisation Scheme for the Crofters and Cottars of the Western Highlands and Islands, Parliamentary Publication, London, 1888.

Meyer, Duane, *The Highland Scots of North Carolina, 1732–1776*, Chapel Hill, 1961.

Middlekauff, Robert, *The Glorious Cause: The American Revolution, 1763–1789*, Oxford, 1982.

Miller, J.R., *Skyscrapers Hide the Heavens: A History of Indian-White Relations in Canada*, Toronto, 1989.

Mitchell, Joseph, *Reminiscences of my Life in the Highlands*, 2 volumes, Newton Abbott, 1971.

Mitchison, Rosalind, *Agricultural Sir John: The Life of Sir John Sinclair of Ulbster, 1754–1835*, London, 1962.

Moore, Christopher, *The Loyalists: Revolution, Exile, Settlement*, Toronto, 1984.

Morgan, R.J. *More Essays in Cape Breton History*, Windsor, 1977.

Morgan, Ted, *Wilderness at Dawn: The Settling of the North American Continent*, New York, 1993.

Morrison, Jean (ed), *The North West Company in Rebellion: Simon MacGillivray's Fort William Notebook*, Thunder Bay, 1988.

Morse, Eric W., *Fur Trade Routes of Canada*, Toronto, 1979.

Morton, Arthur S. (ed), *The Journal of Duncan McGillivray of the North West Company, 1794–95*, Toronto, 1929.

Morton, Arthur S., *Under Western Skies*, Toronto, 1937.

Morton, Arthur S., *A History of the Canadian West to 1870–71*, second edition, Toronto, 1973.

Morton, Tom, *Going Home: The Runrig Story*, Edinburgh, 1991.

Morton, W.L., *Manitoba: A History*, Toronto, 1957.

Moss, Bobby G., *Muster of the Loyalists in the Battle of Moore's Creek Bridge*, Blacksburg, 1992.

Munro, R.W., *Taming the Rough Bounds: Knoydart, 1745–1784*, Isle of Coll, 1984.

Murdoch, Alexander, 'A Document concerning Emigration to North Carolina in 1772', *North Carolina Historical Review*, LXVII, 1990.

Nash, Roderick, *Wilderness and the American Mind*, third edition, Yale, 1982.

Newman, Peter, *Company of Adventurers: The Story of the Hudson's Bay Company*, Penguin edition, London, 1987.

Newman, Peter, *Caesars of the Wilderness: The Story of the Hudson's Bay Company*, Penguin edition, London, 1988.

Newman, Peter, *Merchant Princes: Company of Adventurers*, Penguin edition, Toronto, 1991.

Nicholson, Ranald, *Scotland: The Later Middle Ages*, Mercat Press edition, Edinburgh, 1989.

O'Gallagher, Marianna, *Grosse Ile: Gateway to Canada, 1832–1937*, Quebec, 1984.

Pannekoek, Frits, *The Fur Trade and Western Canadian Society, 1670–1870*, Ottawa, 1987.

Papers Relative to Emigration to the North American Colonies, Parliamentary Papers, London, 1852.

Parker, James, *Emporium of the North: Fort Chipewyan and the Fur Trade to 1835*, Regina, 1987.

Partoll, Albert J., 'Angus MacDonald: Frontier Fur Trader', *Pacific Northwest Quarterly*, XLII, 1951.

Patterson, George G., *History of Victoria County*, Sydney, 1978.

Peckham, Howard H., *The Colonial Wars, 1689–1762*, Chicago, 1964.

Perdue, Theda, *Native Carolinians: The Indians of North Carolina*, Raleigh, 1985.

Philbrick, Thomas, *St John de Crevecoeur*, New York, 1970.

Phillipson, N.T., and Mitchison, R. (eds), *Scotland in the Age of Improvement*, Edinburgh, 1970.

Powell, William S., *North Carolina: A History*, Chapel Hill, 1988.

Prebble, John, *Culloden*, Penguin edition, London, 1967.

Prebble, John, *Glencoe*, Penguin edition, London, 1968.

Prebble, John, *The Highland Clearances*, Penguin edition, London, 1969.

Prebble, John, *Mutiny: Highland Regiments in Revolt, 1743–1804*, Penguin edition, London, 1977.

Prebble, John, *Landscapes and Memories: An Intermittent Autobiography*, London, 1993.

Purich, Donald, *The Metis*, Toronto, 1988.

Pritchett, John P., *The Red River Valley, 1811–1849*, New Haven, 1942.

Raban, Jonathan, *Hunting Mr Heartbreak*, Picador edition, London, 1991.

Rankin, Hugh F., *The North Carolina Continentals*, Chapel Hill, 1971.

Rankin, Hugh F., *The Moore's Creek Bridge Campaign*, Conshohocken, 1986.

Ranlet, Philip, *The New York Loyalists*, Knoxville, 1986.

Rawlyk, G.A. (ed), *Historical Essays on the Atlantic Provinces*, Toronto, 1967.

BIBLIOGRAPHY

Ray, Arthur J., *Indians in the Fur Trade: Their Role as Trappers, Hunters and Middlemen in the Lands Southwest of Hudson Bay, 1660–1870*, Toronto, 1974.

Rea, J., *Bishop Alexander MacDonell and the Politics of Upper Canada*, Toronto, 1974.

Redmond, Gerald, *The Sporting Scots of Nineteenth-Century Canada*, Toronto, 1982.

Reid, W. Stanford (ed), *The Scottish Tradition in Canada*, Toronto, 1976.

Reports from the Select Committee appointed to enquire into Emigration, Parliamentary Publication, London, 1826–27.

Reports from the Select Committee on Emigration, Scotland, Parliamentary Publication, London, 1841.

Reports of the Select Committee on Emigrant Ships, Parliamentary Publication, London, 1854.

Reports of Her Majesty's Commissioners appointed to carry out a scheme of Colonisation in Canada of Crofters and Cottars from the Western Highlands and Islands, Parliamentary Publications, London, 1890–1906.

Rich, E.E., *The Fur Trade and the Northwest to 1857*, London, 1968.

Richards, Eric, *A History of the Highland Clearances: Agrarian Transformation and the Evictions, 1746–1886*, London, 1982.

Richards, Eric, *A History of the Highland Clearances: Emigration, Protest, Reasons*, London, 1985.

Roberts, Leslie, *The Mackenzie*, New York, 1949.

Robinson, Neil, *Lion of Scotland*, Auckland, 1974.

Ross, Alexander, *The Red River Settlement*, London, 1856.

Ross, Alexander, *Adventures of the First Settlers on the Oregon or Columbia River*, Cleveland, 1904.

Ross, Alexander, *The Fur Hunters of the Far West*, Chicago, 1924.

Ross, Peter, *The Scot in America*, New York, 1896.

Royal Commission of Inquiry into the the Condition of the Crofters and Cottars of the Highlands and Islands of Scotland, Report and Evidence, Parliamentary Publications, London, 1884.

Sage, Donald, *Memorabilia Domestica: Or Parish Life in the North of Scotland*, second edition, Wick, 1899.

Sale, Kirkpatrick, *The Conquest of Paradise: Christopher Columbus and the Columbian Legacy*, Papermac edition, London, 1992.

Sampson, Anthony, *The Seven Sisters: The Great Oil Companies and the World They Made*, Coronet edition, London, 1976.

Saum, Lewis O., *The Fur Trader and the Indian*, Seattle, 1965.

Schaitberger, Lillian B., *Scots of McIntosh*, Darien, 1986.

Schwantes, Carlos A., *The Pacific Northwest*, Lincoln, 1989.

Scotus Americanus, *Informations concerning the Province of North Carolina addressed to Emigrants from the Highlands and Western Isles of Scotland*, as reprinted in William K. Boyd (ed), *Eighteenth-Century Tracts Concerning North Carolina*, Raleigh, 1927.

Shaw, Alexander M., *Historical Memoirs of Clan MacIntosh*, 2 volumes, London, 1880.

Shaw, C. John, *A History of Clan Shaw*, Chichester, 1983.

Sheppe, Walter, *First Man West: Alexander Mackenzie's Journal of his Voyage to the Pacific Coast of Canada in 1793*, Berkeley, 1962.

Sher, Richard B. and Smitten, Jeffrey R. (eds), *Scotland and America in the Age of Enlightenment*, Edinburgh, 1990.

Sinton, Thomas, *The Poetry of Badenoch*, Inverness, 1906.

Smailes, Helen, *Scottish Empire*, Edinburgh, 1981.

Smith, Annette M., *The Jacobite Estates of the Forty-Five*, Edinburgh, 1982.

Smith, Cynthia M., *Sir John A.: An Anecdotal Life of John A. Macdonald*, Toronto, 1989.

Somers, Robert, *Letters from the Highlands on the Famine of 1846*, Inverness, 1977.

Spalding, Phiziny, *Oglethorpe in America*, Chicago, 1977.

Stacey, C.P., *Quebec 1759: The Siege and the Battle*, Toronto, 1959.

Steele, Samuel B., *Forty Years in Canada*, London, 1916.

Stewart, David, *Sketches of the Highlanders of Scotland*, second edition, 2 volumes, Edinburgh, 1977.

Stewart, John, *The Camerons: A History of Clan Cameron*, Stirling, 1974.

Storrie, Margaret C., *Islay: Biography of an Island*, Port Ellen, 1981.

Stuart, Kent, 'The Scottish Crofter Colony, Saltcoats, 1889–1904', *Saskatchewan History*, XXIV, 1971.

Sullivan, Buddy, *Early Days on the Georgia Tidewater: The Story of McIntosh County and Sapelo*, third edition, Darien, 1992.

Talman, James J. (ed), *Loyalist Narratives from Upper Canada*, Toronto, 1946.

Taylor, John H., *Ottawa: An Illustrated History*, Toronto, 1986.

Telford, Thomas, *A Survey and Report of the Coasts and Central Highlands of Scotland with Reports of the Select Committee to whom the Report was Referred*, Parliamentary Publication, London, 1802–3.

Thomson, Derick, *Introduction to Gaelic Poetry*, London, 1974.

Trafzer, Clifford E., *The Nez Perce*, New York, 1992.

Traill, Catherine P., *The Backwoods of Canada*, London, 1836.

Tuchman, Barbara W., *The March of Folly*, London, 1984.

Upton, L.F.S., *Micmacs and Colonists: Indian-White Relations in the Maritimes, 1713–1867*, Vancouver, 1979.

Vining, Elizabeth G., *Flora MacDonald: Her Life in the Highlands and America*, London, 1967.

Wagenknecht, Edward, *Washington Irving: Moderation Displayed*, New York, 1962.

Waite, P.B., *Macdonald: His Life and World*, Toronto, 1975.

Walker, Edward E., *Indians of Idaho*, Moscow, 1978.

Wallace, W. Stewart (ed), *John McLean's Notes of a Twenty-Five Year's Service in the Hudson's Bay Territory*, Toronto, 1932.

Wallace, W. Stewart (ed), *Documents Relating to the North West Company*, Toronto, 1934.

West, John, *The Substance of a Journey During a Residence at the Red River Colony*, second edition, London, 1828.

Wilkie, Jim, *Metagama: A Journey from Lewis to the New World*, Edinburgh, 1987.

Willson, Beckles, *The Life of Lord Strathcona*, Toronto, 1915.

Wood, John D., 'Transatlantic Land Reform: America and the Crofters Revolt, 1878–1888', *Scottish Historical Review*, LXIII, 1984.

Woodcock, George, *A Social History of Canada*, London, 1989.

Woodcock, George, *The Century That Made Us; Canada, 1814–1914*, Toronto, 1989.

Wright, J.F.C., *Saskatchewan: The History of a Province*, Toronto, 1955.

Wright, Louis B., *The Dream of Prosperity in Colonial America*, New York, 1965

Youngson, A.J., *After the Forty-Five: The Economic Impact on the Scottish Highlands*, Edinburgh, 1973.

Index

INDEX